CCNP BSCI Official Exam Certification Guide, Fourth Edition

Brent D. Stewart
Clare Gough, CCIE No. 2893

Cisco Press

800 East 96th Street
Indianapolis, Indiana 46240 USA

About the Author

Brent D. Stewart, CCNP, CCSI, is a network administrator at CommScope, where he focuses on design and implementation of an international IP network. Brent has worked in fiber-optic manufacturing R&D, as a network consultant, and as a certified Cisco instructor. Brent participated in the development of BSCI while with Global Knowledge and developed Internet-based versions of several CCNP classes. Brent received a B.S. in physics from Lenoir-Rhyne College and is currently finishing an M.S. in computer science/information security from James Madison University.

Brent lives in Hickory, North Carolina, with his beautiful wife, Karen, and their wonderfully mischievous children, Benjamin, Kaitlyn, Madelyn, and William.

About the Contributors

Wayne Lewis, Ph.D., is an associate professor at Honolulu Community College. Since 1992, he has served as a math instructor, as the state school-to-work coordinator, and as the lead instructor for the Cisco Academy Training Center (CATC). He has authored seven Cisco Press books on network troubleshooting, multilayer switching, and, most recently, intermediate routing and basic switching. As a consultant for Cisco, he coordinated the development of several iterations of the curriculum for the CCNP and served as a project manager for the development of the Securing Cisco LAN Devices course for the Critical Infrastructure Assurance Group. When he is not managing, teaching, writing, consulting, or spending time with his wife and kids, he enjoys surfing the North Shore of Oahu during the winter months and the South Shore of Oahu during the summer months.

Diane Teare, CCNP, CCDP, CCSI, is a professional in the networking, training, and e-learning fields. She has more than 20 years of experience in designing, implementing, and troubleshooting network hardware and software and has also been involved in teaching, course design, and project management. She has extensive knowledge of network design and routing technologies and is an instructor with one of the largest authorized Cisco Learning Partners. She was also recently the Director of e-Learning for the same company, responsible for planning and supporting all the company's e-learning offerings in Canada, including Cisco courses. Diane was part of the team that developed the latest version of the BSCI course. She has a bachelor's degree in applied science in electrical engineering (BASc) and a master's degree in applied science in management science (MASc). She co-authored the Cisco Press titles *Campus Network Design Fundamentals* and three editions of the *Building Scalable Cisco Internetworks (BSCI) Authorized Self-Study Guide*; she also edited *CCDA Self-Study: Designing for Cisco Internetwork Solutions (DESGN)* and *Designing Cisco Networks*.

About the Technical Reviewers

Clare Gough, CCIE No. 2893, has worked as a network engineer for 17 years, during which time she has managed and designed large-scale networks. In 1997 she was one of the first women to gain her CCIE. In addition to being a network design consultant, she is an acknowledged authority on the development and delivery of technical training. She is the author of several Cisco Press books, including the first three editions of the *BSCI Official Exam Certification Guide.* At Digital Equipment Corporation in Atlanta, she was part of the development team responsible for the production of all training materials. She also created PATHworks System Management courses. As the third employee hired by Protocol Interface, which was the first Cisco Training Partner, Clare eventually became the company's first training manager and saw it grow to become a part of Global Knowledge.

Jerold Swan, CCIE No. 17783, is currently a senior network engineer for the Southern Ute Indian Tribe Growth Fund, where he works on routing/switching, VoIP, and security projects. Previously, he was an instructor with Global Knowledge, where he taught CCNA and CCNP courses. He has also worked in networking in the service provider and higher education fields. He holds bachelor's and master's degrees in English from Stanford University. He lives with his wife and son in Durango, Colorado, and is involved in trail running, search and rescue, and martial arts.

Dedications

This book is dedicated to Karen. Without her love, patience, and encouragement, this book would not have been possible.

Acknowledgments

A book of this nature requires a constellation of intelligent and hardworking people to bring it together, and I appreciate all the help I've received.

Jay Swan and Clare Gough were tremendously helpful technical editors. They offered corrections and suggestions that have improved this book enormously.

I'd especially like to thank the editors at Cisco Press who have guided this book to completion: Mary Beth Ray and Dayna Isley.

This Book Is Safari Enabled

The Safari® Enabled icon on the cover of your favorite technology book means the book is available through Safari Bookshelf. When you buy this book, you get free access to the online edition for 45 days.

Safari Bookshelf is an electronic reference library that lets you easily search thousands of technical books, find code samples, download chapters, and access technical information whenever and wherever you need it.

To gain 45-day Safari Enabled access to this book:

1. Go to http://www.ciscopress.com/safarienabled.

2. Complete the brief registration form.

3. Enter the coupon code WUDT-P5UC-JD1D-6NCE-ZNVX.

If you have difficulty registering on Safari Bookshelf or accessing the online edition, please e-mail customer-service@safaribooksonline.com.

x

Contents at a Glance

Contents

Icons Used in This Book

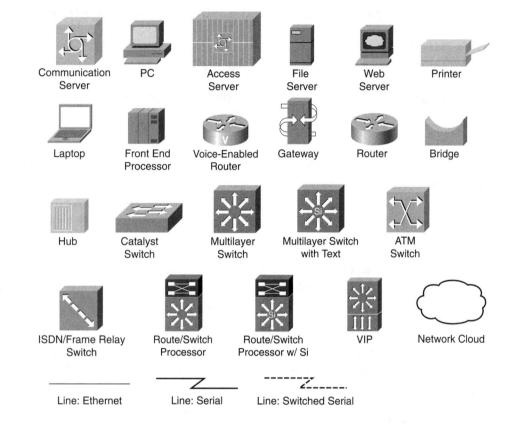

Command Syntax Conventions

The conventions used to present command syntax in this book are the same conventions used in the IOS Command Reference. The Command Reference describes these conventions as follows:

- **Boldface** indicates commands and keywords that are entered literally as shown. In actual configuration examples and output (not general command syntax), boldface indicates commands that are manually input by the user (such as a **show** command).

- *Italics* indicate arguments for which you supply actual values.

- Vertical bars (I) separate alternative, mutually exclusive elements.

- Square brackets [ ] indicate optional elements.

- Braces { } indicate a required choice.

- Braces within brackets [{ }] indicate a required choice within an optional element.

Foreword

CCNP BSCI Official Exam Certification Guide is an excellent self-study resource for the CCNP BSCI exam. Passing the exam validates the knowledge, skills, and understanding needed to use advanced IP addressing and routing in implementing scalability for Cisco ISR routers connected to LANs and WANs. It is one of several exams required to attain the CCNP certification.

Gaining certification in Cisco technology is key to the continuing educational development of today's networking professional. Through certification programs, Cisco validates the skills and expertise required to effectively manage the modern enterprise network.

Cisco Press exam certification guides and preparation materials offer exceptional—and flexible—access to the knowledge and information required to stay current in your field of expertise, or to gain new skills. Whether used as a supplement to more traditional training or as a primary source of learning, these materials offer users the information and knowledge validation required to gain new understanding and proficiencies.

Developed in conjunction with the Cisco certifications and training team, Cisco Press books are the only self-study books authorized by Cisco; these books offer students a series of exam practice tools and resource materials to help ensure that learners fully grasp the concepts and information presented.

Additional authorized Cisco instructor-led courses, e-learning, labs, and simulations are available exclusively from Cisco Learning Solutions Partners worldwide. To learn more, visit http://www.cisco.com/go/training.

I hope that you find these materials to be an enriching and useful part of your exam preparation.

Erik Ullanderson
Manager, Global Certifications
Learning@Cisco
February, 2007

Introduction

Cisco's professional certifications—CCNP (Routing and Switching), CCDP (Design), CCIP (Service Provider), CCSP (Network Security), and CCVP (Voice)—are very popular and meaningful measurements of progress in your career. Successfully completing any of these tracks demonstrates exposure and familiarity with a range of important concepts and a deep commitment to your career. Details about all Cisco certifications may be found online at www.cisco.com/go/certification.

The BSCI exam is a requirement for CCNP, CCDP, and CCIP, and generally shows that you have the theoretical understanding and implementation know-how to build and support large, complex IP networks. The BSCI exam is not an easy exam. Cisco wants to ensure that everyone who passes the test thoroughly understands the subject matter both at a conceptual level and at an implementation level.

Although this is a difficult exam, networking professionals can expect to pass if they meet the prerequisites and spend the proper amount of time on training, on-the-job experience, and study. As with most certification exams, you might not pass the first time. Taking the exam a second time, however, is likely to be easier because you will have a better idea of what to expect.

There are many questions on the BSCI exam that you might already know through your professional background and experiences, if you meet the prerequisites. This book offers you the opportunity to solidify that knowledge as you make your final preparations to take the BSCI exam.

Exam Overview

The BSCI exam is a computer-based exam. You can take the exam at any Prometric or Pearson VUE testing center. See the Cisco Training and Events page (http://www.cisco.com/web/learning/index.html) for more information about registering for your exam.

Your testing center can tell you the exact length of the exam. Be aware that when you register for the exam, you might be told to allow a certain amount of time to take the exam that is longer than the testing time indicated by the testing software when you begin. This is to allow time to get settled and take the tutorial about the testing engine.

The exam is difficult in subject matter and also in format. Questions may be multiple-choice/single answer, multiple choice/multiple answer, fill-in-the-blank, drag-and-drop, or simulations. Expect questions that require you to pick the correct answer based on output screens and configuration output. Also be prepared to configure a router or organize a diagram to demonstrate your understanding of the practical application of routing. Visit Cisco.com for a certification exam tutorial: http://www.cisco.com/web/learning/le3/learning_certification_exam_tutorial.html.

Another difficult aspect of the exam format is that you are not allowed to go back and change an answer. Candidates who are unsure about an answer will be forced to guess rather than have an extra 15 minutes to think about it at the end of the exam.

> **NOTE**   One of the prerequisites for professional-level certification is CCNA. If you have completed the CCNA then you are already familiar with the formats and techniques used in Cisco tests and the BSCI test will not surprise you in that regard.

Goals and Methods

The goal of this book is to help you efficiently study for and ultimately pass the Cisco BSCI exam (642-901). You cannot pass the BSCI exam through rote memorization. The goal of this book is to ensure that you understand and retain the topics. A happy side effect is that you will also be prepared to apply these concepts on the job.

The first step in efficient study is to recognize your own strengths and weaknesses and to delegate study time accordingly. The methodology used in this book helps you assess your current understanding of the topics and then review those topics, quizzing yourself at the end to ensure you've retained what you've learned. By "dipping into" the sections that you need, you can quickly access and review the information you need.

Who Should Read This Book?

This book is intended for anyone interested in passing the Cisco BSCI exam or interested in learning the material that is included on that exam. BSCI is attractive both as a step toward certification and as a way to prepare for important job roles.

This book is intended as a final-stage preparation tool. Before reading this book and taking the exam, you should have either taken the Building Scalable Cisco Internetworks (BSCI) v3.0 CCNP course; read through *Building Scalable Cisco Internetworks (BSCI)*, Third Edition (Authorized Self-Study Guide); have a couple of years of LAN switching experience; or have some combination of these prerequisites.

In addition, this book assumes that you have achieved the CCNA certification and understand the following concepts:

- Common networking terms
- Binary, hexadecimal, and decimal numbering and translation
- OSI reference model
- TCP/IP protocols

- IP addressing and subnetting, including complex variable-length subnetting.

- Routing protocol theory and configuration of simple networks using

  — Static routes and default routes

  — EIGRP (Enhanced Internet Gateway Routing Protocol)

  — Single-area OSPF (Open Shortest Path First)

- Standard and extended access-lists

- Point-to-point WAN links using HDLC or PPP

- Frame Relay WAN links, including point-to-point and multipoint subinterfaces

How This Book Is Organized

Although you can read this book cover-to-cover, it is designed to be flexible and allow you to easily move between chapters and sections of chapters to cover just the material that you need more work with. Each chapter covers a subset of topics on the BSCI exam. This book is divided into five parts.

Part I: Introduction to Scalable Networks

- Chapter 1, "Network Design," describes how scalability and multiplexing simplify network design; compares the enterprise composite model to the older hierarchical model; describes Services-Oriented Network Architecture (SONA) and Intelligent Information Network (IIN); and introduces the routing protocols covered in detail in later chapters.

- Chapter 2, "IP Address Planning and Summarization," acts as a bridge between CCNA and CCNP topics by reviewing IP addressing fundamentals and explaining summarization.

Part II: EIGRP

- Chapter 3, "EIGRP Principles," describes the key features and advantages of EIGRP; explains EIGRP neighbor, topology, and routing tables; and describes factors that impact EIGRP network scalability.

- Chapter 4, "Scalable EIGRP," describes EIGRP configuration, authentication, and troubleshooting.

Part III: OSPF

- Chapter 5, "Understanding Simple Single Area OSPF," reviews OSPF fundamentals and describes configuring and troubleshooting OSPF in a single area.

- Chapter 6, "OSPF Network Topologies," describes OSPF network topology options and how to configure different types of OSPF networks.

- Chapter 7, "Using OSPF Across Multiple Areas," describes the features and operation of an OSPF multi-area network and explains how to configure, verify, and troubleshoot multi-area OSPF.

- Chapter 8, "OSPF Advanced Topics," describes how OSPF design uses stub, totally stubby, and not-so-stubby areas to optimize resource utilization, and explains OSPF authentication.

Part IV: IS-IS

- Chapter 9, "Fundamentals of the Integrated IS-IS Protocol," introduces Integrated IS-IS, including the ISO addressing structure, adjacencies, and design considerations.

- Chapter 10, "Using IS-IS with IP," covers basic IS-IS configuration, optional IS-IS commands, and commands for verifying and troubleshooting the IS-IS operation.

Part V: Cisco IOS Routing Features

- Chapter 11, "Implementing Redistribution and Controlling Routing Updates," introduces redistribution fundamentals and describes controlling routing updates, important configuration commands, and when to use **traceroute** and **ping.**

- Chapter 12, "Controlling Redistribution with Route Maps," describes configuring and monitoring route maps.

- Chapter 13, "Dynamic Host Control Protocol," describes the process of allocating IP addresses with DHCP; defines the server, relay, and client used by DHCP; and outlines the process for troubleshooting DHCP

Part VI: BGP

- Chapter 14, "BGP Concepts," introduces fundamental concepts such basic BGP operation, multihoming, load sharing, synchronization, and BGP states.

- Chapter 15, "BGP Neighbors," describes basic BGP configuration commands, commands for managing and verifying the BGP configuration, and methods for resetting neighbors.

- Chapter 16, "Controlling BGP Route Selection," describes BGP attributes, path selection, and commands that you can use to display output related to BGP attributes.

Part VII: Multicasting

- Chapter 17, "What Is Multicasting?," explains styles of IP addresses, the process to convert a multicast IP address to a multicast MAC address, and some of the problems that limit the use of multicasting.

- Chapter 18, "IGMP and Multicast Routing Protocols," describes data link layer support for multicast, introduces the features of IGMP, and describes enabling IGMP groups and configuring IGMP snooping.

- Chapter 19, "Configuring Multicast," describes multicast routing protocols and the commands necessary to implement multicasting.

Part VIII: IPv6

- Chapter 20, "Introduction to IPv6 and IPv6 Addressing," describes the need for IPv6, the IPv6 packet header, IPv6 addressing and address assignments, and IPv6 mobility.

- Chapter 21, "IPv6 Routing Protocols, Configuration, and Transitioning from IPv4," describes the various routing protocols that support IPv6, provides the commands to configure and verify IPv6 and OSPFv3, and discusses the transition from IPv4 to IPv6.

Each chapter in the book uses several features to help you make the best use of your time in that chapter. The features are as follows:

- **Assessment**—Each chapter begins with a "Do I Know This Already?" quiz that helps you determine the amount of time you need to spend studying that chapter. If you intend to read the entire chapter, you can save the quiz for later use. Questions are all multiple-choice to give a quick assessment of your knowledge.

  A more lengthy "Q&A" section appears near the end of each chapter. The Q&A section presents many open-ended review questions to test your retention and comprehension of the subject matter presented in the chapter.

  Appendix A, "Answers to Chapter 'Do I Know This Already?' Quizzes and Q&A Sections," list the answers to both quizzes.

- **Foundation Topics**—This is the core section of each chapter that explains the protocols, concepts, and configuration for the topics in the chapter.

- **Foundation Summary**—At the end of each chapter, a Foundation Summary collects key concepts, methodologies, and commands into an easy-to-review format.

- **Scenarios**—Where appropriate, some chapters conclude with a Scenarios section that provides an in-depth examination of a network implementation. Instead of posing a simple question asking for a single fact, the scenarios let you design, configure, and troubleshoot networks (at least on paper) without the clues inherent in a multiple-choice quiz format.

- **CD-based practice exam**—The companion CD-ROM contains two separate test banks—one composed of the questions from the book and an entirely new test bank of questions to reinforce your understanding of the book's concepts. In addition to the multiple-choice questions, you encounter some configuration simulation questions for which you actually perform configurations. This is the best tool for helping you prepare for the actual test-taking process.

BSCI Exam Topics

The exact questions that appear on the BSCI exam are a very closely guarded secret. Only those who write the questions for Cisco and who have access to the entire question database truly know what is on the exam. Cisco reveals only general details about the contents and objectives of the BSCI exam. Because Cisco maintains the right to change this information without notice, it is important that you check the web site for the most current information. You can find a list of Cisco exams and the general outline that accompanies each exam at http://www.cisco.com/go/certification.

Table I-1 lists the BSCI 642-901 exam topics posted on the Cisco website at the publication time of this book. The table reflects the part of the book in which each topic is discussed.

Table I-1 *Cisco Exam Topics*

Exam Topic	Part of This Book That Covers the Exam Topic
Explain the functions and operations of EIGRP (e.g., DUAL).	Part II*
Configure EIGRP routing (e.g., Stub Routing, authentication, etc.).	Part II
Verify or troubleshoot EIGRP routing configurations.	Part II
Explain the functions and operations of multiarea OSPF.	Part III
Configure multiarea OSPF routing (e.g., Stub, NSSA, authentication, etc.).	Part III
Verify or troubleshoot multiarea OSPF routing configurations.	Part III
Describe the features and benefits of integrated IS-IS.	Part IV
Configure and verify integrated IS-IS.	Part IV
Describe, configure, or verify route redistribution between IP routing IGPs (e.g., route-maps, default routes, etc.).	Part V
Describe, configure, or verify route filtering (i.e., distribute-lists and passive interfaces).	Part V
Describe and configure DHCP services (e.g., Server, Client, IP helper address, etc.).	Part V
Describe the functions and operations of BGP.	Part VI
Configure or verify BGP operation in a non-transit AS (e.g., authentication).	Part VI
Configure BGP path selection (i.e., Local Preference, AS Path, Weight, or MED attributes).	Part VI
Describe IP Multicast (e.g., Layer-3 to Layer-2 mapping, IGMP, etc.).	Part VII
Describe, configure, or verify IP multicast routing (i.e., PIM Sparse-Dense Mode).	Part VII
Describe IPv6 addressing operations.	Part VIII
Describe IPv6 interoperation with IPv4.	Part VIII
Describe, configure, or verify OSPF routing with IPv6 addressing.	Part VIII

* Part I, "Introduction to Scalable Networks," provides an overview of network design. Although not directly tied to official exam topics, understanding concepts described in Part I is essential for passing the exam.

For More Information

Cisco might make changes that affect the CCNP certification from time to time. You should always check cisco.com for the latest details. Also, you can look to this book's website http://www.ciscopress.com/title/158720147x for information pertinent to how you might use this book differently in light of Cisco's future changes.

The *CCNP BSCI Official Exam Certification Guide* is designed to help you attain CCNP, CCDP, or CCIP certification. It is a certification book from the only Cisco-authorized publisher. We at Cisco Press believe that this book will help you achieve certification, but the real work is up to you. We hope you find your time well-spent with this book. Good luck!

Part I: Introduction to Scalable Networks

This chapter covers the following topics:

- **Building Scalable Networks**—Describes how scalability and multiplexing simplify network design.

- **Enterprise Architecture**—Describes the older hierarchical model and the newer enterprise composite model.

- **SONA and IIN**—Describes the three phases of the Intelligent Information Network (IIN) and how Services-Oriented Network Architecture (SONA) applies the IIN ideas to enterprise networks.

- **Comparing Routing Protocols**—Compares the different features of RIP (versions 1 and 2), OSPF, EIGRP, IS-IS, and BGP.

Network Design

This first chapter includes a variety of concepts, some of which are expanded on later in the book, some of which are simply here to expose you to a set of ideas. Regardless of the motivation, all the topics covered in this chapter are on the Building Scalable Cisco Internetworks (BSCI) exam and should be understood.

Network design is an important topic and is covered here at the depth necessary to define terms and standards about implementation. These terms form a foundation for the rest of the book.

Services-Oriented Network Architecture (SONA) and Intelligent Information Network (IIN) are also broadly described in this chapter. They are only covered to the extent you might expect to see them on the exam.

This is a book about routing protocols, and a comparison and theoretical discussion of the different routing protocols is found here. Again, this section is important because it helps describe similarities and unique features and sets the stage for the chapters to come.

"Do I Know This Already?" Quiz

The purpose of the "Do I Know This Already?" quiz is to help you decide which parts of this chapter to use. If you already intend to read the entire chapter, you do not necessarily need to answer these questions.

The 12-question quiz, derived from the major sections in the "Foundation Topics" portion of the chapter, helps you determine how to spend your limited study time.

Table 1-1 outlines the major topics discussed in this chapter and the corresponding quiz questions.

Table 1-1 *"Do I Know This Already?" Foundation Topics Section-to-Question Mapping*

Foundation Topics Section	Questions Covered in This Section	Score
Building Scalable Networks	1–2	
Enterprise Architecture	3–5	
SONA and IIN	6–8	
Comparing Routing Protocols	9–12	
Total Score		

CAUTION The goal of self-assessment is to gauge your mastery of the topics in this chapter. If you do not know the answer to a question or are only partially sure of the answer, you should mark the question wrong for purposes of the self-assessment. Giving yourself credit for an answer you correctly guessed skews your results and might provide you with a false sense of security.

1. How many links are required to form a full mesh of eight devices?

    a. 7

    b. 28

    c. 80

    d. Not possible

2. What does a "scalable" design indicate?

    a. The design can be "unfolded" to fit various sizes.

    b. The design grows without causing the endpoint costs to grow.

    c. Only large enterprises can use this design.

    d. The design uses EIGRP and BGP.

3. Which of the following describe the hierarchical network model?

    a. Switching, Routing, Provider

    b. Access, Distribution, Core

    c. Physical, Data Link, Network

    d. Red, Blue, Black

4. In the standard hierarchical design, what elements are found within a switch block?

    a. Two core switches and some number of distribution switches

    b. Two distribution Layer-2 switches and some number of Layer-1 access switches

    c. Two distribution Layer-3 switches and some number of Layer-2 access switches

    d. One access switch per department

5. What are the key differences between traditional hierarchical design and the enterprise composite model?

    a. Hierarchical design has three layers, the Enterprise Composite Model has five.

    b. Servers and WAN connections are defined.

    c. The hierarchical design model is Cisco-specific.

    d. The enterprise composite model is superseded by AON.

6. What is the goal of the SONA network infrastructure layer?

    a. Provide a hierarchical and converged network

    b. Allow for integration of Service and Network

    c. Support dynamic resource allocation

    d. Provide for accounting and billing services

7. Which SONA layer corresponds to IIN phase two?

    a. Network infrastructure

    b. Application

    c. Session

    d. Interactive services

8. What is the goal of IIN phase three?

    a. To create service-aware networks

    b. To converge voice and data networks

    c. To provide complete redundancy

    d. To allow for pervasive network management

9.   Which of the following routing protocols is proprietary?

    a. RIP

    b. OSPF

    c. EIGRP

    d. BGP

10.   Which of the following routing protocols is meant to work between autonomous systems?

    a. RIP

    b. OSPF

    c. EIGRP

    d. BGP

11.   Which of the following routing protocols converge much more quickly than the others?

    a. RIP

    b. IGRP

    c. OSPF

    d. EIGRP

12.   Which of the following routing protocols are classless?

    a. RIP

    b. OSPF

    c. EIGRP

    d. BGP

The answers to the "Do I Know This Already?" quiz are found in Appendix A, "Answers to Chapter 'Do I Know This Already?' Quizzes and Q&A Sections." Compare your score with the following suggestions to determine how to proceed:

■   **8 or less overall score**—Read the entire chapter. This includes the "Foundation Topics," "Foundation Summary," and "Q&A" sections.

- **9 or 10 overall score**—Begin with the "Foundation Summary" section, and then go to the "Q&A" section at the end of the chapter. If you have trouble answering the Q&A questions, read the appropriate sections in "Foundation Topics."

- **11 or 12 overall score**—If you want more review on these topics, skip to the "Foundation Summary" section and then go to the "Q&A" section at the end of the chapter. Otherwise, move to the next chapter.

Foundation Topics

Building Scalable Networks

Because this book has not yet discussed large data networks, this chapter uses the phone system as an easily understandable example of network design.

Originally, folks needed to run wires to every home they might want to call. Phone companies provided a more efficient way to form connections by using one line from a home to a central point to switch traffic to arbitrary locations. Another type of consolidation came when the T1 carrier was introduced. Before T1 a business needing 20 phone lines would have needed 20 pairs of copper run out from the telephone central office (CO). A T1 uses 2 pairs and supports 24 concurrent conversations.

Although this example might seem far afield, it points out two techniques that are used to simplify networks: scalability and multiplexing.

Scalability

This book is about building *scalable* Cisco internetworks, but what does "scalable" mean? The definition of scalability affects every subject in this book. Therefore, it is important to begin with an idea of what a "scalable" network looks like.

Imagine that to use the phone, folks in a town would need to run a telephone line from every home to every other house. This is called a *full-mesh design*. If there are n homes in the town, the total number of lines required is

$$\text{lines} = n(n - 1)/2$$

Table 1-2 relates town size to the number of lines required to support the town.

Table 1-2 *Links in a Full-Mesh Network*

Homes	Lines Required
10	45
100	4,950
1000	499,500

Figure 1-1 illustrates this same point with a town of five homes. Notice that for five homes, 10 lines are required: $5(4)/2 = 10$.

Figure 1-1 *Full-Mesh Phone Network*

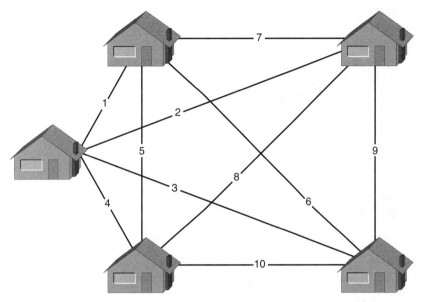

Adding one more home to the diagram would require five new lines, taking the town from 10 lines to 15. This type of growth is called *exponential growth* because the number of lines is growing proportional to an n^2 pace. In this system, the 100th house must have 99 lines (one to each of the preceding homes), while the 101st house will need 100 lines. It therefore becomes progressively more expensive to expand the network. It is easy to see that the town could not expand too much using this type of wiring.

On the other hand, the town might run one phone line from each house back to a central switching station. This type of topology is called a hub and spoke. With this topology, any line could arbitrarily be connected to any other line. In this system, the total number of lines required is calculated simply (where *n* is the number of endpoints, that is, every home plus the CO):

$$\text{lines} = n - 1$$

Table 1-3 relates town size to the number of lines required to support the town. Remember that the CO counts as an endpoint, so for 10 homes n = 11 (10 + CO) .

Table 1-3 *Links in a Hub and Spoke Network*

Homes	Lines Required
10	10
100	100
1000	1000

Figure 1-2 illustrates this same point with a town of five homes. Notice that for five homes, five lines are required.

Figure 1-2 *Hub and Spoke Phone Network*

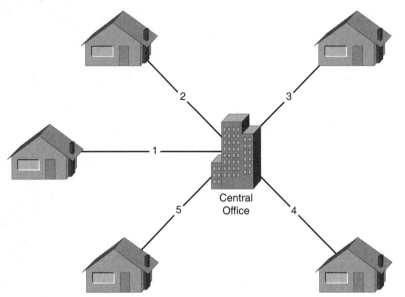

Each new home added now requires only one new line. This type of growth is called *linear growth* because the number of lines increases at the same pace as the number of homes. As the town grows, the price of installing the 101st house will be the same as the cost of the installation of the 100th house.

Scalability is a term that indicates that a network can support arbitrary growth and that the cost per endpoint will remain constant. One of the primary goals for any network designer is to support scalable growth.

Multiplexing

Historically, voice traffic has used one set of circuits and data traffic has used another. In the 1980s, data traffic was even segregated into separate networks for mainframe traffic (SNA) and LAN traffic (such as IPX or IP).

A T1 places 24 phone conversations onto two copper pairs by time division multiplexing (using short slices of time for each channel). The T1 saves the phone company a lot of expense in building out subscriber lines. However, T1s cannot dynamically adjust as usage requirements change.

It was very common to find a T1 where 12 of the 24 channels were dedicated to voice, 6 to IPX, and 6 to SNA. This works, but what happens when IPX runs out of capacity and no one is talking on the phone? Nothing, because this segregated system lacks a mechanism to dynamically adjust.

Modern networks are designed to carry voice, enterprise applications, normal LAN traffic, and management traffic all on a single secure infrastructure. This practice is called *convergence*. The traffic is forced, or *statistically multiplexed*, to share access to the network.

Recognizing the types of traffic modern converged networks have to bear will be important in just a bit, so hold this thought. The next topic discussed is design; after this, the chapter will again focus on traffic flow and how it impacts design.

Enterprise Architecture

With new networks, it is important to take the time to consider how addressing will take place and how routing protocols will run. Many modern networks have grown organically to meet business conditions; this lack of deliberation creates problems. Therefore, it is important to consider good design principles and to prune those organic networks back to something that is manageable.

A firm idea of what good design looks like is an important tool in building and maintaining networks. The Cisco description of a well-designed network has evolved over time, and this section presents the older hierarchical model and the newer enterprise composite model.

Hierarchical Design Model

Cisco has used the three-level hierarchical design model for years. This older model provided a high-level idea of how a reliable network could be conceived but was largely conceptual, because it did not provide specific guidance.

Figure 1-3 shows a prototypical picture of the hierarchical design model. This is a simple drawing of how the three-layer model might have been built out. A distribution Layer 3 switch is used for each building on campus, tying together the access switches on the floors. The core switches link the various buildings together.

Access devices are Layer 2 switches based on price per port and are chosen to get the needed number of ports. Access switches are responsible for attaching end systems to the network and assigning them to virtual LANs (VLANs).

Distribution devices are Layer 3 switches and act as intermediate devices that route between VLANs and apply traffic policies such as firewalling and quality of service (QoS) decisions.

Figure 1-3 *Hierarchical Design*

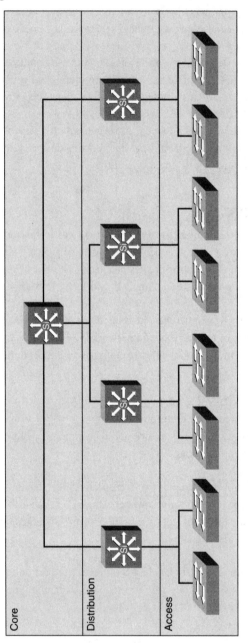

Core devices, also known as the backbone, provide high-speed paths between distribution devices.

Note that the distribution layer is the "sweet spot" for managing the network. Implementing policy on access devices would drive up the complexity and costs of those devices and slow them down, plus it would mandate complex management of a large number of devices. Implementing policy at the core would slow down devices that are primarily tasked with moving traffic quickly.

This early model was a good starting point, but it failed to address key issues, such as

- Implementing redundancy

- Adding Internet access and security

- Accounting for remote access

- Locating workgroup and enterprise services

Cisco developed the enterprise composite network model to addresses these issues.

Enterprise Composite Network Model

Later versions of the hierarchical model showed redundant distribution and core devices and connections to make the model more fault tolerant. A set of distribution devices and their accompanying access layer switches were called a *switch block*. Figure 1-4 shows a switch block design.

Switch block design helped explain how redundancy fit in networks, but still did not adequately specify other parts of network design. Cisco therefore developed a newer design model—the enterprise composite model—that is significantly more complex. This model attempts to address the major shortcomings of the hierarchical model by expanding the older version and making specific recommendations about how and where certain network functions should be implemented. This model is based on the principles described in Cisco's description of converged networks.

The enterprise composite model is broken up into three large pieces:

- Enterprise campus

- Enterprise edge

- Service provider edge

Figure 1-5 shows the complete enterprise composite model.

Figure 1-4 *Campus Design with Switch Blocks*

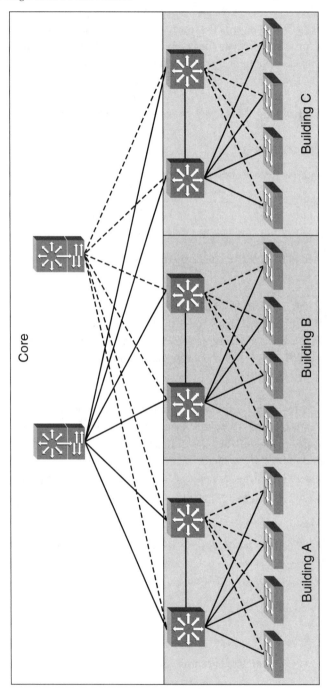

Figure 1-5 *Enterprise Composite Model*

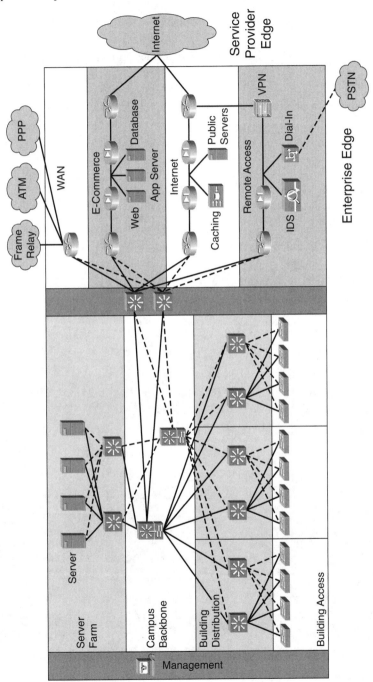

The following sections describe each piece of the enterprise composite model.

Enterprise Campus

The *enterprise campus* looks like the switch block design with some added details. It features five sections:

- Campus backbone (like the core layer of the hierarchical model)

- Building distribution

- Building access

- Management

- Server farm (for enterprise services)

Figure 1-6 shows the enterprise campus.

Figure 1-6 *Enterprise Campus*

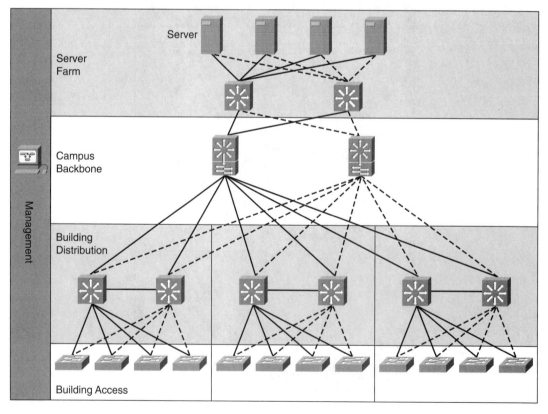

As you can see, the enterprise campus builds on the switch block idea but gives specific guidance about where to place servers and management equipment. Notice that the server farm looks like a switch block, but here all the servers are directly and redundantly attached (also called *dual-homed*) to the switches.

Enterprise Edge

The *enterprise edge* details the connections from the campus to the wider area and includes

- E-Commerce

- Internet connectivity

- Remote access (dial-up and VPN)

- WAN (internal links)

Note that the enterprise edge is basically just another switch block with redundant distribution elements and resources within, only with some extra definition. Figure 1-7 shows the enterprise edge.

Service Provider Edge

The *service provider edge* includes the public networks that facilitate wide-area connectivity:

- Internet service provider (ISP)

- Public Switched Telephone Network (PSTN) for dialup

- Frame Relay, ATM, and PPP for private connectivity

Figure 1-7 *Enterprise Edge*

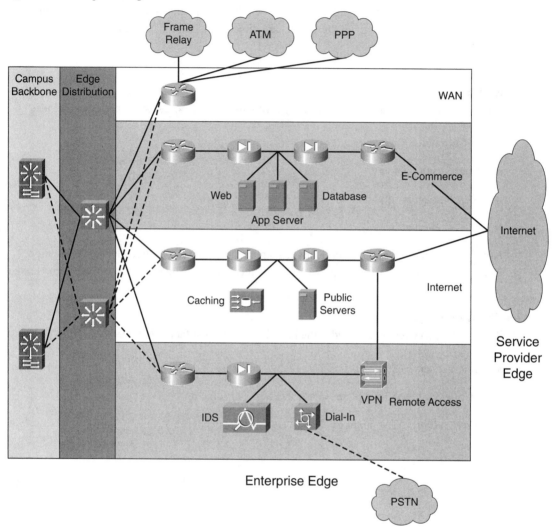

SONA and IIN

The "Multiplexing" section of this chapter described the idea of a converged network as a system that integrates what were previously disparate systems (such as voice, video, and data). The contents of a converged network include the following traffic types:

- Voice signaling and bearer traffic

- Core application traffic, such as enterprise resource planning or customer relationship management

- Transactional traffic related to database interaction

- Network management traffic for monitoring and maintaining the network structure (including routing protocol traffic)

- Multicast multimedia

- "Other" traffic, such as web pages, e-mail, and file transfer

Each of these traffic types has unique requirements and expectations that govern its execution. These requirements include security, QoS, transmission capacity, and delay.

Security, in particular, is a constant requirement. Data can be stolen, erased, or corrupted through malicious attack. Safeguarding the secure operation of the network is the first goal, which should be accomplished before looking at speed or efficiency.

The other parameters vary—for example, interactive traffic tends to use little capacity but needs quick response, whereas "default" applications such as file transfer really only care about capacity.

To support this mixture of multiplexed traffic, Cisco routers are able to implement filtering, compression, prioritization, and policing (dedicating network capacity). Except for filtering, these capabilities are referred to collectively as QoS.

NOTE   The absolute best way to meet capacity requirements is to have twice as much bandwidth as needed. QoS is needed only when there is not enough bandwidth. In most cases this strategy is a bit of a dream, however.

As an alternative to QoS, Cisco espouses an ideal called the Intelligent Information Network (IIN).

IIN describes a vision of a network that integrates network and application functionality cooperatively and allows the network to be smart about how it handles traffic to minimize the footprint of applications. For instance, security can be handled at the switch port instead of at a central server, or XML contents can be used to make routing decisions. IIN is built on top of the enterprise composite model and describes additional functionality overlaid on the composite template.

IIN is an evolutionary approach, where functionality is added as required. The IIN evolution is described in three phases:

- Phase 1: Integrated Transport

- Phase 2: Integrated Services

- Phase 3: Integrated Applications

The following sections describe each phase in more detail.

Phase 1: Integrated Transport

Phase 1, Integrated Transport, describes a converged network, built along the lines of the enterprise composite model and based on open standards. The industry has been transitioning to this phase over the past few years and Cisco Integrated Services Routers are a tangible example of this trend.

Phase 2: Integrated Services

Phase 2, Integrated Services, attempts to virtualize resources such as servers, storage, and network access, and move to an "on-demand" model.

Virtualization of resources is a phrase that at first hearing sounds like marketing-speak; however, by this, Cisco means that services are not associated with a particular device or location. Instead, many services may reside in one device to ease management, or many devices may provide one service to provide more reliable service.

An example of providing many services on one device is the Integrated Services Router, which brings together routing, switching, voice, network management, security, and wireless. Another example is load balancers, which make many servers look like one in order to grow out the capacity.

The opposite of this is taking one resource and making it look like many. The new generation of IOS is capable of having a router present itself as many "virtual router" instances, allowing your company to deliver different logical topologies on the same physical infrastructure. Server virtualization is another example. Virtual servers allow one physical machine to support many installations.

Of course, the classic example of taking one resource and making it appear to be many resources is VLANs. VLANs allow one physical infrastructure to support multiple network implementations.

However you slice it, virtualization provides flexibility in configuration and management.

Phase 3: Integrated Applications

Phase 3, Integrated Applications, uses application-oriented networking (AON) to make the network "application aware" and allow the network to actively participate in service delivery.

An example of this phase three IIN holistic approach to service delivery is Network Admission Control (NAC). Before NAC, authentication, VLAN assignment, and anti-virus updates were separately managed. With NAC in place, the network is able to check the policy stance of a client and admit, deny, or remediate based on policies.

IIN allows the network to deconstruct packets, parse fields, and take actions based on the values it finds. An Integrated Services Router equipped with an AON blade might be set up to route traffic from a business partner. The AON blade could examine traffic, recognize the application, and rebuild XML files in memory. Corrupted XML fields might represent an attack (called *schema poisoning*), so the AON blade could react by blocking that source from further communication. In this example, routing, an awareness of the application data flow, and security are combined to allow the network to contribute to the success of the application.

Services-Oriented Network Architecture

Services-Oriented Network Architecture (SONA) is the application of the IIN ideas to enterprise networks. SONA breaks down the IIN functions into three layers. The SONA Network Infrastructure is comparable to IIN Phase 1. IIN Phase 2 is analogous to the SONA Interactive Services layer, while the Application layer has the same concepts as IIN Phase 3. More specifically, the three SONA layers are

- Network Infrastructure, which describes a hierarchical converged network and the attached end-systems.

- Interactive Services, which allocates resources to applications.

- Application, which includes business policy and logic integration

Figure 1-8 shows the mapping between IIN and SONA.

Figure 1-8 *IIN and SONA*

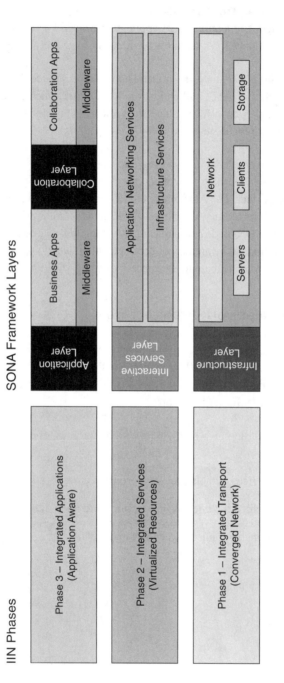

Comparing Routing Protocols

The majority of this book is devoted to understanding how routing protocols work and how they are optimized. Before delving into the details, though, it's worth thinking about the characteristics of routing protocols, how the protocols differ, and how those differences impact design. This section discusses RIP (versions 1 and 2), OSPF, EIGRP, IS-IS, and BGP.

NOTE This book assumes that you have completed CCNA or have equivalent experience. Basic knowledge and techniques used with RIP, EIGRP, and OSPF will be found with the CCNA material.

Distance Vector and Link State Routing Protocols

Routing protocols are built to employ one of two basic strategies to communicate routing information. Distance vector routing protocols work by passing copies of their routing table to their neighbors (this is also known as "routing by rumor" because neighbors talk to neighbors and not the source of the route). Link state routing protocols work by advertising a list of their neighbors and the networks attached to their neighbors until all routers have a copy of all lists. The routers then run the Shortest Path First algorithm to analyze all paths and determine best paths.

Distance vector routing is less processor- and memory-intensive than link state routing, but can have loops because decisions are made on incomplete information (solely the portion of the routing table sent by a neighbor). Link state routing is loop-proof because routers know all possible routes, but link state routing requires more CPU time and memory.

Table 1-4 shows the various routing protocols and the technique they employ.

Table 1-4 *Distance Vector and Link State Protocols*

Protocol	Technique
RIP	Distance Vector
RIPv2	Distance Vector
EIGRP	Distance Vector
OSPF	Link State
IS-IS	Link State
BGP	Path Vector

Classless and Classful Routing

Another characteristic of routing protocols is the manner in which they advertise routes. Older routing protocols pass just the prefix, such as "192.168.1.0." Given that example, there is no way for a router to understand if the network advertised uses a 24-bit mask or a 27-bit mask.

Older routing protocols, such as RIP and IGRP, assume the subnet mask is the same as the one on the receiving interface or that it is the default mask. The default mask for Class A networks is /8, for Class B it is /16, and for Class C it is /24. This behavior is called *classful*, because the assumption is based on the class of the IP address.

Example 1-1 shows an advertisement from a Routing Information Protocol (RIP) router. Notice that no subnet mask is advertised. For instance, the first route is 10.0.0.0 with no indication of the appropriate subnet mask. This shows that RIP is a classful routing protocol.

Example 1-1   *Classful RIP Advertisements*

```
Router1#debug ip rip
RIP protocol debugging is on
00:03:40: RIP: received v1 update from 172.16.2.200 on Serial1/0
00:03:40:       10.0.0.0 in 1 hops
00:03:40:       172.16.4.0 in 1 hops
00:03:40:       172.16.6.0 in 1 hops
00:03:40:       172.16.44.0 in 2 hops
00:03:40:       172.16.66.0 in 2 hops
```

Modern routing protocols (OSPF, IS-IS, and EIGRP) explicitly advertise the mask. There is no assumption involved, the mask is clearly indicated. This behavior is referred to as *classless*.

Variable Length Subnet Masks (VLSM) refers to the property of a network that allows different subnet masks to be mixed throughout the network. For instance, office networks might each use /24 while point-to-point lines use /30. Classless Interdomain Routing (CIDR) is a property of a network that allows classful networks to be aggregated—for example, combining 192.168.0.0/24 and 192.168.1.0/24 into a "supernet" that includes 512 addresses. Classless routing protocols support VLSM and CIDR. In fact, the three terms are so closely linked that they are sometimes used synonymously.

Example 1-2 shows RIP version 2 (RIPv2) enabled on Router1. Notice that the subnet mask is now advertised. RIPv2 is a classless routing protocol.

Example 1-2   *Classless RIPv2 Advertisements*

```
Router1#configure terminal
Enter configuration commands, one per line.  End with CNTL/Z.
Router1(config)#router rip
```

Example 1-2 *Classless RIPv2 Advertisements (Continued)*

```
Router1(config-router)#version 2
Router1(config-router)#end
Router1#debug ip rip
RIP protocol debugging is on
00:11:07: RIP: sending v2 update to 224.0.0.9 via FastEthernet0/0 (172.16.22.1)
00:11:07: RIP: build update entries
00:11:07:        10.0.0.0/8 via 0.0.0.0, metric 2, tag 0
00:11:07:        172.16.2.0/24 via 0.0.0.0, metric 1, tag 0
00:11:07:        172.16.4.0/24 via 0.0.0.0, metric 2, tag 0
00:11:07:        172.16.6.0/24 via 0.0.0.0, metric 2, tag 0
00:11:07:        172.16.44.0/24 via 0.0.0.0, metric 3, tag 0
00:11:07:        172.16.66.0/24 via 0.0.0.0, metric 3, tag 0
```

The Internet has been classless for years and the vast majority of enterprise networks are classless. In fact, classful routing protocols should be considered outdated. Classless routing protocols are necessary in today's network. Table 1-5 shows the protocols and whether each is classful or classless.

Table 1-5 *Classless and Classful Routing*

Protocol	Classless or Classful
RIP	Classful
RIPv2	Classless
EIGRP	Classless
OSPF	Classless
IS-IS	Classless
BGP	Classless

Interior and Exterior Gateway Protocols

Most protocols are interior gateway protocols, meaning that they are designed to run inside your network. Inside a network, routers can trust each other and—because all links are owned by the organization—can choose paths without regard to who owns a link.

BGP is an exterior gateway protocol (EGP), meaning that BGP is the routing protocol used between autonomous systems in the public Internet. Because it is the only EGP, you will have to consider using it if you connect your network to the Internet.

Table 1-6 shows the routing protocols and whether each is intended for interior or exterior use.

Table 1-6 *Interior and Exterior Routing Protocols*

Protocol	Interior or Exterior Gateway Protocol
RIP	IGP
RIPv2	IGP
EIGRP	IGP
OSPF	IGP
IS-IS	IGP
BGP	EGP

Convergence Times

Another distinguishing characteristic of routing protocols is speed. Convergence times are generally grouped as slow or fast. Fast convergence means that the routing protocol is able to recognize a problem and fix it faster than a user can call to report the problem. Slow protocols, such as RIP and IGRP, can take minutes to converge. Fast protocols, such as OSPF, IS-IS, and EIGRP, generally converge in less than ten seconds.

Table 1-7 shows the convergence speeds of the routing protocols to help in your selection.

Table 1-7 *Convergence Times*

Protocol	Convergence Speed
RIP	Slow
RIPv2	Slow
EIGRP	Fast
OSPF	Fast
IS-IS	Fast
BGP	Slow

Proprietary and Open Protocols

The important aspects of routing protocols are that they are fast and that they are classless. Three routing protocols fit that description: OSPF, IS-IS, and EIGRP. All three protocols are wholly acceptable; however, there are some small differences between them from a support perspective.

OSPF and IS-IS are public standards, and are therefore supported on a wider variety of equipment than proprietary protocols. This protects against incompatibilities with legacy equipment or "vendor lock-in." On the other hand, these protocols can be complicated to build and maintain.

EIGRP is the easiest to configure of the three, as it does many smart things automatically. EIGRP, however, is a Cisco proprietary protocol and using it locks you in to Cisco equipment.

Obviously, different organizations will weigh factors such as ease of use and public standards. The "best" protocol is the one that is most appropriate for a given situation.

Table 1-8 shows the routing protocols and points out which are proprietary.

Table 1-8 *Proprietary Protocols*

Protocol	Proprietary
RIP	No
RIPv2	No
EIGRP	Yes
OSPF	No
IS-IS	No
BGP	No

Summarizing Routing Protocol Characteristics

Older routing protocols (RIP versions 1 and 2 and IGRP) are slow and modern routing protocols (OSPF, IS-IS, EIGRP, and BGP) are fast. Older routing protocols are slow because they send a full copy of all their information periodically. These older protocols, like RIP and IGRP, have to use that periodic transmission as both a routing advertisement and a keepalive message (to let the receiver know that they are still alive). Because they are sending a lot of information, they talk less often (every 30 seconds for RIP). In addition to being slow, they also consume a lot of bandwidth relative to their function.

Modern routing protocols are fast because they separate the keepalive and update functions. Updates are only sent when connections change and new networks need to be advertised or old networks need to be withdrawn. Otherwise, routers simply have to verify that their neighbors are still alive. Because they send small keepalives, routers can afford to check on each other more often (every 5 seconds for EIGRP).

This distinction is at the heart of what makes modern routing protocols so much faster than their predecessors.

RIP and IGRP are older distance vector routing protocols that are slow and classful. There is no reason to run either of these today. Some legacy systems—such as some UNIX systems—expect to learn their default gateway by eavesdropping on RIP advertisements. If you have to deploy RIP, RIPv2 at least has the advantage of being classless.

EIGRP is a modern distance vector routing protocol. It is classless and fast, easy to set up and maintain, but is proprietary to Cisco. Some organizations refuse to consider proprietary standards. The counter argument to this, however, is that EIGRP provides equivalent performance to OSPF but requires less expertise and less time to maintain. By far the most expensive part of your network is the people it takes to maintain it, so this is a powerful argument.

OSPF is a modern classless and fast link-state routing protocol. The "O" stands for "open," meaning public standard. OSPF, however, has a steep learning curve and uses more processor time and memory than EIGRP. If your organization supports a heterogeneous mixture of routers, or has chosen to abstain from proprietary protocols for philosophical reasons, OSPF is a good fit.

IS-IS was developed to compete with OSPF and the two protocols are similar in more ways than they are dissimilar. Today it is moderately difficult to find anyone who has experience working with IS-IS, which makes IS-IS a difficult choice. In every other regard—it is open, fast, and classless—it is a great routing protocol. There is still some interest in IS-IS because it can be adapted to support MPLS and to support IPv6, and, probably because of that, IS-IS is included on this test.

There are only two good reasons to choose one interior routing protocol over another: because it is fast and because it is classless. EIGRP and OSPF each meet these criteria. The other reasons to prefer one over another are largely based on situational requirements or company philosophy. It is not that those values are not important, just that they are not quantifiable. For instance, EIGRP and OSPF are both fine choices, but if your organization does not use proprietary standards then you must go with OSPF. In this case, you are not choosing OSPF because EIGRP does not work equally well, but rather because it is not as good a fit for the policies and management objectives of your company.

BGP is the routing protocol used between autonomous systems in the public Internet and you will have to use it if you connect your network to the Internet.

This book analyzes the modern routing protocols—EIGRP, OSPF, IS-IS, and BGP—and then talks about how to use them cooperatively. There are situations where you must run more than one—for instance, you might run RIP to support an old UNIX host, OSPF for internal routes, and BGP to connect to the Internet.

Foundation Summary

The Foundation Summary provides a convenient review of many key concepts in this chapter. If you are already comfortable with the topics in this chapter, this summary might help you recall a few details. If you just read this chapter, this review should help solidify some key facts. If you are doing your final prep before the exam, the following lists and tables are a convenient way to review the day before the exam.

Figure 1-9 shows the complete enterprise composite model.

Figure 1-9 *Enterprise Composite Model*

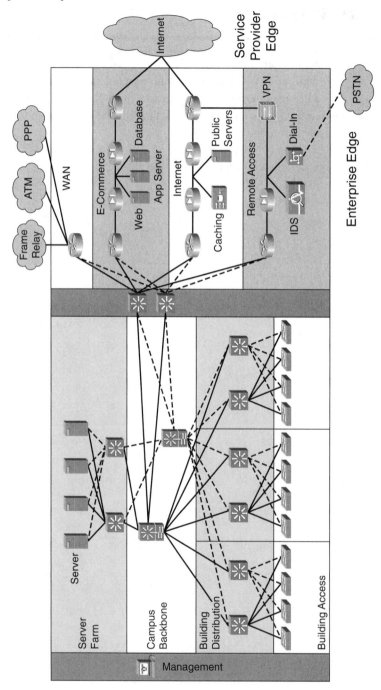

Figure 1-10 shows the IIN and SONA layers.

Figure 1-10   *IIN and SONA*

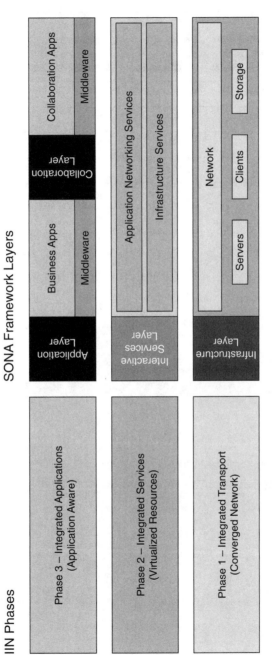

Table 1-9 summarizes the different routing protocols.

Table 1-9 *Comparing Routing Protocols*

Protocol	Distance Vector or Link State	Classless	Interior/ Exterior Gateway Protocol	Convergence Speed	Proprietary
RIP	DV	No	IGP	Slow	No
RIPv2	DV	Yes	IGP	Slow	No
EIGRP	DV	Yes	IGP	Fast	Yes
OSPF	LS	Yes	IGP	Fast	No
IS-IS	LS	Yes	IGP	Fast	No
BGP	Path Vector	Yes	EGP	Slow	No

Q&A

The questions and scenarios in this book are designed to be challenging and to make sure that you know the answer. Rather than allowing you to derive the answers from clues hidden inside the questions themselves, the questions challenge your understanding and recall of the subject.

You can find the answers to these questions in Appendix A. For more practice with exam-like question formats, use the exam engine on the CD-ROM.

1. List the layers of the hierarchical network model and give a short description of each one.

2. Describe the enterprise campus component of the enterprise composite model.

3. How is the enterprise campus component of the enterprise composite model different from the hierarchical model?

4. How do WAN services fit into the enterprise composite model?

5. How many links does it take to make a full mesh of seven locations?

6. How many links are required to make a hub and spoke connection if there are seven locations including the hub?

7. In the hierarchical design model, where would network policy be implemented?

8. What are the differences between a server farm and a switch block?

9. From a design perspective, what is a "converged" network?

10. What is the difference between IIN, SONA, and AON?

11. Briefly describe the SONA framework in terms of layers and responsibilities.

12. List the routing protocols that converge quickly and are classless.

13. What is a classful routing protocol?

14. Describe the advantages and disadvantages of the routing protocols from the answer to question 12.

This chapter covers the following topics:

- **Understanding IP Addresses**—Describes the structure of IP addresses and reviews binary, classful addressing, and the steps to calculate subnets.

- **Understanding Summarization**—Proposes a way to take a list of addresses and convert them into a single summary or to provide a "best fit" set of summaries.

CHAPTER 2

IP Address Planning and Summarization

This chapter discusses IP addressing and summarization. It begins with a short review of CCNA concepts, including binary and IP subnetting. It then uses those concepts as a springboard to discuss summarization and address planning.

The first section, "Understanding IP Addresses," describes the structure of an IPv4 address and provides classful and classless methods that can be used to calculate the range of a given subnet.

The second section, "Understanding Summarization," builds on the range of calculation methods by describing how larger groups of addresses can be advertised in the simplest possible manner. This section reviews why summarization is important and discusses how to apply summarization to network design.

The topics in this chapter are indirectly important for the BSCI exam. Although you will not be tested directly on these topics, each routing protocol will introduce a technique to create summaries and you will be tested with questions that combine your understanding of summarization and the commands necessary to apply summarization.

"Do I Know This Already?" Quiz

The purpose of the "Do I Know This Already?" quiz is to help you decide which parts of this chapter to use. If you already intend to read the entire chapter, you do not necessarily need to answer these questions.

The 11-question quiz, derived from the major sections in the "Foundation Topics" portion of the chapter, helps you determine how to spend your limited study time.

Table 2-1 outlines the major topics discussed in this chapter and the corresponding quiz questions.

Table 2-1 *"Do I Know This Already?" Foundation Topics Section-to-Question Mapping*

Foundation Topics Section	Questions Covered in This Section	Score
Understanding IP Addresses	1–9	
Understanding Summarization	10–11	
Total Score		

> **CAUTION**   The goal of self-assessment is to gauge your mastery of the topics in this chapter. If you do not know the answer to a question or are only partially sure of the answer, you should mark the question wrong for purposes of the self-assessment. Giving yourself credit for an answer you correctly guessed skews your results and might provide you with a false sense of security.

1. What is the binary for 172?

    a. 1 111 10

    b. 1010 1100

    c. 1100 0000

    d. 1011 1111

2. What is the binary for 128?

    a. 1 10 1000

    b. 1010 1010

    c. 1000 0000

    d. 1011 1111

3. What is the decimal for 1100 0000?

    a. 192

    b. 194

    c. 200

    d. 202

4. What class is 172.16.1.1?

    a. Class A

    b. Class B

    c. Class C

    d. Class D

5. What class is 10.37.5.11?

    a. Class A

    b. Class B

c. Class C

d. Class D

6. What is the CIDR-notation equivalent of 255.255.255.0?

a. /20

b. /22

c. /24

d. /26

7. What is the dotted-decimal equivalent of /27?

a. 255.255.255.0

b. 255.255.224.0

c. 255.255.255.224

d. 255.255.0.0

8. What is the network for the address 192.168.37.62/26?

a. 192.168.37.0

b. 255.255.255.192

c. 192.168.37.64

d. 192.168.37.32

9. What is the broadcast address for the host address 192.168.190.55/27?

a. 192.168.190.59

b. 255.255.190.55

c. 192.168.190.63

d. 192.168.190.0

10. Given the addresses 10.1.8.0/24 and 10.1.9.0/24, which of the following is the best summary?

a. 10.0.0.0/8

b. 10.1.0.0/16

c. 10.1.8.0/23

d. 10.1.10.0/24

11.   Given the addresses 10.1.138.0/27, 10.1.138.64/26, and 10.1.138.32/27, which of the following is the best summary?

    a.   10.0.0.0/8

    b.   10.1.0.0/16

    c.   10.1.138.0/24

    d.   10.1.138.0/25

You can find the answers to the "Do I Know This Already?" quiz in Appendix A, "Answers to Chapter 'Do I Know This Already?' Quizzes and Q&A Sections." The suggested choices for your next step are as follows:

- **7 or less correct**—Read the entire chapter. This includes the "Foundation Topics" and "Foundation Summary," and the "Q&A" section.

- **8 or 9**—Begin with the "Foundation Summary" section, and then go to the "Q&A" section at the end of the chapter. If you have trouble with these exercises, read the appropriate sections in "Foundation Topics."

- **10 or more**—If you want more review on these topics, skip to the "Foundation Summary" section and then go to the "Q&A" section. Otherwise, move to the next chapter.

Foundation Topics

Understanding IP Addresses

Although the BSCI exam might not ask direct questions about IP addressing, IP addressing is a central topic of the test. Scalability (the "S" in BSCI) in IP routing is found by summarization, and you must understand how to summarize using each routing protocol to be successful on this test.

This section also reviews binary numbering fundamentals by guiding you through the math behind turning the numbers we use in everyday life—decimal—into the numbers used by our computers—binary. This section also reviews calculating classfully assumed network ranges, reviews the concept of address classes (used to assume a mask in the early days of IP), and describes the modern classless approach of calculating network ranges using subnet masks.

Reviewing IP

IP version 4 (IPv4) uses 32-bit numbers that combine a network address and host address. IP addresses are written in four decimal fields separated by periods. Each number represents a byte. The far right bits are the *network address* because all hosts on this network have addresses that start with that pattern. The left bits are the *host address* because each host has a different value. A sample IP address might look like 192.168.1.5/24. In this example, the network portion of the address is 192.168.1 and the host portion is ".5."

Reviewing Binary Numbering Fundamentals

Binary numbering, or base two, uses 0 and 1 for counting, and each digit to the left represents an increasing power of two. By comparison, decimal numbers use ten symbols, with each digit to the left representing an increasing power of ten.

> **NOTE** A more complete description of binary and the conversion process may be found in the *CCNA Exam Certification Guide*.

Figure 2-1 shows an example of a decimal and a binary number.

IP addresses are composed of four bytes—eight bits—and you will work with them one byte at a time. You only need to be able to convert binary and decimal numbers between 0000 0000 and 1111 1111 (0 to 255).

Figure 2-1 *Interpreting Decimal and Binary Numbers*

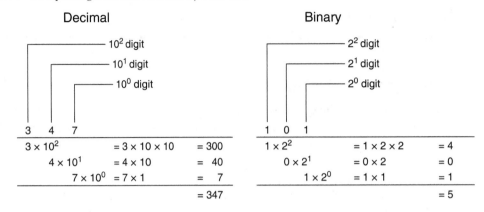

To convert a binary byte to decimal, the easiest method is to label each bit position with its decimal value. The far-right bit is 1, and the values double as you move to the left, as follows:

128   64   32   16   8   4   2   1

Then, take the binary value of the byte at each bit position and multiply the byte by the value. For instance, 0101 1010 could be interpreted in this way:

Values: 128   64   32   16   8   4   2   1
Bits: 0   1   0   1   1   0   1   0
=   0 + 64 + 0 + 16 + 8 + 0 + 2 + 0 = 90

To convert a decimal number to binary, ask if the number is equal to or larger than the bit value at each position, starting from the left. If it is, write a 1 in that space and subtract the value from the number. An example for the number 137 is as follows:

Values: 128   64   32   16   8   4   2   1

Is 137 equal to or greater than 128? Yes.

1

Subtract 128 from 137, leaving a remainder of 9. Is 9 equal to or greater than 64? No.

0

Is 9 equal to or greater than 32? No. *16?* No. *8?* Yes, 9 is greater than 8.

0   0   1

Because 9 – 8 = 1, is 1 equal to or greater than 4? 2? 1? Because 1 = 1, the last bit is 1.

0   0   1

So the decimal 137 is converted to binary as 1000 1001.

IP addressing uses a binary operation called AND. Figure 2-2 shows the truth table for AND. AND is only true if both inputs are true, so 0 AND 1 is 0, but 1 AND 1 is 1.

Figure 2-2   *Truth Table for AND*

AND	0	1
0	0	0
1	0	1

Calculating Classfully Assumed Network Ranges

A common task in addressing is to take an IP address and to understand the range of addresses that are on the same network. Originally, this was done by reading the first bits of the address to determine a class; this is called *classful addressing*. The portion of the address consumed by the network prefix was then assumed, based on that class. Table 2-2 shows the first bits of an IP address, the corresponding classes, and the number of bytes assumed to be in the network portion of the address.

Table 2-2   *IP Address Classes*

First Bits of IP	Range of First Byte	Class	Network Bytes
0 _ _ _ _ _ _ _	0–127	A	1
1 0 _ _ _ _ _ _	128–191	B	2
1 1 0 _ _ _ _ _	192–223	C	3
1 1 1 0 _ _ _ _	224–239	D—Multicast	
1 1 1 1 _ _ _ _	240–255	E—Experimental	

The address 192.168.1.5 starts with the byte 192. In binary, 192 is **1100** 0000, so this is a Class C address. Since it is a Class C address, the network portion of the address is assumed to be 192.168.1 and all IP speakers in this network will have addresses that start with that prefix. However, the last octet will be unique for each of them.

The address 150.159.216.202 starts with the byte 150, which is **10**10 0110 in binary. Based on the first two bits, this is a Class B address and the first two bytes establish the network prefix. All devices on this network will have an address that starts 150.159.

Classful addressing is not flexible enough to meet the needs of the modern network. Class C networks are too small for large organizations, and even large organizations do not need 65,000 addresses in one office (which they would have if the first two octets were the prefix).

Calculating Network Ranges Using Subnet Masks

Subnetting is the action of taking the assigned network and breaking it up into smaller pieces. Because the prefix length can no longer be classfully assumed just by looking at the address, the prefix length is now specified. For instance, an address might be written 172.20.1.5/23. This *slash notation* indicates that the first 23 bits are a routing prefix, and are common to all devices on a subnet. Another way of expressing the same address is to create a subnet mask where 1 shows the position of the network portion and 0 shows the host portion. In this example:

/23 =1111 1111.1111 1111.1111 1110.0000 0000 =255.255.254.0

Hosts use subnet masks to determine whether a destination is local or on a remote subnet. Consider a case where three computers need to communicate, as shown in Figure 2-3.

Figure 2-3 *Example of Subnets*

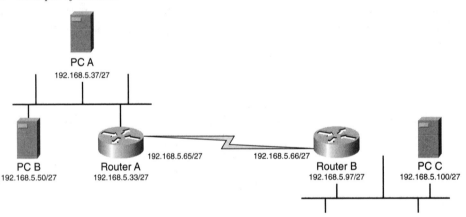

PC A needs to be able to compare its address with the addresses of the destination to determine if devices are local or remote. If a device is local, PC A will use ARP to determine its MAC address and then will transmit directly to it. If a device is remote, PC A will use ARP to get the MAC address of the default gateway and will transmit through that router.

To determine the topology, an IP device takes a bit-wise binary AND of its own address and subnet mask and compares it to an AND of the destination address. Since any devices that share a link will also share the same prefix, if both numbers are the same then they are both on the same network.

Remember the AND truth table shown in the "Reviewing Binary Numbering Fundamentals" section. In the case of PC A communicating with PC B, PC A starts by taking a bit-wise binary AND of its source address and its subnet mask. Remember that /27 means that the first 27 bits of the subnet mask are on, which translates to 255.255.255.224.

```
PC A 192.168.5.37       11000000.10101000.00000101.00100101
Mask 255.255.255.224    11111111.11111111.11111111.11100000
Subnet 192.168.5.32     11000000.10101000.00000101.00100000
```

This shows that the network address of PC A is 192.168.5.32. Notice that the subnet mask "masks" the host portion of the address. Performing the same operation against PC B yields the same result, so PC A knows they are on the same network.

```
PC B 192.168.5.50       11000000.10101000.00000101.00110010
Mask 255.255.255.224    11111111.11111111.11111111.11100000
Subnet 192.168.5.32     11000000.10101000.00000101.00100000
```

However, when PC A tries to communicate with PC C a different network number is determined. Because PC C is on the 192.168.5.96 network, PC A must pass traffic through its default gateway to reach this peer.

```
PC C 192.168.5.100      11000000.10101000.00000101.01100100
Mask 255.255.255.224    11111111.11111111.11111111.11100000
Subnet 192.168.5.96     11000000.10101000.00000101.01100000
```

A common task in network support involves performing the same kind of operation. Imagine that you have to support the network that PC A and PC B reside on. If you need to add another PC, what IP address could be used for the new PC? The following procedure may be used to determine the range of addresses supported by a network.

Step 1   If the mask is given in dotted decimal notation, convert it to CIDR notation.

Step 2   To determine the network address, copy the network bits from the address as shown by the CIDR notation. Fill in the remaining bits with zeros.

Step 3   The last address in the range is the broadcast address. Again, copy the network bits from the address and then fill in the remaining bits with ones.

Step 4   The usable set of addresses on this network falls between these two numbers.

Step 5   To check your math, subtract the CIDR notation from 32 to determine the number of host bits. There should be 2n-2 host addresses, where n is the number of host bits.

As an example, consider PC C (192.168.5.100).

1. The mask in CIDR notation is /27.

2. Step 2 says to "Copy the network bits from the address as shown by the CIDR notation. Fill in the remaining bits with zeros." The first three bytes (24 bits) are all within the /27 so those portions may be copied directly. The last octet is converted to binary and the first three bits are copied, while the remaining bits are changed to zeros.

    PC C 192.168.5.100 11000000.10101000.00000101.01100000

    The result is a network address of 192.168.5.96.

3. To determine the broadcast address, copy the network bits and fill in the remaining bits with ones:

    PC C 192.168.5.100 11000000.10101000.00000101.01111111

    The broadcast address is 192.168.5.127.

4. The usable set of addresses on this network falls between these two numbers (from 96 to 127), so addresses from 192.168.5.97 through 192.168.5.126 are usable.

5. To check ourselves, subtract 32–27 = 5. There are five host bits. There should be $2^5-2=30$ hosts on this network, which matches what step four told us.

Understanding Summarization

This section describes the process of summarization. Summarization is the technique of grouping IP networks together to minimize advertisements. For instance, imagine that a division's network consisted of the subnets 172.21.0.0/24 through 172.21.255.0/24. To advertise each network using a routing protocol, the division will send 256 advertisements to other divisions.

To extend the example, consider Figure 2-4. There are many routers in this company, but the three routers shown are the three that tie the divisions together. If each router announces every route in its division, there will be 768 advertisements!

As an alternative, Router A could advertise 172.21.0.0/16. This would be equivalent to saying "all the addresses that start with the 16 bits 172.21 can be found behind Router A. Do not worry about the details—let Router A worry about how to forward your traffic within the division." This is the process of summarization—replacing a large set of individual advertisements with a smaller set that advertise the same range.

Figure 2-4 *Advertisements in a Fictional Company*

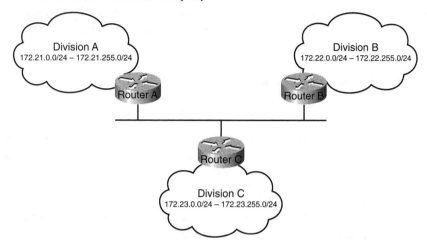

Summarization Advantages

Summarization hides details to simplify the routing process. One of the keys to scalable routing is to take large complicated sets of advertisements and reduce them as much as possible.

Summarization reduces router resource consumption (CPU and memory) required to store and process routes by reducing the number of routes. Summarization also saves network capacity, because fewer advertisements are required and each advertisement is smaller.

Summarization also hides unimportant details, such as flapping links. A flapping link is a network that goes up and down, sometimes several times per minute. In Figure 2-4, imagine that the 172.23.5.0/24 link interior to division C began to flap. In an unsummarized network, Router C has to advertise 172.23.5.0/24 every time the link comes up and withdraw it every time the link goes down. In a summarized network, Router C does not pass on this level of detail. Traffic to 172.23.5.0/24 will simply be dropped within the division if the network is down.

This might strike you as counter-intuitive, but IP devices are capable of recognizing when responses are not received. The inefficiency of allowing some traffic to pass and then be dropped is less than the inefficiency of re-advertising the route.

Convergence is sped up in a summarized network because each router has a smaller set of routes to consider, because each router can receive updates faster, and because each router has fewer routes to process.

Summarization Solutions

Subsequent chapters show techniques for summarizing routes for each of the routing protocols described in this book. However, it is important that you understand how to compose the summary address.

The method for determining the summary is

Step 1   Write each network in binary.

Step 2   Determine the number of bits that match. This gives a single summary that includes all the routes, but may include a range of addresses that is too large (also called *over-summarization*).

Step 3   If step two unacceptably over-summarizes, start from the first address and add bits to the prefix until a portion of the range is summarized. Take the remaining addresses and start this process again.

Suppose a network is composed of the links 172.16.0.0/24 through 172.16.3.0/24. Following the procedure:

Step 1   Write each network in binary.

172.16.0.0 = 1010 1010.0001 0000.0000 0000 0000.0000 0000

172.16.1.0 = 1010 1010.0001 0000.0000 0000 0001.0000 0000

172.16.2.0 = 1010 1010.0001 0000.0000 0000 0010.0000 0000

172.16.3.0 = 1010 1010.0001 0000.0000 0000 0011.0000 0000

Step 2   Determine the number of bits that match.

172.16.0.0 = **1010 1010.0001 0000.0000 0000 00**00.0000 0000

172.16.1.0 = **1010 1010.0001 0000.0000 0000 00**01.0000 0000

172.16.2.0 = **1010 1010.0001 0000.0000 0000 00**10.0000 0000

172.16.3.0 = **1010 1010.0001 0000.0000 0000 00**11.0000 0000

In this example, the first 22 bits match. A summary of 172.16.0.0/22 is a candidate, although we know that this may over-summarize. To determine if it over-summarizes, use the technique described in the "Calculating Network Ranges Using Subnet Masks" section to determine the range of addresses covered.

In this case, you will find that 172.16.0.0/22 covers the exact same set of addresses as the combination of 172.16.0.0/24, 172.16.1.0/24, 172.16.2.0/24, and 172.16.3.0/24

Step 3   Step 2 did not result in an over-summarization, so the process is complete.

On the BSCI exam, you may see cases where a range of addresses can be summarized in a neat and tidy fashion, just like the previous example. In the real world, there will be times when you will need to go a step further. One more example will help you in those cases. Consider a case where the following networks need to be summarized:

■   192.168.0.0/24

■   192.168.1.0/24

■   192.168.2.0/24

■   192.168.3.0/24

■   192.168.4.0/24

■   192.168.5.0/24

■   192.168.6.0/24

■   192.168.7.0/24

■   192.168.8.0/24

■   192.168.9.0/24

Following the procedure:

Step 1   Write each network in binary.

Step 2   Determine the number of bits that match.

192.168.0.0 = **1100 0000.1010 1000.0000** 0000.0000 0000

192.168.1.0 = **1100 0000.1010 1000.0000** 0001.0000 0000

192.168.2.0 = **1100 0000.1010 1000.0000** 0010.0000 0000

192.168.3.0 = **1100 0000.1010 1000.0000** 0011.0000 0000

192.168.4.0 = **1100 0000.1010 1000.0000** 0100.0000 0000

192.168.5.0 = **1100 0000.1010 1000.0000** 0101.0000 0000

192.168.6.0 = **1100 0000.1010 1000.0000** 0110.0000 0000

192.168.7.0 = **1100 0000.1010 1000.0000** 0111.0000 0000

192.168.8.0 = **1100 0000.1010 1000.0000** 1000.0000 0000

192.168.9.0 = **1100 0000.1010 1000.0000** 1001.0000 0000

The first 20 bits match. However, upon reflection, a summary of 192.168.0.0/20 covers the range from 192.168.0.0 to 192.168.15.255 and over-summarizes.

Step 3   Because step 2 over-summarized, add a bit to the prefix and consider 192.168.0.0/21. This summarizes 192.168.0.0 through 192.168.7.0. So that will be one advertisement. We take the remaining portion of addresses and start again.

Step 4   Write each network in binary.

Step 5   Determine the number of bits that match.

192.168.8.0 = **1100 0000.1010 1000.0000 1000**.0000 0000

192.168.9.0 = **1100 0000.1010 1000.0000 1001**.0000 0000

The first 23 bits match. A summary of 192.168.8.0/23 describes addresses from 192.168.8.0 to 192.168.9.255, which matches exactly the required address space.

Step 6   Because step 2 did not over-summarize, the process is complete. Two advertisements (192.168.0.0/21 and 192.168.8.0/23) will be required.

This process results in advertising 192.168.0.0/21 and 192.168.8.0/23, which is better than the ten advertisements that would have been required.

Address Planning

Summarization is not possible as an after-thought. If network numbers are randomly assigned within an organization, it will be difficult or impossible to find ways to adequately summarize. When designing a network, it is extremely important that careful attention is paid to the requirements for summarization.

Figure 2-5 shows that an example corporation might have multiple levels of summarization— within plants, within manufacturing groups, at the divisional level, and to the Internet. In particular, notice that the Internet is being summarized back to the company as a default route.

Figure 2-5   *An Example of Summarization*

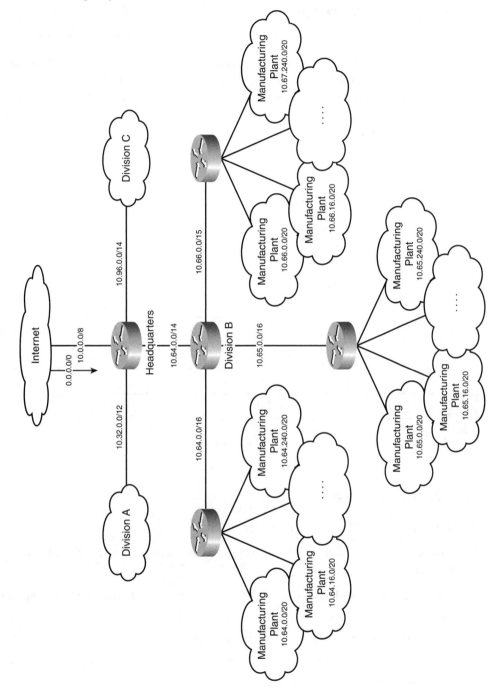

Foundation Summary

The Foundation Summary provides a convenient review of many key concepts in this chapter. If you are already comfortable with the topics in this chapter, this summary might help you recall a few details. If you just read this chapter, this review should help solidify some key facts. If you are doing your final prep before the exam, the following lists and tables are a convenient way to review the day before the exam.

IP addresses are

■ 32-bit numbers (written as four bytes)

■ Divided into a network portion and host portion

Table 2-3 shows the first bits of an IP address, the corresponding classes, and the number of bytes assumed to be in the network portion of the address.

Table 2-3 *IP Address Classes*

First Bits of IP	Range of First Byte	Class	Network Bytes
0 _ _ _ _ _ _ _	0–127	A	1
1 0 _ _ _ _ _ _	128–191	B	2
1 1 0 _ _ _ _ _	192–223	C	3
1 1 1 0 _ _ _ _	224–239	D—Multicast	
1 1 1 1 _ _ _ _	240–255	E—Experimental	

To determine the range of addresses:

1. If the mask is dotted decimal, convert it to CIDR.

2. To determine the network address, copy the network bits from the address. Fill in the remaining bits with zeros.

3. The last address is the broadcast. Copy the network bits and fill in the remaining bits with ones.

4. The usable addresses fall between these two numbers.

5. To check, subtract the CIDR length from 32 to determine the number of host bits. There are 2^n-2 host addresses.

Summarization:

- Hides details and protects against flaps

- Reduces router CPU and memory consumption

- Saves network capacity

The method for determining the summary is

Step 1 Write each network in binary.

Step 2 Determine the number of bits that match. This gives a single summary that includes all the routes.

Step 3 If step 2 unacceptably over-summarizes, start from the first address and add bits to the prefix until a portion of the range is summarized. Take the remaining addresses and start this process again.

Q&A

The questions and scenarios in this book are designed to be challenging and to make sure that you know the answer. Rather than allowing you to derive the answers from clues hidden inside the questions themselves, the questions challenge your understanding and recall of the subject.

You can find the answers to these questions in Appendix A. For more practice with exam-like question formats, use the exam engine on the CD-ROM.

1. Convert the following numbers to binary:

   — 181

   — 202

   — 152

   — 109

2. Convert the following binary numbers to decimal:

   — 10101111

   — 10000001

   — 00111100

   — 01001001

3. What is the binary representation of 192.168.0.1?

4. Specify the IP address class for each of the following addresses:

   — 12.150.146.181

   — 150.159.216.202

   — 209.209.158.152

   — 224.137.116.109

5. What are the assumed subnet masks for Class A, Class B, and Class C addresses?

6. How many host IPs are included in the following prefixes?

   — /24

   — /27

   — /20

7. For each address in the following list, compute the range of host addresses found on its subnet:

— 24.177.78.62/27

— 135.159.211.109/19

— 207.87.193.1/30

8. Summarize the following addresses without over-summarizing:

— 192.168.160.0/24

— 192.168.162.0/23

— 192.168.161.0/24

— 192.168.164.0/22

9. Summarize the following addresses without over-summarizing:

— 172.30.31.0/24

— 172.30.32.0/24

— 172.30.33.0/24

— 172.30.34.0/23

— 172.30.36.0/23

— 172.30.38.0/24

10. List three reasons why summarization is important.

Part II covers the following Cisco BSCI exam topics related to implementing EIGRP operations:

- Explain the functions and operations of EIGRP (e.g., DUAL).
- Configure EIGRP routing (e.g., Stub Routing, authentication, etc.).
- Verify or troubleshoot EIGRP routing configurations.

This list reflects the exam topics posted on Cisco.com at the publication time of this book.

Part II: EIGRP

This chapter covers the following topics:

- **EIGRP Features and Advantages**— Describes the key features and advantages of EIGRP, including neighborship and reliable incremental updates, neighbor discovery and recovery, the sophisticated metric used by EIGRP, DUAL, and queries.

- **Understanding EIGRP Tables**—Describes neighbors, topology, and routing tables.

- **EIGRP Network Design**—Describes the factors that affect the scaling of EIGRP.

EIGRP Principles

Enhanced Interior Gateway Routing Protocol (EIGRP) is a distance vector protocol that uses the same sophisticated metric as IGRP and uses the Diffusing Update Algorithm (DUAL) convergence algorithm. EIGRP is able to converge quickly and use little bandwidth because it— like OSPF—has separate keepalives and reliable updates. EIGRP is sometimes referred to as a *hybrid routing protocol*, although *advanced distance vector routing protocol* is probably a more accurate description.

EIGRP is an efficient but proprietary solution for large networks. Its ability to scale is limited only by the design of the network.

This chapter covers EIGRP used with IPv4. You can find a short discussion of EIGRP support for IPv6 in Chapter 21, "IPv6 Routing Protocols, Configuration, and Transitioning from IPv4," but the concepts of EIGRP are essentially the same.

This chapter provides a theoretical description of how EIGRP works. The operation of EIGRP, available options, and design considerations are explained in this chapter, particularly in reference to scaling EIGRP and its use over a nonbroadcast multiaccess (NBMA) WAN environment.

The topics in this chapter directly reflect questions on the BSCI exam. EIGRP is designed for use in large networks. As a proprietary routing protocol for Cisco, it is therefore an obligatory subject in a Cisco exam on IP routing protocols.

"Do I Know This Already?" Quiz

The purpose of the "Do I Know This Already?" quiz is to help you decide which parts of this chapter to use. If you already intend to read the entire chapter, you do not necessarily need to answer these questions.

The 13-question quiz, derived from the major sections in the "Foundation Topics" portion of the chapter, helps you determine how to spend your limited study time.

Table 3-1 outlines the major topics discussed in this chapter and the corresponding quiz questions.

Table 3-1   *"Do I Know This Already?" Foundation Topics Section-to-Question Mapping*

Foundation Topics Section	Questions Covered in This Section	Score
EIGRP Features and Advantages	1–7	
Understanding EIGRP Tables	8–12	
EIGRP Network Design	13	
Total Score		

CAUTION   The goal of self-assessment is to gauge your mastery of the topics in this chapter. If you do not know the answer to a question or are only partially sure of the answer, you should mark the question wrong for purposes of the self-assessment. Giving yourself credit for an answer you correctly guessed skews your results and might provide you with a false sense of security.

1.   Which of the following describes how a reply to an EIGRP query is sent?

   a. Multicast

   b. Best effort unicast

   c. A reliable unicast

   d. A reliable multicast

2.   Which of the following are advantages to using EIGRP as a routing protocol instead of RIP?

   a. Rapid convergence

   b. Reduced bandwidth consumption

   c. Link state routing

   d. Increased vendor support

3.   Cisco identifies four main components of EIGRP. Select the two correct components from the following list.

   a. Neighbor discovery

   b. SPF algorithm

   c. Areas

   d. RTP

4.   Given the default constant values, which variables are included in the EIGRP metric?

   a. Bandwidth

   b. Load

    c. Reliability

    d. Delay

5. For EIGRP to form a neighbor relationship, which of the following must be true?

    a. Authentication must be enabled.

    b. The K-values of the metric must be the same on both routers.

    c. The autonomous system number must be the same on both routers.

    d. The holddown timer must be the same.

6. What do the letters SIA stand for?

    a. Stuck in Active

    b. Shortest IP Address

    c. Stuck in Area

    d. Simple IP Address

7. What is the EIGRP reserved Multicast address?

    a. 224.0.0.1

    b. 224.0.0.5

    c. 224.0.0.9

    d. 224.0.0.10

8. The neighbor table contains which of the following information?

    a. The administrative distance

    b. The metric of neighbors

    c. The feasible distance between neighbors

    d. The status of the links between neighbors

9. What do the letters SRTT stand for?

    a. Shortest Remote-Trip Time

    b. Smooth Round-Trip Time

    c. Shortest Reliable-Trip Time

    d. Single Remote Timer Test

10. Which of the following would trigger the topology table to recalculate?

    a. LSP received

    b. SRT packet received

    c. A new router coming online

    d. Link loss detected

11. Feasible successor information is stored in which table?

    a. Topology

    b. Routing

    c. Neighbor

    d. Autonomous System

12. What is EIGRP Active Mode?

    a. When the router is actively forwarding

    b. When the router is actively recalculating paths

    c. When the router is searching for replacement paths

    d. When the router is discovering neighbors

13. The factors that can affect the scaling of EIGRP include which of the following?

    a. The amount of information sent between neighbors

    b. The number of routers that receive updates

    c. The distance between neighboring routers

    d. The number of alternative paths to remote networks

You can find the answers to the "Do I Know This Already?" quiz in Appendix A, "Answers to Chapter 'Do I Know This Already?' Quizzes and Q&A Sections." The suggested choices for your next step are as follows:

■ **9 or less correct**—Read the entire chapter. This includes the "Foundation Topics," "Foundation Summary," and "Q&A" sections.

■ **10 or 11**—Begin with the "Foundation Summary" section, and then go to the "Q&A" section at the end of the chapter. If you have trouble answering the Q&A questions, read the appropriate sections in "Foundation Topics."

■ **12 or 13 overall score**—If you want more review on these topics, skip to the "Foundation Summary" section and then go to the "Q&A" section at the end of the chapter. Otherwise, move to the next chapter.

Foundation Topics

EIGRP Features and Advantages

The goal of EIGRP is to solve the scaling limitations that IGRP faces, while keeping the advantages of distance vector routing protocols: simplicity, economy of memory, and economy of processor resources. EIGRP is scalable in terms of hardware resources and network capacity. EIGRP is also lightning fast.

Cisco identifies four principal components of EIGRP:

- **Protocol-dependent modules**—EIGRP supports several routed protocols independently. The two that are of interest today are IP and IPv6.

- **Reliable Transport Protocol**—EIGRP sends some packets reliably using a reliable transport protocol.

- **Neighbor discovery and recovery**—EIGRP uses hellos to identify its neighbors quickly and to recognize when those neighbors are down.

- **Diffusing Update Algorithm (DUAL)**—DUAL identifies the procedure used to sort the list of available paths and select best paths and feasible fail-over routes.

The following sections describe the key features and advantages of EIGRP, including neighborship and reliable incremental updates, neighbor discovery and recovery, the sophisticated metric used by EIGRP, DUAL, and queries.

Neighborship and Reliable Incremental Updates

EIGRP produces reliable updates by identifying its packets using IP protocol 88. *Reliable*, in a networking context, means that the receiver acknowledges that the transmission was received and understood. EIGRP only repeats itself if an advertisement is lost, so EIGRP is less "chatty" than other protocols.

EIGRP uses the following five types of packets to communicate. These packets are directly encapsulated by IP.

- **Hello**—Identifies neighbors. Hellos are sent as periodic multicasts and are not acknowledged directly.

- **Update**—Advertises routes. Updates are sent as multicasts only when there is a change.

- **Ack**—Acknowledges receipt of an update.

- **Query**—Used to ask about routes for which the previous best path has been lost. If an update indicates that a path is down, multicast queries are used to ask other neighbors if they still have a path. If the querier does not receive a reply from each of its neighbors, it repeats the query as a unicast to each unresponsive neighbor until it either gets a reply or gives up after sixteen tries.

- **Reply**—Used to answer a query. Each neighbor responds to the query with a unicast reply indicating an alternative path or the fact that it does not have a path.

Neighbor Discovery and Recovery

Using reliable updates produces two new problems:

- The router needs to know how many other routers exist, so it knows how many acknowledgements to expect.

- The router needs to know whether a missing advertisement should be interpreted as "no new information" or "neighbor disconnected."

EIGRP uses the concept of neighborship to address these problems. EIGRP produces hellos periodically. The first hellos are used to build a list of neighbors; thereafter, hellos indicate that the neighbor is still alive. If hellos are missed over a long period of time—the *hold time*—then the neighbor is removed from the EIGRP table and routing reconverges.

EIGRP starts by discovering its neighbors. Advertisements are multicast, and individual unicast acknowledgements come back. The neighbor table is used to make sure that each neighbor responds. Unresponsive neighbors receive a follow-up unicast copy, repeatedly, until they acknowledge. If a neighbor is still unresponsive after 16 attempts, the neighbor is removed from the neighbor table and EIGRP continues with its next task.

Presumably, the neighbor will at some point be able to communicate. When it is able to do so, it will send a hello and the process of routing with that neighbor will begin again.

Sophisticated Metric

EIGRP uses a sophisticated metric that considers bandwidth, load, reliability, and delay. That metric is

$$metric = 256 * (K_1 * bandwidth + \frac{K_2 * bandwidth}{256 - load} + K_3 * delay) * \frac{K_5}{reliability + K_4}$$

Although this equation looks intimidating, a little work will help you understand the math and the impact the metric has on route selection.

You first need to understand that EIGRP selects path based on the fastest path. To do that it uses K-values to balance bandwidth and delay. The K-values are constants that are used to adjust the relative contribution of the various parameters to the total metric. In other words, if you wanted *delay* to be much more relatively important than *bandwidth*, you might set K_3 to a much larger number.

You next need to understand the variables:

- **Bandwidth**—Bandwidth is defined as 107 kbps divided by the slowest link along the path. Because routing protocols select the lowest metric, inverting the bandwidth (using it as the divisor) makes faster paths have lower costs.

- **Load and reliability**—Load and reliability are 8-bit calculated values based on the performance of the link. Both are multiplied by a zero K-value, so neither is used.

- **Delay**—Delay is a constant value on every interface type, and is stored in terms of microseconds. For example, serial links have a delay of 20,000 microseconds and Ethernet lines have a delay of 1000 microseconds. EIGRP uses the sum of all delays along the path, in tens of microseconds.

By default, $K_1=K_3=1$ and $K_2=K_4=K_5=0$. Those who followed the math will note that when $K_5=0$ the metric is always zero. Because this is not useful, EIGRP simply ignores everything outside the parentheses. Therefore, given the default K-values the equation becomes

$$metric = 256 * \left(1 * bandwidth + \frac{0 * bandwidth}{256 - load} + 1 * delay\right) * \frac{0}{reliability + 0}$$

$$= 256 * (bandwidth + delay)$$

Substituting the earlier description of variables, the equation becomes 10,000,000 divided by the chokepoint bandwidth plus the sum of the delays:

$$metric = 256 * \left(\frac{10^7}{min(bandwidth)} + \Sigma \frac{delays}{10}\right)$$

An example of the metric in context will make its application clear. Figure 3-1 shows a simple network topology, with routers labeled A, B, C, D, and E. Using the metric equation, which path would be used to pass traffic from Router A to Router D?

Figure 3-1 *EIGRP Metric Topology*

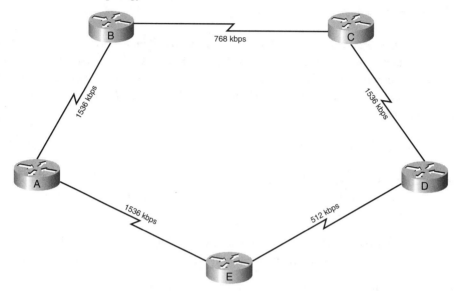

The top path (ABCD) metric would have a chokepoint bandwidth of 768 Kbps and would go across three serial lines:

$$metric = 256 * \left(\frac{10^7}{768} + \frac{20,000 + 20,000 + 20,000}{10} \right) = 256(13,020 + 6000) = 4,869,120$$

The bottom path (AED) metric would have a chokepoint bandwidth of 512 Kbps and would go across two serial lines:

$$metric = 256 * \left(\frac{10^7}{512} + \frac{20,000 + 20,000}{10} \right) = 256(19,531 + 4000) = 6,023,936$$

EIGRP chooses the top path based on bandwidth.

> **NOTE** Routers will not become EIGRP neighbors unless they share K-values. There really is not a compelling reason to change the default K-values and Cisco does not recommend it.

DUAL

The Diffusing Update Algorithm (DUAL) is a modification of the way distance-vector routing typically works that allows the router to identify loop-free failover paths. This concept is easier to grasp if you imagine it geographically. Consider the map of North Carolina shown in Figure 3-2. The numbers show approximate travel time by car, in minutes. Pretend that you live in Hickory. From Hickory, you need to determine the best path to Raleigh.

Figure 3-2 *North Carolina*

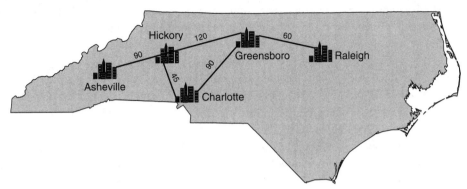

Imagine that each of Hickory's neighbors advertises a path to Raleigh. Each neighbor advertises its cost (travel time) to get to Raleigh and the cost Hickory would use. The cost from the neighbor to the destination is called the *advertised distance*. The cost from Hickory is called the *feasible distance*.

In this example, Greensboro reports that if Hickory routed to Raleigh through Greensboro, the total cost (feasible distance) is 180 minutes, and that the remaining cost once the traffic gets to Greensboro is only 60 minutes. Table 3-2 shows distances reported from Hickory to Raleigh going through each of Hickory's neighbors.

Table 3-2 *Feasible and Advertised Distance*

City	Feasible Distance	Advertised Distance
Asheville	360	270
Charlotte	195	150
Greensboro	180	60

Hickory will select the route with the lowest feasible distance, which is the path through Greensboro.

If the Hickory-Greensboro link goes down, Hickory knows it may fail-over to Charlotte without creating a loop. Notice that the distance from Charlotte to Raleigh (150 minutes) is less than the distance from Hickory to Raleigh (180 minutes). Because Charlotte is closer to Raleigh, routing through Charlotte does not involve driving to Charlotte and then driving back to Hickory before going to Raleigh. Charlotte is a guaranteed loop-free path.

This idea that a path through a neighbor is loop free if the neighbor is closer is called the *feasibility requirement* and can be restated as "using a path where the neighbor's advertised distance is less than our feasible distance will not result in a loop."

The neighbor with the best path is referred to as the *successor*. Neighbors that meet the feasibility requirement are called *feasible successors*. In emergencies, EIGRP understands that using feasible successors will not cause a routing loop and instantly switches to the backup paths.

Notice that Asheville is not a feasible successor. Asheville's AD (270) is higher than Hickory's FD (180). For all we know, driving to Raleigh through Asheville involves driving from Hickory to Asheville, then turning around and driving back to Hickory before continuing on to Raleigh (in fact, it does). Asheville will still be queried if the best path is lost and no feasible successors are available because potentially there could be a path that way; however, paths that do not meet the feasibility requirement will not be inserted into the routing table without careful consideration.

Now consider how DUAL works in terms of routers and networks. Figure 3-3 shows the EIGRP topology while Table 3-3 shows each router's options for routing to 192.168.5.0/24 (the Ethernet network on the right).

Figure 3-3 *EIGRP DUAL*

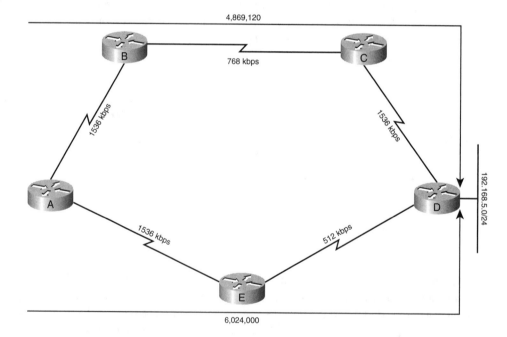

Table 3-3 *EIGRP DUAL Results to 192.168.5.0/24*

Router	Clockwise	Counter-Clockwise
A	Through B—Successor Min(BW)=768, Delay=60000 FD=4,869,120 AD=4,357,120	Through E Min(BW)=512, Delay=40000 FD=6,023,936 AD=5,511,936
B	Through C—Successor Min(BW)=768, Delay=40000 FD=4,357,120 AD=2,178,560	Through A Min(BW)=512, Delay=60000 FD=6,535,936 AD=6,023,936
C	To D—Successor Min(BW)=1536, Delay=20000 FD=2,178,560 AD=0	Through B Min(BW)=512, Delay=80000 FD=7,047,936 AD=6,535,936
E	To A—Successor Min(BW)=768, Delay=80000 FD=5,381,120 AD=4,869,120	To D—Feasible Successor Min(BW)=512, Delay=20000 FD=5,511,936 AD=0

Notice that Router E has a feasible successor because the advertised distance of the alternative path is less than the Feasible Distance of the best path (0 < 5,381,120). On the other hand, A, B, and C do not have feasible successors because their counterclockwise path does not meet the feasibility requirement.

In practical terms, what does this mean for the network? If Router E loses its path through A, it can fail-over to the D path instantly and without consulting neighbors because it knows this will not create a problem. If Router A loses its path through B, it has to query its remaining neighbor (E) and ask whether a path is still available. The query process results in the counterclockwise path being used as a backup but with a very short additional delay.

Queries

Having a feasible successor provides the best convergence. A feasible successor is a backup path, and it can be substituted for a lost path at any point. When a path is lost and no feasible successor exists, the router will send queries to its remaining neighbors. If a neighbor does not know of an alternative path, it will recursively ask its neighbors.

Recursive queries can loop without being resolved, forcing the router to time-out the query. This situation is known as stuck in active (SIA). Fortunately, it is uncommon; understanding its causes can prevent it entirely.

EIGRP uses split-horizon, which says that a router should not advertise a network on the link from which it learned about the network. As shown in Figure 3-3, because Router A learned about 192.168.5.0 from Router B, A does not advertise the network to B.

If the link between B and C goes down, B loses its only path to 192.168.5.0. The query process allows B to actively search remaining neighbors for a replacement route. When B asks A, "Do you have a route to 192.168.5.0/24?," Router A realizes that its route (through B) is down and recursively queries E. Router E has a route and so replies to A, which passes the news on to B.

Queries continue propagating until an answer is found or until no one is left to ask. When queries are produced, the router changes to an active state and sets a timer (typically three minutes). If the timer expires before an answer comes back then the router is considered stuck in active. SIA typically occurs because queries loop or are not properly limited to an area. The primary way to limit how far queries travel (called *query scoping*) is to summarize.

Queries will not cross summarization because the summary answers the query—the route is either behind the summary or not. For this reason, summarization is extremely important on EIGRP networks. The concepts of summarization are discussed in more detail in Chapter 2, while the EIGRP commands to summarize are found in Chapter 4.

The query process allows EIGRP to avoid periodically transmitting entire routing tables. When new networks are added or advertisements are withdrawn, routers may ask each other for additional information, allowing EIGRP to converge quickly even when there is not a feasible successor.

Additional EIGRP Advantages

The preceding section discussed the key advantages of EIGRP, but some smaller issues relating to network efficiency remain.

Incremental Updates

EIGRP periodically sends hellos to maintain neighborship, but only sends updates when a change occurs. When a route is added or withdrawn, an incremental update is sent (that includes only those changes). This is an important feature because it prevents EIGRP from monopolizing link access, which was occasionally a problem with older protocols.

Multicast Addressing for Updates

EIGRP uses both multicast and unicast addressing. Some packets are sent reliably using Real-Time Protocol (RTP), a Cisco proprietary protocol that oversees the communication of EIGRP packets. These packets are sent with sequence numbers to make the transmission of data reliable. Hellos and ACKs do not require acknowledgement.

Incremental updates cannot be anticipated; therefore, update, query, and reply packets must be acknowledged by the receiving neighbor.

Updates are sent using a reliable multicast. The address is the reserved class D address, 224.0.0.10. When the neighbor receives a multicast, it acknowledges receipt of the packet with an unreliable unicast.

The use of multicast by EIGRP to send updates is also important because it represents an improvement over other protocols. Older protocols used broadcast, which created issues. Multicast allows hosts to filter out the traffic while preserving the "one to all" aspect of broadcasts.

> **NOTE**   A broadcast domain identifies devices that are within the same Layer 2 domain. Although they might not be directly connected to the same physical cable, if they are in a switched environment, from a logical Layer 2 or Layer 3 perspective, they are on the same link. If a broadcast is sent out, all the devices within the broadcast domain will hear the message and will expend resources determining whether it is addressed to them. A Layer 3 device is a broadcast firewall in that a router does not forward broadcasts.

Unequal-Cost Load Sharing

All IP routing protocols on Cisco routers support equal-cost load sharing. EIGRP is unique in its support for unequal-cost load sharing.

Unequal-cost load balancing takes the best FD and multiplies it by variance. Any other path with an FD less than this product is used for load sharing. That is exciting because now a 256 kbps link and a 384 kbps link can work together—but EIGRP actually goes one better than that.

EIGRP does proportional unequal-cost load sharing. EIGRP will pass a relative portion of the traffic to each interface. The 384 kbps link would get 60 percent and the 256 kbps link would handle 40 percent of the traffic. This allows all links to a destination to be used to carry data without saturating the slower links or limiting the faster links.

Understanding EIGRP Tables

EIGRP builds and maintains three tables. A neighbor table is used to make sure all acknowledgements are received. A topology table is used to understand paths through the network. Finally, the best paths from the topology table are fed into the IP routing table. The following sections describe how EIGRP creates and maintains each table.

Creating the Neighbor Table

The neighbor table is maintained by means of Hello packets. Hello packets are multicast announcements that the router is alive. Hello packets place the router into adjacent routers' neighbor tables. Reciprocal hellos build the local neighbor table. Once neighbor tables are built, hellos continue periodically to maintain neighborship ("I'm still here!").

Each Layer 3 protocol supported by EIGRP (IPv4, IPv6, IPX, and AppleTalk) has its own neighbor table. Information about neighbors, routes, or costs is not shared between protocols.

Contents of the Neighbor Table

The neighbor table includes the following information:

- The Layer 3 address of the neighbor.

- The interface through which the neighbor's Hello was heard.

- The holdtime, or how long the neighbor table waits without hearing a Hello from a neighbor, before declaring the neighbor unavailable and purging the database. Holdtime is three times the value of the Hello timer by default.

- The uptime, or period since the router first heard from the neighbor.

- The sequence number. The neighbor table tracks all the packets sent between the neighbors. It tracks both the last sequence number sent to the neighbor and the last sequence number received from the neighbor.

- Retransmission timeout (RTO), which is the time the router will wait on a connection-oriented protocol without an acknowledgment before retransmitting the packet.

- Smooth Round Trip Time (SRTT), which calculates the RTO. SRTT is the time (in milliseconds) that it takes a packet to be sent to a neighbor and a reply to be received.

- The number of packets in a queue, which is a means by which administrators can monitor congestion on the network.

Becoming a Neighbor

All EIGRP routers periodically announce themselves with the Hello protocol using a multicast address of 224.0.0.10. On hearing Hellos, the receiving routers add an entry in their neighbor table. The continued receipt of these packets maintains the neighbor table. If a Hello from a known neighbor is not heard within the holdtime, the neighbor is treated as no longer operational and removed from the table. The holdtime, by default, is three times the Hello timer. Therefore, if the router misses three Hellos, the neighbor is declared dead. The Hello timer on a LAN is set to 5 seconds; the holdtime, therefore, is 15 seconds. On DS1 (1.5 Mbps) or slower WAN links, the Hello timer is 60 seconds and the holdtime is 180 seconds.

To become a neighbor, the following conditions must be met:

■ The router must hear a Hello packet from a neighbor.

■ The EIGRP autonomous system number in the Hello must be the same as that of the receiving router.

■ K-values used to calculate the metric must be the same.

Example 3-1 demonstrates a neighbor table.

Example 3-1 *The* **show ip eigrp neighbors** *Command*

```
Router#show ip eigrp neighbors
IP-EIGRP neighbors for process 1
H        Address        Interface      Hold    Uptime    SRTT    RTO Q   Seq
                        (sec)          (ms)    Cnt                       Num
172.16.0.1     S0/0            14      01:16:26 149       894 0   291
```

Creating the Topology Table

After the router knows who its neighbors are, it is able to create a topological database and assign successors and feasible successors for each route. The topology table has a record not only of feasible successors and successors but also of all received routes. The other routes are referred to as *possibilities*. The topology table in EIGRP manages the selection of routes to be added to the routing table.

The topology table includes the following information:

■ Whether the route is passive or active.

■ Whether an update has been sent to the neighbor.

- Whether a query packet has been sent to the neighbor. If this field is positive, at least one route will be marked as active.

- Whether a query packet has been sent; if so, another field will track whether any replies have been received from the neighbor.

- That a reply packet has been sent in response to a query packet received from a neighbor.

- Prefixes, masks, interface, next-hop, and feasible and advertised distances for remote networks.

The topology table is built from the update packets that are exchanged by the neighbors and by replies to queries sent by the router.

The queries and responses used by EIGRP for DUAL are sent reliably as multicasts using RTP, which is a Cisco proprietary protocol. If a router does not hear an acknowledgment within the allotted time, it retransmits the packet as a unicast. If there is no response after 16 attempts, the router marks the neighbor as dead. Each time the router sends a packet, RTP increments the sequence number by one. The router must hear an acknowledgment from every router before it can send the next packet. The capability to send unicast retransmissions decreases the time that it takes to build the tables.

When the router has an understanding of the topology, it runs DUAL to determine the best path to the remote network. The result is entered into the routing table.

Maintaining the Topology Table

The topology table may be recalculated because a new network is added to the network, successors change, or because a network is lost. Figure 3-4 illustrates the traffic flow seen when a router loses a connection.

Just as the neighbor table tracks the receipt of the EIGRP packets, the topology table records the packets that have been sent by the router to the neighbors. It also identifies the status of the networks in the table. Like a Sunday afternoon, passive is good and active is bad. A healthy network is marked passive; a lost route is active because the router is actively attempting to find an alternative path to the remote network.

Because the routing table is built from the topology table, the topology table must have all the information required by the routing table. This includes the next hop or the address of the neighbor that sent the update, and the metric (which is taken from the feasible distance).

Figure 3-4   *Traffic Flow Used to Maintain the Topology Table*

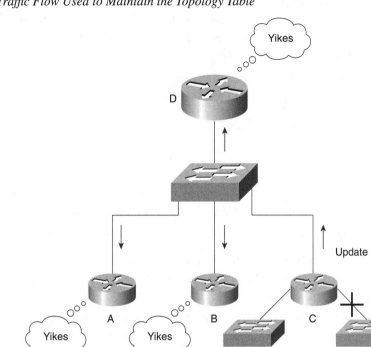

Adding a Network to the Topology Table

Imagine an access layer router (Router A) that connects to a new network via an Ethernet interface. The administrator has configured another interface to service a department that has moved into the building. At the start of this process, the old interface has converged routing. The following list describes how the new network is propagated to all the routers in the EIGRP autonomous system:

1.   As soon as Router A becomes aware of the new network, it starts to send Hello packets out of the new interface. No one answers—no other routers are on the segment.

    There are no new entries in the neighbor table because no neighbors have responded to the Hello protocol. There is a new entry in the topology table, however, because it is attached to a new network.

2.   EIGRP, sensing a change, is obliged to send an update to all its neighbors on the old interface, informing them of the new network. These updates are tracked in the topology table and the neighbor table because the updates are connection-oriented and the acknowledgments from the neighbors must be received within a set timeframe.

3.   Router A has completed its work. However, its neighbors on the old network still have work to do. On hearing the update from Router A, they will update the sequence number in their neighbor table and add the new network to the topology table. They calculate the FD and the successor to place in the routing table.

The next section describes the process for removing a router or path from the topology table.

Removing a Path or Router from the Topology Table

The process of removing a path or router from the topology table is far more complex and gets to the crux of EIGRP.

1.   If a network connected to Router A is disconnected, Router A updates its topology and routing table and sends an update to its neighbors.

2.   When a neighbor receives the update, it updates the neighbor table and the topology table.

3.   The neighbor searches for an alternative route to the remote network. It examines the topology table for alternatives. Because there is only one path to the remote network, no alternatives are found.

4.   The neighbor then sends out a query to its neighbors requesting that they look in their tables for paths to the remote network. The route is marked active in the topology table at this time.

5.   The query number is tracked, and when all the replies are in, the neighbor and topology tables are updated.

6.   DUAL, which starts to compute as soon as a network change is registered, runs to determine the best path, which is placed in the routing table.

7.   Before they respond, they query their own neighbors; in this way, the search for an alternative path extends or diffuses throughout the organization.

8.   If no alternative route is available, the neighbors reply to the query stating that they have no path.

9.   When no router can supply a path to the network, all the routers remove the network from their routing and topology tables.

The next section describes what happens if a neighbor does have an alternative route.

Finding an Alternative Path to a Remote Network

When the path to a network is lost, EIGRP goes to a lot of trouble to find an alternative path. The method that EIGRP uses to find alternative paths is very reliable and very fast.

The following list describes the process after a neighbor goes offline:

1.   The router marks the routes that were reached by sending the traffic to that neighbor.

2. The router looks in the topology table, which has every advertisement received, to determine whether there is an alternative route. It is looking for a FS.

3. If a successor is found, the router adds the FS route to its routing table. If the router did not have a FS, it would have placed the route into an active state while it actively queried other routers for an alternative path.

4. After interrogating the topology table, if a feasible route is found, the neighbor replies with the alternative path. This alternative path is then added to the topology table.

5. If no answer is heard, the messages are propagated.

When the router sends a query packet, it is recorded in the topology table. This is to ensure a timely reply. If the router does not hear a reply, the neighbor is removed from the neighbor table and all networks held in the topology table from that neighbor are removed from the topology table. Occasionally, problems can occur because of slow links and burdened routers in a large network. In particular, a router might not receive a reply from all the queries that it sent out. This leads to the route being declared SIA; the neighbor that failed to reply is removed from the neighbor table.

Creating the Routing Table

The routing table is built from the topology table using DUAL. The topology table holds all routing information known to the router and from this information successors and feasible successors are selected. Successor paths are then transferred to the routing table and used as the basis for routing decisions.

EIGRP Path Selection

The DUAL algorithm uses the metric to select the best path or paths to a destination. Up to sixteen paths can be held for one destination. There are three different types of paths. These three path types are described in Table 3-4.

Table 3-4   *EIGRP Route Types*

Route Type	Description
Internal	Paths placed directly into EIGRP
Summary	Internal paths that have been summarized
External	Routes redistributed into EIGRP

The metric is discussed in greater detail earlier in the chapter in the section "Sophisticated Metric" and is calculated from bandwidth and delay.

Updating the Routing Table in Passive Mode with DUAL

When a path is lost, DUAL first looks in the topology table for a feasible successor. If one is found, the router stays in passive mode (passive, in this sense, means that the router is not actively querying for an alternative path).

Figure 3-5 provides an example network.

Figure 3-5 *The Use of Feasible and Advertised Distance—Passive Mode*

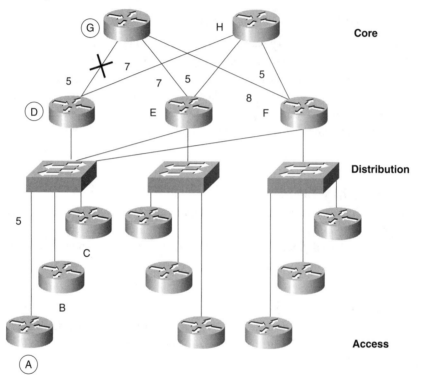

The following list explains Figure 3-5 with the metrics and actions that EIGRP takes in determining the path:

- The feasible distance from Router A to Router G is 10 (A to D to G).

- The advertised distance from Router A to Router G is 5 (advertised from Neighbor D).

- Because 10 > 5, feasible distance > advertised distance. This means that the feasible distance meets the feasibility condition, allowing it to become a feasible distance. If you follow the diagram, it is very straightforward and less algebraic.

- If the link between Router D and Router G were down, Router A would look in its topology table.

- The alternative routes through Router A to D to H to E to G have an advertised distance of 19 (7 + 5 + 7).

- Because 19 is greater than the original feasible distance of 10, it does not qualify as an feasible successor.

- The path through Router D to H to F to G has an advertised distance of 20 and cannot be a feasible successor.

- The path through Router A to E to G has an advertised distance of 7, however, which is less than the original 10. Therefore, this is a feasible successor and can be replaced as a route without Router A changing from passive to active mode.

- The original topology table would show that the primary route (successor) is Router D, while the backup route (feasible successor) is Router E. After the link between D and G dies, the routing table would be updated from the topology table while the route remains passive.

The following section illustrates what happens when the topology table is interrogated and no feasible route is found.

Updating the Routing Table in Active Mode with DUAL

Figure 3-6 shows feasible and advertised distance.

Figure 3-6 *Feasible and Advertised Distance—Active Mode*

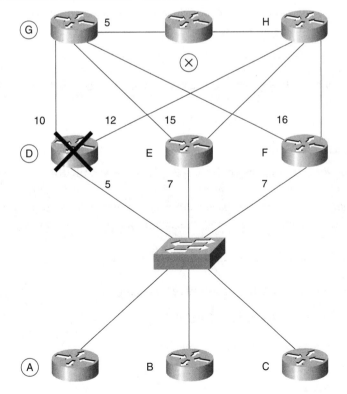

When no alternative route is found in the routing table, the following actions are taken (using the network in Figure 3-6 as an example). The topology table of Router A starts with a path (successor) of A to D to G to X. The feasible distance is 20, and the advertised distance from Router D is 15. When Router D dies, Router A must find an alternative path to X.

■ The router rejects neighbors B, C, E, and F as feasible successors. These neighbors have advertised distances of 27, 27, 20, and 21, respectively. Because all the neighbors have an advertised distance that is the same or greater than the successor feasible distance, they do not meet the feasibility requirement.

■ Router A goes into active mode and sends queries to the neighbors.

■ Both Routers E and F reply with a feasible successor because both have an advertised distance of 5 from Router G. Remember that equation feasible distance > advertised distance; the Routers E and F have a feasible distance of 21, and 21 > 5.

■ The network returns to passive mode. The feasible distance is acceptable, the topology and routing tables will be updated, and there is no need for further convergence.

■ From this information received from Routers E and F, the router selects the path through E as the best route because it has the lower feasible distance.

■ The result is placed in the routing table as the valid neighboring router. EIGRP refers to this neighboring router as a successor.

■ Router F will be stored as an FS in the topology table.

The details on how EIGRP computes successors are complex, but the concept is simple, as described in the next section.

EIGRP Network Design

EIGRP is designed to work in very large networks. However, EIGRP is design-sensitive. Scaling a network is a major concern in organizations. New demands are constantly driving the networks to use applications that require more bandwidth and less delay; at the same time networks are becoming larger and more complex. Mergers and acquisitions, for instance, do nothing for good design.

The factors that can affect the scaling of EIGRP include

■ The amount of information sent between neighbors

■ The number of routers that receive updates

■ The distance between neighboring routers

■ The number of alternative paths to remote networks

Poorly scaled EIGRP networks can result in

- A stuck-in-active route

- Network congestion

- Lost routing information

- Flapping routes

- Retransmission

- Low router memory

- Overutilized router CPU

Other factors, such as poor design, cause some of these symptoms because resources are overwhelmed by the tasks assigned. Often, a route flagged as SIA characterizes many of these symptoms, because the router waits for a reply from a neighbor across a network that cannot handle the demands made upon it. Careful design and placement of network devices can remedy many of the problems seen in a network.

EIGRP Design Issues

The major concerns in scaling an organizational network are controlling advertisements and limiting query range. These are particularly important over slow WAN links. By sending less information about the network, the capacity available for the data between clients and servers increases. Although sending less routing information relieves the network and speeds convergence, it provides less information for finding alternate routes. A balance between summarization and full information must be struck, but generally this balance will tilt toward more summarization and not less.

EIGRP automatically summarizes at classful network boundaries because summarization is generally helpful and the EIGRP process is built to recognize opportunities such as this to optimize the network. However, most administrators find that automatic summarization sometimes does not match what their network needs and choose to disable it. Instead, they choose to manually configure summarization at the interface level.

Certain topologies pose problems for the EIGRP network. This is true in particular for the hub-and-spoke design often seen implemented between remote sites and regional offices. The popular dual-hub configuration provides redundancy and allows the potential for routers to reflect queries back to one another. Summarization and filters make this network design work well while also allowing queries to be managed effectively.

Guideline to Address Scaling Issues

The design of the network is very important to the ability to scale any network. The following actions are critical to a well-designed network:

- Assign addresses and organize links so that natural points for summarization exist. A hierarchical network design meets this criteria.

- Provide sufficient hardware resources (memory and CPU) on network devices.

- Use sufficient bandwidth on WAN links.

- Use filters to limit advertisements.

- Monitor the network.

Foundation Summary

The "Foundation Summary" section of each chapter lists the most important facts from the chapter. Although this section does not list every fact from the chapter that will be on your exam, a well-prepared candidate should, at a minimum, know all the details in each "Foundation Summary" before going to take the exam.

The key features of EIGRP include

- Neighborship and reliable incremental updates

- Neighbor discovery and recovery

- Sophisticated metric

- DUAL

- Queries

EIGRP uses five types of packets to communicate:

- Hello

- Ack

- Update

- Query

- Reply

EIGRP uses a sophisticated metric that considers bandwidth, load, reliability, and delay. When default constant values are taken into consideration, the equation simplifies to

$$metric = 256 * \left(\frac{10^7}{min(bandwidth)} + \sum \frac{delays}{10} \right)$$

Additional EIGRP advantages include

- Incremental Updates

- Multicast Addressing for Updates

- Easy Configuration

- Unequal-Cost Load Sharing

EIGRP builds and maintains three tables:

- Neighbor table

- Topology table

- Routing table

To become a neighbor, the following conditions must be met:

- The router must hear a Hello packet from a neighbor.

- The EIGRP autonomous system must be the same.

- K-values must be the same.

Q&A

The questions and scenarios in this book are designed to be challenging and to make sure that you know the answer. Rather than allowing you to derive the answers from clues hidden inside the questions themselves, the questions challenge your understanding and recall of the subject.

You can find the answers to these questions in Appendix A. For more practice with exam-like question formats, use the exam engine on the CD-ROM.

1. If a router does not have a feasible successor, what action will it take?

2. Which timers are tracked in the neighbor table?

3. What is the difference between an update and a query?

4. When does EIGRP recalculate the topology table?

5. State two rules for designing a scalable EIGRP network.

6. Which EIGRP packets are sent reliably?

7. How long is the holdtime by default?

8. What is an EIGRP topology table, and what does it contain?

9. What is the advertised distance in EIGRP, and how is it distinguished from the feasible distance?

10. What EIGRP algorithm is run to create entries for the routing table?

11. When does EIGRP place a network in active mode?

12. By default, EIGRP summarizes at which boundary?

13. What is Stuck in Active?

14. State two factors that influence EIGRP scalability.

15. What are reply packets in EIGRP?

16. What conditions must be met for a router to become a neighbor?

This chapter covers the following topics:

- **Configuring EIGRP**—This section describes the basic configuration commands necessary to support routing.

- **Verifying the EIGRP operation**—This section describes **show** and **debug** commands that will help evaluate the status of EIGRP.

- **Troubleshooting EIGRP**—This section describes the process of diagnosing and repairing EIGRP problems.

CHAPTER 4

Scalable EIGRP

This chapter details steps to configure EIGRP for IP routing. This chapter assumes general knowledge of routing protocols and the terminology, concepts, and operation of EIGRP (from Chapter 3, "EIGRP Principles"). This chapter introduces EIGRP configuration commands by explaining the required commands and then discussing the optional configuration commands that you can use.

"Do I Know This Already?" Quiz

The purpose of the "Do I Know This Already?" quiz is to help you decide what parts of this chapter to use. If you already intend to read the entire chapter, you do not necessarily need to answer these questions now.

The 12-question quiz, derived from the major sections in the "Foundation Topics" portion of the chapter, helps you determine how to spend your limited study time.

Table 4-1 outlines the major topics discussed in this chapter and the "Do I Know This Already?" quiz questions that correspond to those topics.

Table 4-1 *"Do I Know This Already?" Foundation Topics Section-to-Question Mapping*

Foundation Topics Section	Questions Covered in This Section	Score
Configuring EIGRP	1–7	
Verifying the EIGRP Operation	8–10	
Troubleshooting EIGRP	11–12	
Total Score		

CAUTION   The goal of self-assessment is to gauge your mastery of the topics in this chapter. If you do not know the answer to a question or are only partially sure of the answer, you should mark the question wrong for purposes of the self-assessment. Giving yourself credit for an answer you correctly guessed skews your results and might provide you with a false sense of security.

1. What command starts the EIGRP routing process?

    a. **router eigrp**

    b. **router eigrp** *autonomous-system-number*

    c. **ip routing eigrp**

    d. **ip eigrp routing**

2. What happens if no **network** command is configured?

    a. The EIGRP process is not activated on any interface.

    b. The EIGRP defaults to all interfaces.

    c. The EIGRP process can receive, but cannot send, updates.

    d. The router prompts you for the networks.

3. What happens immediately after the **network** command is configured?

    a. Updates are sent.

    b. The routing table is created.

    c. Hellos are sent on appropriate interfaces.

    d. Networks are advertised.

4. Where in the EIGRP network is it possible to summarize IP addresses?

    a. At a classful network boundary

    b. At the ASBR

    c. At the ABR

    d. At an interface

5. Where is the command **ip summary-address eigrp** *autonomous-system-number address mask* configured?

    a. At the routing process

    b. At the interface

    c. After the network command

    d. At the EXEC command prompt

6. What command is used to change the hello timer?

    a. **eigrp hello-interval** *seconds*

    b. **hello interval seconds**

    c. **ip hello-interval eigrp** *autonomous-system-number seconds*

    d. **ip eigrp hello timer** *seconds*

7. Which of the following commands will show the hold time?

    a. **show ip eigrp topology**

    b. **show ip eigrp traffic**

    c. **show ip eigrp holdtime**

    d. show ip eigrp neighbors

8. Which command is used to display the current status of EIGRP neighbors?

    a. **show ip eigrp traffic**

    b. **show ip eigrp neighbors**

    c. **show ip eigrp adjacencies**

    d. **show ip eigrp database**

9. Which command is used to see the types of packets sent and received, as well as the statistics on routing decisions?

    a. **show ip eigrp traffic**

    b. **show eigrp events**

    c. **debug ip eigrp packets**

    d. **debug ip eigrp traffic**

10. What types of information are shown by the **show ip eigrp traffic** command?

    a. Updates

    b. Hellos

    c. Queries and replies

    d. ACKs

11. What is displayed in the command **debug ip eigrp summary**?

    a. A summary of EIGRP activity

    b. A summary of the contents of the neighbor database

    c. The process taken when a change is made in a summary route

    d. A summary of the topology database

12. Which command could be used to show that EIGRP is able to contact neighbors?

    a. **debug ip eigrp traffic**

    b. **debug ip eigrp packets**

    c. **debug ip eigrp events**

    d. **debug ip eigrp**

The answers to the "Do I Know This Already?" quiz are found in Appendix A, "Answers to Chapter 'Do I Know This Already?' Quizzes and Q&A Sections." The suggested choices for your next step are as follows:

■ **8 or less overall score**—Read the entire chapter. This includes the "Foundation Topics" and "Foundation Summary" sections, the "Q&A" section, and the "Scenarios" section at the end of the chapter.

■ **9-10 overall score**—Begin with the "Foundation Summary" section, and then go to the "Q&A" section and the "Scenarios" at the end of the chapter. If you have trouble with these exercises, read the appropriate sections in "Foundation Topics."

■ **11 or 12 overall score**—If you want more review on these topics, skip to the "Foundation Summary" section, and then go to the "Q&A" and "Scenarios" sections at the end of the chapter. Otherwise, move to the next chapter.

Foundation Topics

Configuring EIGRP

Routers are able to route IP out of the box, but you need to configure static routes or a routing protocol so they can reach networks that are not directly connected.

EIGRP is classless, meaning that it advertises both a prefix and a mask with each route. Classless routing protocols are also able to arbitrarily summarize. EIGRP summarizes automatically at classful network boundaries, but you will also want to summarize within your network. EIGRP can summarize at any interface on any router, and summarization is extremely important in building a scalable EIGRP network.

The commands for EIGRP are similar to IP routing protocols.

This section covers the following:

■ Required commands for configuring EIGRP

■ Optional commands for EIGRP

■ Optional EIGRP commands specific to WANs

Required Commands for Configuring EIGRP

Like other interior routing protocols, the template for an EIGRP configuration involves turning on the protocol and identifying participating interfaces. EIGRP also uses an autonomous system (AS) to group routers. To run EIGRP, you must enable the following three items:

■ **The EIGRP process**—The routing protocol needs to be started on the router.

■ **The EIGRP autonomous system number**—Routers in the same administrative domain should be identified and grouped by a common AS number. This 16-bit number is arbitrary. Organizations that have a BGP AS will sometimes use that number; others just make up a number or use "AS 1." The significance of the AS is that a router will not become a neighbor with a router in a foreign AS.

■ **Participating router interfaces**—You can activate EIGRP on some or all interfaces. For instance, a router might run EIGRP on internal interfaces and BGP on external interfaces.

To enable EIGRP as an active routing protocol, use the **router** command. Remember that the AS must be consistent between routers to exchange updates.

```
Router(config)#router eigrp autonomous-system-number
```

At this point, EIGRP is enabled but not active on an interface. EIGRP will not produce hellos or advertise networks until it is activated on particular links.

> **NOTE**   Most versions of the IOS software do not offer an error message when the configuration is incomplete, which can make troubleshooting more difficult. Refer to the section titled "Verifying the EIGRP Operation" later in this chapter for more information.

Interfaces are then attached to the EIGRP process with the **network** command. The **network** command is a pattern-matching tool: interfaces with IP addresses that match the pattern are active EIGRP speakers and those subnets are advertised through EIGRP.

There are two ways to utilize the network command. The first way is by classful network number.

```
Router(config-router)#network network-number
```

In this case, the **network** command in EIGRP is similar to the **network** command in RIP. A router with three interfaces—10.0.0.1, 10.1.1.1, and 192.168.0.1—configured with the **network 10.0.0.0** command would speak EIGRP on two interfaces, but not on the 192.168.0.1 port.

In some cases, you might want to leave an interface that is within the classful network out of EIGRP. The command to do this is **passive-interface**. The **passive-interface** command prevents EIGRP from speaking on an interface; it does not send hellos or advertisements. Neighbors are not found on the passive interface and routes are not exchanged; however, the prefix of the passive interface is advertised to EIGRP neighbors on other interfaces.

The **passive-interface** command can be used on interfaces with no neighbors, or on interfaces that run another routing protocol (such as BGP).

For example, a router with two interfaces addressed 172.17.0.1 and 172.17.55.1 is configured in Example 4-1. EIGRP should run only on fastethernet0/0. Configuring the classful network (network 172.17.0.0) enables EIGRP on both interfaces. The **passive-interface** command is then used to suppress fastethernet0/1. Because EIGRP is active but quiet on fastethernet 0/1, the attached subnet (172.17.55.0/24) is advertised to neighbors through fastethernet0/0.

Example 4-1   *The EIGRP* **passive-interface** *Command*

```
Router(config)#interface fastethernet0/0
Router(config-if)#ip address 172.17.0.1 255.255.255.0
Router(config-if)#interface fastethernet0/1
```

Example 4-1 *The EIGRP* **passive-interface** *Command (Continued)*

```
Router(config-if)#ip address 172.17.55.1 255.255.255.0
Router(config-if)#router eigrp 100
Router(config-router)#network 172.17.0.0
Router(config-router)#passive-interface fastethernet0/1
```

> **NOTE** As shown in Example 4-1, you do not have to exit back to global-configuration mode to move between sub-configuration modes.

The **network** command for EIGRP can also be stated with a mask option. This allows you to identify specific interfaces for EIGRP. Routes that match the network and mask will run EIGRP and those subnets will be advertised.

This alternative syntax (first supported in IOS 12.0(4)T) is

```
Router(config-router)#network network-number [wildcard-network-mask]
```

To repeat the previous example, a router with interfaces numbered 172.17.0.1 and 172.17.55.1 needs to run EIGRP only on fastethernet0/0. Using the mask option allows the administrator to identify a specific interface, as shown in Example 4-2.

Example 4-2 *EIGRP* **network** mask *Command*

```
Router(config)#interface f0/0
Router(config-if)#ip address 172.17.0.1 255.255.255.0
Router(config-if)#interface f0/1
Router(config-if)#ip address 172.17.55.1 255.255.255.0
Router(config)#router eigrp 100
Router(config-router)#network 172.17.0.1 0.0.0.0
```

There is an important difference between the **passive-interface** and **network** *mask* techniques. The **passive-interface** command forces an interface to be quiet, but advertises the connected network out other interfaces. Interfaces left out of **network** *mask* do not speak EIGRP and subnets attached to those interfaces are not advertised.

Once interfaces have been selected for EIGRP, the next order of business is to meet and greet neighbors and exchange routes.

At this point, EIGRP is completely configured. It is possible to "tune" it a bit, and the following sections describe how to do so with optional commands. As the discussion turns to these optional commands, do not lose sight of one of the most important features of EIGRP: EIGRP makes smart decisions (such as bandwidth utilization and summarization) automatically and is thus easy to configure and troubleshoot. Many of the optional tuning commands are unnecessary because EIGRP defaults are effective in most cases.

Optional Commands for Configuring EIGRP

Optional commands described in this section are summarized in Table 4-2.

Table 4-2 *Optional Commands for Configuring EIGRP*

Command	Description
no auto-summary	Turns off automatic classful summarization.
ip summary-address	Manually configures summarization.
eigrp stub	Configures a stub router.
variance	Configures unequal proportional load balancing.
ip hello-interval eigrp *autonomous-system-number seconds*	Changes the hello frequency.
ip hold-time eigrp *autonomous-system-number seconds*	Changes the length of time before a neighbor is considered dead.
bandwidth	Changes the bandwidth setting on an interface, which is used to calculate the EIGRP metric and the maximum percentage of bandwidth to which EIGRP traffic will limit itself.
ip bandwidth-percent eigrp *as-number*	Changes the maximum amount of bandwidth EIGRP traffic will use. The default is 50%.

Summarization with EIGRP

It cannot be said enough: Scalability comes from summarization. Like other routing protocols, summarization is important to EIGRP because it limits advertisements, minimizes the size and optimizes the speed of the routing table, limits route recalculation, and holds down the amount of memory and processor resources consumed. Smaller routing tables make for faster networks.

Summarization in EIGRP also solves a problem unique to EIGRP: *query scoping*. EIGRP queries do not stop until they come to a dead-end; because of this, they can loop. Route convergence cannot proceed until all replies have been received. Summarization limits queries by stating: "only these routes are found past this point." Summarizing at logical points in the network is important to prevent stuck in active (SIA).

In IOS versions before 12.2(8), summarization automatically happens at classful network boundaries. Automatic summarization is an example of EIGRP trying to be helpful; however, if your network uses more than one classful network—for example, some enterprises use 10.0.0.0/8 and 192.168.x.0/24 networks concurrently—automatic summarization may create problems in some situations and should be disabled.

Summarization may be manually applied at any point in the network. You can configure manual summarization on any router interface. Consider summarization for both upstream and downstream neighbors. Upstream neighbors should receive a consolidated route, and downstream neighbors can receive a default route.

There are two commands for summarization with EIGRP: **no auto-summary** and **ip summary-address eigrp** *autonomous-system-number address mask*. The **no auto-summary** command disables automatic summarization. With **no auto-summary** configured, all known subnets are advertised out of each interface, limited only by split-horizon.

The **ip summary-address eigrp** command is used to announce a specific range on a particular interface. This allows bidirectional summarization and allows summarization to be more widely utilized.

Manual summarization is configured at the interface level, as shown here:

```
Router(config)#interface S0
Router(config-if)#ip summary-address eigrp autonomous-system-number address mask
```

For example, imagine a router that connects to the corporate network and to a division with IP subnets such as 172.20.0.0/24, 172.20.1.0/24 . . . 172.20.31.0/24 on serial 1/1. It also has a default route on serial 1/0. Configuration of manual summarization is done at the interface level. The corporation uses AS 100. This is shown in Example 4-3.

Example 4-3 *EIGRP Summarization*

```
Router(config)#interface S1/0
Router(config-if)#ip summary-address eigrp 100 172.20.0.0 255.255.224.0
Router(config-if)#interface S1/1
Router(config-if)#ip summary-address eigrp 100 0.0.0.0 0.0.0.0
```

Thus the division is summarized to the larger network and receives back a simple default route.

CAUTION   Summarizing the default route can be a useful technique. However, if used in cases where there are multiple default paths, this will reduce routing options and prevent failover to alternate paths when the primary path fails.

Stub Routers

Cisco IOS software release 12.0 made it possible for you to configure a remote router as an EIGRP stub router. Stub routers in EIGRP networks use EIGRP to send limited information between the stub and the core routers. A stub router is typically used on routers to minimize memory and processor utilization; as such it is a good candidate for slow routers with minimal memory.

The stub router has only one neighbor, a distribution layer router. The remote router only needs a default route pointing to the distribution router—everywhere else can be reached via that router.

Configuring a router as a stub also helps the rest of the network. Queries are responded to much quicker and convergence happens much faster. Sometimes a query can cause delays that result in the path being SIA. If the stub configuration is applied, the router responds to queries as inaccessible, thus limiting the scope of the query range and preventing SIA from occurring.

The following command structure shows the syntax of the **eigrp stub** command:

```
Router(config-router)# eigrp stub [receive-only | connected | redistributed | static |
    summary]
```

Table 4-3 explains the options further. The third column shows that some optional commands may be combined on a single command line, while others require a separate **eigrp stub** command.

Table 4-3 *The **eigrp stub** Option Syntax and Description*

Parameter	On by Default	May Be Combined	Description
receive-only	No	No	(optional) Prevents the router from advertising routes.
connected	Yes	Yes	(optional) Permits advertisement of connected routes.
static	No	Yes	(optional) Permits redistribution of static routes.
summary	Yes	Yes	Advertises summary routes.

Figure 4-1 shows a group of routers connected over WAN links. These routers are stub routers because they have no other networks connected to them.

Example 4-4 is the configuration for Router B in Figure 4-1.

Figure 4-1 *Stub Routers*

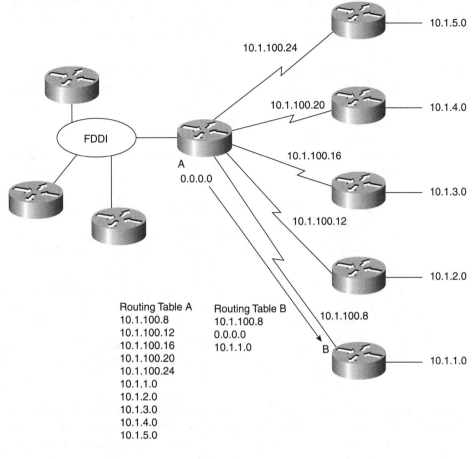

Example 4-4 *The* **eigrp stub** *Router Command*

```
RouterB(config)#router eigrp 100
RouterB(config-router)#network 10.0.0.0 255.0.0.0
RouterB(config-router)#eigrp stub
```

This is obviously a simplified example, but it does raise an interesting point. This network could be configured with static routes. By using **eigrp stub**, the on-site technician can simply copy an example configuration into the router and change the IP addresses without having to understand EIGRP. Some organizations use EIGRP in hub-and-spoke topologies because it standardizes the configuration and fits situations where on-site technicians are not as familiar with IP and EIGRP.

Load Balancing in EIGRP

EIGRP automatically load balances across equal-cost links. The exact mechanism depends on the internal switching process of the router. You can also configure EIGRP to load balance proportionally across unequal-cost paths using the **variance** command.

When **variance** is used, the metric of the best path is multiplied by the variance. Alternate paths with a feasible distance lower than that product are used for load balancing. The command syntax is simply the keyword **variance** and the whole number multiplier:

```
Router(config-router)#variance multiplier
```

The *multiplier* argument is a whole number from 1 to 128. The default is 1, which means equal-cost load balancing.

CAUTION   When using variance, remember the following important points:

- A variance of two or three is almost always appropriate—use higher values with caution. At a certain point, EIGRP will start activating old 28.8 modems to load-balance with DS1s.

- Variance should be used cautiously with delay-sensitive traffic. A DS1 link takes 8 ms to transmit a 1500 B packet, while a 256-kbps link takes 47 ms. Voice over IP (VoIP) traffic, if shared between the two links, would perceive the difference as 39 ms of jitter.

  Cisco Voice over IP (CVoice), Second Edition, by Kevin Wallace, is a great resource for more information about delay and its effect on voice (Cisco Press, 2006).

If the variance number is higher than the default value of 1, the EIGRP process multiplies the best (lowest) metric by the variance. All paths to the same destination that have metrics less than this product are now included in load balancing. The amount of traffic sent over each link is proportional to the metric for the path.

Figure 4-2 shows EIGRP metrics to 192.168.5.0/24. To demonstrate the **variance** command, consider Router B.

Example 4-5 shows the configuration of the **variance** command.

Example 4-5 *The **variance** Command*

```
RouterB(config)#router eigrp 100
RouterB(config-router)#variance 2
```

Figure 4-2 *EIGRP Distance and the* **variance** *Command*

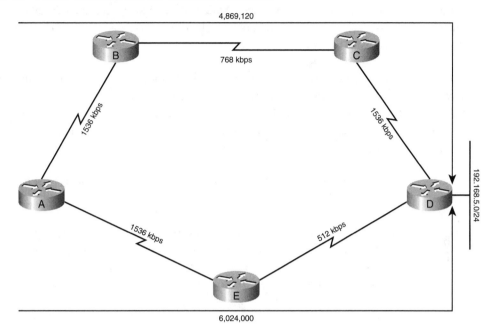

Because the clockwise metric is about five million, a variance of two will load-balance with paths less than ten million. Because the counterclockwise metric is about six million, six packets will go clockwise for every five that go counterclockwise.

> **NOTE**   Only those paths that are in the topology table as feasible successors are eligible to be included in the **variance** command.

Tuning the EIGRP Process

You can tune a network in many ways. Load balancing and summarizing routes are probably the two most important ways, but other techniques include reducing the frequency of the hello and hold timers.

There is a trade-off between reducing the hello traffic and maintaining the stability of the network. Fewer hellos, for example, result in the network taking longer to notice a failure, which in turn delays convergence. When the network does not have an accurate understanding of the available routes, the router cannot forward packets correctly.

EIGRP only sends updates when a new route is advertised or an existing route is withdrawn (changes state to down). Link failure causes an interface to change state without delay. But when a failed neighbor is not directly connected (on the other side of an Ethernet switch, for example), the only way to notice the change is to notice that hellos are no longer received. Neighborship is important because it alerts the router to topology changes and because the router is responsible to the rest of the network to publicize the lost routes.

Change the timers only after careful consideration. In the majority of cases, the default values are reasonable. Instead of improving performance, changing timers can create issues if not done deliberately. For instance, timers are changed per interface and changing the timers on only one side of a link can create a problem where a neighborship forms and dissolves periodically.

Timer values default based on the speed of the interface. Because the timers are assumed based on speed, they will usually be the same.

Timers are not communicated between neighbors and are not a requirement for neighborship. If Router A has a hello interval of 5 seconds and a hold timer of 15 seconds and Router B has a hello interval of 30 seconds, then the two routers will be neighbors for 15 seconds and then down for 15 seconds. Both the hello timer and the hold timer are discussed in the next sections.

The Hello Timer

Tuning the hello timer directly affects the ability of the network to notice a change in the state of a neighbor. Only after a router's interface is recognized as being down, or the router has failed to hear from a neighbor after a certain amount of time, does the router declare the neighbor dead and take action to update the routing table and neighbors.

For these reasons, the **ip hello-interval eigrp** command is typically used to decrease the time between hellos to ensure that the network converges quickly.

The defaults for the hello timer are as follows:

- High-bandwidth links (every 5 seconds):

    — Broadcast media, such as Ethernet, Token Ring, and FDDI

    — Point-to-point serial links, such as PPP or HDLC leased circuits, Frame Relay point-to-point subinterfaces, and ATM

    — Point-to-point subinterfaces

    — High bandwidth (greater than T1) multipoint circuits, such as ISDN PRI and Frame Relay

■ Low-bandwidth links (every 60 seconds):

— Multipoint circuits T1 bandwidth or slower, such as Frame Relay multipoint interfaces, ATM multipoint interfaces, and ATM

— Switched virtual circuits and ISDN BRIs

The command to change how often the hellos are sent to neighbors is

```
Router(config-if)#ip hello-interval eigrp autonomous-system-number seconds
```

Notice that the command is applied to an interface and does not affect the default interval on other interfaces. The autonomous system number ties the command to a particular EIGRP process. The last variable then changes the default hello interval. Example 4-6 shows the hello interval on serial0/0 changing to 10 seconds.

Example 4-6 *Hello Timer*

```
Router(config)#interface Serial 0/0
Router(config-if)#ip hello-interval eigrp 100 10
```

This command is very useful with nonbroadcast multiaccess (NBMA) WAN links. EIGRP uses a 60-second hello timer for Frame Relay by default.

The Hold Timer

The *hold time* is how long the router waits for a hello before pronouncing a neighbor unavailable. By default, the hold time is three times the hello time but changing the hello interval does not automatically change the hold time. The hold timer for an interface must be changed manually using the **ip hold-time eigrp** command, as follows:

```
Router(config-if)#ip hold-time eigrp autonomous-system-number seconds
```

The command is specific to an interface and EIGRP AS. Example 4-7 shows the hold interval on serial0/0 changing to 30 seconds.

Example 4-7 *Hold Timer*

```
Router(config)#interface serial0/0
Router(config-if)#ip hold-time eigrp 100 30
```

Authentication

EIGRP supports two forms of authentication: simple passwords and MD5 hashes. Simple passwords are sent as plain-text and matched to the key on the receiver. Simple passwords are not secure, because any listener can see this traffic and read the key value. Because simple passwords do not accomplish a change in the security structure in your network, the commands to implement them are not discussed here.

Hashed keys, sent as MD5 values, are secure because a listener cannot use the value in one transmission to compute the key.

Using MD5 Authentication, the router generates a hash value for every EIGRP transmission and checks the hash of every received EIGRP packet.

To specify MD5 authentication, the command is

```
router(config-if)#ip authentication mode eigrp autonomous-system md5
```

Once MD5 is specified, the command to set the key is

```
router(config-if)#ip authentication key-chain eigrp autonomous-system chain-name
```

Finally, the key-chain is configured and the key is specified:

```
router(config-if)#key chain chain-name
router(config-if)#key key-id
router(config-keychain-key)#key-string key
```

An example configuration in AS 100 might therefore look like the following:

```
router(config-if)#ip authentication mode eigrp 100 md5
router(config-if)#ip authentication key-chain eigrp 100 my-chain
router(config)#key chain my-chain
router(config-keychain)#key 1
router(config-keychain-key)#key-string secret
```

Authentication results are not shown under the **show** commands; authentication must be assumed based on the successful establishment of neighborship. However, the **debug eigrp packets** command does show the process.

Optional EIGRP Commands over WANs

There are EIGRP design and configuration issues concerning WANs. Here you must deal with limited capacity to a greater degree than at other points in the network. Furthermore, routing updates and data transmissions compete for that limited space.

EIGRP is unique in that it restricts its use of bandwidth. By default, it uses no more than half the link capacity, which is superior to the scant consideration shown by every other routing protocol. Although the default setting for EIGRP is usually sufficient, you may need to adjust it at times. The following sections describe the commands necessary to make these changes.

EIGRP Defaults in Bandwidth Utilization

Routers usually understand link capacity. Serial interfaces are problematic in this regard, though, because they usually attach through a DSU. The router therefore assumes a default serial speed of 1544 kbps.

If the link is 56 kbps, however, EIGRP would calculate an inaccurate metric and—even limiting itself to 772 kbps—could saturate the link. This could result in dropped EIGRP and data packets because of congestion.

The **show interface** command allows you to check that the interface bandwidth is accurate. The output shows the configured bandwidth of the link.

Example 4-8 shows the bandwidth of serial0.

Example 4-8 *Bandwidth*

```
Router# show interface serial 0
Serial0 is up, line protocol is up
Hardware is HD64570
Description: to Internet
Internet address is 172.25.146.182/30
MTU 1500 bytes, BW 1280 Kbit, DLY 20000 usec, rely 255/255, load 1/255
...
```

Note that, in this case, the bandwidth has been adjusted to 1280 kbps.

The bandwidth does not affect the actual speed of the link. It is used for routing-protocol calculations and load calculations. The following sections provide additional guidelines about bandwidth configuration.

In general, the bandwidth is set using the **bandwidth** command. The following syntax shows the structure of the command:

```
Router#interface S0
Router(config-if)#bandwidth speed-of-line
```

Configuring Bandwidth over an NBMA Cloud

EIGRP works well over all WANs, including point-to-point and NBMA environments such as Frame Relay or ATM. The NBMA topology can include either point-to-point subinterfaces or multipoint interfaces.

Cisco identifies three rules that you should follow when configuring EIGRP over an NBMA cloud:

■ EIGRP traffic should not exceed the committed information rate (CIR) capacity of the virtual circuit (VC).

■ EIGRP aggregated traffic over all the VCs should not exceed the access line speed of the interface.

■ The bandwidth allocated to EIGRP on each VC must be the same in both directions.

If you understand and follow these rules, EIGRP works well over the WAN. If you do not take care in the configuration of the WAN, EIGRP can swamp the network.

> **NOTE**   Come back and look through this section after you have read about OSPF support for Frame Relay. OSPF over Frame Relay is complicated and contrasts with the simple implementation of EIGRP over Frame Relay. EIGRP handles whatever topology that is thrown at it without requiring a special configuration.

Configuring Bandwidth over a Multipoint Network

In addition to being used in the EIGRP metric, the **bandwidth** command influences how EIGRP uses NBMA virtual circuits (VCs). If the serial line has many VCs in a multipoint configuration, EIGRP will assume that each VC has an even share of bandwidth. EIGRP will confine itself to using half that share for its traffic. This limitation is important—no other routing protocol does this—but will work best if the bandwidth is correctly defined. A 56-kbps link that has a bandwidth set to 128 kbps will not benefit from restraint shown by EIGRP.

The **bandwidth** command should reflect the access-link speed into the Frame Relay cloud. Your company might have five PVCs from your router's serial interface, each carrying 56 kbps. The access link will need a capacity of 5 * 56 kbps (280 kbps).

Configuring Bandwidth over a Hybrid Multipoint Network

If the multipoint network has differing speeds allocated to the VCs, a more complex solution is needed. There are two main approaches:

- Take the lowest CIR and multiply it by the number of circuits. Apply the product as the bandwidth of the physical interface. The problem with this configuration is that EIGRP will underutilize the higher-bandwidth links.

- If possible, it is much easier to configure and manage an environment that has used subinterfaces, where a VC is logically treated as if it were a separate interface. The **bandwidth** command can be configured on each subinterface, which allows different speeds on each VC. In this solution, subinterfaces are configured for each VC and the CIR is configured as the bandwidth. Cisco recommends this as the preferred solution.

Configuring the Pure Point-to-Point Network

If there are many VCs, there might not be enough bandwidth at the access speed of the interface to support the aggregate EIGRP traffic. The subinterfaces should be configured with a bandwidth that is much lower than the real speed of the circuit. In this case, it is necessary to use the **bandwidth-percent** command to indicate to the EIGRP process that it can still function.

The **ip bandwidth-percent-eigrp** command adjusts the percentage of capacity that EIGRP may use from the default fifty percent. You would use this command because the **bandwidth** command does not reflect the true speed of the link. The **bandwidth** command might have been altered to manipulate the routing metric and path selection of a routing protocol (but it might be better to use other methods of controlling the routing metric and return the bandwidth to a true value). The following shows the structure of the **ip bandwidth-percent eigrp** command:

```
Router(config)#interface S0
Router(config-if)#ip bandwidth-percent eigrp autonomous-system-number percent
```

Verifying the EIGRP Operation

It is important to understand the output of the **show** commands to prepare for the exam. The ability to interpret these **show** command output examples in conjunction with the physical and logical topology diagrams of your organization will ensure your understanding of the operation of EIGRP.

This section describes the **show** commands shown in Table 4-4.

Table 4-4 *EIGRP* **show** *Commands*

Command Option	Description
show ip eigrp neighbors	Gives detailed information about neighbors. This command records the communication between the router and the neighbors in addition to the interface and address by which they communicate.
show ip eigrp topology	Gives details about the routes held in the topology table, detailed information on the networks that the router is aware of and the preferred paths to those networks, and the next hop in the path. Also allows the router to track EIGRP packets that have been sent to neighbors.
show ip eigrp traffic	Gives information about the aggregate traffic sent to and from the EIGRP process.

The EIGRP **show** commands are highly detailed and give a comprehensive understanding of the state of the network. Troubleshooting EIGRP should start with the generic routing commands **show ip route** and **show ip protocols**, before continuing with EIGRP-specific troubleshooting.

The show ip eigrp neighbors Command

The **show ip eigrp neighbors** command shows the neighbor table. The syntax is

```
Router#show ip eigrp neighbors [type number]
```

Example 4-9 shows the output of this command.

Example 4-9 *The* **show ip eigrp neighbors** *Command Output*

```
Router# show ip eigrp neighbors
IP-EIGRP Neighbors for process 100
Address          interface   Holdtime    Uptime     Q      Seq    SRTT    RTO
                             (secs)      (h:m:s)    Count  Num    (ms)    (ms)
140.100.48.22    Ethernet1   13          0:00:41    0      11     4       20
140.100.32.22    Ethernet0   14          0:02:01    0      10     12      24
140.100.32.31    Ethernet0   12          0:02:02    0      4      5       2
```

Table 4-5 explains the meaning of the important fields in Example 4-9.

Table 4-5 *Explanation of the* **show ip eigrp neighbors** *Command Output*

Field	Explanation
process 100	Autonomous system number.
Address	IP address of the EIGRP neighbor.
Interface	Interface the router receives hellos on.
Holdtime	Length of time, in seconds, that the router will wait before declaring the link down.
Uptime	Time (in hours, minutes, and seconds) since the router first heard from this neighbor.
Q Count	Number of EIGRP packets (update, query, and reply) that the router has queued.
Seq Num	The sequence number of the last packet received from the neighbor.
SRTT	Smooth round-trip time. The time (in milliseconds) from the sending of the packet to the receipt of an acknowledgment from the neighbor.
RTO	Retransmission timeout, in milliseconds. This shows how long the router will wait for an acknowledgment before it retransmits the packet.

The show ip eigrp topology Command

The **show ip eigrp topology** command shows the topology table. This command shows the effect of DUAL, which is described in Chapter 3. It shows whether the successor or the route is in an active or passive state and if there is a feasible successor. The syntax is

```
Router#show ip eigrp topology [autonomous-system-number | [[ip-address] mask]]
```

Example 4-10 shows the output of this command.

Example 4-10 *The* **show ip eigrp topology** *Command Output*

```
Router# show ip eigrp topology
IP-EIGRP Topology Table for process 100
Codes:P - Passive, A - Active, U - Update, Q - Query, R - Reply, r - Reply status
P 140.100.56.0 255.255.255.0, 2 successors, FD is 0
via 140.100.32.22 (46251776/46226176), Ethernet0
via 140.100.48.22 (46251776/46226176), Ethernet1
via 140.100.32.31 (46277376/46251776), Ethernet0
P 140.100.48.0 255.255.255.0, 1 successors, FD is 307200
via Connected, Ethernet1
via 140.100.48.22 (307200/281600), Ethernet1
140.100.32.22 (307200/281600), Ethernet0
via 140.100.32.31 (332800/307200), Ethernet0
```

Table 4-6 explains the meaning of the important fields in Example 4-10.

Table 4-6 *Explanation of the* **show ip eigrp topology** *Command Output*

Field	Explanation
P	Passive—The router has not received any EIGRP input from a neighbor, and the network is assumed to be stable.
A	Active—When a route or successor is down, the router attempts to find an alternative path. The router is currently actively querying for a backup path.
U	Update—A value in this field identifies that the router has sent an update packet to a neighbor.
Q	Query—A value in this field identifies that the router has sent a query packet to a neighbor.
R	Reply—A value here shows that the router has sent a reply to the neighbor.
r	This is used in conjunction with the query counter; the router has sent out a query and is awaiting a reply.
140.100.48.0	Destination IP network number.
255.255.255.0	Destination subnet mask.
successors	This is the number of routes or the next logical hop. The number stated here is the same as the number of applicable routes in the routing table.
via	This is the next-hop address. The first of these entries are the current successors. The remaining entries on the list are feasible successors.
(46251776/46226176)	The first number is the EIGRP metric. After the slash is the EIGRP metric the peer advertised, or the advertised distance.
Ethernet0	The interface through which the EIGRP advertisement was received and the outgoing interface.

The show ip eigrp traffic Command

The **show ip eigrp traffic** command shows the EIGRP traffic received and generated by the router. The command syntax is

```
Router#show ip eigrp traffic [autonomous-system-number]
```

Example 4-11 shows the output of this command.

Example 4-11 *The* **show ip eigrp traffic** *Command Output*

```
Router# show ip eigrp traffic
IP-EIGRP Traffic Statistics for process 100
Hellos sent/received: 218/205
Updates sent/received: 7/23
Queries sent/received: 2/0
Replies sent/received: 0/2
Acks sent/received: 21/14
```

Table 4-7 explains the meaning of the important fields in Example 4-11.

Table 4-7 *Explanation of the* **show ip eigrp traffic** *Command Output*

Field	Explanation
process 100	Autonomous system number
Hellos sent/received	Number of hello packets sent and received by the router
Updates sent/received	Number of update packets sent and received by the router
Queries sent/received	Number of query packets sent and received by the router
Replies sent/received	Number of reply packets sent and received by the router
Acks sent/received	Number of acknowledgment packets sent and received by the router

Troubleshooting EIGRP

Having many methods and tools helps in troubleshooting any network. One of the most beneficial tools is documentation, for several reasons. For example, you can see progress and easily eliminate the obvious in a checklist manner, and you can clearly explain the problem and the steps taken thus far in solving it if you need to call in expert help. Cisco provides many tools, both on its web page and in service contracts, to help solve your network problems. One of the mainstays in troubleshooting any routing protocol is the group of debug commands, which provide the ability to see traffic and router processes in real time.

Exercise care when using the **debug** command, because it can be very greedy in terms of the resources that it consumes. You should use it only for a specific option and for a finite time. When debugging is complete, the **undebug all** command will disable debugging.

The options available for monitoring EIGRP are covered in Table 4-8.

Table 4-8   *The* **debug** *Command Options for EIGRP*

Command Option	Description
debug ip eigrp packet	Shows the EIGRP packets sent and received by the router. The packet types to be monitored can be selected. Up to 11 types are available.
debug ip eigrp neighbors	Shows the hello packets sent and received by the router and the neighbors discovered by this process.
debug ip eigrp	Shows dynamic changes made to the routing table.
debug ip eigrp summary	Shows the process taken when a summary (manual or auto) is changed on the router.

Foundation Summary

The Foundation Summary provides a convenient review of many key concepts in this chapter. If you are already comfortable with the topics in this chapter, this summary might help you recall a few details. If you just read this chapter, this review should help solidify some key facts. If you are doing your final prep before the exam, the following tables are a convenient way to review the day before the exam.

Table 4-9 summarizes the commands covered in this chapter.

Table 4-9 *Summary of EIGRP Commands*

Command	Function
Router(config)#**router eigrp** *autonomous-system-number*	Starts the EIGRP processes on the router with the specified autonomous system number.
Router(config-router)#**network** *network-number [wildcard-mask]*	Advertises the networks that match the *network mask*.
Router(config-router)#**no auto-summary**	Disables automatic summarization.
Router(config-if)#**ip summary-address eigrp** *autonomous-system-number address mask*	Enables manual summarization.
Router(config-router)#**eigrp stub** [**receive-only** | **connected** | **static** | **summary**]	Used on single-neighbor routers in a hub-and-spoke environment. Minimizes local routing table and advertises local subnets to core.
Router(config-if)#**bandwidth** *speed-of-line*	Identifies bandwidth on interfaces where router cannot automatically determine them. Used primarily on serial lines.
Router(config-if)#**ip bandwidth-percent eigrp** *autonomous-system-number percent*	EIGRP, by default, will take only 50% of bandwidth for routing protocol traffic. Allows adjustment of that percentage.
Router(config-router)#**variance** *multiplier*	Allows unequal-cost paths to proportionally load share.
Router(config-if)#**ip hello-interval eigrp** *autonomous-system-number seconds*	Changes hello interval. May be used to lengthen interval (reducing overhead) or to shorten the interval (decreasing convergence time).

Table 4-9 *Summary of EIGRP Commands (Continued)*

Command	Function
Router(config-if)#**ip hold-time eigrp** *autonomous-system-number seconds*	Defines how long to wait without hearing a hello from a neighbor before declaring it dead. By default, it is three times the length of the hello-interval.
Router#**show ip eigrp neighbors**	Displays information drawn from the neighbor table.
Router#**show ip eigrp topology**	Displays information drawn from the topology table.
Router#**show ip eigrp traffic**	Shows statistics about the EIGRP traffic reaching the router.
Router#**debug eigrp packet**	Shows EIGRP packets sent and received.
Router#**debug ip eigrp neighbors**	Shows the hello packets sent and received by the router and the neighbors discovered by this process.
Router#**debug ip eigrp summary**	Shows when a summary is changed on the router.

Q&A

The questions and scenarios in this book are designed to be challenging and to make sure that you know the answer. Rather than allowing you to derive the answers from clues hidden inside the questions themselves, the questions challenge your understanding and recall of the subject.

You can find the answers to these questions in Appendix A. For more practice with exam-like question formats, use the exam engine on the CD-ROM.

1. Imagine a router that has two interfaces—fastethernet 0/0 is 10.1.1.1 and serial 0/0 is 10.2.2.2. Nominally, EIGRP would be run with the "network 10.0.0.0" command, which would enable both interfaces. There are two ways discussed in this chapter that could be used to specify that one interface run EIGRP and not the other. What are those two techniques?

2. What is the preferred configuration for a hybrid multipoint NBMA network when one VC has a CIR of 56 kbps and the other five VCs each have a CIR of 256 kbps?

3. Four Frame Relay PVCs exist on a multipoint interface. On the multipoint interface, the command **bandwidth 224** is used. How much bandwidth will EIGRP assign to each PVC, and how much of that amount will EIGRP use for advertisements?

4. Explain the purpose of the command **no auto-summary**.

5. Explain the meaning of the command **ip bandwidth-percent eigrp 63 100**.

6. How long is the default hold time?

7. How is the **variance** command used?

8. What command is used to display the passive and active state of the routes?

9. What command is used in EIGRP to perform manual summarization?

10. Which command is used to display all types of EIGRP packets that are both received and sent by a router?

11. What problems can you solve by configuring summarization?

12. Why would you configure an EIGRP router as a stub router?

13. Explain the parameters **receive-only**, **connected**, **static**, and **summary** used in the command **eigrp stub**:

    ```
    router(config-router)# eigrp stub [receive-only | connected | static |
        summary]
    ```

14. When configuring the **variance** command, which routes can be used?

15. Give two reasons why you might wish to change the hello timer.

16. If a multipoint serial interface uses five PVCs with CIRs of 56-, 128-, 128-, 128-, and 256-kbps, how should the bandwidth command be implemented on the interface?

17. On what occasions should you consider configuring the bandwidth on subinterfaces?

Scenarios

The following scenarios and questions are designed to draw together the content of the chapter and to exercise your understanding of the concepts. There is not necessarily a right answer. The thought process and practice in manipulating the concepts are the goals of this section. The answers to the scenario questions are found at the end of this chapter. The information used in these scenarios was adapted from the Cisco web page, "Cisco Configuration Guidelines."

Scenario 4-1

The multinational company Gargantuan, Inc., has a private network addressed using the 10.0.0.0/8 space. Figure 4-3 shows the addressing scheme.

Figure 4-3 *Diagram for Scenario 4-1*

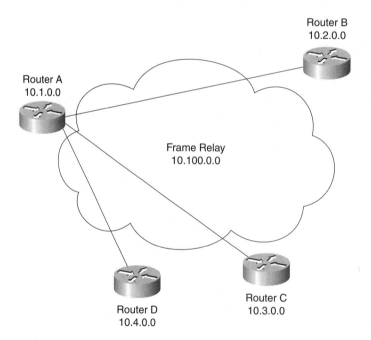

The network is experiencing timeouts and network crashes. In addition, EIGRP appears to be losing routes from its routing tables, which is adding to the problem.

Review the Gargantuan, Inc., addressing scheme and answer the following questions:

1. What changes to addressing or EIGRP could affect the route drops and network problems? State the configuration commands necessary to activate this solution on Router A.

2. The WAN is a Frame-Relay cloud, and Router A is the hub in the hub-and-spoke configuration. Each VC is 56 kbps. Give the commands to configure Router A for EIGRP over this NBMA cloud.

3. Give the commands to configure Router B for EIGRP over this NBMA cloud.

Scenario 4-2

Given the configuration of EIGRP in Example 4-12, perform the tasks and answer the questions listed. The WAN has light user traffic and is a hub-and-spoke configuration, as shown in Figure 4-4.

Example 4-12   *Scenario 4-2 Configuration for Router A*

```
Router#show config
interface Serial 0
   encapsulation frame-relay

   interface Serial 0.1 point-to-point
   bandwidth 25
   ip bandwidth-percent eigrp 123 90

   interface Serial 0.2 point-to-point
   bandwidth 25
   ip bandwidth-percent eigrp 123 90

   ...
```

Figure 4-4 *Diagram for Scenario 4-2*

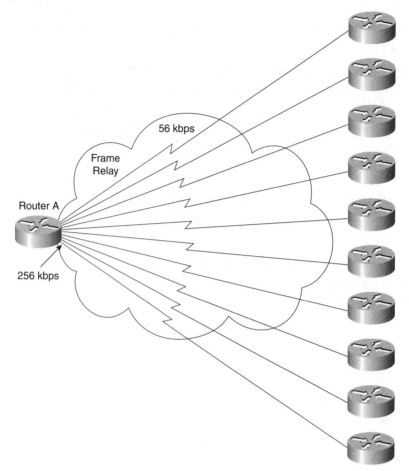

The 256-kbps access line to the hub has 56-kbps access lines to each of ten spoke sites. Each link has a Frame Relay CIR of 56 kbps. The access line to each router reflects the CIR. The access line to the hub router, Router A, is 256 kbps, but the CIR of the hub is the same as its access line.

From a Frame Relay perspective, a circuit is considered oversubscribed when the sum of CIRs of the remote circuits is higher than the CIR of the hub location. With ten links, each with a CIR of 56 kbps, this circuit is oversubscribed.

1. How much bandwidth has each circuit been allocated? Why was this value chosen by the administrator?

2. What bandwidth utilization is available to EIGRP? Why was this value chosen by the administrator?

3. If Router A fails, what would the effect be on the network?

4. Is summarization possible only on the routers entering the WAN cloud, or is it possible on the networks not shown in the figure that are on the other side of the routers? Give reasons for your answers.

Scenario Answers

The answers provided in this section are not necessarily the only possible answers to the questions. The questions are designed to test your knowledge and to give practical exercise in certain key areas. This section is intended to test and exercise skills and concepts detailed in the body of this chapter.

If your answer is different, ask yourself whether it follows the tenets explained in the answers provided. Your answer is correct not if it matches the solution provided in the book, but rather if it has included the principles of design laid out in the chapter.

If you do not get the correct answer, refer back to the text and review the subject tested. Be certain to also review your notes on the question to ensure that you understand the principles of the subject.

Scenario 4-1 Answers

1. What needs to be done in addition to solve the problems caused by EIGRP? State the configuration commands necessary to activate this solution on Router A.

   The WAN is a Frame Relay cloud, and Router A is the hub in the hub-and-spoke configuration. Each VC is 56 kbps.

   In addition to readdressing the network, summarization would limit the query range of the routers. This would prevent the routes in the topology table being SIA, which seriously affects the performance of the network.

   The commands required are as follows:

   ```
   RouterA(config)# router eigrp 63
   RouterA(config)# no auto-summary
   RouterA(config)# network 10.0.0.0
   RouterA(config)# int serial 0
   RouterA(config-if)# ip summary-address eigrp 63 10.1.0.0 255.255.0.0
   ```

2. Give the commands to configure Router A for EIGRP over this NBMA cloud.

   The configuration on Router A is as follows:

   ```
   RouterA(config)# interface serial 0
   RouterA(config-if)# frame-relay encapsulation
   RouterA(config-if)# bandwidth 178
   ```

3. Give the commands to configure Router B for EIGRP over this NBMA cloud.

The configuration on Router B is as follows:

```
RouterB(config)# interface serial 0
RouterB(config-if)# frame-relay encapsulation
RouterB(config-if)# bandwidth 56
```

Scenario 4-2 Answers

1. How much bandwidth has each circuit been allocated? Why was this value chosen by the administrator?

Because a maximum of 256 kbps is available, you cannot allow any individual PVC to handle more than 25 kbps (256/10). Note that EIGRP will not use more than 22.5 kbps (90 percent of 25 kbps) on this interface, even though its capacity is 56 kbps. This configuration will not affect user data capacity, which will still be able to use the entire 56 kbps, except when EIGRP is using 22 kbps.

2. What bandwidth utilization is available to EIGRP? Why was this value chosen by the administrator?

Because this data rate is low, and because you do not expect very much user data traffic, you can allow EIGRP to use up to 90 percent of the bandwidth.

3. If Router A fails, what would the effect be on the network?

If Router A fails, there would be no communication between the routers in the WAN because Router A is the hub. Each site would function, but they would all be isolated from each other. The neighbor tables would fail to hear the hellos from the other routers connecting to the WAN and would time out all routes that they had heard from these routers. The topology table would be updated, and the routers would send updates to all their other neighbors.

4. Is summarization possible only on the routers entering the WAN cloud, or is it possible on the networks not shown in the figure, that are on the other side of the routers? Give reasons for your answers.

Summarization is possible on all interfaces in EIGRP, as long as the addressing scheme allows for it to be implemented. This is one of the major advantages of EIGRP over OSPF. OSPF can summarize only at ABRs.

Part III covers the following Cisco BSCI exam topics related to implementing multiarea OSPF operations:

- Explain the functions and operations of multiarea OSPF.

- Configure multiarea OSPF routing (e.g., Stub, NSSA, authentication, etc.).

- Verify or troubleshoot multiarea OSPF routing configurations.

This list reflects the exam topics posted on Cisco.com at the publication time of this book.

Part III: OSPF

This chapter covers the following topics:

- **Understanding OSPF Fundamentals**— This section reviews fundamental concepts related to OSPF operation.

- **Configuring OSPF in a Single Area**—This section describes required and optional commands for configuring OSPF in a single area.

- **Checking the Configuration of Single-Area OSPF**—This section describes commands used to troubleshoot the OSPF configuration.

CHAPTER 5

Understanding Simple Single-Area OSPF

This chapter explores the routing protocol Open Shortest Path First (OSPF). You should already be familiar with the basic concepts of link-state routing protocols and single-area OSPF. This chapter briefly reviews single-area OSPF and then introduces multiple-area OSPF. The chapter concludes with techniques for configuring, verifying, and troubleshooting OSPF.

"Do I Know This Already?" Quiz

The purpose of the "Do I Know This Already?" quiz is to help you decide what parts of this chapter to use. If you already intend to read the entire chapter, you do not necessarily need to answer these questions now.

The 14-question quiz, derived from the major sections in the "Foundation Topics" portion of the chapter, helps you determine how to spend your limited study time.

Table 5-1 outlines the major topics discussed in this chapter and the "Do I Know This Already?" quiz questions that correspond to those topics.

Table 5-1 *"Do I Know This Already?" Foundation Topics Section-to-Question Mapping*

Foundation Topics Section	Questions Covered in This Section	Score
Understanding OSPF Fundamentals	1–10	
Configuring OSPF in a Single Area	11–12	
Checking the Configuration of Single-Area OSPF	13–14	
Total Score		

> **CAUTION** The goal of self-assessment is to gauge your mastery of the topics in this chapter. If you do not know the answer to a question or are only partially sure of the answer, you should mark this question wrong for purposes of the self-assessment. Giving yourself credit for an answer you correctly guess skews your self-assessment results and might provide you with a false sense of security.

1. What is a neighbor on a local LAN segment in OSPF?

    a. A neighbor is a router in the same area.

    b. A neighbor is a router in the same classful network.

    c. A neighbor is a router on a multiaccess link, with an adjacency with a DR.

    d. A neighbor is another router with the same network address.

2. What is an adjacency in OSPF?

    a. An adjacency is when another router has received an LSA from another area. The areas are adjacent.

    b. An adjacency is the state that two neighbors can achieve after they have synchronized their OSPF databases.

    c. An adjacent router is one that has received a hello packet from a neighbor.

    d. Routers connected across a WAN but not directly connected, for example Frame Relay, are considered adjacent to each other.

3. What is a designated router?

    a. The router responsible for maintaining the SPF tree for a totally stubby area

    b. The router responsible for summarizing routes to other areas

    c. A router responsible for making adjacencies with all routers on a multiaccess link and maintaining those adjacencies

    d. The router responsible for forwarding all the traffic across the global Internet

4. By default, how often does OSPF send out hello packets on a broadcast multiaccess link?

    a. By default, OSPF sends out hello packets every 30 seconds on a broadcast network.

    b. By default, OSPF sends out hello packets every 40 seconds on a broadcast network.

    c. By default, OSPF sends out hello packets every 3.3 seconds on a broadcast network.

    d. By default, OSPF sends out hello packets every 10 seconds on a broadcast network.

5. When a router sends an LSA on a multiaccess link, to what is it sent?

    a. The DR, which updates the BDR every *hello* interval.

    b. The DR and the BDR.

    c. All routers on the link; all routers maintain adjacencies, but only the DR updates the rest of the network.

    d. The DR, which updates the BDR every 3.3 minutes.

6. What does it mean when an interface shows that it is in the init state?

    a. That an interface is coming online, determining the IP address and OSPF parameters

    b. That a router sees a hello packet from a neighbor but the packet does not contain its own router ID

    c. That this is a point-to-multipoint interface and is waiting to connect to the WAN cloud

    d. Seen only on broadcast links, it shows that the election of the DR is in progress

7. If the network is stable and sees no changes, how often will it send LSAs? Why are these updates sent out periodically?

    a. Every 30 minutes by default. This is to ensure the integrity of the topological databases.

    b. Every 30 seconds by default. This is to ensure that the network is fully connected.

    c. Never; there is no need if the network is stable.

    d. Whenever an LSA is received; this means there is a problem on the network that needs to be flooded through the network.

8. In learning a new route, what will an internal OSPF router do if a received LSA is not found in the topological database?

    a. The LSA is flooded immediately out of all the OSPF interfaces, except the interface from which the LSA was received.

    b. The LSA is dropped and a message is sent to the transmitting router.

    c. The LSA is placed in the topological database and an acknowledgement is sent to the transmitting router.

    d. The sequence numbers are checked, and if the LSA is valid, it is entered into the topology database.

9. What would the default cost of a 1-Mbps link be?

   a. 1

   b. 10

   c. 100

   d. 1000

10. If a router has an OSPF priority set to 0, what does this indicate?

   a. A router with the OSPF priority set to 0 is one that can participate in the election of a DR. It has the highest priority.

   b. A router with the OSPF priority set to 0 is one that will switch OSPF packets before it does anything else.

   c. A router with the OSPF priority set to 0 is one that cannot participate in the election of a DR. It can become neither a DR nor a BDR.

   d. A router with the OSPF priority set to 0 is one that cannot participate in the election of a DR, but it can become a BDR.

11. Which of the following IP addresses are subsumed by this command:

```
Router(config-router)# network 10.1.32.0 0.0.31.255 area 0
```

   a. 10.1.32.255

   b. 10.1.34.0

   c. 10.1.64.0

   d. 10.1.64.255

12. What is the default OSPF cost for a T1 link?

   a. 1

   b. 10

   c. 32

   d. 64

13. On a LAN segment, what is the maximum number of neighbors that can be designated as DROTHER in the **show ip ospf neighbor** output?

   a. 1

   b. 8

   c. 32

   d. None of these options is correct

14. Which command would include output such as "SPF algorithm executed 10 times?"

   a. **show ip ospf**

   b. **show ip ospf interface**

   c. **show ip ospf neighbor**

   d. **show ip ospf database**

The answers to this quiz are found in Appendix A, "Answers to Chapter 'Do I Know This Already?' Quizzes and Q&A Sections." The suggested choices for your next step are as follows:

■ **10 or less overall score**—Read the entire chapter. This includes the "Foundation Topics," "Foundation Summary," "Q&A," and "Scenarios" sections at the end of the chapter.

■ **11–12 overall score**—Begin with the "Foundation Summary" section, and then go to the "Q&A" and "Scenarios" sections. If you have trouble with these exercises, read the appropriate sections in "Foundation Topics."

■ **13–14 overall score**—If you want more review on these topics, skip to the "Foundation Summary" section, and then go to the "Q&A" and "Scenarios" sections. Otherwise, move to the next chapter.

Foundation Topics

Understanding OSPF Fundamentals

Rarely is a name as descriptive as the one given to this protocol—Open Shortest Path First (OSPF). OSPF is an open standard, defined in detail in many RFCs, including RFC 2328. OSPF uses the SPF algorithm to compute the best path to destinations. OSPF builds loop-free paths that converge quickly, but it often requires more processor power and memory than distance vector routing protocols. OSPF can also be more complicated because there are many topology and configuration options to consider.

OSPF is designed to offer flexibility in network design and, as an open standard, support linking routers from various vendors.

This section describes OSPF operation with the assumption that you have some experience with OSPF. Many of the details specific to the underlying OSPF operation are omitted, to focus on the important concepts appropriate to an Exam Certification Guide.

OSPF Snapshot

A *link-state routing protocol* is a sophisticated routing protocol based on the Dijkstra Shortest Path First (SPF) algorithm. When compared to distance-vector routing, link-state routing processes more information locally to reduce network traffic, trading additional memory and processor time for less bandwidth consumption. Link-state routing protocols record all possible routes, and therefore avoid many of the techniques required by distance-vector protocols to avoid loops.

OSPF, in particular, is a link-state routing protocol used within an autonomous system. It has a number of advantages over distance-vector routing protocols, including the following:

- OSPF is classless and allows summarization.

- It converges very quickly.

- OSPF is a standard, and ubiquitous support can be expected in a heterogeneous environment.

- It conserves network bandwidth.

- It uses multicasts instead of broadcasts.

- It sends incremental change-based updates.

- It uses cost as the metric.

Distance-vector routing protocols advertise routes to neighbors, but a link-state routing protocol advertises a list of its connections. When a link comes up or goes down, a link-state advertisement (LSA) is generated. In the context of link-state routing, a *neighbor* is simply a directly connected router, or a router on the opposing end of a WAN link, with the same network address (an exception to this is a virtual link, discussed in Chapter 7, "Using OSPF Across Multiple Areas"). LSAs are shared with neighbors and a topological database, also called a link-state database (LDSB) or topology table, is built. LSAs are marked with sequence numbers so that older or newer versions of an advertisement can be recognized; sequence numbers start at 0x8000 0001 and iterate to 0xFFFF FFFF before wrapping back around to 0x0000 00000. Eventually, every router in the same "area" has the same LSDB. Each router then processes this database using SPF and places the best routes into its routing table.

The topology database is the router view of the network within the area. It includes every OSPF router within the area and all the connected networks. This database is essentially a routing table—a routing table for which no path decisions have been made.

To view the current status of the link-state database, use the **show ip opsf database** command as shown in Example 5-1.

Example 5-1   *The **show ip ospf database** Command Output*

```
SanJose# show ip ospf database

OSPF Router with ID (140.100.32.10) (Process ID 100)


Router Link States (Area 3)

Link ID         ADV Router       Age      Seq#        Checksum Link count
140.100.17.131  140.100.17.131   471      0x80000008 0xA469   1
140.100.17.132  140.100.17.132   215      0x80000007 0xA467   1
140.100.17.194  140.100.17.194   1489     0x8000000B 0xFF16   1
140.100.23.1    140.100.23.1     505      0x80000006 0x56B3   1
140.100.32.10   140.100.32.10    512      0x8000000C 0x46BA   3
140.100.32.11   140.100.32.11    150      0x80000006 0x6A73   1
140.100.32.12   140.100.32.12    1135     0x80000002 0x8E30   1


Net Link States (Area 3)

Link ID         ADV Router       Age      Seq#        Checksum
140.100.17.130  140.100.23.1     220      0x80000007 0x3B42
140.100.17.194  140.100.17.194   1490     0x80000002 0x15C9
140.100.32.11   140.100.32.11    150      0x80000004 0x379E
```

To reiterate, the topology database is updated by the LSAs and each router within an area has exactly the same topology database. All routers must have the same view of the network; otherwise, routing loops or loss of connectivity will result.

As soon as a router realizes that there has been a change in the network topology, the router is responsible for informing the rest of the routers in the area. Typically, it will identify a change in the state of one of its links for one of the following reasons:

■   The router loses the physical or data-link layer connectivity on a connected network.

■   The router does not receive a predetermined number of consecutive OSPF hello messages.

■   The router receives an LSA update from an adjacent neighbor, informing it of the change in the network topology.

In any of these instances, the router will generate an LSA and flood it to all its neighbors with the following stipulations:

■   If the LSA is new, the route is added to the database, the route is flooded out other links so other routers are updated, and SPF is rerun.

■   If the sequence number is the same as the current entry in the topology table, the router ignores the advertisement.

■   If the sequence number is older, the router sends the newer copy (from memory) back to the advertiser to make sure that all neighbors have the latest LSA.

All OSPF operations center on populating and maintaining the following tables:

■   Neighbor table

■   Topology database

■   Routing table

It is useful now to take a step back and focus on the relationships between pairs of OSPF speakers.

Neighbors and Adjacencies

OSPF develops neighbor relationships with routers on the same link by exchanging *hello messages* (sometimes shortened to *hellos*). Upon initial exchange of hello messages, the routers add each other to their respective neighbor tables. A neighbor table is a list of connected *OSPF speakers* (devices running OSPF). OSPF speakers send multicast hellos with destination address 224.0.0.5 on all OSPF-enabled interfaces. OSPF sends out hello packets every 10 seconds on a broadcast link and every 30 seconds on a nonbroadcast link. The contents of a hello message are shown in Table 5-2.

Table 5-2 *OSPF Hellos*

Value	Description
Router ID	A 32-bit number that is unique to this router.
Hello and dead interval	Period of time between hellos and the timeout.
Neighbor list	List of neighbor Router IDs.
Area ID	Area number.
Priority	Highest priority is elected the designated router.
DR and BDR	IP address of designated routers.
Authentication	Password, if enabled.
Stub Area Flag	TRUE if this is a stub area.

After two routers complete an initial exchange based on hellos, they go through a process of exchanging information about the network. After the routers have synchronized their information, they are *adjacent*. Figure 5-1 outlines the formal states that a neighbor relationship transitions through in the process of forming a "full" adjacency. Once full state is reached, tables must be kept up-to-date. LSAs are re-sent whenever there is a change, or every 30 minutes to keep them "fresh."

The following list describes each possible state of a neighbor relationship:

- **Down**—This is the first OSPF neighbor state. It means that no information (hellos) has been received from this neighbor.

- **Attempt**—This state is only valid for manually configured neighbors in an NBMA environment. In Attempt state, the router sends unicast hello packets every poll interval to the neighbor from which hellos have not been received within the dead interval.

- **Init**—This state indicates that the router has received a hello packet from its neighbor, but the receiving router's ID was not included in the hello packet.

- **2-Way**—This state indicates that bi-directional communication has been established between two routers.

- **Exstart**—Once the DR and BDR are elected, the actual process of exchanging link-state information can start between the routers and their DR and BDR.

- **Exchange**—In the exchange state, OSPF routers exchange database descriptor (DBD) packets.
- **Loading**—In this state, the actual exchange of link-state information occurs.
- **Full**—In this state, routers are fully adjacent with each other. All the router and network LSAs are exchanged and the router databases are fully synchronized.

Figure 5-1 *The States of Updating the Routers About the Network*

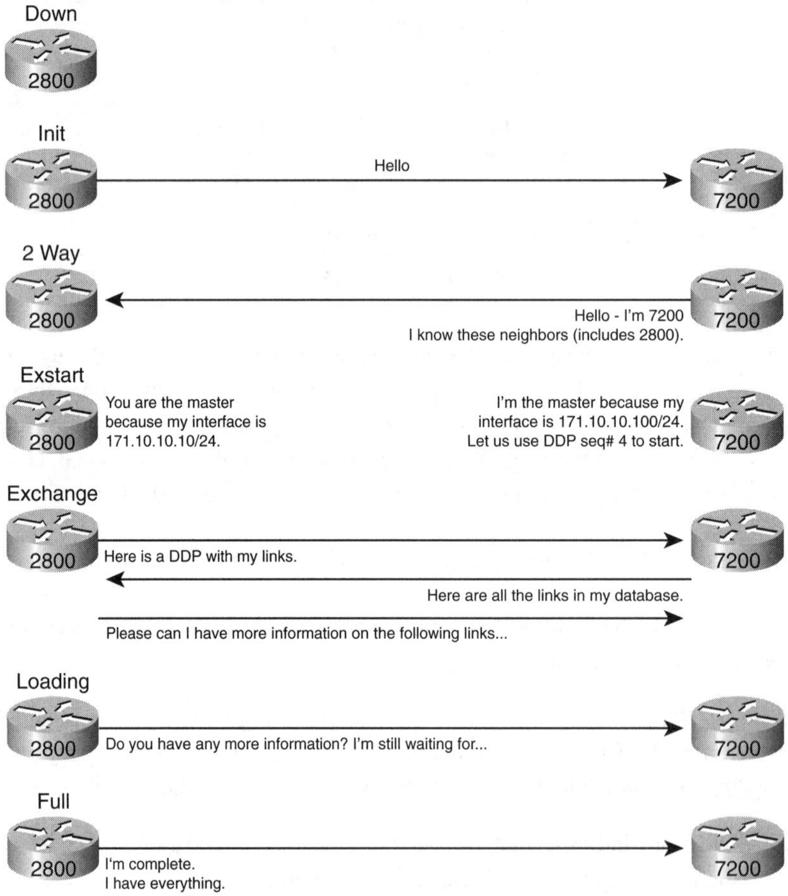
Down
2800
Init
Hello
2800
7200
2 Way
2800
Hello - I'm 7200
I know these neighbors (includes 2800).
7200
Exstart
2800
You are the master
because my interface is
171.10.10.10/24.
I'm the master because my
interface is 171.10.10.100/24.
Let us use DDP seq# 4 to start.
7200
Exchange
2800
Here is a DDP with my links.
7200
Here are all the links in my database.
Please can I have more information on the following links...
Loading
2800
Do you have any more information? I'm still waiting for...
7200
Full
2800
I'm complete.
I have everything.
7200

Hellos continue to be sent periodically and the adjacency is maintained as long as hellos are exchanged. Missing hello messages result in a router declaring the adjacency *dead*.

As soon as OSPF identifies a problem, it modifies its LSAs accordingly and sends the updated LSAs to the remaining neighbors (with full adjacencies). Being event-driven, this LSA process intrinsically improves convergence time and reduces the amount of information that needs to be sent across the network.

One key piece of information exchanged in LSAs is OSPF metric information.

Many OSPF vendor implementations assign each link a cost of 10. The Cisco implementation makes cost inversely proportional to 100 Mbps, as follows:

$$Cost = \frac{100,000,000 \ bps}{LinkSpeed}$$

An administrator can override this default cost. Typically, this is done for compatibility with other OSPF speakers or because some links are faster than 100 Mbps.

Sometimes the metric is equivalent for multiple paths to a destination. In this case, OSPF will load balance over each of the equivalent interfaces. Cisco routers will automatically perform equal-cost load balancing for up to four paths, but this parameter can be increased by configuration to as many as sixteen paths.

The cost is applied to the outgoing interface. The routing process will select the lowest cumulative cost to a remote network.

Designated Router and Backup Designated Router

If routers are connected to a broadcast segment (for example, when several routers in one VLAN are on the same switch) then one router on the segment is assigned the duty of maintaining adjacencies with all other segment routers. This job is known as the *designated router (DR)* and the responsible router is selected using information in hello messages. For redundancy, a *backup designated router (BDR)* is also elected.

DRs are created on multiaccess links because the number of adjacencies grows at a quadratic rate. For a network of *n* routers, the number of adjacencies required would be

$$\frac{n(n-1)}{2}$$

Two routers require the following adjacencies:

$$\frac{2(2-1)}{2} = 1$$

Four routers require the following adjacencies:

$$\frac{4(4-1)}{2} = 6$$

Ten routers require the following adjacencies:

$$\frac{10(10-1)}{2} = 45$$

As you can see, maintaining the segment consumes increasingly more bandwidth and processing as the number of routing devices increases.

The purpose of a DR is to be the one router to which all other routers are adjacent. Using a DR reduces the number of adjacencies that consume bandwidth and processing to $n - 1$. Yes, larger networks still involve more processing, but with a DR, the adjacencies scale with the network. This growth rate is shown in Table 5-3 and illustrated in Figure 5-2.

Table 5-3 *Adjacencies Required in Various Scenarios*

Routers	Adjacencies Needed Without a DR	Adjacencies Needed with a DR Only	Adjacencies Needed Using a DR and BDR
1	0	0	1
2	1	1	3
3	3	2	5
4	6	3	7
5	10	4	9
6	15	5	11
7	21	6	13
8	28	7	15
9	36	8	17
10	45	9	19

The role of the DR is to receive updates and distribute them to each segment router, making sure that each router acknowledges receipt and has a synchronized copy of the LSDB. Routers advertise changes to the "AllDRs" multicast address, 224.0.0.6. The DRs then advertise the LSA using the "AllSPF" multicast address, 224.0.0.5. Each router then acknowledges receipt.

The BDR listens passively to this exchange and maintains a relationship with all the routers. If the DR stops producing hellos, the BDR promotes itself and assumes that role.

Note that DRs and BDRs are only useful on multiaccess links because they reduce adjacencies. The concept of a DR is not used on point-to-point links because there can be only one adjacency.

Figure 5-2 *Adjacencies from Table 5-3*

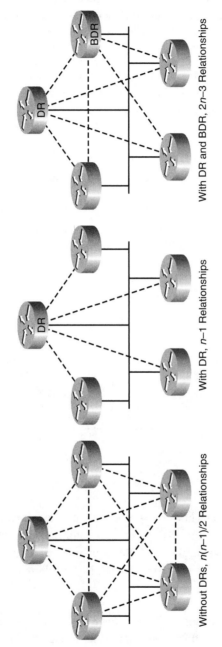

> **NOTE** DRs are elected on point-to-point Ethernet links, which are very common in modern networks. Because the DR and BDR are not necessary on a point-to-point Ethernet link, some current design guides recommend changing the Ethernet interfaces to point-to-point mode.

If a DR fails, the BDR is promoted. The BDR is elected on the basis of highest OSPF priority and ties are broken in favor of the highest IP address. The default priority is 1 and a priority of 0 prevents a router from being elected. Priority can be set from 0–255; to change the priority from its default for a particular interface, use the following command:

```
Router(config-if)# ip ospf priority number
```

DRs are stable—even if a better candidate joins the network the DR will not change.

To put this description in context, consider the network shown in Figure 5-3. There are five routers, A through E, with priorities ranging from zero to three. Intuitively, you might expect that A would be the DR, that B would be the BDR, and that E would never let itself be elected. Generally, this is true, but it neglects some important details.

Figure 5-3 *Example OSPF Segment, with Priorities*

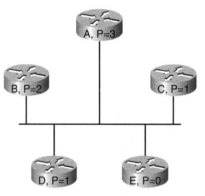

Imagine that Router C starts first. Router C sends out hellos and waits the dead time for a response. Receiving no response, Router C conducts an election and becomes the BDR. Because there is no DR, Router C promotes itself to DR. Next, suppose that Router E starts. Router E has a priority of zero, so it will not become the BDR. Router B starts third and is elected BDR. Router A and Router D start last.

In this scenario, Router C is the DR and Router B is the BDR—not what we expected. This is because designated routers do not preempt—once elected they serve until they are rebooted. If Router C restarts, Router B promotes itself to DR and Router A is elected BDR while Router C is down. If Router B goes down, Router A promotes itself and elects Router C or Router D (whichever has the highest IP address). Finally, when the BDR is rebooted, Router B wins the election for BDR.

> **NOTE**   In addition to rebooting, clearing the OSPF process using the Privilege EXEC mode command **clear ip ospf process *** on the DR will force a DR/BDR election.

Multiple Areas

An OSPF area is a logical grouping of routers that are running OSPF with identical topological databases. An area is a subdivision of the OSPF routing domain. Each area runs SPF separately and summaries are passed between each area.

This section begins with a description of the problems associated with single-area networks, and then discusses how multiple-area structures overcome problems specific to a large single area.

Problems with OSPF in a Single Area

Consider a growing OSPF network with a single area. Several problems emerge in relation to capacity:

- The SPF algorithm runs more frequently. The larger the network, the greater the probability of a network change and a recalculation of the entire area. Each recalculation in a large network takes longer and involves more work than recalculations in a small area.

- The larger the area, the greater the size of the routing table. The routing table is not sent out wholesale, as in a distance vector routing protocol. However, the greater the size of the table, the longer each lookup becomes. The memory requirements on the router also increase as the size of the table increases.

- In a large network, the topological database increases in size and eventually becomes unmanageable. The topology table is exchanged between adjacent routers at least every 30 minutes.

As the various databases increase in size and the calculations increase in frequency, the CPU utilization increases while the available memory decreases. This can affect network latency or cause link congestion, resulting in various additional problems, such as convergence time, loss of connectivity, loss of packets, and system hangs.

Area Structure

OSPF creates a two-level hierarchy of areas. Area zero (also called the *backbone area* or *transit area*) is always the central area; all other areas attach to area zero. Area zero forms the top level in the hierarchy and the remaining areas form the bottom level of the hierarchy. This hierarchical design supports summarization and minimizes routing table entries.

Routers in area zero are called *backbone routers*. Routers that link area zero and another area are called *Area Border Routers (ABR)*. OSPF routers that redistribute routing information from another routing protocol are called *Autonomous System Boundary Routers (ASBR)*.

OSPF Packet Types

As OSPF link-state information is shared between areas, an intricate set of mechanisms is followed, relying on a number of different OSPF packet types. All OSPF traffic is transmitted inside IP packets. Receivers recognize OSPF traffic because it is marked as IP protocol 89.

OSPF includes five packet types:

- **Hello packets**—Establish communication with directly attached neighbors.

- **Database Descriptor (DBD)**—Sends a list of router IDs from whom the router has an LSA and the current sequence number. This information is used to compare information about the network.

- **Link State Requests (LSR)**—Follow DBDs to ask for any missing LSAs.

- **Link State update (LSU)**—Replies to a link-state request with the requested data.

- **Link-state acknowledgements (LSAck)**—Confirm receipt of link-state information.

All OSPF packets have a common format that contains the following nine fields:

- **Version**—All packets are assumed to be version 2 in this chapter. OSPF version 3 is discussed in the context of IPv6 in Part VIII of this book.

- **Type**—There are five packet types, numbered 1 to 5.

- **Packet Length**—The length in bytes.

- **Router ID**—32-bit identifier for the router.

- **Area ID**—32-bit identifier for the area.

- **Checksum**—Standard 16-bit checksum.

- **Authentication Type**—OSPFv2 supports three authentication methods:

  — no authentication

  — plaintext passwords

  — MD5 hashes

- **Authentication Data**—64-bit data, either empty, with a plain-text word, or with a "message digest" of a shared secret.

- **Data**—Values being communicated.

Configuring OSPF in a Single Area

This section examines the configuration of a Cisco router for OSPF within a single area. The commands are few in number and relatively simple; the implications of the commands on the network are somewhat more complicated.

Required Commands for Configuring OSPF Within a Single Area

In this section, you learn to configure an *internal* OSPF router. An internal router is one in which all interfaces lie within a single area. The sole OSPF function of an internal router is to route within the area.

The router needs to understand how to participate in the OSPF network, as defined by the following parameters:

- **OSPF process**—Declare an OSPF process.

- **Participating interfaces**—Identify the interfaces to be used by OSPF.

- **Area**—Define area per interface. This discussion assumes that all active interfaces are in the same area.

- **Router ID**—A unique 32-bit ID, usually drawn from an interface IP address.

The following subsections describe the commands required for configuring OSPF on a single internal router.

Enabling the OSPF Routing Protocol

To configure OSPF as the routing protocol, use the following command:

```
Router(config)# router ospf process-number
```

Here, *process-number* is not globally significant. It is possible to have more than one process running on a router (although that would be an unusual configuration) and two OSPF processes could route for different parts of the network. The process number does not have to be the same on every router in the area.

The OSPF network Command

Once OSPF is turned on, you must define the interfaces that are to participate in OSPF and the area that they reside in by using the following command:

```
Router(config-router)# network network-number wildcard-mask area area-number
```

CAUTION   Be careful with this command. It is the cause of many errors in configuration, normally due to a misapplication of the *wildcard-mask* parameter, either including too many or too few interfaces in a particular OSPF area.

Like RIP, the **network** command identifies the interfaces on which OSPF is to be active. Unlike RIP, this command has a wildcard mask that allows it to be very specific. All interfaces that match the network wildcard pattern will be active in OSPF in the given area.

The **area** parameter places the interface in an area. A router can have different interfaces in different areas (and thus be an ABR). The *area-number* is a 32-bit field and the format can either be a simple decimal or in dotted-decimal format. Some implementations of OSPF might only understand one of the formats, but the Cisco IOS accepts either form.

After identifying the interfaces on the router that are participating in the OSPF domain, hellos are exchanged, LSAs are sent, and the router inserts itself into the network.

NOTE   If there are stub networks connected to a router, it is useful to issue the command **redistribute connected subnets**. This command includes the connected subnets in OSPF advertisements without actually running OSPF on them. A route-map is often used with this command to exclude interfaces that are explicitly configured with OSPF.

You can apply the **network** command in different ways, yet each way achieves similar results.

Imagine that a router has the following interfaces:

- FastEthernet 0/0: 192.168.100.1/24

- FastEthernet 0/1: 192.168.101.1/24

- FastEthernet 0/2: 192.168.102.1/24

- FastEthernet 0/3: 192.168.103.1/24

- Serial 1/0: 10.100.100.1/30

- Serial 1/1: 10.100.100.5/30

It is possible to enable OSPF area 0 on all interfaces with the following command:

```
Router(router-config)# network 0.0.0.0 255.255.255.255 area 0
```

Another way of achieving the same result is to break up the command into the 10 networks and the 192 networks, as follows:

```
Router(router-config)# network 10.0.0.0 0.255.255.255 area 0
Router(router-config)# network 192.168.100.0 0.0.3.255 area 0
```

A third way is to enable it independently on each interface, as follows:

```
Router(router-config)# network 192.168.100.1 0.0.0.0 area 0
Router(router-config)# network 192.168.101.1 0.0.0.0 area 0
Router(router-config)# network 192.168.102.1 0.0.0.0 area 0
Router(router-config)# network 192.168.103.1 0.0.0.0 area 0
Router(router-config)# network 10.100.100.1 0.0.0.0 area 0
Router(router-config)# network 10.100.100.5 0.0.0.0 area 0
```

These three examples achieve exactly the same result. All six interfaces are enabled, placed in area 0, and begin to process OSPF traffic.

By using the first approach (one all-encompassing statement), you may inadvertently include interfaces that you might not want included. The third option involves a lot of typing, but gives the administrator more control. The technique you choose to use is a function of your particular network topology, and generally you should choose the technique that is the most straightforward to document and explain. You need to be intimately familiar with the use of the wildcard mask with the **network** command to enable OSPF on router interfaces.

Configuration Options for an Internal Router

The following options allow you to tune the OSPF configuration of an internal router:

■ Router ID

■ Loopback interface

■ **cost** command

■ **priority** command

Defining the Router ID and Loopback Interfaces

The router needs an ID to participate in the OSPF domain. The router ID is used to identify LSAs in the OSPF database. The router ID can be defined by an administrator or left to the discretion of the router. Most people define the ID so that it is easier to track events in the network, for internal documentation, and for other system-administration purposes.

The OSPF router ID can be defined by the **router-id** command. If the **router-id** command is not present, then the router ID will be the highest IP address of a loopback interface. If no loopbacks are present, then the router ID will be the highest IP address of the first active interface.

Generally, using the **router-id** command is not recommended because BGP and OSPF normally pick a router ID the same way. Manually specifying a router ID can result in these IDs differing, which can be a source of problems with BGP operation.

```
Router(config)# router ospf
Router(config-router)# router-id ip-address
```

The preferred way to control the router ID is to use a *loopback interface* address. A loopback interface is a virtual interface and is always active. The following shows how to configure a loopback interface:

```
Router(config)# interface loopback interface-number
Router(config-if)# ip address ip-address subnet-mask
```

Loopbacks are typically assigned a /32 mask to minimize their use of address space.

Once the router ID of the router has been chosen, the router ID is stable and is not subject to the flippancy of physical interfaces on a router. Changing the router ID can break some OSPF configurations, such as virtual links. Loopback interfaces, which do not physically exist, can never go down and are therefore more stable than physical interfaces.

> **NOTE**   Consider including the loopback interface address in the **network** commands. This gives you an easy point to ping to, regardless of the state of the network.

Changing the Default Cost

The cost metric is calculated as 100,000,000 bps divided by the bandwidth of the interface in bits per second. Sometimes—especially when dealing with faster lines or other vendor routers that use a different cost—it is useful to change this default value. The **cost** command manually overrides the default:

```
Router(config-if)# ip ospf cost cost
```

Cost is a 16-bit value (0 to 65,535) and lower values are preferred. Table 5-4 shows examples of default costs

As shown in Table 5-4, the calculation of bandwidth gives Fast Ethernet and Gigabit Ethernet a metric of 1. In this situation, you might want to manipulate the default cost to prefer the faster path.

Table 5-4 *Default Costs in OSPF*

Link Type	Default Cost
56-kbps serial link	1785
T1 (1.544-Mbps serial link)	64
Ethernet	10
Fast Ethernet	1
Gigabit Ethernet	1

A second way to deal with high-bandwidth paths is to change the numerator in the automatic calculation. The **ospf auto-cost reference-bandwidth** router-configuration command changes the numerator in the metric formula to account for higher speeds:

```
Router(config-router)# ospf auto-cost reference-bandwidth reference-bandwidth
```

Here, *reference-bandwidth* is in megabytes per second. The range is 1 to 4,294,967; the default is 100. Set it to 1000 to give Gigabit links a cost of 1 and FastEthernet paths a cost of 10.

> **NOTE**   It is strongly recommended that changes to the **ospf auto-cost reference-bandwidth** command be replicated on all routers in an area. Also, note that the **ip ospf cost** command overrides the calculated cost resulting from changes in **auto-cost reference-bandwidth**

Determining the Designated Router Using the priority Command

Remember that hello messages include a priority field and thus provide a mechanism by which the DR and BDR are elected. To be "up for election," the priority must be a positive integer between 1 and 255. If its priority is 0, the router cannot participate in the election. Otherwise, highest priority wins. All Cisco routers have a default priority of 1, and the highest router ID is used as a tiebreaker. As previously discussed in the "Electing DRs and BDRs" section, the command to adjust priority on an interface-by-interface basis is

```
Router(config-if)# ip ospf priority number
```

A Working Configuration of OSPF on a Single Router

Example 5-2 is a working configuration of OSPF on a single router. The Charlotte router will be the DR on F1/0 unless another device on the segment has a priority greater than 100. The link attached to F1/0 has a cost of 1. The cost on F3/0 has been changed to 10.

Example 5-2 *Configuring OSPF*

```
Charlotte(config)# router ospf 100
Charlotte(config-router)# network 140.100.0.0 0.0.255.255 area 3
Charlotte(config-router)# interface FastEthernet1/0
Charlotte(config-if)# ip address 140.100.17.129 255.255.255.240
Charlotte(config-if)# ip ospf priority 100
Charlotte(config-if)# interface FastEthernet3/0
Charlotte(config-if)# ip address 140.100.17.193 255.255.255.240
Charlotte(config-if)# ip ospf cost 10
```

Checking the Configuration of Single-Area OSPF

The set of commands shown in Table 5-5 configuration and maintenance of a live OSPF network.

Table 5-5 *The **show** Command Options for OSPF*

Command Option	Description
show ip ospf	Shows OSPF process details—for example, how many times the router has recalculated its routing table.
show ip ospf database	Shows contents of the topological database.
show ip ospf interface	Gives information about how OSPF has been configured on each interface.
show ip ospf neighbor	Displays neighbor information. Used to verify that all neighbors are present.
show ip protocols	Shows IP routing protocol configuration on the router.
show ip route	Shows networks of which the router is aware. Also shows preferred paths and gives next hop for each path.

The OSPF **show** commands are very detailed and give a comprehensive understanding of the state of the network. You need to understand the concepts in this chapter to interpret the output of the **show** commands provided in subsequent sections.

The show ip ospf Command

The **show ip ospf** command shows how OSPF is running on a particular router. It includes the number of times that the SPF routing algorithm has run, which is indicative of the stability of the network. To issue the command, use the following syntax:

```
Router# show ip ospf [process-id]
```

Example 5-3 shows the output of this command. Table 5-6 explains how to interpret this information.

Example 5-3 *The* **show ip ospf** *process-id Command Output*

```
SanJose# show ip ospf 100
 Routing Process "ospf 100" with ID 140.100.32.10
 Supports only single TOS(TOS0) routes
It is an internal router
 SPF schedule delay 5 secs, Hold time between two SPFs 10 secs
 Minimum LSA interval 5 secs. Minimum LSA arrival 1 secs
 Number of external LSA 0. Checksum Sum 0x0
 Number of DCbitless external LSA 0
 Number of DoNotAge external LSA 0
 Number of areas in this router is 1. 1 normal 0 stub 0 nssa
    Area 3
    Number of interfaces in this area is 3
    Area has no authentication
    SPF algorithm executed 10 times
    Area ranges are
    Link State Update Interval is 00:30:00 and due in 00:18:54
    Link State Age Interval is 00:20:00 and due in 00:08:53
    Number of DCbitless LSA 2
    Number of indication LSA 0
    Number of DoNotAge LSA 0
```

Table 5-6 *Explanation of the* **show ip ospf** *process-id Command Output*

Field	Explanation
Routing Process "ospf 100" with ID 140.100.32.10	Shows the local process ID and the router ID for OSPF.
It is an internal router	Type of router (internal, ABR, or ASBR).
SPF schedule delay	Specifies how long to wait to start SPF after receiving an LSA to prevent running SPF too often.
Hold time between two SPFs	Specifies the minimum time between SPF calculations.
Number of DCbitless external LSA	Used with OSPF demand circuits.
Number of DoNotAge external LSA	Used with OSPF demand circuits, such as ISDN.

continues

Table 5-6 *Explanation of the* **show ip ospf** *process-id Command Output (Continued)*

Field	Explanation
Area 3 Number of interfaces in this area is 3 Area has no authentication SPF algorithm executed 10 times Area ranges are	Specifies the number of areas of which this router is a member. It is an internal router because it is only configured for a single area. It is possible to see how many of the router's interfaces are in an area and whether the router is using MD5 security. It is useful to see the number of times that the SPF algorithm has been executed. The area ranges show summarization that has been configured.
Link State Update Interval is 00:30:00 and due in 00:18:54	The default for the LSA update timer is 30 minutes. This is used to ensure the integrity of the topological database. This field shows when the next update is and that the default has not been changed.
Link State Age Interval is 00:20:00 and due in 00:08:53	Specifies the MAX-AGED deletion interval and shows when out-of-date routes will next be purged.

The show ip ospf database Command

The **show ip ospf database** command displays the contents of the router's topological database and the different LSAs that have populated the database:

Internal routers, the primary subject of this chapter, will only display router and network LSAs. This command has many parameters that enable you to examine very specific information.

Example 5-4 shows the output of the **show ip ospf database** command. Table 5-7 explains the important fields.

Example 5-4 *The* **show ip ospf database** *Command Output*

```
SanJose# show ip ospf database

        OSPF Router with ID (140.100.32.10) (Process ID 100)


        Router Link States (Area 3)

Link ID          ADV Router       Age       Seq#        Checksum Link count
140.100.17.131   140.100.17.131   471       0x80000008 0xA469    1
140.100.17.132   140.100.17.132   215       0x80000007 0xA467    1
140.100.17.194   140.100.17.194   1489      0x8000000B 0xFF16    1
```

Example 5-4   *The* **show ip ospf database** *Command Output (Continued)*

```
140.100.23.1    140.100.23.1    505      0x80000006 0x56B3   1
140.100.32.10   140.100.32.10   512      0x8000000C 0x46BA   3
140.100.32.11   140.100.32.11   150      0x80000006 0x6A73   1
140.100.32.12   140.100.32.12   1135     0x80000002 0x8E30   1

        Net Link States (Area 3)
Link ID         ADV Router      Age      Seq#       Checksum
140.100.17.130  140.100.23.1    220      0x80000007 0x3B42
140.100.17.194  140.100.17.194  1490     0x80000002 0x15C9
140.100.32.11   140.100.32.11   150        0x80000004 0x379E
```

Table 5-7   *Explanation of the* **show ip ospf database** *Command Output*

Field	Explanation
OSPF Router with ID (140.100.32.10) (Process ID 100)	Router ID and process ID of this router.
Router Link States (Area 3)	The router LSAs, showing the links connecting the router to neighbors discovered via the Hello protocol.
Link ID	The link ID, which is the same as the OSPF router ID.
ADV Router	Router ID of the advertising router.
Age	Time (in seconds) since the last update.
Seq #	The sequence number.
Checksum	The checksum on the entire LSA update. Ensures integrity.
Link count	The number of links that the router has configured for OSPF.
Net Link States (Area 3)	Information from network LSAs that have been received by the router.

The show ip ospf interface Command

The **show ip ospf interface** command shows how OSPF has been configured and how it is working on an interface. This level of detail is excellent for troubleshooting configuration errors. Use the following syntax:

```
Router# show ip ospf interface [type number]
```

This command shows important information such as the DR, the BDR, a list of neighbors, and the network type. Example 5-5 shows the output of this command. Table 5-8 explains how to interpret this information.

Example 5-5 *The* **show ip ospf interface** *[type number] Command Output*

```
SanJose# show ip ospf interface fastethernet1/0
FastEthernet1/0 is up, line protocol is up
  Internet Address 140.100.17.129/28, Area 3
  Process ID 100, Router ID 140.100.32.10, Network Type BROADCAST, Cost: 1
  Transmit Delay is 1 sec, State DR, Priority 100
  Designated Router (ID) 140.100.32.10, Interface address 140.100.17.129
  Backup Designated router (ID) 140.100.23.1, Interface address 140.100.17.130
  Timer intervals configured, Hello 10, Dead 40, Wait 40, Retransmit 5
    Hello due in 00:00:06
  Neighbor Count is 3, Adjacent neighbor count is 2
    Adjacent with neighbor 140.100.17.132
    Adjacent with neighbor 140.100.17.131
    Adjacent with neighbor 140.100.23.1   (Backup Designated Router)
  Suppress hello for 0 neighbor(s)
```

Table 5-8 *Explanation of the* **show ip ospf interface** *[type number] Command Output*

Field	Explanation
FastEthernet1/0 is up, line protocol is up	The first "up" indicates the physical line is operational. The second indicates that the data-link layer is working.
Internet Address 140.100.17.129/28	The IP address and mask configured on the interface.
Area 3	Area of the interface.
Process ID 100, Router ID 140.100.32.10	The OSPF process ID and router ID.
Network Type BROADCAST	The type of network, which indicates how neighbors are found and adjacencies formed.
Cost: 1	The cost of the link.
Transmit Delay is 1 sec	Anticipated time taken to send an update to the neighbor. The default is 1 second.

Table 5-8 *Explanation of the* **show ip ospf interface** *[type number] Command Output (Continued)*

Field	Explanation
State DR	Possible DR states include the following: DR—The router is the DR on the network to which this interface is connected, and it establishes OSPF adjacencies with all other routers on this broadcast network. In this example, this router is the BDR on the Ethernet segment to which the Ethernet0 interface is connected. BDR—The router is the BDR on the network to which this interface is connected, and it establishes adjacencies with all other routers on the broadcast network. DROTHER—The router is neither the DR nor the BDR on the network to which this interface is connected, and it establishes adjacencies only with the DR and the BDR. Waiting—The interface is waiting to declare the state of the link as DR. The amount of time the interface waits is determined by the wait timer. This state is normal in a nonbroadcast multiaccess (NBMA) environment. Point-to-Point—This interface is point-to-point for OSPF. In this state, the interface is fully functional and starts exchanging hello packets with all of its neighbors. Point-to-Multipoint—This interface is point-to-multipoint for OSPF.
Priority 100	The priority is sent in the Hello protocol, used for DR election.
Designated Router (ID) 140.100.32.10, Interface address 140.100.17.129	The address of the elected DR.
Backup Designated router (ID) 140.100.23.1, Interface address 140.100.17.130	The address of the BDR.
Timer intervals configured, Hello 10, Dead 40, Wait 40, Retransmit 5	It is possible to change these timers, but they should be consistent throughout your organization. Routers cannot become adjacent if their timers differ.
Hello due in 00:00:06	When the next hello packet is due.

continues

Table 5-8 *Explanation of the* **show ip ospf interface** *[type number] Command Output (Continued)*

Field	Explanation
Neighbor Count is 3, Adjacent neighbor count is 2	The number of routers that have neighbor relationships. Note that the number of routers with which adjacency is established is less than the number of neighbors. This is because there is a DR and a BDR, whose responsibility it is to maintain the adjacencies with all routers on the LAN.
Adjacent with neighbor 140.100.23.1 (Backup Designated Router)	The router ID of the adjacent router, which is the BDR in this case.

The show ip ospf neighbor Command

The **show ip ospf neighbor** command shows OSPF neighbors. All the neighbors known to the router can be viewed, or the command can be made more granular and the neighbors can be shown on a per-interface basis with the following syntax:

Router# **show ip ospf neighbor** [*type number*] [*neighbor-id*] [**detail**]

Example 5-6 shows the output of the **show ip ospf neighbor** command.

Example 5-6 *The* **show ip ospf neighbor** *Command Output*

```
SanJose# show ip ospf neighbor
Neighbor ID      Pri   State          Dead Time   Address          Interface
140.100.17.132    1    FULL/DROTHER   00:00:36    140.100.17.132   FastEthernet1/0
140.100.17.131    1    FULL/DROTHER   00:00:37    140.100.17.131   FastEthernet1/0
140.100.23.1      1    FULL/BDR       00:00:38    140.100.17.130   FastEthernet1/0
140.100.32.12     1    FULL/DROTHER   00:00:35    140.100.32.12    Fddi2/0
140.100.32.11     1    FULL/DR        00:00:32    140.100.32.11    Fddi2/0
140.100.17.194    1    FULL/DR        00:00:31    140.100.17.194   FastEthernet3/0
```

It is also possible to focus on viewing information regarding neighbors that have been discovered on a particular interface, as seen in Example 5-7.

Example 5-7 *Neighbors That Have Been Discovered on a Particular Interface*

```
SanJose# show ip ospf neighbor fddi 2/0
Neighbor ID      Pri   State          Dead Time   Address          Interface
140.100.32.12     1    FULL/DROTHER   00:00:36    140.100.32.12    Fddi2/0
140.100.32.11     1    FULL/DR        00:00:32    140.100.32.11    Fddi2/0
```

To see all the neighbors in as much detail as possible, use the command displayed in Example 5-8.

Example 5-8 *Using the* **show ip ospf neighbor detail** *Command*

```
SanJose# show ip ospf neighbor detail
Neighbor 140.100.17.132, interface address 140.100.17.132
    In the area 3 via interface FastEthernet1/0
    Neighbor priority is 1, State is FULL, 6 state changes
    DR is 140.100.17.129 BDR is 140.100.17.130
    Options 2
    Dead timer due in 00:00:35
Neighbor 140.100.17.131, interface address 140.100.17.131
    In the area 3 via interface FastEthernet1/0
    Neighbor priority is 1, State is FULL, 6 state changes
    DR is 140.100.17.129 BDR is 140.100.17.130
    Options 2
    Dead timer due in 00:00:34
Neighbor 140.100.23.1, interface address 140.100.17.130
    In the area 3 via interface FastEthernet1/0
    Neighbor priority is 1, State is FULL, 6 state changes
    DR is 140.100.17.129 BDR is 140.100.17.130
    Options 2
    Dead timer due in 00:00:36
Neighbor 140.100.32.12, interface address 140.100.32.12
    In the area 3 via interface Fddi2/0
    Neighbor priority is 1, State is FULL, 6 state changes
    DR is 140.100.32.11 BDR is 140.100.32.10
    Options 2
    Dead timer due in 00:00:32
Neighbor 140.100.32.11, interface address 140.100.32.11
    In the area 3 via interface Fddi2/0
    Neighbor priority is 1, State is FULL, 6 state changes
    DR is 140.100.32.11 BDR is 140.100.32.10
    Options 2
    Dead timer due in 00:00:38
Neighbor 140.100.17.194, interface address 140.100.17.194
    In the area 3 via interface FastEthernet3/0
    Neighbor priority is 1, State is FULL, 9 state changes
    DR is 140.100.17.194 BDR is 140.100.17.193
    Options 2
    Dead timer due in 00:00:38
```

Table 5-9 explains the key output fields in Examples 5-6 through 5-8.

Table 5-9 *Explanation of the* **show ip ospf neighbor** *Command Output*

Field	Explanation
Neighbor	Router ID.
Neighbor priority	Priority sent out with the hello messages to elect the DRs.
State	Shows the functional state of the neighbor router: Down Attempt Init 2-Way Exstart Exchange Loading Full
Dead Time	Time the router will wait without hearing the periodic hello from its neighbor before it is declared dead.
Address	Address of the neighbor. Note that router ID is not the same as the interface address.
Interface	Outgoing interface of the router, upon which neighbor routers were heard.
Options	Identifies whether this is a stub area.

The show ip protocols Command

The **show ip protocols** command shows the configuration of IP routing protocols on the router. It details how the protocols were configured and how they interact with one another. It also indicates when the next updates will occur. This command is excellent for troubleshooting configuration errors and understanding how the network is communicating about its routes:

```
Router# show ip protocols
```

Example 5-9 shows the output of this command. Table 5-10 explains how to interpret this information.

Example 5-9 *The* **show ip protocols** *Command Output*

```
SanJose# show ip protocols
Routing Protocol is "ospf 100"
  Sending updates every 0 seconds
  Invalid after 0 seconds, hold down 0, flushed after 0
  Outgoing update filter list for all interfaces is not set
  Incoming update filter list for all interfaces is not set
  Redistributing: ospf 100
  Routing for Networks:
    140.100.0.0
  Routing Information Sources:
    Gateway          Distance      Last Update
    140.100.17.131        110      00:50:23
    140.100.17.132        110      00:50:23
    140.100.17.194        110      00:07:39
    140.100.23.1          110      00:50:23
    140.100.32.11         110      00:07:39
    140.100.32.12         110      00:07:39
  Distance: (default is 110)
```

Table 5-10 *Explanation of the* **show ip protocols** *Command Output*

Field	Explanation
Routing Protocol is "ospf 100"	Routing protocols configured on the router, listed in turn.
Sending updates every 0 seconds	Frequency of routing updates.
Invalid after 0 seconds	For distance-vector protocols, this indicates the time a route is considered valid.
hold down 0	Holddown timers are used only in distance-vector protocols.
flushed after 0	Distance-vector protocols will flush invalid paths from the routing table after this timer has expired.
Outgoing update filter list for all interfaces is not set	Access lists can be set on an interface to filter networks from the routing update. Note that outgoing distribution lists have no effect in OSPF.
Incoming update filter list for all interfaces is not set	The access list can filter either outgoing or incoming updates.

continues

Table 5-10 *Explanation of the* **show ip protocols** *Command Output (Continued)*

Field	Explanation
Redistributing: ospf 100	Shows any configured redistribution.
Routing for Networks: 140.100.0.0	This reflects the use of the network commands when the protocol was configured.
Routing Information Sources	These are the addresses of the routers sending updates to this router.
Gateway	Address of the router providing updates.
Distance	Administrative distance.
Last Update	Time since the last update was received from that source.
Distance: (default is 110)	The administrative distance can be changed for the entire routing protocol (the example here is OSPF), or per source.

The show ip route Command

The **show ip route** command shows the IP routing table on the router. It details how the network is known to the router and how the router discovered the route. The syntax follows:

```
Router# show ip route
Codes: C - connected, S - static, I - IGRP, R - RIP, M - mobile, B - BGP
       D - EIGRP, EX - EIGRP external, O - OSPF, IA - OSPF inter area
       N1 - OSPF NSSA external type 1, N2 - OSPF NSSA external type 2
       E1 - OSPF external type 1, E2 - OSPF external type 2, E - EGP
       i - IS-IS, L1 - IS-IS level-1, L2 - IS-IS level-2, ia - IS-IS inter area
       * - candidate default, U - per-user static route, o - ODR
       P - periodic downloaded static route

Gateway of last resort is 10.122.22.129 to network 0.0.0.0

C    10.0.0.0/8 is directly connected, FastEthernet0/1
     10.122.0.0/25 is subnetted, 1 subnets
C       10.122.22.128 is directly connected, FastEthernet0/0
O IA 6.0.0.0/8 [110/65] via 5.0.0.2, 00:00:18, Serial0/0
S*   0.0.0.0/0 [1/0] via 10.122.22.129
Router#
```

The commands covered in this section are useful for verifying that the configuration is right and that the OSPF network is functioning correctly. In a single-area environment, the full complexity of OSPF is not present. The full complexity of OSPF comes into play with the design and configuration of a multiarea network.

The debug Commands

An excellent, though potentially dangerous, troubleshooting tool is the **debug** command. The **debug** command has the highest process priority and is therefore capable of consuming all the resources on the router. It is important to turn on **debug** for a specific task and to turn it off as soon as the data is gathered. The **no** form of this command disables debugging output.

You might want to direct the output to the log file so that the data can be perused offline. The **debug** commands are EXEC commands.

The debug options available for monitoring OSPF are listed in Table 5-11.

Table 5-11   *The **debug** Command Options for OSPF*

Command Option	Description
debug ip ospf events	Displays information about OSPF-related events, such as adjacencies, flooding information, designated router selection, and SPF calculation.
debug ip packet	IP debugging information includes packets received, generated, and forwarded. Fast-switched packets do not generate messages.

Foundation Summary

The Foundation Summary provides a convenient review of many key concepts in this chapter. If you are already comfortable with the topics in this chapter, this summary might help you recall a few details. If you just read this chapter, this review should help solidify some key facts. If you are doing your final prep before the exam, the following lists and tables are a convenient way to review the day before the exam.

OSPF is an interior gateway link-state routing protocol. It has a number of advantages:

■ OSPF is classless and allows summarization.

■ It converges very quickly.

■ OSPF is a standard, and ubiquitous support can be expected in a heterogeneous environment.

■ It conserves network bandwidth.

■ It uses multicasts instead of broadcasts.

■ It sends incremental change-based updates.

■ It uses cost as the metric.

OSPF uses three tables:

■ Neighbor table

■ Topology table

■ Routing table

The OSPF metric is calculated based on interface speed:

$$Cost = \frac{100,000,000 \; bps}{LinkSpeed}$$

There are five types of OSPF packets:

■ Hello

■ DBD

■ LSR

- LSU

- LSAck

All OSPF packets have a common format that contains nine fields:

- Version

- Type

- Packet Length

- Router ID

- Area ID

- Checksum

- Authentication Type

- Authentication Data

- Data

The following two commands are required for configuring OSPF on a single internal router:

- **router ospf** *process-number*

- **network** *network wildcard-mask* **area** *area*

The OSPF router ID will be one of the following:

- Address defined by the **router-id** command

- Highest IP address of a loopback interface

- Highest IP address of an interface configured to run OSPF

The set of commands shown in Table 5-12 is invaluable in both configuration and maintenance of a live network.

Table 5-12 *The* **show** *Command Options for OSPF*

Command Option	Description
show ip ospf	Shows OSPF process details—for example, how many times the router has recalculated its routing table.
show ip ospf database	Shows contents of the topological database.

continues

Table 5-12 *The* **show** *Command Options for OSPF (Continued)*

Command Option	Description
show ip ospf interface	Gives information about how OSPF has been configured on each interface.
show ip ospf neighbor	Displays neighbor information. Used to verify that all neighbors are present.
show ip protocols	Shows IP routing protocol configuration on the router.
show ip route	Shows networks the router is aware of and preferred paths. Also gives next hop for each path.

The **debug** options available for monitoring OSPF are listed in Table 5-13.

Table 5-13 *The* **debug** *Command Options for OSPF*

Command Option	Description
debug ip ospf events	Displays information about OSPF-related events, such as adjacencies, flooding information, designated router selection, and SPF calculation.
debug ip packet	IP debugging information includes packets received, generated, and forwarded. Fast-switched packets do not generate messages.

Q&A

The questions and scenarios in this book are designed to be challenging and to make sure that you know the answer. Rather than allowing you to derive the answers from clues hidden inside the questions themselves, the questions challenge your understanding and recall of the subject.

You can find the answers to these questions in Appendix A. For more practice with exam-like question formats, use the exam engine on the CD-ROM.

1. What command is used to manually determine which router on a LAN will become the DR?

2. What parameter is used to calculate the metric of a link in OSPF on a Cisco router?

3. It is possible to have more than one OSPF process on a router. How would you do this?

4. The address 192.100.56.10/21 has been allocated to an interface on the router. This interface alone is to be included in the OSPF process. State the command that would start the process on this interface.

5. The metric used by OSPF is cost. How would you change the metric on an interface?

6. What command shows which router on a LAN is the BDR?

7. Explain briefly what **show ip ospf database** will reveal.

8. What command is used to show the state of adjacencies?

9. Which command is used to show OSPF packets being sent and received in real time?

10. How would you show the OSPF process ID of the router?

11. What is the sequence number and where is it held?

12. In the **show ip ospf** command, there is a field called the SPF schedule delay. What is the purpose of this field, and what is the default time?

13. What is the advantage of the command **show ip ospf interface** in troubleshooting?

Scenarios

The following scenarios and questions are designed to draw together the content of the chapter and to exercise your understanding of the concepts. There is not necessarily a right answer. The thought process and practice in manipulating the concepts is the goal of this section. The answers to the scenario questions are found at the end of this chapter.

Scenario 5-1

For a given network, all routers share a common multiaccess segment. One router is elected the DR and another is elected the BDR.

1. Which parameter determines the router that will be selected as the DR in an OSPF network?

2. Could a router with a priority value of zero assume the role of a DR or a BDR in the OSPF?

3. How is the OSPF router ID determined on a Cisco router?

4. What is the role of the DR and BDR in the OSPF network?

Scenario Answers

The answers provided in this section are not necessarily the only possible answers to the questions. The questions are designed to test your knowledge and to give you practical exercise in certain key areas. This section is intended to test and exercise skills and concepts detailed in the body of this chapter.

If your answer is different, ask yourself whether it follows the tenets explained in the answers provided. Your answer is correct not if it matches the solution provided in the book, but rather if it has included the principles of design laid out in the chapter.

In this way, the testing provided in these scenarios is designed to challenge you intellectually: It examines not only your knowledge, but also your understanding and ability to apply that knowledge to problems.

If you do not get the correct answer, refer to the text and review the subject tested. Be certain to also review your notes on the question to ensure that you understand the principles of the subject.

Scenario 5-1 Answers

1. *Which parameter determines the router that will be selected as the DR in an OSPF network?*

    The router with the highest OSPF priority on a segment will become the DR for that segment. The default priority is 1. If multiple routers have the same priority, the router with the highest RID will be selected as the DR.

2. *Could a router with a priority value of zero assume the role of a DR or BDR in the OSPF?*

    No. A priority value of zero indicates that an interface is not to be elected as a DR or BDR. The state of the interface with priority zero will be DROTHER.

3. *How is the OSPF router ID determined on a Cisco router?*

    The OSPF router ID, if not manually configured, is the highest IP address on the box, or the highest loopback address, if one exists.

4. *What is the role of the DR and the BDR in the OSPF network?*

    Instead of each router exchanging updates with every other router on the segment, every router will exchange the information with the DR and the BDR. The DR and the BDR will relay the information to everyone else. In mathematical terms, the number of adjacencies required for a full mesh is $n(n-1)/2$ and for a DR/BDR situation is $2n-2$.

This chapter covers the following topics:

- **OSPF Network Topology Options**—Describes the differences between these OSPF network types, the use of subinterfaces, and how to select an OSPF design.

- **Configuring OSPF in a Nonbroadcast Environment**—Describes how to configure different types of OSPF networks.

CHAPTER **6**

OSPF Network Topologies

This chapter details OSPF support for nonbroadcast multiaccess (NBMA) interfaces. Several OSPF network topologies are possible in an NBMA environment. In particular, the various options for configuring OSPF over Frame Relay on Cisco router physical interfaces and subinterfaces are explored. This chapter assumes knowledge of the previous chapter, which introduced OSPF.

"Do I Know This Already?" Quiz

The purpose of the "Do I Know This Already?" quiz is to help you decide what parts of this chapter to use. If you already intend to read the entire chapter, you do not necessarily need to answer these questions now.

The 12-question quiz, derived from the major sections in the "Foundation Topics" portion of the chapter, helps you determine how to spend your limited study time.

Table 6-1 outlines the major topics discussed in this chapter and the "Do I Know This Already?" quiz questions that correspond to those topics.

Table 6-1 *"Do I Know This Already?" Foundation Topics Section-to-Question Mapping*

Foundation Topics Section	Questions Covered in This Section	Score
OSPF Network Topology Options	1–11	
Configuring OSPF in a Nonbroadcast Environment	12	
Total Score		

CAUTION The goal of self-assessment is to gauge your mastery of the topics in this chapter. If you do not know the answer to a question or are only partially sure of the answer, you should mark this question wrong for purposes of the self-assessment. Giving yourself credit for an answer you correctly guess skews your self-assessment results and might provide you with a false sense of security.

1. Which of the following is *not* an OSPF network type?

   a. Broadcast multiaccess

   b. Point-to-point nonbroadcast

   c. Point-to-multipoint nonbroadcast

   d. NBMA

2. What OSPF network type is a workaround used to account for the lack of multicast and broadcast support inherent in the default behavior of Cisco router interfaces in a nonbroadcast environment?

   a. Broadcast multiaccess

   b. Point-to-point

   c. Point-to-multipoint

   d. Nonbroadcast multiaccess

3. How often, by default, does OSPF send out hello packets on a broadcast multiaccess link?

   a. Every 30 seconds

   b. Every 40 seconds

   c. Every 3.3 seconds

   d. Every 10 seconds

4. If a router has an OSPF priority set to 0, what does this indicate?

   a. It has the highest priority.

   b. It will switch OSPF packets before it does anything else.

   c. It cannot participate in the election of a DR.

   d. It cannot participate in the election of a DR, but it can become a BDR.

5. Which two of the following are valid OSPF network types that do not support DR election?

   a. Point-to-point

   b. NBMA

   c. Broadcast

   d. Point-to-multipoint

6.   True or False: It is possible to create a full mesh environment emulating a broadcast network topology using the NBMA OSPF network type.

7.   RFC 2328 describes the operation of OSPF in two modes across an NBMA cloud. What are they?

    a.   Point-to-point and broadcast

    b.   Nonbroadcast multiaccess and broadcast

    c.   Point-to-point and point-to-multipoint

    d.   Nonbroadcast multiaccess and point-to-multipoint

8.   You want to set up a newly created point-to-point subinterface to use the OSPF point-to-point network type. What command should you use?

    a.   No additional commands required

    b.   Router(config-subif)# **ip ospf network non-broadcast**

    c.   Router(config-subif)# **ip ospf network point-to-multipoint**

    d.   Router(config-subif)# **ip ospf network point-to-multipoint non-broadcast**

    e.   Router(config-subif)# **ip ospf network point-to-point**

9.   Router A has a priority of one, but is configured on Router B with the following command:

        `RouterB(config-if)# neighbor 12.150.146.3 priority 7`

    What value does Router B use for the priority of Router A?

    a.   0

    b.   1

    c.   7

    d.   10

10. Look at Figure 6-1. If this topology were configured with the NBMA OSPF network type, which of the following are true?

Figure 6-1 *Sample Topology*

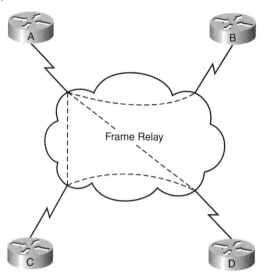

a. There are three adjacencies.

b. There are four adjacencies.

c. Router A must be the DR.

d. Router B must be the DR.

e. Router C must be the DR.

f. Router D must be the DR.

g. Any router may be the DR.

11. Referring to Figure 6-1, with the point-to-multipoint OSPF network type, which of the following are true about this topology?

a. There are three adjacencies.

b. There are four adjacencies.

c. Router A must be the DR.

d. Router B must be the DR.

e. Router C must be the DR.

f. Router D must be the DR.

g. Any router may be the DR.

12. You want to set up an interface to use a DR, but do not want to have to manually identify neighbors. What command should you use?

  a. Router(config-if)# **ip ospf network broadcast**

  b. Router(config-if)# **ip ospf network non-broadcast**

  c. Router(config-if)# **ip ospf network point-to-multipoint**

  d. Router(config-if)# **ip ospf network point-to-multipoint non-broadcast**

  e. Router(config-if)# **ip ospf network point-to-point**

The answers to this quiz are found in Appendix A, "Answers to Chapter 'Do I Know This Already?' Quizzes and Q&A Sections." The suggested choices for your next step are as follows:

■ **8 or less overall score**—Read the entire chapter. This includes the "Foundation Topics," "Foundation Summary," and "Q&A" sections.

■ **9 or 10 overall score**—Begin with the "Foundation Summary" section and follow up with the "Q&A" section at the end of the chapter. If you need additional review, read the appropriate sections in "Foundation Topics."

■ **11 or 12 overall score**—If you want more review on these topics, skip to the "Foundation Summary" section and then go to the "Q&A" section at the end of the chapter. Otherwise, move to the next chapter.

Foundation Topics

OSPF Network Topology Options

OSPF is capable of routing over every type of data link, but OSPF makes assumptions that do not hold true for all topologies. OSPF assumes that—within a subnet—all routers can communicate directly using multicasts and that no router is uniquely positioned in the topology. Both assumptions are fine for Ethernet: If five routers are attached to a switch, a multicast from one reaches the other four and each would be fine as a designated router (DR).

The aforementioned assumptions do not hold for nonbroadcast multiaccess (NBMA) environments. In a Frame Relay network, for example, multicasts and broadcasts are not supported on "NBMA" OSPF-network-type interfaces on Cisco routers. The following are the OSPF network types available on Cisco router interfaces:

- Broadcast multiaccess

- Point-to-point

- Point-to-multipoint (default is point-to-multipoint broadcast; nonbroadcast option is available)

- Nonbroadcast multiaccess (NBMA)

To account for the lack of multicast and broadcast support inherent in NBMA OSPF-network-type interfaces on Cisco routers, multicasts are simulated by replicating an advertisement to each neighbor. This chapter describes several strategies for dealing with neighbor discovery and communication in an NBMA topology.

Any-to-any communication within a subnet cannot be assumed in NBMA. DRs need to be able to communicate with all other devices, which leads to design considerations. This chapter discusses the strategies available for overcoming this limitation.

> **NOTE** Neither of these issues applies to LANs or to point-to-point links. Ethernet links are automatically recognized as broadcast links. Point-to-point links, such as DS3, are also automatically recognized.

Multipoint interfaces on Cisco routers automatically start in nonbroadcast mode, but there are times when this needs to be manually adjusted. Each of the four OSPF network types has its own advantages and disadvantages, as described in this section. After explaining the differences between these OSPF network types and the use of subinterfaces, this section describes how to select an OSPF design.

Understanding the Differences Between OSPF Network Types

The key differences between the four OSPF network types revolve around the use of DRs, support for partial mesh Frame Relay topologies, support for standards, neighbor recognition, and timers. The following sections compare the properties of each OSPF network type.

Designated Routers and Topology Support

DRs minimize topology traffic, but a DR works under the assumption that it is in contact with all devices. Multiaccess topologies, such as those found in NBMA and broadcast OSPF network types, rely on DRs and so are best applied to full-mesh topologies. If the topology is not a full mesh, then the DR should be manually selected, using priorities, to be a router with permanent virtual circuits (PVCs) connecting it to all other routers. For example, in a hub-and-spoke topology, the DR should be the hub and all spokes should have a priority of zero (there will not be a separate BDR).

The point-to-multipoint OSPF network type does not involve a DR election; this OSPF network type is less efficient in a full mesh, but fine with a partial mesh. It is more tolerant of network changes than the broadcast option. The point-to-multipoint OSPF network type also has a Cisco-specific option called *point-to-multipoint nonbroadcast*.

The point-to-point OSPF network type also does not involve a DR election.

Standards

OSPF network types can be described as either RFC-compliant or Cisco proprietary, as follows:

- **RFC-compliant**—RFC-compliance offers a vendor-neutral routing platform. There are two nonbroadcast OSPF network types (RFC 2328):

  — NBMA

  — Point-to-multipoint

- **Cisco-specific**—Of the broadcast, point-to-multipoint (broadcast), point-to-multipoint nonbroadcast, point-to-point, and NBMA OSPF network type options on a Cisco router that can be used in nonbroadcast environment, three of these are Cisco proprietary:

  — Point-to-multipoint nonbroadcast

  — Broadcast

  — Point-to-point

Neighbor Recognition

With the NBMA OSPF network type, routers cannot dynamically discover their neighbors, so the neighbors must be manually identified. The broadcast OSPF network type is similar to the NBMA OSPF network type in that both use DRs and expect a full mesh, but with the broadcast OSPF network type routers are capable of discovering their neighbors automatically. This simplification is very attractive.

The RFC point-to-multipoint mode discovers neighbors automatically; however, point-to-multipoint nonbroadcast requires neighbors to be manually entered. Point-to-multipoint nonbroadcast differs in this regard, and is designed for links that do not have a broadcast capability or even an ability to emulate broadcasts.

The neighbor on point-to-point links is obvious (it is the *other* router).

Timers

OSPF sends out hellos at regular intervals to discover neighbors and to verify that the neighbor list remains current. Neighbors time-out of the list after a "dead" time, which is four times the hello time by default.

Broadcast links use a 10-second hello timer because capacity is assumed to be plentiful. Point-to-point also uses a faster hello time, because of the simplicity of the network. The other OSPF network types all use 30-second hello and 120-second dead timers, reducing the load on the network.

Table 6-2 compares the five OSPF network types in a nonbroadcast environment.

Table 6-2 *OSPF Network Types in a Nonbroadcast Environment*

	Nonbroadcast	Point-to-Multipoint (Broadcast)	Point-to-Multipoint Nonbroadcast	Broadcast	Point-to-Point
DR/BDR	Yes	No	No	Yes	No
Identify Neighbor?	Yes	No	Yes	No	No
Timer Intervals (Hello/Dead)	30/120	30/120	30/120	10/40	10/40
RFC 2328 or Cisco	RFC	RFC	Cisco	Cisco	Cisco
Network Supported	Full mesh	Any	Any	Full mesh	Point-to-point

Subinterfaces

On a Cisco router, it is possible to configure a physical interface with two logical subinterface options. You can configure these subinterfaces to be point-to-point or multipoint. (Note: The default OSPF network type for a physical serial interface is nonbroadcast multiaccess.)

Frame Relay multipoint subinterfaces support multiple PVCs. A Frame Relay multipoint subinterface can be configured using any of the OSPF network types except point-to-point. Do not allow the similar terminology to confuse you! Two distinct things are going on at the same time: OSPF network types and subinterface types.

Multipoint subinterfaces are treated like other interfaces, so the default OSPF network type is NBMA.

Point-to-point subinterfaces are treated by the router exactly as if they were point-to-point circuits. These interfaces automatically use the point-to-point OSPF network type.

Selecting an OSPF Design

Full-mesh Frame Relay networks may be handled using any of the OSPF network types, but are generally left as NBMA. Switching to the broadcast OSPF network type gives automatic neighbor discovery. Because NBMA and broadcast OSPF network types are functionally optimal for a full-mesh nonbroadcast environment, they are generally preferred to the point-to-multipoint OSPF network-type option.

Partial-mesh Frame Relay networks are more difficult. The designated router idea does not work as well in a partial mesh because the router elected may not be able to reach all the other routers. Pick one of the following techniques for dealing with this situation:

- Use NBMA and pick your DR.

- Use point-to-multipoint.

- Break up the network into point-to-point connections.

- Divide the network into a fully meshed region and some extra point-to-point circuits.

To examine these options consider Figure 6-2, which shows a partial-mesh Frame Relay network.

The first option—picking a DR—is available only if your network has at least one router with connections to all other routers. In Figure 6-2, Router A has PVCs to all other routers. Set the priority of B, C, and D to zero to make sure that A is the DR and that this network can be configured with interfaces using the NBMA OSPF network type. This should not be your first choice, because if A goes down then C and D cannot communicate, even though they are directly connected.

Figure 6-2 *Partial-Mesh Frame Relay Network*

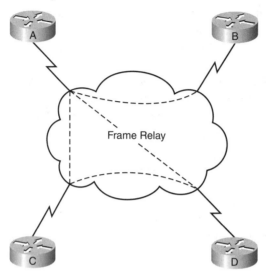

The second option is to use the point-to-multipoint OSPF network type. This is a good option. Neighbors will automatically recognize each other, so this is easy to set up. Relationships will form along PVCs, so there will be four adjacencies (and using a DR would only reduce this to three adjacencies).

The third option is to treat each PVC as a separate point-to-point circuit. This is the easiest method to document and to troubleshoot, but creates a more involved configuration. This is a very common way to handle this situation.

The final option is to create two subinterfaces on Router A. A multipoint interface would use NBMA or broadcast OSPF network types on the interfaces in the A-C-D full mesh, while a point-to-point subinterface would be used on Router A to connect to Router B.

Each of these options is appropriate in some situations. Generally, point-to-point subinterfaces are a safe, straightforward, and easily understandable way to build out partial mesh networks.

Configuring OSPF in a Nonbroadcast Environment

This section illustrates the configuration commands needed for implementing OSPF in a nonbroadcast environment. Interfaces default to the NBMA OSPF network type in a nonbroadcast environment. To change this, apply the **ip ospf network** command on the interface, as follows:

```
Router(config-if)# ip ospf network {broadcast | non-broadcast | point-to-point | {point-
    to-multipoint [non-broadcast]}}
```

For example, to change the OSPF network type to point-to-multipoint the command would be **ip ospf network point-to-multipoint**. Note that if point-to-point subinterfaces are created, they will automatically be assigned the OSPF point-to-point network type.

Configuring OSPF with the Nonbroadcast OSPF Network Type

Configuring a router to support OSPF in a nonbroadcast environment with the NBMA OSPF network type involves two steps: identifying neighbors and picking an OSPF network type for the cloud. Because NBMA is the default OSPF network type, it is only necessary to identify neighbors.

Remember that the DR and BDR need direct connectivity to the other routers. Pick candidates based on PVC attachments and use priorities to prevent poor candidates from being elected DR or BDR.

The syntax of the **neighbor** command is

```
Router(config-if)# neighbor ip-address [priority number ] [poll-interval sec]
    [cost number]
```

Use the **neighbor** command to configure interconnecting OSPF routers within a nonbroadcast environment. Three options exist:

- Priority may be adjusted from the default value of 1. If the **ip ospf priority** command on the neighbor is set, then the higher value of the two is used. Priority is an eight-bit value.

- In some situations, it is necessary to continue sending hellos to inactive neighbors. These hello packets will be sent at a reduced rate, called the *poll interval*, to ensure connectivity is maintained while preserving bandwidth. The default poll interval is 120 seconds.

- The **cost** option adjusts the cost value used by the local router to reach this neighbor. It does not affect the cost reported by the neighbor.

Example 6-1 shows how the **neighbor** command is used. Remember that the NBMA OSPF network type (the default) is in use in this example.

Example 6-1 *The OSPF **neighbor** Command*

```
Router(config)# interface Serial0
Router(config-if)# ip address 131.144.10.100 255.255.255.0
Router(config-if)# encapsulation frame-relay
Router(config)# router ospf 1
Router(config-router)# network 131.144.10.100 0.0.0.255 area 0
Router(config-router)# neighbor 131.144.10.2
Router(config-router)# neighbor 131.144.10.3
Router(config-router)# neighbor 131.144.10.5
```

Configuring the OSPF Point-to-Multipoint Network Type

Point-to-multipoint forms an adjacency automatically along any PVC, which causes more overhead but is more resilient than the NBMA option. With point-to-multipoint, no DR is elected and neighbors are automatically discovered, so the only configuration command is to change from the default OSPF NBMA network type.

> **NOTE** The **ip ospf network point-to-multipoint non-broadcast** command was introduced with Cisco IOS Release 11.3a. You can find more information online at Cisco.com by searching for "OSPF point-to-multipoint network with separate costs per neighbor." This feature was added to support customers using point-to-multipoint on nonbroadcast media, such as classic IP over ATM.

The commands **ip ospf network point-to-multipoint** and **ip ospf network point-to-multipoint non-broadcast** change the OSPF network type on the interface. Point-to-multipoint non-broadcast requires that neighbors are identified.

Example 6-2 shows the necessary configuration for the point-to-multipoint OSPF network type. There is no need to configure neighbors, although you can do so.

Example 6-2 *Configuring Point-to-Multipoint Networks*

```
Router(config)# interface Serial0
Router(config-if)# ip address 10.1.1.1 255.255.255.0
Router(config-if)# encapsulation frame-relay
Router(config-if)# ip ospf network point-to-multipoint
Router(config)# router ospf 1
Router(config-router)# network 10.1.1.0 0.0.0.255 area 0
```

Configuring OSPF with the Broadcast Network Type

With the broadcast OSPF network type, neighbors are automatically discovered and the hello timer is faster than with NBMA. Configuring a broadcast interface just involves changing the OSPF network type—no neighbor statements are required.

The broadcast OSPF network type works best with a fully meshed network. Example 6-3 shows a typical configuration of the broadcast OPSF network type.

Example 6-3 *Configuring a Broadcast Network*

```
Router(config)# interface Serial0
Router(config-if)# ip address 10.1.1.1 255.255.255.0
Router(config-if)# encapsulation frame-relay
Router(config-if)# ip ospf network broadcast
Router(config)# router ospf 1
Router(config-router)# network 10.1.1.0 0.0.0.255 area 0
```

Configuring OSPF with the Point-to-Point Network Type on a Frame Relay Subinterface

With the point-to-point OSPF network type, each subinterface behaves as a physical point-to-point network. Therefore, the communication between the routers is direct and the adjacency is automatic.

Simply creating a point-to-point subinterface with an IP address that is matched by a network statement is the only step. Example 6-4 shows the necessary configuration required for a point-to-point Frame Relay subinterface.

Example 6-4 *Configuring a Point-to-Point Frame Relay Subinterface*

```
Router(config)# interface Serial0
Router(config-if)# no ip address
Router(config-if)# encapsulation frame-relay
Router(config)# interface Serial0.1 point-to-point
Router(config-subif)# ip address 10.1.1.1 255.255.255.0
Router(config-subif)# frame-relay interface-dlci 51
Router(config)# interface Serial0.2 point-to-point
Router(config-subif)# ip address 10.1.2.1 255.255.255.0
Router(config-subif)# frame-relay interface-dlci 52
Router(config)# router ospf 1
Router(config-router)# network 10.1.0.0 0.0.255.255 area 0
```

Foundation Summary

The Foundation Summary provides a convenient review of many key concepts in this chapter. If you are already comfortable with the topics in this chapter, this summary might help you recall a few details. If you just read this chapter, this review should help solidify some key facts. If you are doing your final prep before the exam, the following lists and tables are a convenient way to review the day before the exam.

Table 6-3 compares the five OSPF network types in a nonbroadcast environment.

Table 6-3 *OSPF Network Types in a Nonbroadcast Environment*

	Nonbroadcast	Point-to-Multipoint (Broadcast)	Point-to-Multipoint Nonbroadcast	Broadcast	Point-to-Point
DR/BDR	Yes	No	No	Yes	No
Identify Neighbor?	Yes	No	Yes	No	No
Timer Intervals (Hello/Dead)	30/120	30/120	30/120	10/40	10/40
RFC 2328 or Cisco	RFC	RFC	Cisco	Cisco	Cisco
Network Supported	Full mesh	Any	Any	Full mesh	Point-to-point

To configure OSPF in a nonbroadcast environment, apply the **ip ospf network** command on the interface, as follows:

```
Router(config-if)# ip ospf network {broadcast | non-broadcast | {point-to-multipoint
   [non-broadcast]}}
```

Q&A

The questions and scenarios in this book are designed to be challenging and to make sure that you know the answer. Rather than allowing you to derive the answers from clues hidden inside the questions themselves, the questions challenge your understanding and recall of the subject.

You can find the answers to these questions in Appendix A. For more practice with exam-like question formats, use the exam engine on the CD-ROM.

1. Which of the following is not a valid OSPF network type configuration option?

   ```
   Router(config-if)# ip ospf network broadcast
   Router(config-if)# ip ospf network non-broadcast
   Router(config-if)# ip ospf network point-to-multipoint broadcast
   Router(config-if)# ip ospf network point-to-multipoint non-broadcast
   ```

2. What command is used to determine manually which router on a LAN will become the DR?

3. How many subnets are required in an OSPF configuration for a router with multiple point-to-point connections?

4. What command is used to support a point-to-multipoint OSPF network topology on nonbroadcast media?

5. What are the three keyword options for the **neighbor** command?

6. What OSPF network types include a DR election?

7. With all OSPF network types, the default settings have the dead interval configured as a multiple of the hello interval. What is the multiple?

8. Which NBMA configuration options are Cisco-specific?

9. What is the difference between a point-to-point interface and a multipoint interface?

10. What is the default OSPF network type for a physical serial interface on a Cisco router?

This chapter covers the following topics:

- **The Purpose of Multi-area OSPF**—Explains OSPF multiple-area networks and the single area network issues they solve.

- **The Features of Multi-area OSPF**—Describes router types, link-state advertisements, and the different types of areas.

- **The Operation of Multi-area OSPF**—Explains LSA propagation, OSPF path selection between areas, and how OSPF calculates the costs of paths to other areas.

- **Design Considerations in Multi-area OSPF**—Describes capacity planning, summarization, and the use of virtual links in multi-area OSPF.

- **Required Configuration Commands for a Multi-area OSPF Network**—Describes configuring OSPF as the routing protocol and explains the **network** command in the context of OSPF.

- **Optional Configuration Commands for a Multi-area OSPF Network**—Describes commands that ensure the multi-area OSPF network runs efficiently.

- **Working Configuration of Multi-area OSPF**—Combines the concepts and commands described in the chapter to show an entire working configuration.

- **Verifying the Configuration of OSPF in a Multi-area Network**—Covers the commands used to verify the configuration and monitor the network.

- **Troubleshooting a Multi-area OSPF Network**—Covers the **log-adjacency-changes** command, the most useful **debug** commands, and common problems that occur in forming adjacencies.

CHAPTER 7

Using OSPF Across Multiple Areas

This chapter discusses using OSPF in large networks—networks large enough to be broken up into multiple smaller areas for routing purposes. In order to design a multi-area OSPF network, you need a comprehensive grasp of the features of multi-area OSPF, the operation of OSPF across multiple areas, and, of course, the design considerations of such a network. This chapter discusses each of these topics.

"Do I Know This Already?" Quiz

The purpose of the "Do I Know This Already?" quiz is to help you decide what parts of this chapter to use. If you already intend to read the entire chapter, you do not necessarily need to answer these questions now.

The 23-question quiz, derived from the major sections in the "Foundation Topics" portion of the chapter, helps you determine how to spend your limited study time.

Table 7-1 outlines the major topics discussed in this chapter and the "Do I Know This Already?" quiz questions that correspond to those topics.

Table 7-1   *"Do I Know This Already?" Foundation Topics Section-to-Question Mapping*

Foundation Topics Section	Questions Covered in This Section	Score
The Purpose of Multi-area OSPF	1	
The Features of Multi-area OSPF	2–6	
The Operation of Multi-area OSPF	7	
Design Considerations in Multi-area OSPF	8–11	
Required Configuration Commands for a Multi-area OSPF Network	12–14	
Optional Configuration Commands for a Multi-area OSPF Network	15–18	

continues

Table 7-1 *"Do I Know This Already?" Foundation Topics Section-to-Question Mapping (Continued)*

Foundation Topics Section	Questions Covered in This Section	Score
Working Configuration of OSPF in a Multi-area Network	19	
Verifying the Configuration of OSPF in a Multi-area Network	20–22	
Troubleshooting a Multi-area OSPF Network	23	
Total Score		

CAUTION   The goal of self-assessment is to gauge your mastery of the topics in this chapter. If you do not know the answer to a question or are only partially sure of the answer, you should mark this question wrong for purposes of the self-assessment. Giving yourself credit for an answer you correctly guess skews your self-assessment results and might provide you with a false sense of security.

1. What is the command to view CPU utilization?

    a. **show memory free**

    b. **show cpu utilization**

    c. **show processes cpu sorted**

    d. **show processor**

2. What is an internal router?

    a. An OSPF process running on a multilayer switch.

    b. The internal router is responsible for managing multiple OSPF processes.

    c. All interfaces on this router are within the same area.

    d. A router running OSPF with no external processes.

3. What is the purpose of an ABR?

    a. A router responsible for connecting to outside the autonomous system

    b. A router responsible for connecting two or more areas

    c. A logical group of nodes forming a backbone that connects other areas

    d. A group of routers running OSPF with no external links

4. What do the initials ASBR represent?

   a. Autonomous System Border Router

   b. Authority Subnet Boundary Router

   c. Automatic Summarization Boundary Router

   d. Autonomous System Boundary Router

5. How is routing information generated within an area propagated throughout the area?

   a. Type 3 and Type 4 LSAs

   b. In the summary LSA sent out every 30 minutes

   c. In the Hello packet between neighbors

   d. Type 1 and Type 2 LSAs

6. Which of the following OSPF characteristics affect how the routing table is created?

   a. Whether there are multiple areas in the domain

   b. Whether MD-5 security has been configured

   c. The role of the router in the area in which the router is located

   d. Whether there are communications outside the autonomous system

   e. Network link LSA

7. Which two LSA types are propagated within an area?

   a. Router

   b. Type 3

   c. Type 4

   d. Type 5

   e. Network

8. Why does the frequency of the SPF algorithm increase with the size of the area?

   a. Each router will have more neighbors, and synchronizing the databases takes priority.

   b. The topology databases will subdivide after a certain size, requiring multiple SPF calculations.

   c. As the area size increases, each recalculation will also take longer, which might result in errors, requiring the algorithm to rerun.

   d. The larger the network, the greater the probability of a network change and, thus, a recalculation of the entire area.

9. Multiple areas are one of the main features of OSPF. Which of the following statements explains why this feature is such an important enhancement to earlier routing protocols?

    a. It is easier to implement security.

    b. All computation is kept within the area, with minimum communication between the areas, allowing the network to scale to larger sizes.

    c. The network domain, when divided into areas, allows for the use of both IANA classful addressing and private addressing.

    d. The use of multiple areas allows for the use of prioritization.

10. Which is the best design for OSPF?

    a. Hierarchical with summarization

    b. Tiered

    c. Flat with summarization

    d. Elliptical

11. Which of the following must be observed when creating a virtual link?

    a. Both routers must share a common area.

    b. Both routers must share the same subnet address.

    c. One of the routers must be connected to Area 0.

    d. Both routers must share the same process ID.

12. What command is used to start an OSPF process?

    a. Router(config)# **router ospf** *process-id*

    b. Router(config)# **router ospf** *router-ID*

    c. Router(config)# **router ospf** *autonomous-system-number*

    d. Router(config-if)# **router ospf** *process-id*

13. Which of the following commands are the correct commands, in conjunction, for placing an interface with IP address 172.16.20.128 in area 1 and the interfaces associated with the 172.16.0.0 class B network in Area 0?

   a. **network 172.16.20.128 0.0.0.0 area 1**

   b. **network 0.0.0.0 255.255.255.255 area 0**

   c. **network 172.16.20.128 0.0.0.255 area 1**

   d. **network 172.16.0.0 0.0.255.255 area 0**

   e. **network 172.16.20.128 0.0.0.0 area 1**

   f. **network 172.16.20.0 255.255.255.255 area 0**

   g. **network 172.16.20.128 0.0.0.7 area 1**

   h. **network 172.16.20.0 255.255.255.255 area 0**

14. Which of the following statements about placing subnets into different areas are true?

   a. The **network** command used to assign interfaces and subnets to different areas can be configured on any OSPF router.

   b. The **network** command is used at the interface level to assign interfaces and their subnets into different areas.

   c. The **network** command uses the subnet mask to identify the portion of the address to consider in assigning areas.

   d. The **network** command uses a wildcard mask to identify the portion of the address to consider in assigning areas.

15. Which of the following statements are true of the command **summary-address 172.16.20.0 255.255.255.0**?

   a. This command would be configured on an ASBR.

   b. This command is used to summarize routes between areas.

   c. This command is used to summarize addresses advertised to the outside world.

   d. This command is configured on ABR routers.

16. Which command would be used on an ABR to configure the cost of a default route propagated into a stub or NSSA area?

   a. **default-cost 30**

   b. **area 1 default-cost 30**

   c. **ip ospf default cost 30**

   d. **ip ospf area 1 default-cost 30**

17. What is the purpose of the command **area 3 stub no-summary**?

    a. To create area 3 as a totally stubby area

    b. To create area 3 as a stub area

    c. To create area 3 as an NSSA area

    d. To filter summaries passing between areas

18. Which of the following commands shows the correct syntax for defining a virtual link?

    a. **area 1 virtual-link 10.10.10.10**

    b. **ip ospf area 1 virtual-link 10.10.10.10**

    c. **ip ospf virtual-link area 1**

    d. **area 1 virtual-link 10.10.10.0 255.255.255.0 172.16.20.131 255.255.255.0**

19. In the following configuration, which areas will have default routes automatically propagated to the routers in the respective areas?

```
RouterA(config)# router ospf 100
RouterA(config-router)# network 140.100.17.128 0.0.0.15 area 3
RouterA(config-router)# network 140.100.17.192 0.0.0.15 area 2
RouterA(config-router)# network 140.100.32.0 0.0.0.255 area 0
RouterA(config-router)# area 2 stub
RouterA(config-router)# area 3 stub no-summary
RouterA(config-router)# area 3 default-cost 15
```

    a. Area 2

    b. Area 3

    c. Neither area

    d. Both areas

20. Which command is used to show the OSPF ABRs and ASBRs for which the internal router has entries in its routing table?

    a. **show ip ospf external routers**

    b. **show ip ospf route**

    c. **show ip ospf border database**

    d. **show ip ospf border-routers**

21. Which of the following is the correct command to show virtual links?

  a. show virtual-links

  b. show ip ospf virtual-links

  c. show ip ospf links

  d. show ip ospf neighbors

22. Which of the following are shown in the **show ip ospf database** command?

  a. Router ID number

  b. Hello timer intervals

  c. Advertising router ID

  d. Number of interfaces detected for the router

23. Which of the following events are shown in the **debug ip ospf events** command?

  a. Adjacencies

  b. Designated router selection

  c. Virtual links

  d. SPF calculations

The answers to this quiz are found in Appendix A, "Answers to Chapter 'Do I Know This Already?' Quizzes and Q&A Sections." The suggested choices for your next step are as follows:

■ **13 or less overall score**—Read the entire chapter. This includes the "Foundation Topics" and "Foundation Summary" sections, the "Q&A" section, and the "Scenarios" at the end of the chapter.

■ **16–19 overall score**—Begin with the "Foundation Summary" section, and then go to the "Q&A" section and the "Scenarios" at the end of the chapter. If you have trouble with these exercises, read the appropriate sections in "Foundation Topics."

■ **20–23 overall score**—If you want more review on these topics, skip to the "Foundation Summary" section, and then go to the "Q&A" section and the "Scenarios" at the end of the chapter. Otherwise, move to the next chapter.

Foundation Topics

The Purpose of Multi-area OSPF

This section explains OSPF multiple-area networks and the single area network issues they solve. Multiple areas in OSPF provide one of the distinguishing features between the distance vector protocols and link-state OSPF.

As you learned, an OSPF area is a logical grouping of routers that are running OSPF with identical topological databases. An area is a subdivision of the greater OSPF domain. Multiple areas prevent a large network from outgrowing its capacity to communicate the details of the network to the routing devices charged with maintaining control and connectivity throughout the network.

The division into areas allows routers in each area to maintain their own topological databases. This limits the size of the topological databases, and summary and external links ensure connectivity between areas and networks outside the autonomous system.

Routers in an area maintain a consistent topological database and any changes within the area have to be communicated to all devices. As the network grows, problems develop because the database is using too much memory or because changes are causing the processor to be overworked.

As the various databases increase in size and the calculations become increasingly frequent, the CPU utilization increases while the available memory decreases. This has the effect of increasing the network response time, as well as increasing congestion on the link. These effects may result in loss of connectivity, packet loss, or system hangs.

> **NOTE** To check the CPU utilization on the router, use the **show processes cpu sorted** command. To check the memory utilization, issue the **show memory free** command.

Breaking the network into smaller pieces allows each area to run a reasonably sized topology and for updates to be contained within an area. The number of routers per area should be limited by the network designer to a number commensurate with the number of active links.

The Features of Multi-area OSPF

Now that you understand why you need to control the size of the areas, you should consider the design issues for the different areas, including the technology that underpins them and their communication (both within and between the areas).

Router Types

In the OSPF hierarchical network there are routers within an area, connecting areas, and connecting to the outside world. Each of these routers has different responsibilities in the OSPF design.

- **Internal router**—Responsible for maintaining a current and accurate database of every LSA within the area. It is also responsible for forwarding data to other networks by the shortest path. Flooding of LSAs is confined to the area. All interfaces on this router are within the same area.

- **Backbone router**—The design rules for OSPF require all areas be connected through a single area, known as the backbone area, or Area 0. A router within this area is referred to as a backbone router.

- **Area border router (ABR)**—An ABR is responsible for connecting two or more areas. It holds a full topological database for each area to which it is connected and sends LSA updates between the areas. These LSA updates are summary updates of the subnets within an area, but are sent as Type 3 LSAs only if summarization is configured on the ABR.

- **Autonomous system boundary router (ASBR)**—An ASBR connects to other routing domains. ASBRs are typically located in the backbone area.

Figure 7-1 shows how the different router types are related.

Figure 7-1 *Router Definitions for OSPF*

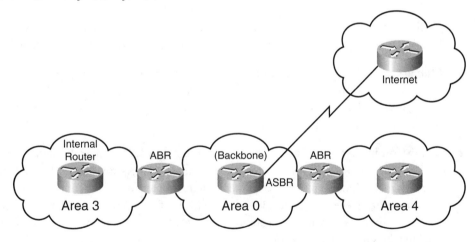

Link-State Advertisements

Link-state advertisements are used to list available routes. The six most common LSA types are described here:

- **Router link LSA (Type 1)**—Each router generates a Type 1 LSA that lists its neighbors and the cost to each. Types 1 and 2 are flooded throughout an area and are the basis of SPF path selection.

- **Network link LSA (Type 2)**—A Type 2 LSA is sent out by the designated router and lists all the routers on the segment it is adjacent to. Types 1 and 2 are flooded throughout an area and are the basis of SPF path selection.

- **Network summary link LSA (Type 3)**—ABRs generate this LSA to send between areas. The LSA lists prefixes available in a given area. If summarization happens within OSPF, summarized routes are propagated using Type 3 LSAs.

- **AS external ASBR summary link LSA (Type 4)**—ASBRs produce this LSA to advertise their presence. Types 3 and 4 are called inter-area LSAs because they are passed between areas.

- **External link LSA (Type 5)**—This LSA is originated by ASBRs and flooded throughout the AS. Each external advertisement describes a route external to OSPF. Type 5 LSAs can also describe default routes out of the AS.

- **NSSA external LSA (Type 7)**—Type 7 LSAs are created by an ASBR residing in a not-so-stubby area (NSSA). Stubby areas do not allow type 5 LSAs, so a Type 7 is a Type 5 tunneled through the NSSA. It is converted into a Type 5 LSA at the ABR.

Different Types of Areas

It is possible to create an OSPF network with only one area—the backbone area or Area 0. In addition to the backbone area, OSPF networks use several other types of areas:

- **Ordinary or standard area**—This area is seen as an SPF domain unto itself. Every router knows about every prefix in the area, and each router has the same topological database.

- **Stub area**—This is an area that will not accept external summary routes (Type 5s). Type 5 LSAs are replaced by the ABR with a default route, and internal routers send external traffic to the closest ABR. Stub areas are useful because they protect slower or less powerful routers from being overwhelmed with routes from outside.

- **Totally stubby area**—This area does not accept summary LSAs from other areas (Types 3 or 4) or external summary LSAs (Type 5). Types 3, 4, and 5 LSAs are replaced by the ABR with a default route. Totally stubby areas protect internal routers by minimizing the routing table and summarizing everything outside the area with a default route. This is a proprietary Cisco solution. Cisco recommends this solution because it keeps the topological databases and routing tables as small as possible.

- **Not so stubby area (NSSA)**—NSSAs are stubby areas that can have ASBRs. Since stubby areas do not support Type 5 LSAs, NSSA uses Type 7 LSAs to disguise external information and the ABR converts the Type 7 LSA to Type 5 when it is sent to Area 0.

NOTE On modern routers, the greatest advantage of special area types is decreased convergence time.

Figure 7-2 shows the connectivity and functionality of the different areas. The routers send out routing updates and other network information through LSAs. The function or type of router determines the LSAs that are sent.

Figure 7-2 *The Different Types of OSPF Areas and LSA Propagation*

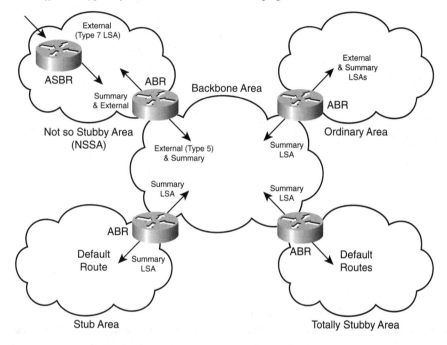

The Operation of Multi-area OSPF

This section describes how OSPF operates across the various areas to maintain a coherent and accurate understanding of the autonomous system.

ABR LSA Propagation

When a router is configured as an ABR, it generates summary LSAs and floods them into the backbone area. Adjacencies within an area are advertised using Type 1 or Type 2 LSAs, and these prefixes are passed to the backbone using Type 3 summaries. These summaries are then injected by other ABRs into their own areas (except for totally stubby areas).

External routes and summaries from other areas are received by the ABR and passed back into the local area.

The flow and propagation of LSAs within and between areas is illustrated in Figure 7-3.

Figure 7-3   *The Propagation of LSAs*

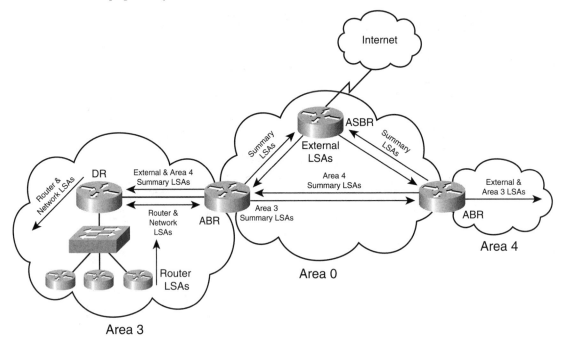

OSPF Path Selection Between Areas

The local routing table on a router depends on its position in the network and the type of area it is in. If there are routes with different routing information sources to the same destination, the router chooses the path with the lowest administrative distance. If both are OSPF, OSPF will select lower type advertisements first and choose lower costs to break ties. OSPF, like all IP routing protocols on Cisco IOS, is capable of load-balancing and will automatically distribute the load over four equal-cost paths.

Remember the sequence of events:

1. The router receives LSAs.

2. The router builds the topological database.

3. The router runs the Dijkstra algorithm, from which the shortest path is chosen and entered into the routing table.

Thus, the routing table is the conclusion of the decision-making process. The routing table displays information on how that decision was made by including the metric for each route. This enables you to view the operation of the network.

Different LSAs are weighted differently in the decision-making process. It is preferable to take an internal route (within the area) to a remote network rather than to traverse multiple areas just to arrive at the same place. Not only does multiple-area traveling create unnecessary traffic, but it can also create a loop within the network.

The routing table reflects the network topology information and indicates where the remote network sits in relation to the local router.

Calculating the Cost of a Path to Another Area

OSPF calculates the costs of paths to other areas differently than it calculates paths to other routing domains. The path to another area is calculated as the smallest cost to the ABR, added to the smallest cost across the backbone. Thus, if there were two paths from the ABR into the backbone, the shortest (lowest-cost) path would be added to the cost of the path to the ABR.

External routes are routes from another routing domain. External routes discovered by OSPF can have their cost calculated in one of two ways:

- **E1**—The cost of the path to the ASBR is added to the external cost to reach the next-hop router outside the AS.

- **E2 (default)**—The external cost of the path from the ASBR is all that is considered in the calculation.

E2 is the default external metric, but E1 is preferred over E2 if two equal-cost paths exist. E2 is useful if you do not want internal routing to determine the path. E1 is useful when internal routing should be included in path selection.

When you look at the routing table by using the **show ip route** command, the first column indicates the source of the information. Typically, this is just the routing protocol the route was learned from. With OSPF, however, it includes the LSA type that provided the path.

Table 7-2 shows the codes used in the routing table.

Table 7-2 *OSPF Routing Table Codes and Associated LSAs*

LSA Type	Routing Table Entry	Description
1 Router	O (short for OSPF)	Generated by a router, listing neighbors and costs. It is propagated within an area.
2 Network	O	Generated by the designated router on a multiaccess network to the area. It is propagated within an area.
3 Summary (between areas)	O IA (short for OSPF interarea)	Type 3 is used to advertise summaries from one area to another.

continues

Table 7-2   *OSPF Routing Table Codes and Associated LSAs (Continued)*

LSA Type	Routing Table Entry	Description
4 Summary (between areas)	O IA	Type 4 is used to advertise the location of an ASBR.
5 External (between autonomous systems)	O E1 or O E2	External to the autonomous system. E1 includes the internal cost to the ASBR added to the external cost. E2 does not compute the internal cost; it reports only the external cost.

Now that you understand the components and operation of multi-area OSPF, you should focus on some of the design implications of creating multiple areas, as described in the next section.

Design Considerations in Multi-area OSPF

The major design consideration in OSPF is how to divide the areas. This is of interest because it impacts the addressing scheme for IP within the network.

In designing a network, consider the resources available and make sure that none of these resources are overwhelmed, either initially or in the future. In the creation of areas, OSPF has tried to provide the means by which the network can grow without exceeding the available resources.

In an OSPF network, summarization takes place at ABRs. You must make summarization part of the initial network design and devise an addressing scheme that supports the use of summarization. With all the interarea traffic disseminated through the backbone, any reduction is beneficial. The entire network benefits when fewer summary LSAs need to be forwarded into the backbone area. When network overhead is minimized, the network grows more easily.

It is also important in a design to allow for transitions or breaks in the network. OSPF provides a device called the *virtual link* that allows areas disconnected from the backbone area to appear directly connected to the backbone as required.

Finally, in any network design, you must consider the WAN topology, in particular the nonbroadcast multiaccess (NBMA) connections.

The following sections consider these topics as they pertain to multi-area OSPF design.

Capacity Planning in OSPF

Although it is possible to have a router attach to more than three areas, the Cisco Technical Assistance Center (TAC) recommends that a greater number of areas be created only after careful consideration. The results of having more areas will vary depending on the router (memory and CPU), as well as network topology and how many LSAs are generated. Various sources recommend that the number of routers per area not exceed 40 to 80; however, this is a rough guideline and not a strict rule. Remember that OSPF is very CPU-intensive in its maintenance of the SPF database and in the flooding of LSAs. Additionally, OSPF is very CPU-intensive when it calculates the routing table—a process based on LSAs. Each ABR maintains a complete picture of the topology map for each area it connects.

Therefore, it is not strictly the number of routers or areas that is important, but also the number of routes and the stability of the network. You must consider these issues because the number of LSAs in your network is proportional to the amount of router resources required.

Major considerations pertinent to capacity planning with OSPF are

- **Type of area (stub, totally stub, or backbone)**—This determines the number of LSAs and how often and how much CPU and memory each SPF computation requires. The area type also affects convergence time.

- **CPU resources of member routers**—Smaller routers are not designed to manage large databases or to continuously run the SPF algorithm.

- **Link speed**—The higher the link speed, the less congestion within the router as it queues the packets for transmission.

- **Stability**—The frequency of LSAs propagation because of topology changes determines the need for bandwidth, CPU, and memory resources.

- **NBMA**—If the area intersects an NBMA network, is the cloud fully meshed? To overcome the resources required to maintain a fully meshed network, Cisco suggests that a well-designed partial mesh over low-bandwidth links reduces the number of links and thus the amount of traffic and resources required.

- **External links**—If the area has external connections, is there a large number of external LSAs? If the external routes are summarized to a default route, far less memory and CPU are required.

- **Summarization**—Do you have a hierarchical design with summarization? The greater the summarization, the smaller and fewer the LSA packets that need to be propagated.

NOTE   Further information is available on Cisco.com in the OSPF Design Guide.

The following sections describe how to determine the appropriate number of neighbors to which a router should be connected, or the number of areas to which an ABR should be connected.

Number of Neighbors per Router

Increasing the number of neighbors increases the resources on the router that are allocated to managing those links. More importantly if there is a designated router (DR), the router that performs the DR function might become overloaded if there are a lot of routers on the link. It's advisable to select the DR through manual configuration to be the router with the most available CPU and memory on the segment. Also, be sure that the router is not selected to be the DR for more than one link.

Number of Areas per ABR

An ABR maintains a full topology table for every area to which it is connected. This not only uses a lot of memory, it also forces the router to recalculate SPF that much more often. The number of areas a router can support depends on the caliber of the router and size of the areas. A good hierarchical design—where the maintenance of the areas is spread over a few routers—not only shares the burden, but also builds in redundancy.

Summarization

OSPF is valuable because it scales—scalability in a routing protocol comes from summarization. Multiple areas are a great way to limit computation and propagation of routing updates; the hierarchical approach imposed by using multiple areas allows for intelligent summarization on ABRs and ASBRs. This section applies summarization to the design and implementation of multi-area OSPF.

In OSPF, two types of summarization exist:

- **Interarea summarization**—Performed at the ABR, creates Type 3 LSAs. Type 4 LSAs advertise the router IDs of ASBRs.

- **External summarization**—Performed at the ASBR, creates Type 5 LSAs.

OSPF benefits from the hierarchical design created by using multiple areas connected to the backbone area. It is important to design the hierarchy to carefully take advantage of interarea and external summarization.

Virtual Links

The main dictate in OSPF is that other areas must connect directly to the backbone area through an ABR. The ABR is resident in both areas and holds a full topological database for each area.

Networks must bend to organizational policies, however. OSPF has provided a solution called a *virtual link* for the unhappy occasion when a direct connection to the backbone is not possible. If the new area cannot connect directly to the backbone area, two ABRs are set up to "bridge" the gap and recreate the connectivity.

The configuration commands pass area information between ABRs in the intermediary area. From the viewpoint of OSPF, each ABR has a direct connection to three areas (Area 0, the outlying area, and the area traversed).

This scenario may emerge in a variety of cases:

■ Merger or failure isolates an area from Area 0.

■ Two Area 0s exist because of merger.

■ The area is critical to the company, and an extra link has been configured for redundancy.

Although the virtual link feature is extremely powerful, virtual links are not recommended as part of the design strategy for your network. They should be a temporary solution to a connectivity problem. You must ensure that you observe the following when creating a virtual link:

■ Both routers must share a common area.

■ The transit area cannot be a stub area.

■ One of the routers must be connected to Area 0.

Figure 7-4 illustrates the use of a virtual link to provide a router in Area 10 connectivity to the backbone in Area 0.

Figure 7-4 *Virtual Links in a Multi-area OSPF Network*

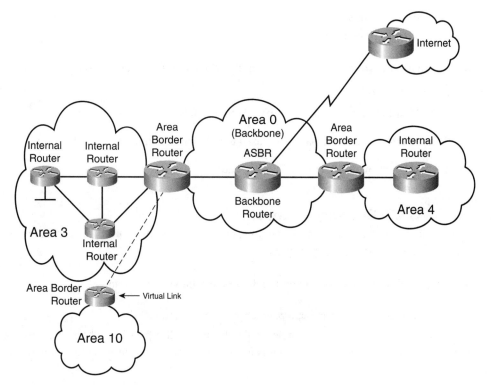

Multi-area OSPF Over an NBMA Network

Another design consideration is the design of the NBMA network as part of the OSPF domain. There are two main ways to approach the inclusion of an NBMA network:

- Define the NBMA network as Area 0. The logic is that if the remote sites are made satellite areas, all traffic will have to traverse the NBMA, so it makes sense to make it the backbone area. This works well in a full-mesh environment, although it results in a large number of LSAs being flooded into the WAN and puts demands on the routers connecting to the NBMA network.

- Define a hub network as Area 0 with remote sites and associated links as spoke areas. This is a good design if the satellite areas are stub areas because it means that the routing information—and network overhead—is kept to a minimum over the NBMA cloud. Depending on the design, the rest of the network might constitute one other area or multiple areas. This will depend on the size and growth expectations of the OSPF domain.

Required Configuration Commands for a Multi-area OSPF Network

The first configuration step is to start OSPF. Many OSPF commands allow "tuning" but the following need to be defined at the startup of the process:

- **Participating router interfaces**—Identify which interfaces should take part in the OSPF process.

- **Identification of the area**—Identify which interfaces are in which areas.

- **Router ID**—Specify the parameter used to uniquely identify the router by a single address.

The next sections review basic OSPF configuration.

Enabling the OSPF Routing Protocol

When configuring the router for the first time, there is no IP routing protocol running on the Cisco router (unless the SETUP script is used).

To configure OSPF as the routing protocol, use the following command:

```
Router(config)# router ospf process-number
```

Recall that *process-number* is a number local to the router. It is possible to have more than one process running on a router, although this is an unusual and expensive configuration in terms of router resources. The process number does not have to be the same on every router in the area or the autonomous system. In the interest of sanity, however, many administrators assign the same number to the routers.

> **NOTE** A common error in configuration is to confuse the process ID with the router ID or the area ID. These are not related in any way. The process ID is simply a mechanism to allow more than one process to be configured on a router. The router ID is the mechanism by which a router is identified within the OSPF domain, and the area ID is a mechanism of grouping routers that share full knowledge of OSPF-derived routes within the OSPF area.

Enabling the network Command

The **network** command was explained in Chapter 5 in terms of identifying the interfaces that participated in the OSPF routing process. In this chapter, the **network** command is used to identify not only the interfaces that are sending and receiving OSPF updates, but also the area in which they reside. Defining the areas connected by an ABR is carried out with the **network** command.

The following is the syntax for the OSPF **network** command:

```
Router(config-router)# network network-number wildcard-mask area area-number
```

> **NOTE** The area requested in the preceding syntax is the area in which the interface or interfaces configured with the network address reside.

You must take care in the use of the wildcard mask. In a single-area configuration, all the interfaces are in the same area. The **network** commands identify only the network numbers in use. Therefore, they can be configured to the classful network address provided by the IANA. The only reason to be more specific would be to exclude some interfaces from the OSPF domain.

Figure 7-5 illustrates the configuration of an ABR. Example 7-1 shows two interfaces on Router A in distinct areas, where each interface lies within subnets of the same major network. The network number has been subnetted into the last octet, where you can see the granularity of the wildcard mask at work. Figure 7-5 illustrates this configuration.

Example 7-1 *The **network** Command for Router A*

```
RouterA(config)# router ospf 100
RouterA(config-router)# network 172.16.20.128 0.0.0.7 area 0
RouterA(config-router)# network 172.16.20.8 0.0.0.7 area 1
```

Figure 7-5 *The **network** Command*

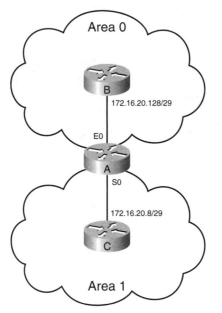

Optional Configuration Commands for a Multi-area OSPF Network

The word *optional* is used here to mean not absolutely necessary, implying that OSPF will run without the optional configuration commands. However, this does not mean that OSPF runs well or efficiently without them. A few of the OSPF commands, optional or not, are necessary in the configuration of an efficient multi-area OSPF network. The following list shows those optional OSPF commands that are important to the maintenance of an efficient network:

- The **area range** command configured on an ABR.

- The **summary-address** command, used to summarize at ASBRs.

- The **area** *area-id* **stub** command to define a stub area.

- The **area** *area-id* **stub no-summary** command to define a totally stubby area.

- The **area default-cost** command for determining the cost of default routes that enter the area.

- The **area virtual-link** commands to create a virtual link.

The area range Command

The **area range** command is configured on an ABR because it dictates the networks that will be advertised out of the area.

Use the **area** router configuration command with the **range** keyword to consolidate and summarize routes at an area boundary. This reduces the size of the databases, which is particularly useful in the backbone area. Use the **no** form of this command to disable for the specified area:

```
Router(config-router)# area area-id range address mask
Router(config-router)# no area area-id range address mask
```

In the preceding syntax, *area-id* is the identifier (ID) of the area about which routes are to be summarized. It can be specified as either a decimal value or an IP address. Here, *address* is the IP address, and *mask* is the IP mask.

Example 7-2 shows the configuration required to summarize the following five individual subnets (which can address six hosts each) into one subnet.

Example 7-2   *The OSPF* **area range** *Command for an ABR*

```
RouterA(config)# router ospf 100
RouterA(config-router)# network 172.16.20.128 0.0.0.15 area 0
RouterA(config-router)# network 172.16.20.144 0.0.0.15 area 0
RouterA(config-router)# network 172.16.20.160 0.0.0.15 area 0
RouterA(config-router)# network 172.16.20.176 0.0.0.15 area 0
RouterA(config-router)# network 172.16.20.8 0.0.0.7 area 1
RouterA(config-router)# area 0 range 172.16.20.128 255.255.255.192
```

The subnets 172.16.20.128/28, 172.16.20.144/28, 172.16.20/160/28, and 172.16.20/28 are summarized to 172.16.20.128/26, saving both bandwidth and CPU.

This one subnet will then be propagated into Area 1 (see Figure 7-6).

NOTE   The area ID requested is the area from which the subnets originated. It is not the destination area.

Figure 7-6 *The OSPF **area range** Command for an ABR*

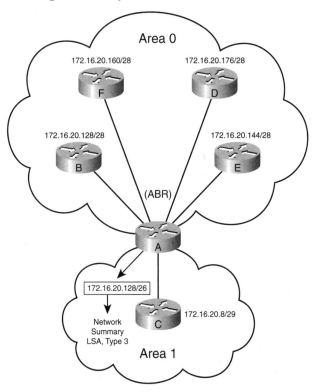

The summary-address Command

The **summary-address** command is used on the ASBR to summarize routes received into OSPF via redistribution. The syntax applied to an ASBR for the **summary-address** command is

```
Router(config-router)# summary-address address mask [not-advertise][tag tag]
```

In the preceding syntax, *address* is the summary address designated for a range of addresses, and *mask* is the IP subnet mask used for the summary route. The design and implementation of the addressing scheme are crucial to the success of the OSPF network.

Figure 7-7 illustrates a scenario where the **summary-address** command is useful.

Example 7-3 shows the summarization of the network address 172.16.20.0, received from the ISP and redistributed into OSPF. The redistribution is not illustrated in this example. (See Chapter 11, "Implementing Redistribution and Controlling Routing Updates.")

Example 7-3 *The OSPF **summary-address** Command for an ASBR*

```
RouterD(config)# router ospf 100
RouterD(config-router)# network 172.16.20.176 0.0.0.7 area 0
RouterD(config-router)# summary-address 172.16.20.0 255.255.255.0
```

Figure 7-7 *The OSPF* **summary-address** *Command for an ASBR*

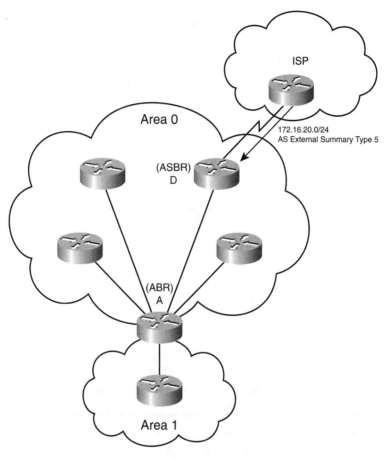

The area stub Command

Any area that has a single ABR, or an area where the choice of exit ABR is not important (because they are co-located, for instance) is a good candidate for a stub area. Areas that shelter underpowered routers demand to be stub areas. Many stub areas could benefit even more by being created as totally stubby. Once areas that could benefit from the stub logic are identified, the syntax to create a stub is

```
Router(config-router)# area area-id stub
```

Figure 7-8 illustrates a scenario with a stub area.

Example 7-4 shows the creation of a stub area. Note that both the ABR and the internal router share the stub area configuration.

Figure 7-8 *The Configuration of a Stub Area*

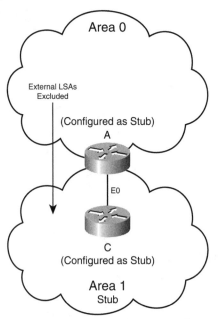

Example 7-4 *The Configuration of a Stub Area*

```
RouterC(config)# router ospf 100
RouterC(config-router)# network 0.0.0.0 255.255.255.255 area 1
RouterC(config-router)# area 1 stub

RouterA(config)# router ospf 100
RouterA(config-router)# network 172.16.20.128 0.0.0.7 area 0
RouterA(config-router)# network 172.16.20.8 0.0.0.7 area 1
RouterA(config-router)# area 0 range 172.16.20.128 255.255.255.192
RouterA(config-router)# area 1 stub
```

> **NOTE** All routers inside a stub or totally stub area must be configured as stub routers. When an area is configured as a stub, interfaces that belong to that area will exchange Hello packets with the stub flag. The flag is a bit in the Hello packet that neighbors must agree on to be neighbors.

The area area-id stub no-summary Command

The syntax for the OSPF command for a totally stubby area is as follows:

```
Router(config-router)# area area-id stub no-summary
```

The addition of the **no-summary** parameter informs the ABR not to pass summary updates (Type 3 LSAs) or external routers (Type 5s) from other areas. This command can be configured only on the ABR. All other routers are configured as stub so that their stub-flag will agree.

Figure 7-9 illustrates a totally stubby area scenario.

Figure 7-9 *The Configuration of a Totally Stubby Area*

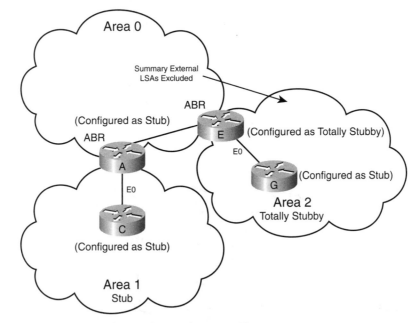

The **stub no-summary** feature is proprietary to Cisco.

Example 7-5 shows the proper configuration for Router E and Router G.

Example 7-5 *The Configuration of a Totally Stubby Area*

```
RouterE(config)# router ospf 100
RouterE(config-router)# network 172.16.20.144 0.0.0.7 area 0
RouterE(config-router)# network 172.16.20.16 0.0.0.7 area 2
RouterE(config-router)# area 2 stub no-summary
RouterG(config)# router ospf 100
RouterG(config-router)# network 0.0.0.0 255.255.255.255 area 2
RouterG(config-router)# area 2 stub
```

As a totally stubby area, no interarea/summary or external LSAs are propagated by the ABR into the area. To reach networks and hosts outside their area, routers use a default route, which the ABR advertises into the area.

The area default-cost Command

An ABR for a stub area replaces external routes with a default cost. The cost of this default route can be set by the **area default-cost** command. If the cost is not specified, the cost will be calculated as the cost to the ABR plus one:

```
Router(config-router)# area area-id default-cost cost
```

Figure 7-10 illustrates the propagation of default cost with OSPF.

Figure 7-10 *The OSPF Command for the Default Route Sent into the Area*

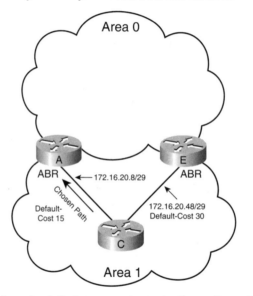

Example 7-6 shows how the default cost can be set in the configuration. Setting a cost on the default route is useful when the stub area has more than one ABR; this allows the administrator to prefer a specific exit.

Example 7-6 *The OSPF Command for the Default Route Propagated into the Area*

```
RouterC(config-router)# router ospf 100
RouterC(config-router)# network 0.0.0.0 255.255.255.255 area 1
RouterC(config-router)# area 1 stub
RouterA(config-router)# router ospf 100
RouterA(config-router)# network 172.16.20.128 0.0.0.7 area 0
RouterA(config-router)# network 172.16.20.8 0.0.0.7 area 1
RouterA(config-router)# area 0 range 172.16.20.128 255.255.255.192
RouterA(config-router)# area 1 stub
RouterA(config-router)# area 1 default-cost 15
RouterE(config-router)# router ospf 100
RouterE(config-router)# network 172.16.20.144 0.0.0.7 area 0
```

Example 7-6 *The OSPF Command for the Default Route Propagated into the Area (Continued)*

```
RouterE(config-router)# area 1 stub
RouterE(config-router)# area 1 default-cost 30
RouterE(config-router)# area 0 range 172.16.20.128 255.255.255.192
```

Configure **area default-cost** only on the ABR. Example 7-6 shows the configuration on both routers to illustrate the choice. The second ABR, Router E, will only be used if Router A fails. If there were no configuration on Router A, it would still be used by all internal routers as the ABR because the default cost is 1.

The area virtual-link Command

When it is not possible to connect an area to Area 0 directly, one solution is to create a virtual link. Although the command is straightforward, many problems can arise. The most common problem is in the address of the other end of the virtual link. The command **area virtual-link** is configured between ABRs that share a common area; at least one of the ABRs must be in Area 0. The command states the transit area and the router ID of the remote destination ABR. This creates a connection through the transit area, which, although it might transit many routers along the way, appears to OSPF on the remote ABRs as a next hop.

> **NOTE**   The **area** *area-id* **virtual-link** command might be included in the BSCI exam and, for that reason, is worth mentioning. In practice, virtual links are a design nightmare and are best avoided. Otherwise, they are useful when mending a network on a temporary basis.

The syntax to configure a virtual link is as follows:

```
Router(config-router)# area area-id virtual-link router-id
```

Here, *area-id* is the transit area and *router-id* is the RID of the other ABR.

Figure 7-11 illustrates an example with an OSPF virtual link.

Example 7-7 shows the setting of the loopback interfaces that provide the router ID. It then shows the configuration of the virtual link through the network.

Example 7-7 *Configuring a Virtual Link*

```
RouterA(config)# interface loopback 0
RouterA(config-if)# ip address 10.10.10.33 255.255.255.255
RouterA(config)# router ospf 100
RouterA(config-router)# network 172.16.20.128 0.0.0.7 area 0
RouterA(config-router)# network 10.10.10.33 0.0.0.0 area 0
RouterA(config-router)# area 0 range 172.16.20.128 255.255.255.192
RouterA(config-router)# area 1 virtual-link 10.10.10.30
```

continues

Example 7-7 *Configuring a Virtual Link (Continued)*

```
RouterM(config)# loopback interface 0
RouterM(config-if)# ip address 10.10.10.30 255.255.255.255
RouterM(config)# router ospf 100
RouterM(config-router)# network 172.16.20.32 0.0.0.7 area 5
RouterM(config-router)# network 10.10.10.30 0.0.0.0 area 0
RouterM(config-router)# area 1 virtual-link 10.10.10.33
```

Figure 7-11 *Configuring a Virtual Link*

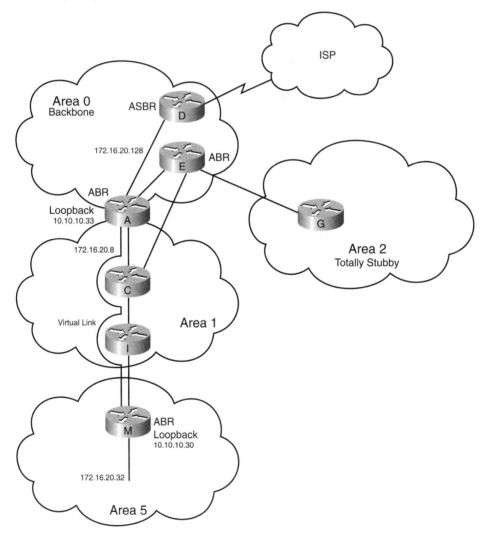

Working Configuration of Multi-area OSPF

Figure 7-12 illustrates a multi-area OSPF network.

Figure 7-12 *Example 7-8 Network*

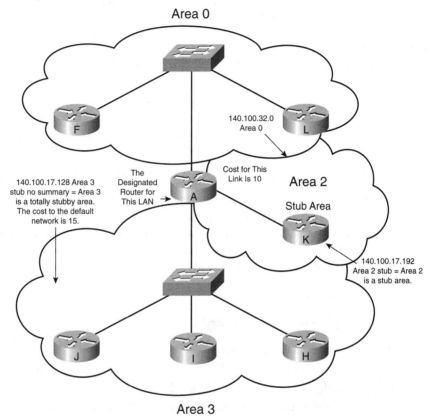

Example 7-8 shows a working configuration of the multi-area OSPF network. It includes many of the commands explained earlier in this chapter. Here you see an entire working configuration rather than just a relevant segment.

Example 7-8 *Configuring OSPF in a Multi-area Network on Router A*

```
RouterA(config)# router ospf 100
RouterA(config-router)# network 140.100.17.128 0.0.0.15 area 3
RouterA(config-router)# network 140.100.17.192 0.0.0.15 area 2
RouterA(config-router)# network 140.100.32.0 0.0.0.255 area 0
RouterA(config-router)# area 2 stub
RouterA(config-router)# area 3 stub no-summary
RouterA(config-router)# area 3 default-cost 15
!
RouterA(config-router)# interface FastEthernet0/0
RouterA(config-if)# ip address 140.100.17.129 255.255.255.240
```

continues

Example 7-8   *Configuring OSPF in a Multi-area Network on Router A (Continued)*

```
RouterA(config-if)# ip ospf priority 100
!
RouterA(config-if)# interface FastEthernet0/1
RouterA(config-if)# ip address 140.100.17.193 255.255.255.240
RouterA(config-if)# ip ospf cost 10
!
RouterA(config-if)# interface FastEthernet1/0
RouterA(config-if)# ip address 140.100.32.10 255.255.255.240
RouterA(config-if)# no keepalive

RouterA(config-if)# exit
```

The following section covers commands to verify the configuration and monitor the network.

Verifying the Configuration of OSPF in a Multi-area Network

The **show** commands described in this section are invaluable in the configuration, troubleshooting, and maintenance of a live network. You can use the following commands in conjunction with the single area commands described in Chapter 5 when verifying OSPF on a multi-area network:

- The **show ip ospf border-routers** command

- The **show ip route** command

- The **show ip ospf virtual-links** command

- The **show ip ospf database** command

The show ip ospf border-routers Command

The **show ip ospf border-routers** command shows the ABRs and ASBRs that the internal router has in its routing table. This command is excellent for troubleshooting configuration errors and understanding how the network is communicating. In a multi-area network, the **show ip ospf border-routers** command can immediately indicate why users cannot connect outside their area:

```
Router# show ip ospf border-routers
```

Example 7-9 shows the output of this command.

Example 7-9   *The **show ip ospf border-routers** Command Output*

```
Router# show ip ospf border-routers
OSPF Process 100 internal Routing Table
Destination      Next Hop        Cost    Type    Rte Type   Area       SPF No
160.89.97.53     144.144.1.53    10      ABR     INTRA      0.0.0.3         3
160.89.103.51    160.89.96.51    10      ABR     INTRA      0.0.0.3         3
160.89.103.52    160.89.96.51    20      ASBR    INTER      0.0.0.3         3
160.89.103.52    144.144.1.53    22      ASBR    INTER      0.0.0.3         3
```

Table 7-3 explains the meaning of the important fields in the output of the **show ip ospf border-routers** command.

Table 7-3 *Explanation of the* **show ip ospf border-routers** *Command Output*

Field	Explanation
OSPF Process 100 internal Routing Table	This is the OSPF routing process ID for the router.
Destination	RID of the destination router, whether an ABR or an ASBR.
Next Hop	Address of the next logical hop in the path to the ABR or ASBR.
Cost	Path metric to the destination.
Type	Classifies router as an ABR, an ASBR, or both.
Rte Type	Type of route, either intra-area or interarea route.
Area	This is the area ID of the area from which this route is learned.
SPF No	This is the SPF calculation number that installed this route into the routing table.

The show ip route Command

The **show ip route** command is one of the most useful commands available for understanding and troubleshooting an IP network. Example 7-10 shows an example of a routing table in a multi-area network.

Example 7-10 *The* **show ip route** *Command Output*

```
Router# show ip route
Codes: C - connected, S - static, I - IGRP, R - RIP, M - mobile, B - BGP
       D - EIGRP, EX - EIGRP external, O - OSPF, IA - OSPF inter area
       N1 - OSPF NSSA external type 1, N2 - OSPF NSSA external type 2
       E1 - OSPF external type 1, E2 - OSPF external type 2, E - EGP
       i - IS-IS, L1 - IS-IS level-1, L2 - IS-IS level-2, * - candidate default
       U - per-user static route, o - ODR

Gateway of last resort is not set

     172.16.0.0/16 is variably subnetted, 3 subnets, 2 masks
O E2    172.16.20.128/29 [110/20] via 172.16.20.9, 00:00:29, Serial1
O IA    172.16.20.128/26 [110/74] via 172.16.20.9, 00:01:29, Serial1
C       172.16.20.8/29 is directly connected, Serial1
O E2 192.168.0.0/24 [110/20] via 172.16.20.9, 00:01:29, Serial1
```

Table 7-4 shows the link-state advertisement (LSA) codes used in the routing table, allowing you to analyze the flow of LSAs both within and between the areas.

Table 7-4 *OSPF Routing Table Codes and Associated LSAs*

LSA Type	Routing Table Entry	Description
1 Router Link	O	Generated by the router, listing all links to which it is connected, their status, and cost. It is propagated within the area.
2 Network Link	O	Generated by the DR on a multiaccess network to the area.
3 or 4 Summary Link (between areas)	OIA	LSA Type 3 includes the networks within an area that might have been summarized and that are sent into the backbone and between ABRs. LSA Type 4 tells how to find an ASBR. These routes are not sent into totally stubby areas.
5 Summary Link/ External Link (between autonomous systems)	OE1 or OE2	External routes that can be configured to have one of two values. E1 includes the internal cost to the ASBR added to the external cost reported by the ASBR. E2 reports only the external cost to the remote destination.

The show ip ospf virtual-links Command

The following command shows the configured virtual links:

```
Router# show ip ospf virtual-links
```

The **show ip ospf neighbors** command is also useful for discovering details about neighbors. Even though virtual-link partners might not be directly attached, they will show as neighbors because of the virtual connection. Example 7-11 shows the output of the **show ip ospf virtual-links** command.

Example 7-11 *The **show ip ospf virtual-links** Command Output*

```
Router# show ip ospf virtual-links
Virtual Link to router 140.100.32.10 is up
Transit area 0.0.0.1, via interface Ethernet0, Cost of using 10
Transmit Delay is 1 sec, State DROTHER
Timer intervals configured, Hello 10, Dead 40, Wait 40, Retransmit 5
Hello due in 0:00:08
Adjacency State FULL
```

Table 7-5 explains the meaning of the important fields in the output of the **show ip ospf virtual-links** command.

Table 7-5   *Explanation of the* **show ip ospf virtual-links** *Command Output*

Field	Explanation
Virtual Link to router 140.100.32.10 is up	The RID of the other end of the virtual link, which is seen as a neighbor.
Transit area 0.0.0.1	The area through which the virtual link is tunneled: Area 0.0.0.1 or Area 1 in this case.
Via interface Ethernet 0	The outgoing interface that connects the virtual link to Area 0.
Cost of using 10	The cost of reaching the neighbor through the virtual link.
Transmit Delay is 1 sec	This is the delay of the link. This value must be less than the retransmit timer setting.
State DROTHER	The state of the OSPF neighbor. The neighbor is a DROTHER, which is a router other than a designated router.
Hello 10	Time between hellos, in seconds. The default is 10 seconds.
Dead 40	The time (in seconds) a router will wait for a Hello before declaring a neighbor dead. The default is 40 seconds.
Retransmit 5	The time (in seconds) the router waits for an acknowledgment for a transmitted LSA. The default is 5 seconds.
Hello due in 0:00:08	Shows the amount of time before the next Hello is expected from the neighbor.
Adjacency State FULL	Specifies the state of neighbor adjacency. The routers have synchronized their topological databases.

The show ip ospf database Command

The **show ip ospf database** command shows all the entries in the OSPF link-state database and the information taken from the LSAs that have been received. It can be tailored to show specific information from the database, such as the Type 2 LSAs. To make the output specific to the LSA that you wish to examine, specify the appropriate parameter.

```
Router# show ip ospf database [router | network | summary | asbr-summary | nssa-
    external | external | database-summary]
```

Another command to use in conjunction with this is **show ip ospf neighbors**.

Example 7-12 shows the output of the **show ip ospf database** command.

Example 7-12 *The **show ip ospf database** Command Output*

```
Router# show ip ospf database

        OSPF Router with ID (172.16.20.130) (Process ID 100)


               Router Link States (Area 0)

Link ID         ADV Router      Age   Seq# Checksum Link count
172.16.20.129   172.16.20.129   295   0x80000003 0x419B   1
172.16.20.130   172.16.20.130   298   0x80000002 0x3E9D   1

               Net Link States (Area 0)

Link ID         ADV Router      Age       Seq#      Checksum
172.16.20.130   172.16.20.130   298       0x80000001 0x19DB

               Summary Net Link States (Area 0)

Link ID         ADV Router      Age       Seq#      Checksum
172.16.20.8     172.16.20.129   291       0x80000001 0x7D1
```

Table 7-6 explains the meaning of the important fields in the output of the **show ip ospf database** command.

Table 7-6 *Explanation of the **show ip ospf database** Command Output*

Field	Explanation
Link ID 172.16.20.129	Router ID number
ADV Router 172.16.20.129	Advertising router ID
Age 295	Link-state age
Seq# 0x80000002	Link-state sequence number
Checksum 0x19DB	Checksum of the contents of the LSA
Link count 1	Number of interfaces detected

Troubleshooting a Multi-area OSPF Network

Troubleshooting OSPF across multiple areas can be complicated, so follow the basic tenets of troubleshooting routing:

■   Maintain clear topology maps of the network.

- Keep current copies of all router configurations.

- Document changes made to the network.

Following these guidelines is imperative in a complex network to make a logical, structured approach. The following sections cover the command **log-adjacency-changes** and the most useful **debug** commands. You will also learn about the most common problems that occur when forming adjacencies, the reasons for them, and how to prevent them from occurring.

The log-adjacency-changes Command

The **log-adjacency-changes** command is similar to **debug** commands but uses fewer resources. The **debug** command provides so much information that it is possible to overrun the logging buffers of the router as well as your own buffers. The **log-adjacency-changes** command offers less detail, which is often easier to assimilate and process. Whenever a change in the state of an adjacency occurs, a message is sent to syslog. This means that immediate updates are sent to the administrator without a massive drain on resources.

```
Router(config-router)# log-adjacency-changes
```

Example 7-13 shows the output of the **log-adjacency-changes** command. In this example, the OSPF process is reconfigured to log adjacency changes. The routing process for OSPF is started and the **network** command allocates all subnets to Area 0. The action is the same whether this is a reconfiguration of the area assignments or OSPF has never been run on this router before. The OSPF process re-initializes all interfaces, requiring the neighbors to be found and the adjacencies formed. With the adjacency changes logged, this example shows the interface Ethernet 0 finding the neighbors at 131.11.84.8 and 131.11.14.14 and all the steps to creating adjacencies being completed.

> **NOTE**   In Cisco IOS software release 12.1, the **ospf log-adjacency-changes** command became **log-adjacency-changes**.

Example 7-13   *OSPF* **log-adjacency-changes** *Command Output*

```
RouterA(config)# router ospf 1
RouterA(config-router)# log-adjacency-changes
RouterA(config-router)# network 0.0.0.0 255.255.255.255 area 0
RouterA(config-router)# end
RouterA#
10:30:15: %SYS-5-CONFIG_I: Configured from console by console
RouterA#
10:30:29: %OSPF-5-ADJCHG: Process 1, Nbr 131.11.14.14 on Ethernet0 from
DOWN to INIT, Received Hello
RouterA#
10:30:38: %OSPF-5-ADJCHG: Process 1, Nbr 131.11.84.8 on Ethernet0 from
DOWN to INIT, Received Hello
```

continues

Example 7-13 *OSPF* **log-adjacency-changes** *Command Output (Continued)*

```
RouterA#
10:30:39: %OSPF-5-ADJCHG: Process 1, Nbr 131.11.14.14 on Ethernet0 from
INIT to 2WAY, 2-Way Received
RouterA#
10:30:48: %OSPF-5-ADJCHG: Process 1, Nbr 131.11.84.8 on Ethernet0 from
INIT to 2 WAY, 2-Way Received
RouterA#
10:30:54: %OSPF-5-ADJCHG: Process 1, Nbr 131.11.84.8 on Ethernet0 from
2WAY to EXSTART, AdjOK?
RouterA#
10:31:18: %OSPF-5-ADJCHG: Process 1, Nbr 131.11.84.8 on Ethernet0 from
EXSTART to EXCHANGE, Negotiation Done
10:31:18: %OSPF-5-ADJCHG: Process 1, Nbr 131.11.14.14 on Ethernet0 from
2WAY to EXSTART, AdjOK?
10:31:18: %OSPF-5-ADJCHG: Process 1, Nbr 131.11.14.14 on Ethernet0 from
EXSTART to EXCHANGE, Negotiation Done
10:31:18: %OSPF-5-ADJCHG: Process 1, Nbr 131.11.14.14 on Ethernet0 from
EXCHANGE to LOADING, Exchange Done
10:31:18: %OSPF-5-ADJCHG: Process 1, Nbr 131.11.14.14 on Ethernet0 from
LOADING to FULL, Loading Done
10:31:18: %OSPF-5-ADJCHG: Process 1, Nbr 131.11.84.8 on Ethernet0 from
EXCHANGE to LOADING, Exchange Done
RouterA#
10:31:18: %OSPF-5-ADJCHG: Process 1, Nbr 131.11.84.8 on Ethernet0 from
LOADING to FULL, Loading Done
```

Useful debug Commands

The **debug** commands are issued from the Privileged EXEC console prompt. Use the following **debug** commands with caution. The resources required by the debug process can overwhelm your system.

The debug ip packet Command

The **debug ip packet** command is useful for analyzing the messages traveling between the local and remote hosts. Any fast-switched packets do not generate messages, so while this command is in effect, turn off fast switching and force all packets to be process switched for the few minutes that you are using the debug tool. IP debugging information includes packets received, generated, and forwarded. This command can easily overwhelm a busy router.

The debug ip ospf events Command

Use the **debug ip ospf events** to display information on OSPF-related events, such as adjacencies, flooding information, designated router selection, and shortest path first (SPF) calculation.

Common Problems with Adjacencies

Many OSPF problems stem from adjacency problems that propagate throughout the network. Problems are often traced back to neighbor discrepancies. The following guidelines are helpful in these situations.

If a router configured for OSPF routing is not seeing an OSPF neighbor on an attached network, do the following:

- Make sure that both routers are configured with the same IP mask, MTU, interface Hello timer, OSPF Hello interval, and OSPF dead interval.

- Make sure that both neighbors are the same area type and part of the same area.

- Use the **debug** and **show** commands to trace the problem.

Foundation Summary

The Foundation Summary provides a convenient review of many key concepts in this chapter. If you are already comfortable with the topics in this chapter, this summary might help you recall a few details. If you just read this chapter, this review should help solidify some key facts. If you are doing your final prep before the exam, the following lists and tables are a convenient way to review the day before the exam.

OSPF Router roles are

- Internal router

- Backbone router

- ABR

- ASBR

The six most common LSA types are

- Router link LSA (Type 1)

- Network link LSA (Type 2)

- Network-summary link LSA (Type 3)

- AS external ASBR summary link LSA (Type 4)

- External link LSA (Type 5)

- NSSA external LSA (Type 7)

OSPF networks use several types of areas:

- Standard

- Stub

- Totally stubby

- Not-so-stubby

LSAs learned by OSPF can have the cost of the path calculated in one of two ways:

- **E1**—Cost of the path to ASBR added to external cost

- **E2**—Only external cost of path from ASBR considered in calculation

Two types of summarization exist:

- **Interarea summarization**—Performed at the ABR, creates Type 3 and Type 4 LSAs.

- **External summarization**—Performed at the ASBR, creates Type 5 LSAs.

Configuration commands for a multi-area OSPF network are as follows:

- **area** *area-id* **range address** *mask*

- **summary-address** *address mask* [**not-advertise**][**tag** *tag*]

- **area** *area-id* **stub**

- **area** *area-id* **stub no-summary**

- **area** *area-id* **default-cost** *cost*

- **area** *area-id* **virtual-link**

- **area** *area-id* **virtual-link** *router-id*

Commands to verify the configuration and monitor the network are

- **show ip ospf border-routers**

- **show ip route**

- **show ip ospf virtual-links**

- **show ip ospf database**

Useful debug commands are as follows:

- **log-adjacency-changes**

- **debug ip packet**

- **debug ip ospf events**

Use the following guidelines when troubleshooting adjacencies:

- Make sure that both routers are configured with the same IP mask, MTU, interface Hello timer, OSPF Hello interval, and OSPF dead interval.

- Make sure that both neighbors are the same area type and part of the same area.

- Use the **debug** and **show** commands to trace the problem.

Q&A

The questions and scenarios in this book are designed to be challenging and to make sure that you know the answer. Rather than allowing you to derive the answers from clues hidden inside the questions themselves, the questions challenge your understanding and recall of the subject.

You can find the answers to these questions in Appendix A. For more practice with exam-like question formats, use the exam engine on the CD-ROM.

1. In a totally stubby area, which routes are not propagated into the area?

2. Can a virtual link transit a stub area?

3. An ABR must be resident in which area?

4. What LSAs will the ABR forward?

5. State two advantages in creating areas in OSPF.

6. What is an external route, and on which type of router will this route be introduced?

7. Why is the use of summarization important in the design of OSPF?

8. What is an estimate of the maximum number of routers that should reside in a given area?

9. What restrictions govern the creation of a stub or totally stubby area?

10. A virtual link in OSPF is used to solve what problem?

11. What issues may emerge when running OSPF within an area containing a Frame Relay NBMA cloud?

12. State one advantage in making centralized routers and network resources reside in Area 0 while the Frame Relay cloud and stub remote LANs reside in satellite stub areas.

13. How does creating multiple areas in OSPF reduce the number of SPF calculations?

14. How does a stub area differ from the backbone area?

15. How does a totally stubby area differ from a stub area?

16. State the different LSA types.

17. Where does the backbone router reside, and what is its function?

18. There are two types of summarization. What are they?

19. Which router type creates LSA Types 3 and 4?

20. Which command in OSPF shows the network LSA information?

21. What command would you use to create a totally stubby area?

22. What is a virtual link, and which command would you use to create it?

23. Where would you issue the command to summarize IP subnets? State the command that is used.

24. How would you summarize external routes before injecting them into the OSPF domain?

25. Give the command for defining the cost of a default route propagated into an area.

26. Give an example of when it would be appropriate to define a default cost.

27. On which router is the area default cost defined?

28. Give the command to configure a stub area and state on which router it is configured.

29. What is the purpose of the **area range** command, and why is it configured on the ABR?

30. Give the commands to configure a router to place subnets 144.111.248.0 through to 144.111.255.0 in Area 1 and to put all other interfaces into Area 0.

31. Give the syntax to summarize the external subnets 144.111.248.0 to 144.111.254.255 into OSPF.

32. Explain (briefly) the difference between the **area range** command and the **summary-address** command.

33. Explain the following syntax and what it will achieve: **area 1 stub no-summary**.

34. Why would you configure the routing process to log adjacency changes as opposed to turning on debug for the same trigger?

35. Give some of the common reasons that neighbors fail to form an adjacency.

36. When configuring a virtual link, which routers are configured?

37. What does the command **area 1 default-cost 15** achieve?

38. Explain what is placed in the parameters *area-id* and *router-id* for the command **area** *area-id* **virtual-link** *router-id*.

Scenarios

The following scenarios and questions are designed to draw together the content of the chapter and to exercise your understanding of the concepts. There is not necessarily a right answer. The thought process and practice in manipulating the concepts is the goal of this section. The answers to the scenario questions are found at the end of this chapter.

Scenario 7-1

A new network administrator recently joined the company and has found little documentation for the network. On drawing the topology of the network, the administrator has found a surprising configuration of a virtual link. Luckily, the administrator has previous experience with such configurations and therefore understands their purpose.

After studying Figure 7-13, answer the following question.

Figure 7-13 *Network Diagram 1 for Scenario 7-1*

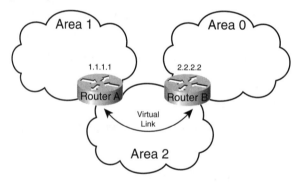

1. Explain the purpose of the virtual link in Figure 7-13.

   Figure 7-14 shows the network of another company for which the administrator worked previously. Examine the figure and then answer the questions.

2. Does the topology map in Figure 7-14 show a valid design?

3. Why would a company implement this design?

Figure 7-14   *Network Diagram 2 for Scenario 7-1*

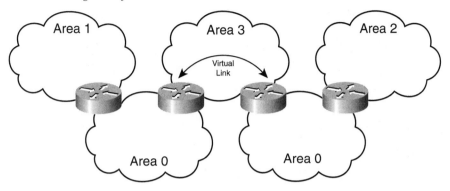

Scenario 7-2

Refer to Figure 7-15 and design the addressing scheme for the network. Then write the configuration for the central router.

Be sure to include the following:

1.   Address the network using the private network 10.0.0.0. Design the addressing scheme so that it allows for the summarization of addresses between areas. Show the summarization that you allocate, and explain your reasons for your choices.

Area 0 is using a prefix of 28 bits within the area.

Area 2 is using a prefix of 22 bits within the area.

Area 3 is using a prefix of 24 bits within the area.

Area 4 is using a prefix of 30 bits for the serial connections. It is using a 28-bit prefix for the connections to the Ethernet routers. Do not include the subnets attached to the LANs in Area 4.

2.   Issue the commands for the main router in Figure 7-15 to configure the following:

— The router ID

— The network commands to place the appropriate interfaces into the correct areas

— The configuration of the totally stubby area (Area 3)

— The configuration of the stub (Area 4)

— Summarization between areas

— The election of the central router as designated router, where appropriate

Figure 7-15 *The Diagram for Configuration Scenario 7-2*

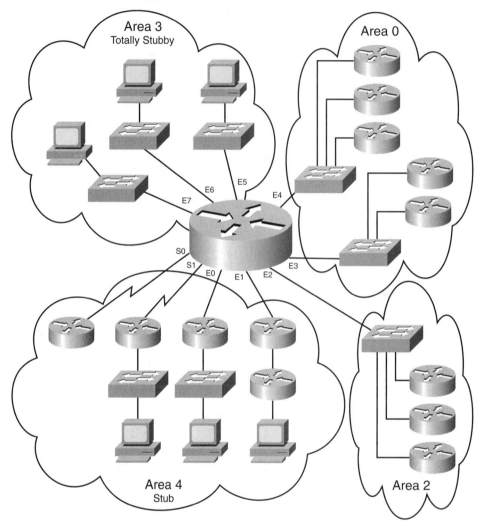

Scenario 7-3

Use Figure 7-16 for this scenario.

The users of the network are complaining about the slowness of the network, particularly when trying to access the Internet. Examine the configuration in Example 7-14 in conjunction with Figure 7-16, and give reasons for any slowness or lack of connectivity that you can see on the network. Provide current configuration commands to correct any errors that you find.

Figure 7-16 *The Diagram for Configuration Scenario 7-3*

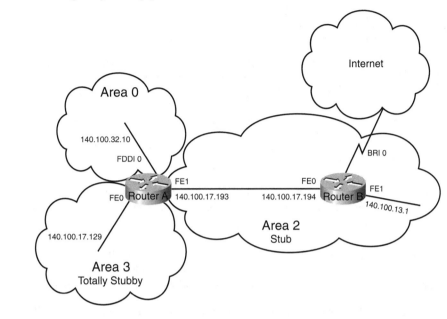

Example 7-14 *Configuring OSPF Example for Scenario 7-3*

```
ROUTER A
Router(config)# router ospf 100
Router(config-router)# network 140.100.17.128 0.0.0.15 area 3
Router(config-router)# network 140.100.17.192 0.0.0.15 area 2
Router(config-router)# network 140.100.32.0 0.0.0.0 area 0
Router(config-router)# area 2 stub
Router(config-router)# area 3 stub no-summary
Router(config-router)# area 3 default-cost 15
!
Router(config-router)# interface FastEthernet0
Router(config-if)# ip address 140.100.17.129 255.255.255.240
!
Router(config-if)# interface FastEthernet1
Router(config-if)# ip address 140.100.17.193 255.255.255.240
!
Router(config-if)# interface Fddi0
Router(config-if)# ip address 140.100.32.10 255.255.255.240
Router(config-if)# exit
ROUTER B
Router(config)# router ospf 100
Router(config-router)# network 140.100.0.0 0.0.255.255 area 2
!
Router(config-router)# interface FastEthernet0
Router(config-if)# ip address 140.100.17.194 255.255.255.240
```

continues

Example 7-14 *Configuring OSPF Example for Scenario 7-3 (Continued)*

```
Router(config-if)# no ip directed-broadcast
Router(config-if)# ip ospf priority 100
!
Router(config-if)# interface FastEthernet1
Router(config-if)# ip address 140.100.13.1 255.255.255.240
Router(config-if)# no ip directed-broadcast
!
Router(config-if)# exit
```

Answer the questions that follow:

1. There are problems with Router B. There is inconsistency in the routing table, and the system is extremely slow. What commands would you use to identify the problem? In examining the diagram and configuration, what problems can you see?

2. Router A is having problems connecting to Area 0. This is causing problems in other areas because Router A is used to connect to Area 0. What commands would you use to identify the problem? In examining the diagram and configuration, what problems can you see?

3. Issue the commands that would be used to correct the configuration problems that you see in the example configuration for Routers A and B.

4. When you issue the **show ip ospf** interface command, you notice that there is a discrepancy in the timers on the link between Routers A and B. The transmit timer on Router A is set to 5, and the retransmit timer is set to 1. What problems would this cause? What command would you use to change the timers, and what are the default settings?

Scenario Answers

The answers provided in this section are not necessarily the only possible answers to the questions. The questions are designed to test your knowledge and to give practical exercise in certain key areas. This section is intended to test and exercise skills and concepts detailed in the body of this chapter.

If your answer is different, ask yourself whether it follows the tenets explained in the answers provided. Your answer is correct not if it matches the solution provided in the book, but rather if it has included the principles of design laid out in the chapter.

In this way, the testing provided in these scenarios is deeper: It examines not only your knowledge, but also your understanding and ability to apply that knowledge to problems.

If you do not get the correct answer, refer to the text and review the subject tested. Be certain to also review your notes on the question to ensure that you understand the principles of the subject.

Scenario 7-1 Answers

1. *Explain the purpose of the virtual link in Figure 7-13.*

    In this example, Area 1 does not have a direct physical connection into Area 0. A virtual link must be configured between Router A and Router B. Area 2 is to be used as a transit area, and Router B is the entry point into Area 0. This way, Router A and Area 1 will have a logical connection to the backbone.

2. *Does the topology map in Figure 7-14 show a valid design?*

    Yes, the topology map in Figure 7-14 shows a valid design.

3. *Why would a company implement this design?*

    OSPF allows linking discontinuous parts of the backbone using a virtual link. In some cases, different Area 0s need to be linked together. This can occur, for example, if a company is trying to merge two separate OSPF networks into one network with a common Area 0. In other instances, virtual links are added for redundancy in case some router failure causes the backbone to be split in two. Whatever the reason might be, a virtual link can be configured between separate ABRs that touch Area 0 from each side and that have a common area between them.

Scenario 7-2 Answers

Refer to Figure 7-15 and design the addressing scheme for the network. Then write the configuration for the central router.

Table 7-7 shows a possible addressing scheme using the criteria stated in Scenario 7-1. Taking the private address 10.0.0.0, there is a great deal of flexibility in the addressing scheme that can be devised. Remember, however, that careful filtering is required if the organization is to connect to the Internet.

The addressing scheme proposed here is broken out by area. It is not exhaustive in terms of designing an addressing policy down to the LAN level; instead, it deals with the principles of addressing and summarization.

Note in the allocation of addresses that this scenario deals with the allocation of subnets. The addresses displayed in this table are the address ranges of the available subnets, given the prefix length.

Table 7-7   *Allocation of Addresses for Scenario 7-2*

Area	Subnet/Prefix	Subnet Range	Reasons
0	10.0.0.0/28	10.0.0.16 to 10.0.255.224	The use of the 0s in the second octet is an easy reminder that you are in Area 0. Because Area 0 is a transit area, it will be small. The addressing within the area would be allocated the prefix of 28 bits, allowing the range of subnets shown. The number of hosts on each of these subnets would be 15.
2	10.2.0.0/22	10.2.0.0 to 10.2.252.0	Again, the private addressing of 10.0.0.0 as a Class A address is so large that full use can be made of the documentation advantages of the addressing scheme. The second octet allows Area 2 to be identified. The prefix of 22 bits is used within the area. This allows 1022 hosts on each network, which is good for further VLSM and VLANs in switched environments.
3	10.3.0.0/24	10.3.0.0	The second octet identifies the area. Within the area, a 24-bit prefix is used to address the LANs.
4	10.4.0.0/28 ... 10.4.100.0/30	Ethernet: 10.4.0.16 to 10.4.255.240 Serial: 10.4.100.0 to 10.4.100.250	The second octet identifies the area. Within the area, a 30-bit mask is used to identify the serial links on which only two addresses are needed. The subnet 10.4.100.0 was chosen as the subnet to sub-subnet for the serial links simply to ease troubleshooting; all serial links in the company in any area would be assigned the third octet of 100. A 28-bit mask was chosen for the Ethernet connections to allow the creation of many subnets.

Example 7-15 demonstrates a sample configuration for Scenario 7-2. The configuration file is for the central router.

Example 7-15   *Sample Configuration of Scenario 7-2*

```
Router(config)# router ospf 100
Router(config-router)# network 10.0.0.0 0.0.255.255 area 0
! Network Commands
Router(config-router)# network 10.2.0.0 0.0.255.255 area 2
Router(config-router)# network 10.3.0.0 0.0.255.255 area 3
Router(config-router)# network 10.4.0.0 0.0.255.255 area 4
Router(config-router)# area 3 stub no-summary
! Totally Stubby Area
Router(config-router)# area 4 stub
! Stub Area
Router(config-router)# area 0 range 10.0.0.0 255.255.0.0
! Summarization between areas
Router(config-router)# area 2 range 10.2.0.0 255.255.0.0
Router(config-router)# area 3 range 10.3.0.0 255.255.0.0
Router(config-router)# area 4 range 10.4.0.0 255.255.0.0
Router(config)# interface e0
Router(config-if)# ip address 10.4.0.33 255.255.255.240
Router(config)# interface e1
Router(config-if)# ip address 10.4.0.17 255.255.255.240
Router(config)# interface e2
Router(config-if)# ip address 10.2.4.1 255.255.252.0
!Election of Designated Router
Router(config-if)# ip ospf priority 64
Router(config)# interface e3
Router(config-if)# ip address 10.0.0.193 255.255.255.240
Router(config-if)# ip ospf priority 0
!Ensures Router not elected as Designated Router
Router(config)# interface e4
Router(config-if)# ip address 10.0.0.129 255.255.255.240
Router(config-if)# ip ospf priority 0
!Ensures Router not elected as Designated Router
Router(config)# interface e5
Router(config-if)# ip address 10.3.3.1 255.255.255.0
Router(config)# interface e6
Router(config-if)# ip address 10.3.2.1 255.255.255.0
Router(config)# interface e7
Router(config-if)# ip address 10.3.1.1 255.255.255.0
Router(config)# interface s0
Router(config-if)# ip address 10.4.0.9 255.255.255.252
Router(config)# interface s1
Router(config-if)# ip address 10.4.0.5 255.255.255.252
Router(config)# interface loopback 0
!Router ID set by configuring loopback command
Router(config-if)# ip address 10.100.100.101 255.255.255.255
```

Scenario 7-3 Answers

1. *There are problems with Router B. There is inconsistency in the routing table, and the system is extremely slow. What commands would be used to identify the problem? In examining the diagram and configuration, what problems can you see?*

    Router B has been configured to be the designated router for the LAN, which means that it is dealing with all the traffic on the LAN associated with the management of OSPF. Given that the system is an older Cisco router, it is a poor choice for a designated router. A better choice would be Router A, which is a larger system that connects directly to Area 0, making it a better choice from the standpoint of the network design. If Router B were a larger system, there could be an argument for making it the designated router to elevate Router A, which would otherwise be functioning as both the ABR and the designated router.

    The router has not been configured as a stub, so the communication between Router A and Router B will be confused, preventing any communication between the two routers.

2. *Router A is having problems connecting to Area 0. This is causing problems in other areas because Router A is used to connect to Area 0. What commands would be used to identify the problem? In examining the diagram and configuration, what problems can you see?*

    Router A is configured incorrectly. The command that would show the problem would be either **show ip route**, **show ip protocols**, or **show ip ospf database**. The lack of LSA traffic would indicate a configuration problem. When examining the configuration, you would see that the mask on the configuration of the network command for Area 0 is wrong. The mask for 140.100.32.0 should be 0.0.0.15. Using the mask of 0.0.0.0 will place only interfaces with the IP address 140.100.32.0, which is a subnet address not an interface address. Therefore, there will be no communication of OSPF LSAs between the areas.

3. *Issue the commands that would be used to correct the configuration problems that you see in the example configuration for Routers A and B.*

    The commands that would solve these problems are as follows:

    On Router A:

    ```
    router ospf 100
    network 140.100.32.0 0.0.0.15 area 0
    interface fastethernet 1
    no ip ospf cost 10
    ip ospf priority 100
    ```

    On Router B:

    ```
    router ospf 200
    network 140.100.13.0 0.0.0.15 area 2
    area 2 stub
    interface FastEthernet0
    no ip ospf priority 100
    ```

4. *When you issue the **show ip ospf interface** command, you notice that there is a discrepancy in the timers on the link between Routers A and B. The transmit timer on Router A is set to 5, and the retransmit timer is set to 1. What problems would this cause? What command would be used to change the timers, and what are the default settings?*

The default setting for the transmit timer is set to 1 second, and the retransmit timer is set to 5 seconds. The transmit timer determines the estimated number of seconds that it takes to send an LSA to a neighbor. The retransmit timer states the number of seconds to wait for an acknowledgment before retransmitting an LSA.

If the transmit timer is not smaller than the retransmit timer, the interface retransmits in the belief that the other side did not receive the LSA. This leads to excess traffic, confusion in the topology database, and the possibility of flapping links. To correct the settings, issue the following subinterface commands:

```
ip ospf retransmit-interval seconds
ip ospf transmit-delay seconds
```

This chapter covers the following topics:

- **Special OSPF Areas**—Describes how OSPF design uses stub, totally stubby, and not-so-stubby areas to optimize resource utilization.

- **Configuring OSPF Authentication**—Describes the crucial topic of configuring specialized OSPF area types and MD5 authentication for OSPF. It also describes a few basic OSPF **show** and **debug** commands, which are sufficient for most verification and troubleshooting needs.

CHAPTER 8

OSPF Advanced Topics

So far, this book has discussed simple OSPF networks and scaling OSPF to enterprise sizes. These discussions have—by necessity—assumed that the network could be built with only network design concerns. Unfortunately, the real world can be messy. Politics and business imperatives often conflict with "best case" design practices, and all designs must assume a hostile environment.

The first part of this chapter looks at some of the special types of OSPF areas and how they help OSPF fit into particular situations. Areas can be stub, totally stubby, and not-so-stubby, and each of these has advantages in some cases.

The second part of this chapter shows how OSPF authentication can "lock down" the routing infrastructure. If an attacker is able to manipulate routers by injecting false packets, he can force traffic to flow past an observer or deny service. Authentication allows OSPF routers to extend trust carefully, instead of indiscriminately exchanging LSAs with any router.

Both topics fit together to help you understand how to take OSPF out of the "perfect world" setting in which it is often presented and fit it into the realities of your enterprise network.

"Do I Know This Already?" Quiz

The purpose of the "Do I Know This Already?" quiz is to help you decide what parts of this chapter to use. If you already intend to read the entire chapter, you do not necessarily need to answer these questions now.

The 9-question quiz, derived from the major sections in the "Foundation Topics" portion of the chapter, helps you determine how to spend your limited study time.

Table 8-1 outlines the major topics discussed in this chapter and the "Do I Know This Already?" quiz questions that correspond to those topics.

Table 8-1 *"Do I Know This Already?" Foundation Topics Section-to-Question Mapping*

Foundation Topics Section	Questions Covered in This Section	Score
Special OSPF Areas	1–7	
Configuring OSPF Authentication	8–9	
Total Score		

> **CAUTION** The goal of self-assessment is to gauge your mastery of the topics in this chapter. If you do not know the answer to a question or are only partially sure of the answer, you should mark this question wrong for purposes of the self-assessment. Giving yourself credit for an answer you correctly guess skews your self-assessment results and might provide you with a false sense of security.

1. Which of the following are *not* OSPF area types?

    a. Special

    b. Stub

    c. Not-so-Stubby (NSSA)

    d. Sorta-Stubby (SSA)

    e. Totally Stubby

2. Which of the following are advantages of stub areas over standard areas?

    a. Stubby areas use less memory.

    b. Stubby areas utilize the processor less.

    c. Stubby areas block type 4 LSAs.

    d. Stubby areas use a distance vector sub-protocol.

3. How are totally stubby areas different from stub areas?

    a. Totally stubby areas block type 1 and 2 LSAs.

    b. Totally stubby areas block type 3 and 4 LSAs.

    c. Totally stubby areas block type 5 and 6 LSAs.

    d. Totally stubby areas use a default route.

4. Which of the following OSPF router types are allowed inside a totally stubby area?

    a. Backbone Router

    b. Area Border Router

    c. Autonomous System Border Router

    d. Virtual Link Router

5. Which of the following OSPF router types are allowed inside a not-so-stubby area?

    a. Backbone Router

    b. Area Border Router

    c. Autonomous System Border Router

    d. Virtual Link Router

6. What command is used on routers inside OSPF area 7 if it is a totally stubby area?

   a. **area 7 stub**

   b. **area 7 nssa**

   c. **area 7 stub no-summary**

   d. **area 7 nssa no-summary**

7. What command is used on the ABR of OSPF area 7 if it is a totally stubby area?

   a. **area 7 stub**

   b. **area 7 nssa**

   c. **area 7 stub no-summary**

   d. **area 7 nssa no-summary**

8. Which of the following are options for OSPF authentication?

   a. AES

   b. Plaintext

   c. Null

   d. MD5

   e. Rijndael

9. Which commands are needed to implement plain-text passwords between OSPF neighbors using a password of cisco?

   a. **ip ospf authentication-key** *cisco*

   b. **ip ospf authentication**

   c. **ip ospf message-digest-key 2 md5** *cisco*

   d. **ip ospf authentication message-digest**

The answers to this quiz are found in Appendix A, "Answers to Chapter 'Do I Know This Already?' Quizzes and Q&A Sections." The suggested choices for your next step are as follows:

■ **7 or less overall score**—Read the entire chapter. This includes the "Foundation Topics," "Foundation Summary," and "Q&A" section.

■ **8 overall score**—Begin with the "Foundation Summary" section and then go to the "Q&A" section at the end of the chapter. If you have trouble with these exercises, read the appropriate sections in "Foundation Topics."

■ **9 overall score**—If you want more review on these topics, skip to the "Foundation Summary" section and then go to the "Q&A" section. Otherwise, move to the next chapter.

Foundation Topics

Special OSPF Areas

OSPF supports several types of areas, including standard areas, stub areas, totally stubby areas, and not-so-stubby (NSSA) areas. These special area types bring flexibility to OSPF network design, allowing OSPF to fit comfortably into the niches that otherwise could not be served, such as branch offices running legacy router hardware.

Remember that an area is a piece of the OSPF routing domain that implements the Dijkstra algorithm to pick paths. Path information is passed as a block between areas. Areas allow a large network to be broken into fractions that are small enough to reasonably run SPF.

The problem that can occur in OSPF is that an area can become too rich in LSA information and routers can become overloaded with information. Routers, particularly slower routers with less memory, can have their memory overwhelmed by the sheer volume of advertisements. Alternatively, even when memory is plentiful, the processor sometimes cannot process OSPF information fast enough to keep up with changes.

Figure 8-1 shows how a standard area handles the various LSA types. An ABR for a standard area passes all routes—external and inter-area—through to the standard area.

Figure 8-1 *Standard-Area ABR Passes All Routes*

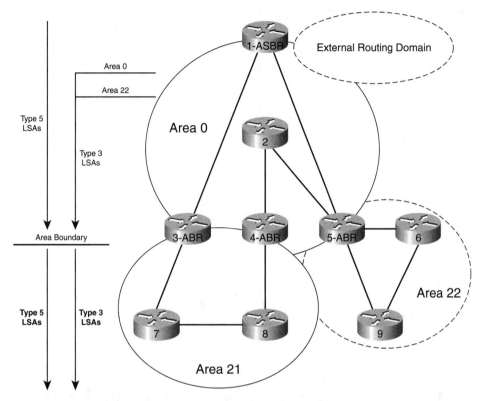

All the stub area types—stub, totally stubby, and not-so-stubby—deal in varying degrees with trying to limit the information that routers in an area must track. Certain characteristics unite all the stub area types:

■ Area 0 cannot be a stub.

■ All routers in the area must agree that it is a stub area.

■ No virtual links may traverse a stub area.

Stub Areas

Stub areas are areas where the ABR filters all external advertisements and replaces them with a default route. Because a large portion of a routing table might come from external routes, this simple substitution can dramatically impact the size of the routing table that must be maintained internally. Recall that external routes are those which are redistributed from another routing process.

Figure 8-2 shows how the ABR for a stub area passes routes. A stub-area ABR passes all inter-area routes, but replaces external routes with a default route.

Figure 8-2   *Stub Area*

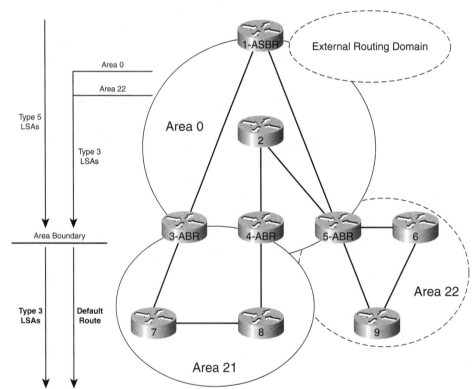

The reduction in routing table size comes with a cost, however. Routers in a stub area will always route external traffic through the closest ABR. Sometimes this will cause inefficient routing, as demonstrated in Figure 8-3. Router 8 wants to send traffic to the Internet through the ASBR. Because both stub-area ABRs are replacing specific Internet routes with a default route, Router 8 sends the traffic toward the closest ABR. Routing through Routers 7 and 3 would probably have been more efficient.

Figure 8-3 *External Path Selection in a Stub Area*

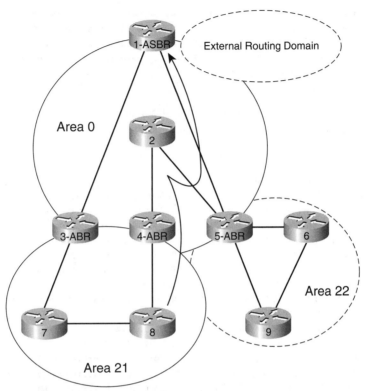

Although Figure 8-3 does not show IP addresses, assume that the routing table in Example 8-1 shows a routing table for Router 8 in a standard area 21.

Example 8-1 *Routes in a Standard Area*

```
         10.0.0.0/32 is subnetted, 4 subnets
O IA     10.0.22.5 [110/782] via 10.21.1.4, 00:01:35, FastEthernet0/0
O IA     10.0.22.6 [110/782] via 10.21.1.4, 00:01:35, FastEthernet0/0
O IA     10.0.22.9 [110/782] via 10.21.1.4, 00:01:35, FastEthernet0/0
O IA     10.0.0.1 [110/1] via 10.21.1.4, 00:01:35, FastEthernet0/0
O IA     10.0.0.2 [110/782] via 10.21.1.7, 00:02:52, Serial0/0/0
                   [110/782] via 10.21.1.4, 00:02:52, FastEthernet0/0
         10.0.0.0/8 is variably subnetted, 7 subnets, 2 masks
O        10.21.1.0/24 [110/10] via 10.21.1.4, 00:03:22, FastEthernet0/0
C        10.21.2.0/24 is directly connected, Loopback0
C        10.21.3.0/24 is directly connected, Serial0/0/0
O        10.0.1.0/24 [110/20] via 10.21.1.7, 00:04:01, Serial0/0/0
O        10.0.2.0/24 [110/30] via 10.21.1.4, 00:04:01, FastEthernet0/0
O        10.0.3.0/24 [110/30] via 10.21.1.4, 00:04:01, FastEthernet0/0
O        10.0.4.0/24 [110/40] via 10.21.1.4, 00:04:01, FastEthernet0/0
```

continues

Example 8-1 *Routes in a Standard Area (Continued)*

```
O IA    10.22.1.0/24 [110/40] via 10.21.1.4, 00:04:01, FastEthernet0/0
O IA    10.22.2.0/24 [110/40] via 10.21.1.4, 00:04:01, FastEthernet0/0
O IA    10.22.3.0/24 [110/40] via 10.21.1.4, 00:04:01, FastEthernet0/0
O E2    10.255.254.0/24 [110/50] via 10.21.1.4, 00:02:39, FastEthernet0/0
O E2    10.255.255.0/24 [110/50] via 10.21.1.4, 00:02:39, FastEthernet0/0
```

Example 8-2 shows the resulting routing table after making area 21 a stub area. Notice that the external routes (marked "E2") have been replaced by a default route.

Example 8-2 *Routes in a Stub Area*

```
        10.0.0.0/32 is subnetted, 4 subnets
O IA    10.0.22.5 [110/782] via 10.21.1.4, 00:02:39, FastEthernet0/0
O IA    10.0.22.6 [110/782] via 10.21.1.4, 00:02:39, FastEthernet0/0
O IA    10.0.22.9 [110/782] via 10.21.1.4, 00:02:39, FastEthernet0/0
O IA    10.0.0.1 [110/1] via 10.21.1.4, 00:02:39, FastEthernet0/0
O IA    10.0.0.2 [110/782] via 10.21.1.7, 00:02:52, Serial0/0/0
                 [110/782] via 10.21.1.4, 00:02:52, FastEthernet0/0
        10.0.0.0/8 is variably subnetted, 7 subnets, 2 masks
O       10.21.1.0/24 [110/10] via 10.21.1.4, 00:03:22, FastEthernet0/0
C       10.21.2.0/24 is directly connected, Loopback0
C       10.21.3.0/24 is directly connected, Serial0/0/0
O       10.0.1.0/24 [110/20] via 10.21.1.7, 00:04:01, Serial0/0/0
O       10.0.2.0/24 [110/30] via 10.21.1.4, 00:04:01, FastEthernet0/0
O       10.0.3.0/24 [110/30] via 10.21.1.4, 00:04:01, FastEthernet0/0
O       10.0.4.0/24 [110/40] via 10.21.1.4, 00:04:01, FastEthernet0/0
O IA    10.22.1.0/24 [110/40] via 10.21.1.4, 00:04:01, FastEthernet0/0
O IA    10.22.2.0/24 [110/40] via 10.21.1.4, 00:04:01, FastEthernet0/0
O IA    10.22.3.0/24 [110/40] via 10.21.1.4, 00:04:01, FastEthernet0/0
O*IA 0.0.0.0/0 [110/2] via 10.1.1.1, 00:01:51, FastEthernet0/0
```

The command to implement a stub area on an ABR is

```
Router(config-router)# area area-id stub
```

All internal routers in a stub area must have this same command so that all hellos agree on the stub area flag.

An example configuration of an ABR is shown in Example 8-3.

Example 8-3 *ABR Configuration to Create a Stub Area*

```
Router ospf 1
 Network 10.0.0.0 0.0.255.255 area 0
 Network 10.21.0.0 0.0.255.255 area 21
Area 21 stub
```

Totally Stubby Areas

Totally stubby areas are areas where the ABR filters all inter-area and external advertisements and replaces them with a default route. Note that the totally stubby option is Cisco proprietary. Because a larger portion of a routing table comes from other areas or external sources, this restricts the routing table to internal routes plus a default.

Figure 8-4 shows how the ABR for a totally stubby area passes routes. A totally stubby ABR removes all inter-area and external routes and replaces them with a default route.

Figure 8-4 *A Totally Stubby Area*

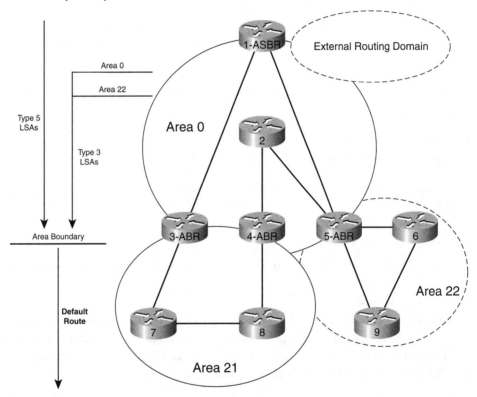

Continuing with the sample routing table from Example 8-2, Example 8-4 shows how the same routing table could be reduced in a totally stubby area.

Example 8-4 *Routes in a Totally Stubby Area*

```
      10.0.0.0/32 is subnetted, 4 subnets
      10.0.0.0/8 is variably subnetted, 7 subnets, 2 masks
O        10.21.1.0/24 [110/10] via 10.21.1.4, 00:03:22, FastEthernet0/0
C        10.21.2.0/24 is directly connected, Loopback0
                                                                    continues
```

Example 8-4   *Routes in a Totally Stubby Area (Continued)*

```
C        10.21.3.0/24 is directly connected, Serial0/0/0
O        10.0.1.0/24 [110/20] via 10.21.1.7, 00:05:59, Serial0/0/0
O        10.0.2.0/24 [110/30] via 10.21.1.4, 00:05:59, FastEthernet0/0
O        10.0.3.0/24 [110/30] via 10.21.1.4, 00:05:59, FastEthernet0/0
O        10.0.4.0/24 [110/40] via 10.21.1.4, 00:05:59, FastEthernet0/0
O*IA 0.0.0.0/0 [110/2] via 10.1.1.1, 00:03:51, FastEthernet0/0
```

The command to implement a totally stubby ABR is

```
Router(config-router)# area area-id stub no-summary
```

The **area** *area-id* **stub no-summary** command is only entered on the ABR of a totally stubby area. The other routers in the totally stubby area are only configured with the **area** *area-id* **stub** command.

All internal routers in a stub area must have the stub area flag set. This can be done with the following **stub** command:

```
Router(config-router)# area area-id stub
```

Example 8-5 shows a sample configuration of an ABR.

Example 8-5   *ABR Configuration to Create a Totally Stubby Area*

```
Router ospf 1
  Network 10.0.0.0 0.0.255.255 area 0
  Network 10.21.0.0 0.0.255.255 area 21
Area 21 stub no-summary
```

Not-So-Stubby Areas

Since stub areas cannot carry external routes, type 5 advertisements are not allowed in stub areas. Since type 5 LSAs are not allowed in stub areas, ASBRs cannot be located in stub areas. The problem is that sometimes the best solution to a design problem is to allow external routes. This problem is solved with not-so-stubby areas (NSSA).

An NSSA can be not-so-stubby or not-so-(totally)-stubby; either way an NSSA is a stub area that allows an ASBR. The ASBR understands that type 5 LSAs are not permitted and so disguises the LSAs as type 7. In all other respects, NSSA operates just like a stub area. NSSA is an Internet standard.

The type 7 advertisements cross the NSSA and are converted back to type 5 LSAs at the ABR. NSSA external routes show up as N1 or N2 instead of E1 or E2.

Note that the ABR of an NSSA does not automatically generate a default route; the **no-summary** or **default-originate** optional keywords must be appended to the **area nssa** *area-id* command for that to happen.

The command to implement a stub or totally stubby NSSA ABR is

```
Router(config-router)# area area-id nssa [no-summary]
```

All internal routers in an NSSA must recognize the NSSA area. This can be done with the **area nssa** command:

```
Router(config-router)# area area-id nssa
```

Troubleshooting

There are several useful **show** commands for looking at stub areas:

- **show ip ospf**

- **show ip route**

- **show ip ospf database**

- **show ip ospf database nssa-external**

When troubleshooting, **show ip protocols** provides an overview of active routing and is a good place to start. The **show ip ospf** command displays common OSPF parameters, while **show ip route** shows the current routing table so that the current routing may be analyzed.

The database commands are useful in particular areas once you identify the problem as pertaining to OSPF. These commands allow you to examine the routes in the topological database. Inter-area and external routes offer a clue about the effectiveness of stub area settings.

Configuring OSPF Authentication

An attacker who could forge OSPF packets could force routes along paths that are easier to intercept, could deny service, or could make forged websites appear to exist at the real IP addresses. OSPF, by default, trusts all OSPF speakers and is susceptible to forged traffic.

As the network became more dangerous, authentication was developed for OSPF. Authentication allows neighbors to identify themselves as legitimate through a shared secret. There are three authentication modes:

- null (no authentication)

- plaintext password

- Message Digest (MD5) hash

The following sections describe the plaintext password and MD5 hash authentication methods.

Plaintext Password Authentication

Password authentication provides little security. Any attacker with access to the medium can capture traffic and easily read the password. Nevertheless, it is presented here as an easy way to introduce the topic before considering the more appropriate method: MD5.

OSPF authentication is configured on an interface. At an interface configuration prompt, a key is set with the **ip ospf authentication** command:

```
Router(config-if)# ip ospf authentication-key password
```

> **NOTE** Prior to Cisco IOS Software version 12.0, authentication was set per-area. All routers in a given area had to share a password. This was less flexible than the newer interface-based shared secret.

Other routers connected through this interface should share this password. Next, enable authentication with the following command:

```
Router(config-if)# ip ospf authentication
```

Message Digest Authentication

MD5 hash authentication provides good security, ensuring that received messages can be trusted because they come from a source that knows the shared secret.

To configure OSPF MD5 authentication, first set a key. A key number is used in combination with the password to create a hash. The key is also useful when changing passwords, because more than one key may be active at a time. Other routers connected through this interface should share this password and key number. Use the following command syntax:

```
Router(config-if)# ip ospf message-digest-key key md5 password
```

Next, enable authentication using the message-digest keyword:

```
Router(config-if)# ip ospf authentication message-digest
```

Example 8-6 shows a configuration for a router that is set up for MD5 authentication.

Example 8-6 *Hash-Based OSPF Authentication*

```
Interface fastethernet0/0
 ip address 10.0.0.1 255.255.255.0
 ip ospf message-digest-key 1 md5 mi5kgbcia
ip ospf authentication message-digest
```

To verify that authentication is taking place, look at **show ip ospf neighbor** and verify that neighbors have become completely adjacent. The **show ip ospf interface** command also yields useful information about authentication.

The **debug ip ospf adjacency** command shows the status of authentication; it shows the progress from DOWN state to full state and—like **show ip ospf neighbor**—authentication success must be inferred. Unlike success, failure to authenticate is clearly shown using this command.

If two routers disagree over whether to use plaintext or MD5, the router will display an authentication type mismatch, as follows:

```
*Dec 03 17:52:17.527: OSPF: Rcv pkt from 10.0.0.1, Fastethernet0/0: Mismatch
    Authentication type.  Input packet specified type 0, we use type 1
```

If the routers disagree over the password, the router shows a key mismatch:

```
*Dec 03 17:55:13.044: OSPF: Rcv pkt from 10.0.0.1, Fastethernet0/0: Mismatch
    Authentication Key - Clear Text
```

Foundation Summary

The Foundation Summary provides a convenient review of many key concepts in this chapter. If you are already comfortable with the topics in this chapter, this summary might help you recall a few details. If you just read this chapter, this review should help solidify some key facts. If you are doing your final prep before the exam, the following lists and tables are a convenient way to review the day before the exam.

There are three special types of OSPF areas:

■ **Stub**—A stub area ABR only injects interarea LSAs and a default route into the area.

■ **Totally Stubby**—A totally stubby area ABR only injects a default route into the area. The totally stubby option is Cisco proprietary.

■ **NSSA**—An NSSA provides a mechanism for ASBRs attached to a (non-backbone) stub area to propagate external routes (via type 7 LSAs) into the routing domain.

The following authentication options are available for securing the OSPF configuration:

■ Plain text

■ MD5

The most useful commands for verifying and troubleshooting OSPF configurations related to the three specialized OSPF areas and OSPF authentication are

■ **show ip ospf neighbor**

■ **show ip ospf interface**

■ **debug ip ospf adjacency**

Q&A

The questions and scenarios in this book are designed to be challenging and to make sure that you know the answer. Rather than allowing you to derive the answers from clues hidden inside the questions themselves, the questions challenge your understanding and recall of the subject.

You can find the answers to these questions in Appendix A. For more practice with exam-like question formats, use the exam engine on the CD-ROM.

1. List the OSPF area types.

2. Which area types permit LSA type 1 and 2?

3. Which area types permit LSA type 3 and 4?

4. Which area type permits type 5?

5. What is OSPF LSA type 7?

6. What is the problem with multiple ABRs in a totally stubby area?

7. List advantages with totally stubby areas.

8. Which area types permit a virtual link?

9. Why must internal routers in a stub area be identified as stub?

10. What is the difference between null, plaintext, and MD5 authentication?

11. What is a message digest?

12. How do ASBR routes appear in the routing table inside an NSSA?

Part IV covers the following Cisco BSCI exam topics related to describing integrated IS-IS:

- Describe the features and benefits of integrated IS-IS.
- Configure and verify integrated IS-IS.

This list reflects the exam topics posted on Cisco.com at the publication time of this book.

Part IV: IS-IS

This chapter covers the following topics:

- **Introduction to Integrated IS-IS**— Describes the history of IS-IS and explains why IS-IS continues to be of interest to networkers.

- **Comparing OSPF and IS-IS**—Describes the similarities and differences between OSPF and IS-IS.

- **ISO Addressing for Integrated IS-IS**— Describes the addressing structure for ISO.

- **IS-IS Adjacency**—Describes how neighborship is formed.

- **Integrated IS-IS Operation**—Discusses the operation of IS-IS.

- **Integrated IS-IS Design Considerations**— Describes design issues, such as where to summarize and how to plan an IS-IS infrastructure.

CHAPTER 9

Fundamentals of the Integrated IS-IS Protocol

The topics in this chapter detail using Intermediate System-to-Intermediate System (IS-IS) as an IP routing protocol. This chapter assumes knowledge of routing protocols and, in particular, link-state routing protocols. This chapter introduces Integrated IS-IS by explaining the protocol's terminology and fundamental concepts.

Because Integrated IS-IS is similar to the Open Shortest Path First (OSPF) protocol, you should read the chapters on OSPF and reinforce your knowledge of the fundamentals of link-state protocols. Differences between Integrated IS-IS and OSPF are clearly outlined within this chapter.

"Do I Know This Already?"Quiz

The purpose of the "Do I Know This Already?" quiz is to help you decide what parts of this chapter to use. If you already intend to read the entire chapter, you do not necessarily need to answer these questions now.

The 22-question quiz, derived from the major sections in the "Foundation Topics" portion of the chapter, helps you determine how to spend your limited study time.

Table 9-1 outlines the major topics discussed in this chapter and the "Do I Know This Already?" quiz questions that correspond to those topics.

Table 9-1 *"Do I Know This Already?" Foundation Topics Section-to-Question Mapping*

Foundation Topics Section	Questions Covered in This Section	Score
Introduction to Integrated IS-IS	1–4	
Comparing IS-IS and OSPF	5–10	
ISO Addressing for Integrated IS-IS	11–13	
IS-IS Adjacency	14–17	
Integrated IS-IS Operation	18–19	
Integrated IS-IS Design Considerations	20–22	
Total Score		

> **CAUTION** The goal of self-assessment is to gauge your mastery of the topics in this chapter. If you do not know the answer to a question or are only partially sure of the answer, you should mark this question wrong for purposes of the self-assessment. Giving yourself credit for an answer you correctly guess skews your self-assessment results and might provide you with a false sense of security.

1. Which of the following packets are used by IS-IS?

   a. Hellos

   b. LSPs

   c. TVLs

   d. SNPs

2. Which of the following are valid hello packet types for IS-IS?

   a. Hello Level 1 LAN

   b. Hello Level 2 LAN

   c. Hello Level 1-2 LAN

   d. Hello Point-to-Point

3. IS-IS uses the Hello protocol to create and maintain adjacencies and neighbor relations. Which of the following are Hello packets used in IS-IS?

   a. A generic Hello

   b. Point-to-point Level 1, point-to-point Level 2, LAN Level 1, LAN Level 2

   c. Point-to-point, LAN Level 1, LAN Level 2

   d. Point-to-point Level 1, point-to-point Level 2, LAN

4. What does TLV stand for?

   a. Total/Length/Verification

   b. Type/Length/Value

   c. Topology/Long/Vector

   d. Temp/Length/Vector

5. What does the acronym CSNP represent?

   a. Current System Node Packet

   b. Complete Sequence Number Protocol

   c. Code Sequence Number Protocol

   d. Complete sequence number packet

6. Which description best fits a Level 1 router?

   a. An interarea router

   b. An HODSP router

   c. An internal router

   d. An intra-area router

7. A Level 2 router is similar to which type of OSPF router?

   a. ASBR

   b. ABR

   c. Stub

   d. Backbone internal router

8. Where are IS-IS areas defined?

   a. On the link

   b. On the interface

   c. At the process

   d. A separate process

9. Which of the following statements is true about Level 2 routers?

   a. Level 2 routers can send updates between routing areas.

   b. Level 2 routers must be placed contiguously.

   c. Level 2 routers are similar to OSPF stub routers.

   d. Level 2 routers must be in the same area.

10. Which of the following do IS-IS and OSPF have in common?

   a. Dijkstra algorithm

   b. Classless routing protocol

   c. Link-state routing protocol

   d. Summarization at the area boundary

11. ISO 10589 defines the NET as having three fields. What are these fields?

   a. IDP, DSP, SEL

   b. Area, System ID, NSEL

   c. IDP, DSP, System ID

   d. AFI, IDP, HODSP

12. Which of the following is a valid NET address?

   a. 47.0005.aa00.0301.16cd.00

   b. 47.0005.aa00.0301.16cd.01

   c. 47.0005.aa00.0301.16cd.ff

   d. 47.0005.aa00.19g6.3309.00

13. The NET system ID for a Level 2 router must be unique across which range?

   a. Interface

   b. Level 1 Area

   c. Backbone

   d. Global

14. For an IS-IS adjacency to be formed and maintained, both interfaces must agree on which of the following?

   a. If Level 1, both must be in the same area.

   b. The system ID must be unique.

   c. Both must be configured at the same level of routing (1 or 2).

   d. Hello timers.

15. How does the pseudonode represent all the routers on the LAN?

    a. Each router on the multiaccess LAN simulates an interface on the pseudonode.

    b. The pseudonode represents the physical link to which the routers are connected.

    c. The pseudonode is the virtual link between two discontiguous areas.

    d. Each link on every router on the LAN is summarized to form a pseudonode for the LAN.

16. A point-to-point link uses which packets to create and maintain neighbor tables and link-state databases?

    a. PSNP

    b. Hellos

    c. CSNP

    d. LSP

17. What is used to elect the DIS automatically?

    a. Highest SNPA address.

    b. Priority defined at the interface.

    c. The DIS must be manually configured.

    d. The highest loopback address.

18. What triggers an LSP update to be flooded to neighbors?

    a. When an adjacency goes up or down

    b. When a change occurs in the state of the interface

    c. When a change occurs in the routing table

    d. When an LSP is received

19. What is the default cost applied to the outgoing interface of a Cisco router configured to run IS-IS?

    a. 15

    b. 10

    c. Inverse of the bandwidth.

    d. There is no default. It must be configured.

20. Which of the following are IS-IS rules for summarization?

   a. All Level 1 routers can summarize routes.

   b. All Level 2 routers can summarize at the area boundary.

   c. If a Level 1-2 router is summarizing routes sent to a Level 2 router, all Level 1-2 routers must summarize in the same way.

   d. All the answers provided are correct.

21. What is the advantage of designing a totally flat network running Level 1-2 routing on every router?

   a. Easy migration to multiple areas.

   b. Easy system administration.

   c. It requires fewer resources from either the network or the router.

   d. Summarization can be configured within the area.

22. What would result if the only Level 1-2 router in an area failed?

   a. Another router would be elected as the Level 1-2 router.

   b. The autonomous system would not be able to communicate with the outside world.

   c. The area would be completely cut off from the rest of the network.

   d. No summary routes would be sent into the backbone area.

The answers to this quiz are found in Appendix A, "Answers to Chapter 'Do I Know This Already?' Quizzes and Q&A Sections." The suggested choices for your next step are as follows:

■ **14 or less overall score**—Read the entire chapter. This includes the "Foundation Topics," "Foundation Summary," and "Q&A" sections.

■ **15–18 overall score**—Begin with the "Foundation Summary" section, and then go to the "Q&A" section at the end of the chapter. If you have trouble with these questions, read the appropriate sections in "Foundation Topics."

■ **19 or more overall score**—If you want more review on these topics, skip to the "Foundation Summary" section and go to the "Q&A" section at the end of the chapter. Otherwise, move to the next chapter.

Foundation Topics

Introduction to Integrated IS-IS

IS-IS is an Interior Gateway Protocol (IGP) developed in the 1980s by DEC and submitted to the International Organization for Standardization (ISO) as the routing protocol for Open System Interconnection (OSI). The creation of IS-IS was part of an attempt to produce an international standard protocol suite that could compete with TCP/IP.

IS-IS was developed to provide

- A nonproprietary protocol

- A large and hierarchical addressing scheme

- An efficient protocol, allowing for fast, accurate convergence and low network overhead

The United States mandated that every system operated by the government be capable of running OSI; IS-IS was extended to pass IP routes to aid in this transition to OSI. In the end, however, the Internet, built on TCP/IP, prevailed as the de facto alternative to an international standard.

When IS-IS is used to support IP, it is properly referred to as *Integrated IS-IS*. This book simplifies that to "IS-IS" in many cases because any mention of IS-IS herein refers to its use as an IP routing protocol.

In recent years there has been renewed interest in IS-IS. This new interest is because IS-IS is protocol independent, scales well, and has the capacity to define type of service (ToS) routing (but ToS routing is not supported by IOS). IS-IS has been dusted off as a routing protocol for IPv6 or for use with MPLS, but this interest has yet to extend to widespread adoption.

Understanding the Lingo

In OSI-speak, a router is referred to as an intermediate-system (IS) and a PC is called an end-system (ES). Thus, IS-IS is a router-to-router protocol.

The network layer protocol in OSI is called the Connectionless Network Protocol (CLNP) and is used for the Connectionless Network Service (CLNS). IS-IS implementers need to understand only one detail of OSI: CLNS addressing. Because IS-IS started as an OSI routing protocol it uses a CLNS address as a router ID and to group the routers into areas. No actual CLNS traffic needs to be passed; the address is only used administratively.

OSI supports four routing levels, with IS-IS used for the middle two:

- Level 0 routing is used to find end-systems and uses end system-to-intermediate system (ES-IS).

- Level 1 routing is used to exchange routes within an area.

- Level 2 is the backbone between areas.

- Level 3 routing is used between autonomous systems and is the province of the Interdomain Routing Protocol (IDRP).

IS-IS is responsible for Levels 1 and 2. Routers may be in a Level 1 area, in the Level 2 backbone, or both. Level 1-2 routers connect areas to the backbone. Each level uses Dijkstra's SPF algorithm to select paths and each level converges quickly.

Network Layer Protocols Used in Integrated IS-IS

The IS-IS protocol data unit (PDU) is encapsulated directly into the data-link frame. All IS-IS packets share the same eight-octet header. After the fixed header, there are a number of optional variable-length fields that contain specific routing-related information. These variable-length fields are called TLV.

Each IS-IS PDU begins with a standard header. Next are the specific fields and the variable-length fields. The following sections describe the three IS-IS packet types: Hellos, LSPs, and SNPs.

Hellos

Adjacencies are formed by exchanging hellos—there are three different types of hellos.

- **End system hellos (ESH)**—ISO end systems use ESHs to attach to routers. IP end systems do not speak ESH, so IS-IS just attaches the local subnet.

- **Intermediate system hellos (ISH)**—Routers use ISHs to announce themselves back to the ES.

- **Intermediate-to-intermediate hellos (IIH)**—Routers use IIHs to meet IS neighbors. IIH is transmitted separately at Level 1 and Level 2.

Because the point-to-point and broadcast media work differently, adjacencies are formed differently. A point-to-point network has only one other router with which to communicate. Broadcast networks are multiaccess networks and can have a mixture of both Level 1 and Level 2 routers. For this reason, the broadcast or LAN network has two Hello formats: the Level 1 format and the Level 2 format. Hellos for broadcast media are referred to as LAN Hellos. Point-to-point Hello packets are used over point-to-point links. LAN Hello packets are used over broadcast links.

Table 9-2 summarizes the hellos used by IS-IS.

Table 9-2 *IS-IS Hellos*

Hello	Goes from	Goes to	Description
ESH	OSI ES	IS	Attaches ES to IS
ISH	IS	OSI ES	Announces IS
Level 1 IIH	L1 IS	L1 IS	Builds area
Level 2 IIH	L2 IS	L2 IS	Passes Level 2 adjacencies

LSP

The LSP from a Level 1 router is flooded to all routers in the area. The LSP contains a list of all the adjacencies.

Likewise, a Level 2 router floods the LSP to every other Level 2 router in the domain. However, this LSP contains the list of adjacencies to other Level 2 routers and the areas that the transmitting router can reach. The TLVs hold the Level 1 and Level 2 information, allowing the LSP format to be the same for both Level 1 and Level 2 routers.

TLVs are one of the strengths of IS-IS. TLVs provide flexibility and extensibility for the protocol. The protocol can adapt to changing needs and advances in technology by simply defining a new TLV.

The following is the structure of the TLV:

■ **Type**—Identifies the advertisement and all characteristics that pertain to it. For example, TLV 128 is an IP advertisement.

■ **Length**—The length of the following field. This is important because the Value field can be variable length.

■ **Value**—The advertisement, which takes the form of IP routes, IS neighbors, or authentication.

It is important to know which TLVs your equipment supports because this determines the design and configuration of the network. The receiving router ignores TLVs that are not supported.

Comparing IS-IS and OSPF

Integrated IS-IS and OSPF share a common heritage. Both protocols were developed around the same time, and reputedly borrowed ideas from one another. Therefore, IS-IS has more similarities than differences to OSPF. In fact, IS-IS could be described as "OSPF using only totally stubby areas."

IS-IS and OSPF are both link-state routing protocols based on the Dijkstra SPF algorithm. Both have a two-level hierarchy, support VLSM, and converge quickly. Both use hellos to meet and greet their neighbors and build a topology.

The main differences between OSPF and IS-IS are

- OSPF has a central area, whereas IS-IS has a backbone on top of its areas.

- IS-IS uses a single designated router (called a *designated intermediate system [DIS]*) and different timers.

- IS-IS sends advertisements in a standard form and in a single set of packets. OSPF advertisements vary based on type and are transmitted by type.

- IS-IS is encapsulated at the data link layer.

- OSPF is more closely associated with TCP/IP and is common in IP networks; IS-IS was deployed to support CLNS and IP concurrently in early ISP backbones.

The following sections elaborate on the differences between the two protocols as a way of describing IS-IS; however, it is important to understand that in all the most important ways the two protocols are similar.

Areas

Both OSPF and IS-IS support a two-level hierarchy. OSPF has a central area (Area 0) to which all other areas attach. OSPF interfaces belong in an area; routers that straddle two areas are called Area Border Routers (ABR).

In IS-IS the router is wholly in a Level 1 area. Level 1-2 routers, which are similar to OSPF ABRs, are in one area at Level 1 and also route separately at Level 2. IS-IS Level 2 may wind through Level 1 areas. Level 1 routers must be in the same area to exchange local routes and receive a default route from a Level 1-2 router. Level 2 routers send Level 2 updates across the backbone. These roles are shown in Figure 9-1.

LAN Topology

Like an OSPF designated router (DR), an IS-IS DIS exists to simulate a point-to-point topology across a multipoint environment. Because of this, a DIS is sometimes called a *pseudonode*. Despite their similarities, the IS-IS DIS is subtly different from OSPF.

The DIS exists separately at Level 1 and Level 2, and there is not a backup DIS. An OSPF DR is elected for life; IS-IS allows preemption if another router comes on line with a higher priority. Fewer adjacencies are formed in OSPF because the routers form adjacencies only with the DR and the BDR. In IS-IS, every router makes an adjacency with every other router on the medium. IS-IS LSPs are sent out only by the DIS on behalf of the pseudonode.

Figure 9-1 *IS-IS Level 1 and Level 2 Routers*

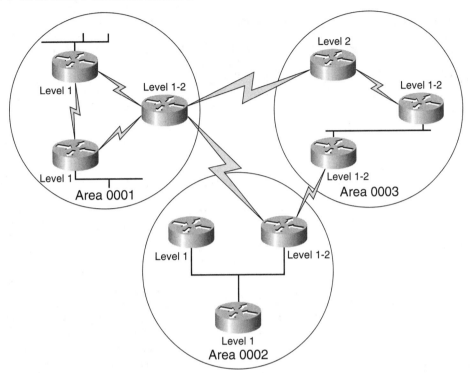

Advertisements

OSPF advertisements are packaged by type and an OSPF router may produce many packets to advertise current connectivity. IS-IS advertisements are all in a standard form: Type, Length, Value (TLV). The TLV structure means that advertisements can be easily grouped and advertised together. This results in fewer packets needed for LSPs and makes IS-IS adaptable. Table 9-3 lists the type codes supported by Cisco IOS.

IS-IS advertisements are called sequence number packets (SNP). SNPs list the LSPs in the transmitting router's link-state database in a condensed format. SNPs are never flooded but only sent between neighbors. SNPs are specific to each level of routing and can be a *complete SNP* (CSNP), which lists every LSP, or a *partial SNP* (PSNP), which lists some of the LSPs.

The way that the LSPs are handled is also slightly different and influences the design of networks running either protocol. Unrecognized LSPs are ignored and flooded in IS-IS; OSPF ignores and drops unrecognized LSAs.

Table 9-3 *TLVs Implemented by Cisco*

TLV	Name	Source	PDU	Description
1	Area Addresses	ISO 10589	Hello and LSPs	Area addresses of the router.
2	IS Neighbors	ISO 10589	LSPs	Lists IS neighbors. Neighbor ID is system ID plus an extra octet. If a pseudonode, the octet is a positive value. If a router, the octet is 0x00.
3	ES Neighbors	ISO 10589	Level 1 LSP	Lists ES neighbors, assuming the same cost as media.
5	Prefix Neighbors	ISO 10589	Level 2 LSP	The same as TLV 3 but stating a prefix rather than an ES.
6	IS Neighbors	ISO 10589	Hello	Lists system IDs from which a valid Hello has been received. Level 1 routers list Level 1 neighbors; Level 2 routers list Level 2 neighbors.
8	Padding	ISO 10589	Hello	Ignored. Used to pad to minimum length.
9	LSP Entries	ISO 10589	SNP	LSP state including remaining Lifetime, LSP ID, sequence number, and Checksum. Identifies LSP and ensures no duplication or corruption.
10	Authentication	ISO 10589	Hello, Level 1 and Level 2 LSP, and SNP	First octet states type of authentication (only clear text is defined in ISO 10589). An interface can be configured with a password and neighbors reject packets if the expected password is not found.
128	IP Internal Reachability	RFC 1195	Level 1 and Level 2 LSP	IP addresses known from interfaces within the area.
129	Protocols Supported	RFC 1195	Hello	Protocols that the transmitter supports (CLNS only, IP only, or both).
131	InterDomain Routing Protocol	RFC 1195	Level 2 LSP	Allows information from external routing protocols to be carried in Level 2 LSPs.
132	IP Interface Address	RFC 1195	Hello, LSP	IP address or addresses of the transmitting interface.

Encapsulation

Another major difference between IS-IS and OSPF is the encapsulation of the two protocols. IS-IS is protocol independent because it runs directly on top of the data link layer. OSPF is encapsulated into IP. This difference means that IS-IS can be adapted to circumstances by simply drafting a new TLV.

One example of the benefit of this approach to encapsulation is IPv6. When a new Layer 3 protocol was developed, IS-IS was quickly adapted to support it by creating new Ipv6 TLVs. OSPF took longer to adapt and its adaptation involved creating a new version of the protocol— OSPFv3.

Future Development

Development of IS-IS has been largely at a standstill for a number of years; however, it has picked up recently and Cisco is committed to bringing it into parity with OSPF in the future. Currently, OSPF has more area types and larger metrics. Information about OSPF is fairly well distributed, so finding good books and engineers prepared to work with OSPF is not difficult. At this point, the IS-IS advantages—encapsulation, TLV structure, and LSP processes—are not appreciated by enterprise users in the same way that OSPF is valued.

ISO Addressing for Integrated IS-IS

IS-IS is the product of a committee, and it has the feel of an academic solution that is intended to resolve every eventuality. Its addressing scheme thinks not just locally, but globally.

Where OSPF uses an IP address for a router id, IS-IS uses an ISO address for that same purpose. The ISO address comes in two forms, depending on what type of device is being addressed:

- Network Service Access Point (NSAP)

- Network Entity Title (NET)

The IS-IS addressing scheme is complex, but is defined by clear rules.

An ISO address varies from 8 to 20 octets (IP uses 4 bytes). ISO 10589 defines three parts to the address:

- **Area**—Area is like an IP subnet, describing a group or location.

- **ID**—ID identifies a particular member at that location, like the host portion of an IP address.

- **SEL**—Similar to a TCP port, SEL identifies a process on the host.

Figure 9-2 shows the complete ISO address.

Figure 9-2 *An ISO Address*

IDP		DSP		
AFI (1 octet)	IDI	High Order DSP	System ID (1-8 octets)	NSEL (1 octet)
AREA			ID	SEL

The following list explains the parts of an ISO address and their relationship:

- **Inter Domain Part (IDP)**—External routing. The IDP is used to route to the autonomous system. IDP is given by ISO and identifies the organization responsible for assigning the format for the rest of the address by defining the DSP structure. The IDP is subdivided into two parts:

    — **Authority and Format Identifier (AFI; also called Address Family Identifier)**— The first octet identifies the authority that dictates the format of the address and issues addresses. This byte is typically either 39 (Country Code), 47 (International Code), or 49 (private).

    — **Initial Domain Identifier (IDI)**—IDI is an organization in the AFI; as an analogy, the U.S. government is the AFI, and the General Services Agency (GSA) is the IDI, otherwise known as GOSIP. Because IS-IS is not used between Autonomous Systems, this can be left out.

- **Domain Specific Part (DSP)**—DSP is used to route within the autonomous system, and contains three fields:

    — **High Order DSP (HODSP)**—High Order DSP is typically the area within the autonomous system.

    — **System ID**—Identifies the system. The standard says a system ID can be either six or eight octets, but Cisco only implements a six-byte system ID. It must be unique and have the same length throughout the autonomous system. There are two easy ways to generate a unique system ID. One method is simply to use a MAC address. A second method is to treat each octet of an IP address as a three-digit number and transfer that to a system ID. Using this method, a system with a loopback of 192.168.77.1 would have a system ID of 1921.6807.7001. You could also just make up a number, but then you would need to track numbers to prevent repetition.

    — **NSEL**—NSEL is one byte and identifies the service at the network layer to which to hand the packet. 0x00 represents the device. An NSAP with a Selector byte of 0x00 is called a Network Entity Title (NET).

The fact that the address can take so many forms can cause confusion; remember, however, that there are only two layers of hierarchy. By providing such flexibility in the address space, the

ISO has ensured a decentralized address allocation and management, in addition to the ability to scale the network.

As with TCP/IP, the addressing scheme within an autonomous system can be the result of the creative genius of the network administrator or can be obtained from the AFI, an authorized ISO body such as ANSI or GOSIP.

The next sections discuss ISO addresses for Integrated IS-IS, and include an explanation of NETs and NSAP and a description of the rules for IS-IS addressing.

NETs and NSAPs

NETs and NSAPs are ISO addresses. The NET address is specifically the NSAP address of the host, with the NSEL set to 0x00. The NET is the form of the address used to identify routers.

Rules of ISO Addressing

The following list indicates a few rules that clarify ISO addressing:

- The ISO address is assigned to the system, not the interface.

- Typically, a router has one NET address. The limit is three NETs in a conventional IS-IS implementation; the limit is three NETs per area in a multi-area Integrated IS-IS implementation. Multiple addresses are used during transitions.

- If multiple NETs are configured on the same router, they all must have the same system ID.

- The area address must be the same for all routers in the same area.

- All Level 2 routers must have a system ID that is unique for the entire Level 2 domain. All Level 1 routers must have a system ID that is unique for the entire Level 1 area. Put simply: All routers must have a unique system ID.

- The system ID must be the same length for all ISs and ESs within a routing domain and Cisco only supports six-byte system IDs.

Example of a NET Address

The following are examples of NET addresses. AFI 49 means "make up your own address structure." Because we only need to differentiate areas, notice that the IDI has been left out.

The first example shows a NET address that uses the host MAC address as the system ID: 49.0005.AA00.0301.16CD.00. When interpreting an address, a Cisco router knows that the first byte is AFI, last byte is SEL, and the preceding six bytes are system ID. Anything between AFI and system ID is interpreted as area, so IDI is not necessary.

4 9 . 0 0 0 5 . A A 0 0 . 0 3 0 1 . 1 6 C D . 0 0
← To the Domain → ← Within the Domain →
Area   System ID   SEL

The second example shows a NET address that transliterates the host's loopback IP address of 144.132.16.19 as the system ID: 49.0001.1441.3201.6019.00.

4 9 . 0 0 0 1 . 1 4 4 1 . 3 2 0 1 . 6 0 1 9 . 0 0
← To the Domain → ← Within the Domain →
Area   System ID   SEL

The following example shows a GOSIP address with external routing information, along with the way IS-IS for IP would interpret it: 47. 0005.80ff.f800.0000. 0001.0000.0c00.1234.00. This structure is overly complicated for the way IS-IS is used today.

AFI	IDI	HODSP	System ID	SEL
47.	0005.80ff.f800.0000.	0001.	0000.0c00.1234.	00
Area			**System ID**	**SEL**

Basic Principles of Area Routing

IP subnets are treated as leaf-objects in the IS-IS SPF tree. Areas—recognized by the format of their NET—produce a summary into Level 2 and the Level 1-2 router and introduce a default route back into Level 1.

Routing to destinations within an area is straightforward. The first IS matches the destination to an entry in its routing table and selects the shortest path in exactly the same way OSPF would.

Routing between areas is only slightly complicated. The first IS receives traffic for an IP destination that is not in its routing table and decides to forward the traffic to the nearest Level 1-2 router. The Level 1-2 router uses its routing table to route it across Level 2 toward the nearest Level 1-2 router advertising a matching summary.

Borders in Integrated IS-IS are defined on the link, meaning that the entire router is in the Level 1 area. For Level 2 routing updates to be exchanged, all the routers capable of sending Level 2 updates must be contiguous. This is shown in Figure 9-3.

IS-IS Adjacency

Routers sharing a common data link layer become IS-IS neighbors if the Hello packets that they exchange meet the criteria for forming an adjacency. Although the process of finding a neighbor differs slightly depending on the media, the information sent in the Hellos is essentially the same.

Figure 9-3 *IS-IS Addresses and Areas*

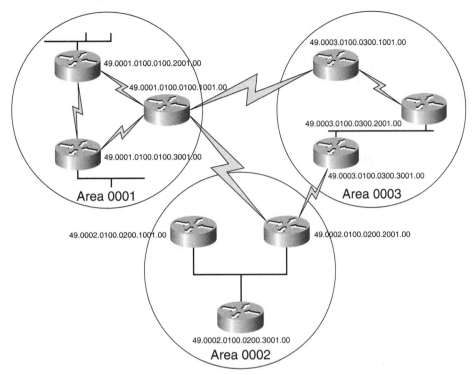

Each Hello states the originator of the Hello and the capabilities of its interface. If the Hellos are exchanged and the criteria are met, an adjacency is formed and the Integrated IS-IS neighbors exchange routing information in the form of LSPs. In this way, every router gathers the connected networks of every other router to create identical detailed topology maps of the network.

For an adjacency to be formed and maintained, both interfaces must agree on the following:

■ The maximum packet size (MTU) of the interface must be the same.

■ Both routers must support the same level of routing. A Level 1 router becomes adjacent to another Level 1 or a Level 1-2 router in the same area. A Level 2 router can become adjacent to a Level 2 or to a Level 1-2 router.

■ To connect to another area, at least one of the routers must be configured as a Level 1-2.

■ The system ID must be unique to each router.

■ If authentication is configured, it must be configured identically on both routers.

■ The Hello and hold timers must match.

Integrated IS-IS defines two network types—broadcast subnetworks and point-to-point networks—whereas OSPF uses five types. A broadcast network, as in OSPF, is a multiaccess data link that supports broadcasts and multicasts. The point-to-point links are deemed to be nonbroadcast and can be permanent virtual circuits (PVC) or dedicated lines.

IS-IS does not have an NBMA link type, so non-broadcast multiaccess links must be setup as either broadcasts or point-to-point networks. The recommended solution is to set them up as point-to-point using subinterfaces.

Establishing Adjacencies on a Point-to-Point Link

When point-to-point links are used, adjacency occurs after a Hello packet has been received. Next, each side sends a CSNP. The CSNP is a list of all the links held in the link-state database, which triggers a synchronization of the link-state database on each machine.

Periodic Hellos maintain the adjacency. If a router does not hear a Hello within the Hello holdtime, the neighbor is declared dead and the database is purged of any entries associated with the router. Cisco sets the default Hello multiplier to three. The holdtime is defined as the Hello time multiplied by the Hello multiplier, which makes the hold timer expire every 30 seconds.

Establishing Adjacencies on a Broadcast Link

On broadcast links, each IS receives packets sent by the DIS, minimizing the amount of traffic that needs to be generated to maintain the adjacencies and databases. The DIS has the responsibility of flooding the LSPs to all connected systems running Integrated IS-IS.

The adjacencies with the other routers are maintained by the DIS, which sends out Hellos every 3.3 seconds, three times the speed of other routers. This is to ensure the integrity of the adjacencies by identifying a problem very quickly. If there is a problem with the DIS, or a router with a higher priority appears, it is quickly identified and a new router is elected in the place of the old DIS, which is forced into retirement. The election is based first on the highest priority and then on the highest data-link address.

Establishing Adjacencies on an NBMA Link

The creation and maintenance of adjacencies becomes more complicated when used over non-broadcast links. An NBMA link is neither a broadcast medium nor a point-to-point link; it is a little of both. Furthermore, IS-IS does not have an NBMA link type. Using PVCs, NBMAs provide multiple connections, which could be viewed as a LAN. The confusion occurs when Integrated IS-IS sees the link is multiaccess. Having no knowledge of multiaccess WAN clouds, Integrated IS-IS believes that the medium is some form of LAN and therefore has broadcast capabilities. Although the LAN can be simulated, the WAN cloud has no inherent broadcast capabilities.

To avoid complications and possible errors, Cisco recommends that you configure the links as a series of point-to-point links. Do not use IS-IS on temporary connections such as dial-up.

Integrated IS-IS Operation

This section describes how the databases for IS-IS are created and maintained.

The routing process for IS-IS is divided into four stages:

- Update

- Decision

- Forwarding

- Receiving

The following sections focus on the update and decision processes.

The Update Process

The router can forward data packets to the remote destination only if it understands the topology. Each router generates an LSP that lists the router's neighbors and propagates it throughout the network. The flooding of LSPs ensures every router has an identical link-state database.

The affected routers generate LSPs whenever there is a change in the network. Any of the following trigger a new LSP to be flooded throughout the network:

- An adjacency either comes up or down.

- An interface changes state or is assigned a new metric.

- A route changes (for example, because of redistribution).

The following sections describe sending and receiving LSPs and determining whether the LSP in the database is valid.

Sending and Receiving LSPs

Routers store new LSPs in the link-state database and mark them for flooding. If the LSP is already present in the database, the router just acknowledges it and ignores it. The router sends the new LSP to its neighbors, which in turn flood to their neighbors and so on. Because Level 1 and Level 2 routers have their own link-state databases, Level 1 LSPs are flooded throughout the area; Level 2 LSPs are sent across all Level 2 adjacencies.

The process of propagating LSPs differs slightly depending on which medium the LSP was received.

Propagating LSPs on a Point-to-Point Interface

A point-to-point link does not need to ensure that multiple systems have synchronized databases. With only one other router with which to work, some reliance is given to the router's capability to determine the need to update so that bandwidth can be optimized.

The following list describes the point-to-point flooding process:

1. When an adjacency is established, both sides send a complete sequence number packet (CSNP) with a compressed version of their link-state database (router ID and the sequence number).

2. If there are any LSPs in the receiving router's database that were not in the received CSNP, the process sends a copy of the missing LSPs to the other router.

3. Likewise, if the database is missing any LSPs received in the CSNP, the receiving router requests the detailed or full LSP to be sent.

4. The individual LSPs are requested, sent, and acknowledged via partial-sequence number packets (PSNP).

5. When an LSP is sent, the router sets a timer, and if no explicit acknowledgement has been received before the timer expires, the LSP is re-sent. This timer is the minimumLSPTransmissionInterval and can be configured; the default on a Cisco router is five seconds.

Propagating LSPs on a Broadcast Link

A psuedonode on a broadcast link may need to send out both Level 1 and Level 2 updates. It sends these updates, using multicast MAC addresses, to all Level 1 routers and all Level 2 routers. Because the pseudonode is just that—a pretend system—a real node or system must enter the charade and perform the tasks of the pseudonode. The designated intermediate system (DIS) takes on much of the responsibility for synchronizing the databases on behalf of the pseudonode (recall that the DIS is comparable to the OSPF DR). The DIS has three tasks:

- Creating and maintaining adjacencies

- Creating and updating the pseudonode LSP

- Flooding the LSPs over the LAN

Following are the main steps in the flooding process:

1. On receipt of a CSNP, the router compares each compressed LSP with the link-state database.

2. If the database has a newer version of the LSP sent in the CSNP, or if there is no instance of a LSP in the CSNP, the router multicasts the LSP onto the LAN.

3. If the database is missing an LSP that was in the CSNP, it sends a PSNP requesting the full LSP. Although the router multicasts, it is only the DIS that responds.

Figure 9-4 summarizes the flow of CSNPs and PSNPs on broadcast and point-to-point links.

Figure 9-4 *Propagating CSNPs and PSNPs*

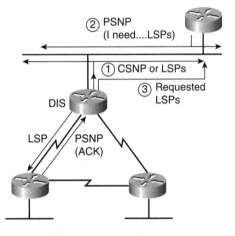

Determining Whether the LSP in the Database Is Valid

The LSP contains three fields that help determine whether the LSP that has been received is more recent than that held in the database, and whether it is intact or has been corrupted. These three fields are as follows:

- **Remaining Lifetime**—This is used to age-out old LSPs. If an LSP has been in the database for 20 minutes, it is assumed that the originating router has died. The refresh timer is set to 15 minutes.

  If the lifetime expires, the LSP has the content removed, leaving only the header. The lifetime is set to show that it is a new LSP, and then it is flooded through the network. All receiving routers accept the mutilated LSP, recognize that this means the route is bad, and purge the existing LSP from their databases.

- **Sequence Number**—This is an unsigned 32-bit linear number. The first LSP is allocated the sequence number 1, and the following LSPs are incremented.

- **Checksum**—If a router receives an LSP and the checksum does not compute correctly, the LSP is flushed and the lifetime is set to 0. The router floods the LSP, all routers purge the LSP, and the originating router retransmits a new LSP.

The Decision Process

After the link-state databases have been synchronized, it is necessary to decide which path to take to reach the destination. Because the routers and hosts may have multiple connections to each other, there may be many paths from which to choose.

To make the best path decision, link-state protocols employ the algorithm defined by Dijkstra. This algorithm creates a tree that shows the shortest paths to all destinations. The tree is used in turn to create the routing table.

If there is more than one path to a remote destination, the criteria by which the lowest cost paths are selected and placed in the forwarding database are as follows:

1. If there is more than one path with the lowest value metric, Cisco equipment places some or all paths into the table. Older versions of IOS support as many as six load-sharing paths, newer versions support more.

2. Internal paths are chosen before external paths.

3. Level 1 paths within the area are more attractive than Level 2 paths.

4. The address with the most specific address in IP is the address with the longest IP subnet mask.

5. If there is no path, the forwarding database sends the packet to the nearest Level 2 router, which is the default router.

The metric defines the cost of the path. Integrated IS-IS has four metrics, only one of which is required and supported. The metrics defined in ISO 10589 are as follows:

- **Default**—Every Integrated IS-IS router must support this metric. Cisco set the default for all interfaces to 10.

- **Delay**—Cisco does not support the transit delay metric.

- **Expense**—Cisco does not support the expense metric.

- **Error**—Cisco does not support the error metric.

By default, six-bit metrics are configured on the outgoing interface. A 10-bit field describes the total path cost. These default metrics are referred to as *narrow*.

Because it considered these inadequate, Cisco increased the metric size to 24 bits. This larger metric field provides more granularity to distinguish between paths and is referred to as *wide*.

To determine shortest path, the lowest metric is chosen, internal paths are chosen over external paths, and Level 1 routes have precedence over Level 2 routes.

The default metric is the only metric supported by Cisco, because each metric used in Integrated IS-IS requires a different link-state database calculation for both the Level 1 and Level 2 routes.

Integrated IS-IS Design Considerations

Optimizing the network relies on careful planning and design. Although each network is constrained by physical and technical limitations, you must strive to design your network to meet the needs of its users and accommodate the demands of various applications.

In Integrated IS-IS, the fundamental design considerations are areas and addressing. The next sections describe the Integrated IS-IS design considerations of area design, route summarization, and nonbroadcast multiaccess (NBMA) modeling solutions.

Area Design of Integrated IS-IS Routers

When designing a network, you have to compromise. Typically, the trade-off is between reliability and speed. What is most efficient for the network is determined by the requirements of the network and the resources available.

In designing Integrated IS-IS networks and the hierarchical design, you need to consider the data flow in addition to the resources required by the routing protocol. Tuning the update process might be sufficient, although this results in compromising resources and reliability. If you reduce the update timers, the databases converge more quickly, but the network could be depleted of resources necessary to route data.

In area design, two SPF databases need to be maintained; this requires the use of additional resources for those routers that straddle more than one level.

Some typical designs include the following:

■ A totally flat network that uses only Level 1 routing. This design will not scale because any change in the network requires a flood of LSPs to all routers, which consequently run the SPF algorithm.

However, this simplified design has some advantages: There will be only one SPF database and no problem with suboptimal routing between areas.

- A totally flat network using only Level 2 routing. As the network expands, Level 1 areas may be added. The Level 2 area has complete internal knowledge with the streamlined advantages of one SPF instance. The Level 1 area may well be a company connecting to the ISP, in which case the areas would be added as new customers came online.

- A totally flat network using the Cisco default of every router running Level 1-2 routing. This allows for easy migration to a hierarchical design and overcomes the problem of suboptimal routing. However, this design requires resources to maintain two SPF databases.

- A hierarchical network where the core is running Level 2 routing, with Level 1 areas connecting into the core. Level 1-2 routers are used to connect the areas. Although this is an excellent design, using the strengths of IS-IS, there are still concerns that need to be considered. This design results in the use of additional resources and the possibility of suboptimal routing. Configuring the metric for the outbound interface determines the routing decision. This requires a careful knowledge of the topology of the network to ensure that the problem is not compounded. Recent developments have allowed for route leaking to be created, which allows the Level 2 routers to pass some specific routing information into Level 1. This facilitates selection of the optimal routing decision.

By default, Cisco routers running Integrated IS-IS operate as Level 1-2 routers. You can configure the router to reflect a true Level 1 and Level 2 design, but the default operation overcomes many potential pitfalls, including the following:

- **Area partitions**—In hierarchical routing between areas, if there is a loss of connection between the Level 1 router and the Level 2 router, the subarea could be completely annexed unless there is an alternative route.

- **Loss of data**—If the area becomes partitioned, a section of the network becomes unavailable through a loss of connectivity.

- **Suboptimal routing decisions**—Level 1 areas have knowledge only of networks within their own areas. To reach another area, packets are sent to the nearest Level 2 router. Without additional configuration, the Level 1 router determines the nearest Level 2 router to be the one with the lowest metric, which translates to the lowest hop count. The metrics used are the default metric of 10, regardless of the bandwidth.

Route Summarization

Summarization has many advantages. It reduces the resource needs of the network and hides network problems within an area. If the router is unaware of a change or problem in the network, the databases are not updated or recalculated, reducing the resources required for SPF calculations. The more details the router knows about the network, the more the router must do to maintain an accurate knowledge of that network; that is, anytime it fails to hear an LSP, however remote and small in terms of its detail of the network, the entire network must flood LSPs and recalculate the SPT. Summarization allows the areas to manage the internal knowledge of the network and to summarize that knowledge across area boundaries.

The rules for summarization using OSPF in multiple areas apply to Integrated IS-IS. The rules for summarizing IP routes in Integrated IS-IS are as follows:

- Level 1-2 routers can summarize the routes held within their area. The summarization is configured at the Level 1-2 router at the edge of the area. This is similar to the OSPF summarization by the ABR.

- If one Level 1-2 router has route summarization configured, you must configure route summarization on every Level 1-2 router in the area injecting updates into Level 2. If one router is advertising without summarization, all traffic destined for the area is sent to that router because Integrated IS-IS uses longest-match routing.

- Level 1 routes cannot be summarized within the area because this is not permitted by the protocol.

Integrated IS-IS NBMA Design Solutions

Designing IS-IS networks across NBMA WANs is not as straightforward as designing other protocols, such as EIGRP, because IS-IS does not explicitly support NBMA. On the other hand, IS-IS over NBMA is not as complicated as OSPF either.

In the good old days, most organizations had a broadcast network (such as Ethernet) for the LAN and point-to-point links (such as serial links) for the WAN. Accommodating these different technologies when building a routing protocol made sense, but technologies have become more complex since then, particularly in the WAN environment.

NBMA networks, such as Frame Relay and ATM, are not accommodated in Integrated IS-IS (unlike OSPF point-to-multipoint). The available options are to use a broadcast configuration (such as would be used for Ethernet) or point-to-point subinterfaces. The recommended solution in the WAN is point-to-point subinterfaces.

Foundation Summary

The Foundation Summary provides a convenient review of many key concepts in this chapter. If you are already comfortable with the topics in this chapter, this summary might help you recall a few details. If you just read this chapter, this review should help solidify some key facts. If you are doing your final prep before the exam, the following lists and tables are a convenient way to review the day before the exam.

Table 9-4 outlines similarities between Integrated IS-IS and OSPF.

Table 9-4   *Integrated IS-IS and OSPF Similarities*

IS-IS	Comparable OSPF Tool
Area	Stub area
Area ID	Area ID
Level 2	Area 0
IS (intermediate system)	Router
ISO Routing Domain	Autonomous system
Level 1 Router	Internal nonbackbone stub area router
Level 1-2 Router	Area border router (ABR)
Level 2 Router	Backbone router
LSP (link-state packet)	LSA (link-state advertisement)
CSNP and PSNP (complete and partial sequence number PDUs)	Link-state acknowledgement packet
PDU (protocol data unit)	Packet
NET (network entity title)	IP destination address (subnet and host), used in a similar way to router ID
NSAP (network service access point)	IP destination address + IP protocol number

Table 9-4 *Integrated IS-IS and OSPF Similarities (Continued)*

IS-IS	Comparable OSPF Tool
Routing technology = link state	Routing technology = link state
• Classless routing protocol • Address summarization between areas • Uses a link-state database • Acknowledges LSPs • Shortest path is computed using Dijkstra's SPF algorithm • Hellos create and maintain adjacencies • Hellos and holdtime may be configured	• Classless routing protocol • Address summarization between areas • Uses a link-state database • Acknowledges LSAs • Shortest path is computed using Dijkstra's SPF algorithm • Hellos create and maintain adjacencies • Hellos and holdtime can be configured
Subnet = data link	Subnet = IP network
SNPA (subnetwork point of attachment)	Layer 2 address; for example, the Ethernet MAC address
System ID	Router ID
Virtual link (defined but not supported)	Virtual link

Figure 9-5 shows the format of an ISO address.

Figure 9-5 *An ISO Address*

IDP		DSP		
AFI (1 octet)	IDI	High Order DSP	System ID (1-8 octets)	NSEL (1 octet)
AREA			**ID**	**SEL**

For an adjacency to be formed and maintained, both interfaces must agree on the following:

■   The maximum packet size (MTU).

■   A common routing level (Level 1 or Level 2) so that they can decode the Hellos sent by the other router.

■   If Level 1, routers must be in the same area.

■   A unique system ID.

■   If authentication is configured, it must be configured identically on both routers.

There are three Integrated IS-IS packets, as the following list describes:

- **Hello**—Hellos create and maintain neighbor relationships.

- **LSP**—LSPs hold information on the neighbors connected to the router. There are two types of LSP, one for each routing level.

- **Sequence number packet (SNP)**—SNPs describe the LSPs in the transmitting router's link-state database. The information is condensed and never flooded but only sent between neighbors. SNPs ensure link-state database synchronization by

  — Distributing groups of LSPs on a LAN without explicit individual acknowledgements

  — Acknowledging individual LSPs

  — Requesting LSPs at startup

  There are two types of SNP for each level of routing:

  — **Complete SNP (CSNP)**—Includes every LSP.

  — **Partial SNP (PSNP)**—Includes a subset of LSPs; used to request LSPs and to acknowledge receipt.

The routing process is divided into four stages:

- The update process

- The decision process

- The forwarding process

- The receive process

Some typical area designs include the following:

- A totally flat network that uses only Level 1 routing.

- A totally flat network using only Level 2 routing. As the network expands, Level 1 areas may be added.

- A totally flat network using the Cisco default configuration of every router running Level 1-2 routing.

- A hierarchical network where the core is running Level 2 routing with Level 1 areas connecting into the core. Level 1-2 routers are used to connect the areas.

Integrated IS-IS does not have a point-to-multipoint configuration option. The alternatives are as follows:

■ Configure the link as multipoint, creating a broadcast environment that requires the election of a DIS.

■ Configure the interfaces with subinterfaces that are point-to-point.

Q&A

The questions and scenarios in this book are designed to be challenging and to make sure that you know the answer. Rather than allowing you to derive the answers from clues hidden inside the questions themselves, the questions challenge your understanding and recall of the subject.

You can find the answers to these questions in Appendix A. For more practice with exam-like question formats, use the exam engine on the CD-ROM.

1. Which system generates the pseudonode?

2. What is a CSNP? When is it used?

3. What is a PSNP? When is it used?

4. A new router comes online on a multiaccess link, and the priority is the same as that of the DIS for the segment. What action is taken?

5. What happens when the DIS is no longer available?

6. Integrated IS-IS can be used to send information about which routed protocols?

7. How often does the DIS send out a Hello packet?

8. What is the name of the link-state algorithm used to create entries for the routing table?

9. What is the relationship between the Hello timer and when the path is considered to have died?

10. Integrated IS-IS areas are similar to which OSPF area types?

11. Describe a design restriction in configuring Level 2 routing.

12. Given the address 49.0001.2222.2222.2222.00, is this a NET or NSAP address?

13. What is a pseudonode and what is its purpose?

14. State two reasons why a router might not be able to become logically adjacent to a neighbor.

15. Explain briefly why two routers cannot have the same system ID within the area.

16. What does TLV stand for? Briefly explain its purpose.

17. How many link-state databases does a Level 1-2 router have?

18. Integrated IS-IS packets run directly on top of which layer?

19. What is the NET address associated with in the IS-IS addressing scheme?

20. Describe the main characteristics of a Level 1 IS.

21. Which systems would you configure as Level 1-2?

22. What are the four stages of the routing process?

23. What does an LSP contain?

24. When are LSPs generated?

25. State at least one of the main steps of the flooding process on a point-to-point link.

26. Which three fields determine if a LSP is valid?

27. Once the link-state database is synchronized, the Dijkstra algorithm is run. Describe where the router places itself in the tree.

28. State two criteria in determining which paths are to be placed in the forwarding database.

29. What is a narrow metric?

30. Where is the IS-IS metric applied?

31. What action will the routing process take if it sees an incomplete LSP fragment?

32. What is a suboptimal routing decision?

33. Where does route summarization take place?

34. When is a DIS elected in a WAN environment?

35. Explain briefly how the IS-IS NBMA cloud is different than the configuration of the OSPF cloud.

This chapter covers the following topics:

- **Basic Configuration of Integrated IS-IS**— Covers essential commands for configuring IS-IS.

- **Optional Integrated IS-IS Commands**— Describes optional commands; however, note that many of these commands are commonly used to tune the required setup.

- **Verifying the Integrated IS-IS Operation**— Looks at **show** commands that verify the setup.

- **Troubleshooting the Integrated IS-IS Operation**—Describes **show** and **debug** commands that you can use to diagnose problems.

Configuring Integrated IS-IS

The first section of this chapter deals with the commands required to create an IS-IS routing environment. Subsequent sections cover optional commands and troubleshooting. The topics in this chapter detail the steps to configuring the IS-IS protocol for integrated routing on a Cisco network. This chapter assumes knowledge of routing protocols—in particular, link-state routing protocols—and the terminology, concepts, and operation of IS-IS.

"Do I Know This Already?" Quiz

The purpose of the "Do I Know This Already?" quiz is to help you decide what parts of this chapter to use. If you already intend to read the entire chapter, you do not necessarily need to answer these questions now.

The 12-question quiz, derived from the major sections in the "Foundation Topics" portion of the chapter, helps you determine how to spend your limited study time.

Table 10-1 outlines the major topics discussed in this chapter and the "Do I Know This Already?" quiz questions that correspond to those topics.

Table 10-1   *"Do I Know This Already?" Foundation Topics Section-to-Question Mapping*

Foundation Topics Section	Questions Covered in This Section	Score
Basic Configuration of Integrated IS-IS	1–3	
Optional Integrated IS-IS Commands	4–6	
Verifying the Integrated IS-IS Operation	7–10	
Troubleshooting the Integrated IS-IS Operation	11–12	
Total Score		

CAUTION   The goal of self-assessment is to gauge your mastery of the topics in this chapter. If you do not know the answer to a question or are only partially sure of the answer, you should mark this question wrong for purposes of the self-assessment. Giving yourself credit for an answer you correctly guess skews your self-assessment results and might provide you with a false sense of security.

1. Which of the following is the correct command to start the Integrated IS-IS routing process?

   a. **ip router isis**

   b. **router isis**

   c. **routing ip isis**

   d. **router clns**

2. Where is the Integrated IS-IS routing process started?

   a. At the exec level

   b. At the interface level

   c. At both the exec and interface levels

   d. Underneath the IP routing process

3. What is the purpose of the **net** command?

   a. To define the summarized address range on the router interface

   b. To define the area into which the interface is to be placed

   c. To define the IS-IS address on the interface

   d. To define the CLNS address for the router

4. Where is the routing level changed from the default of Level 1-2?

   a. At the exec level

   b. At the interface level

   c. Underneath the routing process or at the interface level

   d. Underneath the IP routing process

5. Which of the following are valid commands for changing the routing level?

   a. **isis level-2**

   b. **isis circuit-type level-1**

   c. **isis router level-1**

   d. **ip router level 1**

6. Which of the following commands summarizes the subnets 140.100.104.0 to 140.100.111.0 at the area boundary?

   a. **summary-address 140.100.104.0 255.255.248.0**

   b. **summary-address 140.100.104.0 0.0.7.255**

   c. **ip isis summary address 140.100.104.0/21**

   d. None of these options are correct; summarization is supported only in OSPF and EIGRP

7. Which of the following are displayed in the command **show clns neighbor**?

   a. The contents of the neighbor table.

   b. The routing level as defined at the interface level.

   c. The System ID of the transmitting neighbor.

   d. All answers provided are correct.

8. Which of the following are displayed in the command **show clns interface**?

   a. The number of LSPs received on the interface

   b. The parity check on the received hellos

   c. The metric of the outgoing interface

   d. The round trip delay

9. Which of the following are displayed in the command **show isis database**?

   a. The root of the SPF tree

   b. The LSPs in the local database

   c. Whether an LSP has been fragmented

   d. The sequence number of the LSPs

10. Which of the following commands shows whether the ATT bit has been set?

    a. **show isis hello packets**

    b. **show isis database**

    c. **debug isis interface**

    d. **debug clns interface**

11. Which of the following are displayed in the command **debug isis update-packets**?

    a. Hellos

    b. LSPs

    c. CSNPs

    d. PSNPs

12. Which of the following are displayed in the command **debug isis adjacency-packets**?

    a. The population of the PATH database

    b. The LSPs

    c. Changes in the state of the adjacencies

    d. Hello packets

The answers to this quiz are found in Appendix A, "Answers to Chapter 'Do I Know This Already?' Quizzes and Q&A Sections." The suggested choices for your next step are as follows:

- **7 or less overall score**—Read the entire chapter. This includes the "Foundation Topics," "Foundation Summary," "Q&A," and "Scenarios" sections.

- **8–9 overall score**—Begin with the "Foundation Summary" section, and then go to the "Q&A" and "Scenarios" sections at the end of the chapter. If you have trouble with these exercises, read the appropriate sections in "Foundation Topics."

- **10–12 overall score**—If you want more review on these topics, skip to the "Foundation Summary" section, and then go to the "Q&A" and the "Scenarios" sections at the end of the chapter. Otherwise, move to the next chapter.

Foundation Topics

Basic Configuration of Integrated IS-IS

Routing always starts with a topology that allows summarization and the selection of addresses that can be summarized. Routing protocols assume that these foundations are in place. When ready, the configuration of Integrated IS-IS is straightforward.

Step 1   Enable the routing process Integrated IS-IS with the **router isis** command.

Step 2   Configure the Network Entity Title (NET) address, which assigns the area: **net** *network-address*.

Step 3   Enable IS-IS for IP on the relevant interfaces with the **ip router isis** interface subcommand.

Figure 10-1 illustrates a simple network to support the working configuration example. The figure shows the topology and addressing scheme of the network.

Figure 10-1 *Basic Integrated IS-IS Configuration*

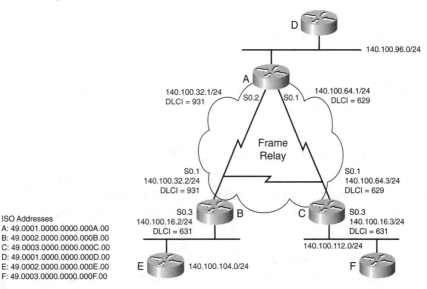

Example 10-1 shows the basic configuration required to run IS-IS. The relevant commands are followed by a brief explanation of the code. Note that the router process is started and the NET address is defined beneath the router process. The ISO address is assigned to the router and is similar to an OSPF router-id, but also implies area assignment. IS-IS is then started on the interfaces.

Example 10-1 *Basic Integrated IS-IS Configuration on Router A*

```
interface Ethernet0
 ip address 140.100.96.1 255.255.255.0
 !assign the IP address and mask
 ip router isis
 !start IS-IS on the interface
 !
interface Serial0
 no ip address
 encapsulation frame-relay
 !
interface Serial0.1 point-to-point
 ip address 140.100.64.1 255.255.255.0
 !assign the IP address and mask
 ip router isis
 !start IS-IS on the interface
 frame-relay interface-dlci 629
 !
interface Serial0.2 point-to-point
 ip address 140.100.32.1 255.255.255.0
 !assign the IP address and mask
 ip router isis
 !start IS-IS on the interface
 frame-relay interface-dlci 931
 !
router isis
 net 49.0001.0000.0000.000a.00
 !Start IS-IS and define ISO address.
```

Remember that by default, Cisco routers are configured as Level 1-2 routers. Also remember that the **clns routing** command, which turns on OSI routing, is not required for IP—only IS-IS.

Optional Integrated IS-IS Commands

The commands in this section are optional in the sense that they are not appropriate for all situations. Frame Relay, for instance, requires some IS-IS customization. Another example of an "optional" issue is area assignment and routing level responsibilities.

Changing the Router from Level 1-2

By default, routers support both Level 1 and Level 2 routing. Routing at both levels means twice as many hellos and advertisements, twice as much memory consumed, and twice as much processing. However, routing at both levels makes configuration easier. One easy way to optimize IS-IS is to reduce the unnecessary duplication of routing at both levels.

IS-IS level is set under the IS-IS process using the **is-type level-1** or **is-type level-2** commands. Once applied, all interfaces communicate only at the given level.

With the topology in Figure 10-2, Routers D, E, and F only need to support Level 1 because they are internal to their areas.

Figure 10-2 *Changing Routing Level*

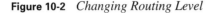
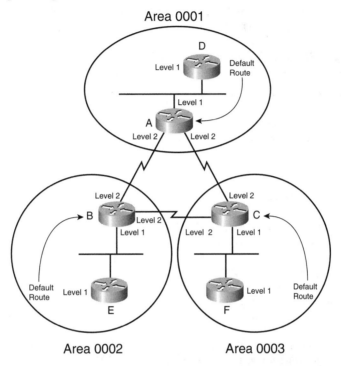

In Example 10-2, Router D is set to route only at Level 1. Note that this command appears under the **router isis** command, changing the behavior of the entire process.

Example 10-2 *Changing the Level of Routing for the Entire Router*

```
interface Ethernet0
 ip address 140.100.96.2 255.255.255.0
 ip router isis
!
router isis
 net 49.0001.0000.0000.000d.00
 is-type level-1
 !Define the router as a Level 1 router
```

Routing level may also be set per-interface by issuing the **isis circuit-type level-1** or **isis circuit-type level-2-only** commands in interface configuration mode. In Figure 10-2, this is done on Routers A, B, and C. The serial interface should be configured as Level 2 by issuing the **isis circuit-type level-2-only** command.

Level 1-2 routers send LSPs with an attached (ATT) bit in their Level 1 LSPs. This indicates that they are attached to another area and is interpreted by the receiver as a default route. Thus the Level 2 router serves as a transit router between areas.

In reference to Figure 10-2, Example 10-3 shows Router A configured as Level 1 on the Ethernet interface pointing to Router D. The other interfaces are configured as Level 2 only.

Example 10-3 *Changing Router A Routing Level on an Interface Basis*

```
interface Ethernet0
 ip address 140.100.96.1 255.255.255.0
 ip router isis
 isis circuit-type level-1
 !Configure Level 1 routing on the interface
!
interface Serial0
 no ip address
 encapsulation frame-relay
!
interface Serial0.1 point-to-point
 ip address 140.100.64.1 255.255.255.0
 ip router isis
 frame-relay interface-dlci 629
 isis circuit-type level-2-only
 ! Configure Level 2 routing on the interface


!
interface Serial0.2 point-to-point
 ip address 140.100.32.1 255.255.255.0
 ip router isis
 frame-relay interface-dlci 931
 isis circuit-type level-2-only
 !Configure Level 2 routing on the interface
!
router isis
```

Configuring Summarization

Once the IP addressing scheme is understood, configuring summarization in IS-IS is straightforward. There are three rules to remember about summarizing IP routes with IS-IS:

■   Summarization is configured on Level 1-2 routers.

■   All the Level 1-2 routers in the area need to summarize equivalently. If one router is offering more specific routes, all traffic to the area will return via this router in accordance with the longest-match rule.

■   Routes cannot be summarized within an area, only between areas.

To configure summarization, enter the **summary-address** command followed by the summary address and mask under the router process. Figure 10-3 shows the topology used to support the working example shown in Example 10-4. In Figure 10-3, the IP routes from Router B are summarized into areas 0001 and 0003. Router B is a Level 1-2 router, straddling more than one area and forming the connectivity between the areas. A Level 1-2 router is similar to an ABR in OSPF. Example 10-4 shows Router B summarizing routes 140.100.104.0 through 140.100.107.0 with a mask summarized from /24 to /22.

Figure 10-3   *Summarizing IP Addresses on Router B Between IS-IS Areas*

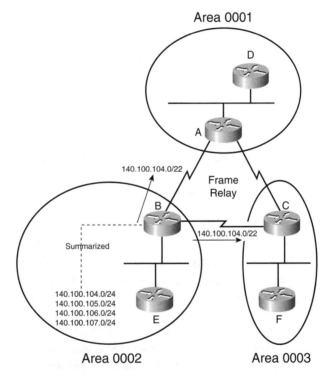

Example 10-4   *Summarization of IP Routes from Router B*

```
interface Ethernet0
 ip address 140.100.104.1 255.255.255.0
 ip router isis
 isis circuit-type level-1
!
interface Serial0
 no ip address
 encapsulation frame-relay
!
```
continues

Example 10-4 *Summarization of IP Routes from Router B (Continued)*

```
interface Serial0.2 point-to-point
 ip address 140.100.32.2 255.255.255.0
 ip router isis
 isis circuit-type level-2-only
 frame-relay interface-dlci 931
!
interface Serial0.3 point-to-point
 ip address 140.100.16.2 255.255.255.0
 ip router isis
 isis circuit-type level-2-only
 frame-relay interface-dlci 631
!
router isis
 summary-address 140.100.104.0 255.255.252.0
 ! Advertises 140.100.104.0/22
 net 49.0002.0000.0000.000b.00
```

Configuring NBMA

IS-IS recognizes two types of network topologies: broadcast and point-to-point. If the network link is not a serial line connecting to a single router (a point-to-point network), IS-IS automatically defines the link as broadcast. Because NBMA is neither a point-to-point nor a broadcast medium, the configuration for IS-IS over NBMA deserves consideration.

For multiaccess WAN interfaces (such as ATM, Frame Relay, and X.25), it is highly recommended that you configure the NBMA cloud as multiple point-to-point subinterfaces. This is a simpler design than trying to use the broadcast mode that makes routing more robust and configuration and support more straightforward.

Frame Relay is an example of an NBMA technology. It supports both point-to-point and meshed environments. The following sections describe both techniques; however, the recommended way to run IS-IS over Frame Relay is to use point-to-point subinterfaces.

Broadcast Configuration over NBMA

If the NBMA cloud is fully meshed, IS-IS broadcast is an option (although it is not recommended). If used, IS-IS treats the cloud as a broadcast medium and elects a DIS. If you manually choose the DIS, you must take into consideration the topology, data flow, and router capacity.

This option is discouraged because of its complexity. The configuration is more involved and the topology is less efficient.

Remember that hello and routing updates are used differently in broadcast environments and point-to-point links. You need to ensure that all the interfaces connecting into the cloud are configured in the same way; otherwise, the hellos will be rejected and no adjacency will form.

The configuration for IS-IS over a fully meshed Frame Relay cloud is illustrated in Figure 10-4. In the figure, the Frame Relay cloud has three fully meshed routers.

Figure 10-4 *NBMA Frame Relay Cloud Running Broadcast Integrated IS-IS*

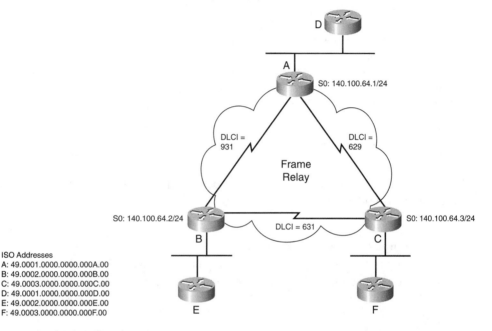

Example 10-5 shows a working example of the configuration shown in the preceding figure. In the example, the **frame-relay map ip** command maps the IP destination address to the outgoing data-link connection identifier (DLCI) and defines the interface as a broadcast interface. Integrated IS-IS uses the links as if they were a broadcast link and elects a DIS.

The **frame-relay map clns** command maps a DLCI to the CLNS process on the destination router. Without this command, no routes appear in the IP routing table because IS-IS does not receive IS-IS frames containing LSPs. IS-IS information does not travel in IP or CLNS packets. IS-IS is encapsulated in a frame similar to CLNS and that frame must be received to build a routing table.

Example 10-5 *Frame Relay Cloud Running Broadcast Integrated IS-IS*

```
interface Ethernet0
 ip address 140.100.96.1 255.255.255.0
 ip router isis
```
continues

Example 10-5   *Frame Relay Cloud Running Broadcast Integrated IS-IS (Continued)*

```
 isis circuit-type level-1
 !
interface Serial0
 ip address 140.100.64.1 255.255.255.0
 ip router isis
 encapsulation frame-relay
 frame-relay map clns 629 broadcast
 !Maps DLCI to the clns process of Router C
 frame-relay map clns 931 broadcast
 !Map DLCI to the clns process of Router B
 frame-relay map ip 140.100.64.2 931 broadcast
 !Maps DLCI to the Destination  IP address of Router B
 frame-relay map ip 140.100.64.3 629 broadcast
 !Maps DLCI to the Destination  IP address of Router C
 isis circuit-type level-2-only
 !
router isis
net 49.0001.0000.0000.000a.00
```

The alternative (and superior) solution to a broadcast configuration is to define subinterfaces and to configure each subinterface as point-to-point.

Point-to-Point Configuration over NBMA

The point-to-point configuration requires an IP subnet for every link. This is the recommended way to run IS-IS over NBMA and the only way to do it on anything less than a full mesh.

The configuration is simpler, because the link is point-to-point and there is no need to configure **frame-relay map** commands.

As shown in Example 10-6, it is only necessary to create subinterfaces, configure those interfaces as point-to-point, start Frame Relay, and define the DLCIs. Do not forget that in addition to configuring Frame Relay, you must start the IS-IS process for each interface.

Figure 10-5 supports the working example for this configuration. It shows the DLCI addresses and the IP addresses for the point-to-point links in addition to the ISO addresses for Routers A, B, and C.

Example 10-6 shows the configuration for Router A to run IS-IS across Frame Relay as a series of point-to-point networks.

Figure 10-5   *NBMA Frame Relay Cloud Running Point-to-Point Integrated IS-IS*

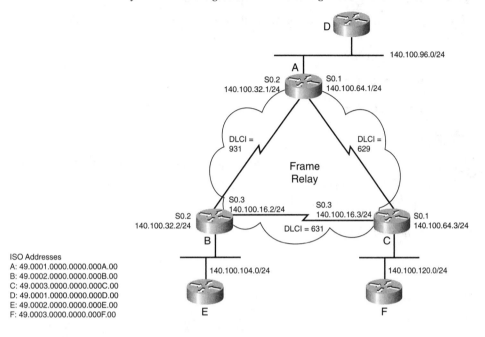

ISO Addresses
A: 49.0001.0000.0000.000A.00
B: 49.0002.0000.0000.000B.00
C: 49.0003.0000.0000.000C.00
D: 49.0001.0000.0000.000D.00
E: 49.0002.0000.0000.000E.00
F: 49.0003.0000.0000.000F.00

Example 10-6   *NBMA Frame Relay Cloud Running Point-to-Point Integrated IS-IS*

```
interface Ethernet0
 ip address 140.100.96.1 255.255.255.0
 ip router isis
!
interface Serial0
 no ip address
 encapsulation frame-relay
 !Configure Frame Relay for the interface
!
interface Serial0.1 point-to-point
 !Configure subinterface to be point-to-point
 ip address 140.100.64.1 255.255.255.0
 ip router isis
 frame-relay interface-dlci 629
 !Define the DLCI to the destination
interface Serial0.2 point-to-point
 ! Configure subinterface as point-to-point
 ip address 140.100.32.1 255.255.255.0
 ip router isis
 Frame-relay interface-dlci 931
 ! Defines DLCI to the destination
!
Router isis
 net 49.0001.0000.0000.000a.00
```

Verifying the Integrated IS-IS Operation

Useful commands to verify the operation of Integrated IS-IS include the following:

- **show clns neighbor**

- **show clns interface**

- **show isis database**

- **show isis database detail**

The following sections explain each of these **show** commands in more detail. The commands explained in this section correspond to the topology illustrated in Figure 10-6 and the configuration shown in Example 10-7 for Router A.

Figure 10-6 *The Network Topology for the **show** Commands*

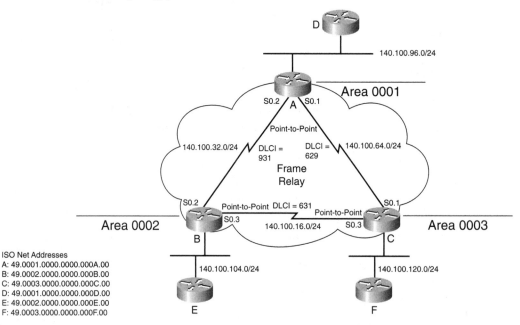

Example 10-7 *The Configuration for Router A in Figure 10-6*

```
interface Ethernet0
 ip address 140.100.96.1 255.255.255.0
 ip router isis
 isis circuit-type level-1
!
```

Example 10-7 *The Configuration for Router A in Figure 10-6 (Continued)*

```
interface Serial0
 no ip address
 encapsulation frame-relay
!
interface Serial0.1 point-to-point
 ip address 140.100.64.1 255.255.255.0
 ip router isis
 isis circuit-type level-2-only
 frame-relay interface-dlci 629
!
interface Serial0.2 point-to-point
 ip address 140.100.32.1 255.255.255.0
 ip router isis
 isis circuit-type level-2-only
 frame-relay interface-dlci 931
!
router isis
 net 49.0001.0000.0000.000a.00
```

The show clns neighbors Command

The **show clns neighbors** command includes some of the contents of the neighbor table and the state of the link. Note that the subnetwork point of attachment (SNPA) is the MAC address of the interface. Level 1-2 routing is used.

The command has the following syntax:

```
show clns area-tag neighbors [type number] [area] [detail]
```

Table 10-2 explains the syntax of this command.

Table 10-2 *Explanation of the* **show clns neighbors** *Command Syntax*

Field	Description
area-tag	Used in multi-process IS-IS configurations, this is a name for a process.
type number	(Optional) Type of interface and interface number (for example, Ethernet 1).
Area	(Optional) Shows CLNS multiarea adjacencies.
detail	(Optional) Shows details of each adjacency.

Example 10-8 shows output for the **show clns neighbors** command.

Example 10-8 *Output for the* **show clns neighbors** *Command*

```
RouterA#show clns neighbors
System Id        Interface   SNPA            State  Holdtime  Type  Protocol
0000.0000.000B   Se0.2       DLCI 931        Up     22        L2    IS-IS
0000.0000.000C   Se0.1       DLCI 629        Up     23        L2    IS-IS
0000.0000.000D   Et0         00e0.1e3d.d56f  Up     8         L1    IS-IS
```

The output of the **show clns neighbors** command shows that Router A has three neighbors. The system ID shows that the serial subinterface S0.1 has heard an LSP from 0000.0000.000C, which has a Frame Relay DLCI of 629. It is running IS-IS Level 2 routing. The link is up and has 23 seconds before another Hello needs to be received. Because the Hello timer is set by default to send Hellos every 10 seconds, it should receive another Hello in 7 seconds, which will reset the holdtime. The Ethernet segment is running Level 1 routing and has a MAC address for the SNPA address.

The **show clns neighbors** command is useful for quickly checking connectivity. This output shows all the neighbors—complete with the DLCI addresses and OSI system IDs—indicating that Frame Relay is correctly configured and working, as is IS-IS.

Adding the parameter **detail** to the **show clns neighbors** command gives information about each neighbor. Example 10-9 shows output for the **show clns neighbors detail** command. The example shows the area address for the neighbor, the IP address of the transmitting interface, and the length of time that the interface has been up. This command gives information that enables you to verify the addressing scheme of the network.

Example 10-9 *Output for the* **show clns neighbors detail** *Command*

```
RouterA#show clns neighbor detail
System Id        Interface   SNPA            State  Holdtime  Type Protocol
0000.0000.000B     Se0.2     DLCI 931        Up     27        L2   IS-IS
  Area Address(es): 49.0002
  IP Address(es):  140.100.32.2*
  Uptime: 00:05:17
0000.0000.000C     Se0.1     DLCI 629        Up     28        L2   IS-IS
  Area Address(es): 49.0003
  IP Address(es):  140.100.64.3*
  Uptime: 00:05:22
0000.0000.000D     Et0       00e0.1e3d.d56f  Up     7         L1   IS-IS
  Area Address(es): 49.0001
  IP Address(es):  140.100.96.2*
Uptime: 00:15:01
```

Table 10-3 explains the meaning of the fields in the detailed output.

Table 10-3 *Explanation of the* **show clns neighbors detail** *Command Output*

Field	Description
System Id	The system address (6 bytes).
Interface	Interface on which the neighbor was learned.
SNPA	Subnetwork point of attachment (data-link address).
State	States are as follows: • Init—Initializing. The router is waiting for an IS-IS Hello message. • Up—Other system reachable. • Down—Other system unreachable.
Holdtime	Seconds before this adjacency times out.
Type	Types of adjacency include • ES—End-system adjacency. • Router adjacency—Discovered via ES-IS or statically configured.
L1	(Optional) Displays Level 1 adjacencies.
L1L2	(Optional) Shows Level 1 and Level 2 adjacencies.
L2	(Optional) Displays Level 2 adjacencies.
Protocol	The routing protocol used to learn the adjacency (ES-IS, IS-IS, ISO IGRP, Static, or DECnet).

The show clns interface Command

Misconfiguration of the interface can result in the inability to create adjacencies. Typically, the error is a simple mismatch of parameters, which can be seen by using the **show clns interface** command.

```
Router#show clns interface [type number]
```

In Example 10-10, Frame Relay is configured with point-to-point links. The circuit ID shows the system ID of a router, rather than a pseudonode. The octet following the system ID indicates whether this ID is a pseudonode representing the multiaccess link. If the ID is that of a pseudonode, the system ID is that of the DIS, with the next octet showing a nonzero value such as 0x01.

This is confirmed when you look at the Ethernet interface. The Ethernet 0 interface has the Level 1 circuit ID as A.01. This indicates that the DIS for Level 1 is Router A and that A is a pseudonode.

Because this is a Level 1-2 router, there is also a circuit ID for the Level 2 adjacency on the Ethernet interface. Note that the value for the Level 2 DIS is that of Router A. Router D has been configured as a Level 1 router and, as such, cannot communicate Level 2 updates.

Example 10-10 shows output for the **show clns interface** command.

Example 10-10   *Output for the* **show clns interface** *Command*

```
RouterA#show clns interface
Ethernet0 is up, line protocol is up
  Checksums enabled, MTU 1497, Encapsulation SAP
  ERPDUs enabled, min. interval 10 msec.
  CLNS fast switching enabled
  CLNS SSE switching disabled
  DEC compatibility mode OFF for this interface
  Next ESH/ISH in 47 seconds
  Routing Protocol: IS-IS
    Circuit Type: level-1-2
    Interface number 0x0, local circuit ID 0x1
    Level-1 Metric: 10, Priority: 64, Circuit ID: A.01
    Number of active level-1 adjacencies: 0
    Level-2 Metric: 10, Priority: 64, Circuit ID A.01
    Number of active level-2 adjacencies: 1
    Next IS-IS LAN Level-1 Hello in 1 seconds
    Next IS-IS LAN Level-2 Hello in 1 seconds
Serial0 is up, line protocol is up
  CLNS protocol processing disabled
Serial0.1 is up, line protocol is up
  Checksums enabled, MTU 1500, Encapsulation FRAME-RELAY
  ERPDUs enabled, min. interval 10 msec.
  CLNS fast switching disabled
  CLNS SSE switching disabled
  DEC compatibility mode OFF for this interface
  Next ESH/ISH in 58 seconds
  Routing Protocol: IS-IS
    Circuit Type: level-1-2
    Interface number 0x1, local circuit ID 0x100
    Level-1 Metric: 10, Priority: 64, Circuit ID: A.00
    Number of active level-1 adjacencies: 0
    Level-2 Metric: 10, Priority: 64, Circuit ID: A.00
    Number of active level-2 adjacencies: 1
    Next IS-IS Hello in 2 seconds
Serial0.2 is up, line protocol is up
  Checksums enabled, MTU 1500, Encapsulation FRAME-RELAY
  ERPDUs enabled, min. interval 10 msec.
  CLNS fast switching disabled
  CLNS SSE switching disabled
  DEC compatibility mode OFF for this interface
  Next ESH/ISH in 24 seconds
```

Example 10-10   *Output for the* **show clns interface** *Command (Continued)*

```
Routing Protocol: IS-IS
  Circuit Type: level-1-2
  Interface number 0x2, local circuit ID 0x101
  Level-1 Metric: 10, Priority: 64, Circuit ID: A.00
  Number of active level-1 adjacencies: 0
  Level-2 Metric: 10, Priority: 64, Circuit ID: A.00
  Number of active level-2 adjacencies: 1
Next IS-IS Hello in 886 milliseconds
```

Table 10-4 explains the meaning of the fields in the output screen.

Table 10-4   *Explanation of the* **show clns interface** *Command Output*

Field	Description
Checksum	This may be either enabled or disabled.
MTU	Maximum transmission size for a packet on this interface. Note that it is not 1500 because 3 bytes are taken by the OSI header.
Encapsulation	The encapsulation is always SAP (ISO1).
Routing Protocol	Indicates whether ES-IS or IS-IS is running and the type of Hellos sent.
Circuit Type	Indicates whether the link is enabled for Level 1, Level 2, or Level 1-2 routing.
Level-1 Metric	Metric value for the outbound interface for Level 1 routing. The default setting is 10.
Priority	Priority setting for DIS election. The default is 64.
Circuit ID	Identifies the DIS for Level 1 if present.
Number of Active Level-1 Adjacencies	The number of Level 1 adjacencies formed on this link.
Level-2 Metric	Metric value for the outbound interface for Level 2 routing. The default setting is 10.
Priority	The priority setting for DIS election.
Circuit ID	Identifies the DIS for Level 2 if present.
Number of Active Level-2 Adjacencies	The number of Level 2 adjacencies formed on this link.
Next IS-IS LAN Level-1 Hello	Number of seconds before next Hello is expected. Repeat the command to see if Hellos are received.
Next IS-IS LAN Level-2 Hello	Number of seconds before next Hello is expected. Repeat the command to see if Hellos are received.

The show isis database Command

The **show isis database** command shows the LSPs held in the local database. The LSP ID shows the system ID of the generating router and whether this LSP is from a router or a pseudonode. The last octet shows whether the LSP was too large to fit into one PDU; a nonzero value in this field indicates that this is a fragment of an LSP (the next number states the fragment number).

Because IS-IS is a link-state protocol, the database should be identical on every router of the same level and area.

```
show isis area-tag database [level-1] [level-2] [l1] [l2] [detail] [lspid]
```

Table 10-5 explains the syntax.

Table 10-5   *Explanation of the* **show isis database** *Command*

Field	Description
area-tag	The name for an IS-IS routing process.
level-1	(Optional) Displays the Level 1 link-state database.
level-2	(Optional) Displays the Level 2 link-state database.
l1	(Optional) Abbreviation for Level 1.
l2	(Optional) Abbreviation for Level 2.
detail	(Optional) Shows each LSP.
lspid	(Optional) Identifier for the link-state PDU. Shows the contents of the specified individual LSP.

Example 10-11 shows output for the **show isis database** command.

Example 10-11   *Output for the* **show isis database** *Command*

```
RouterA#show isis database

IS-IS Level-1 Link State Database:
LSPID                   LSP Seq Num  LSP Checksum  LSP Holdtime    ATT/P/OL
A.00-00                 * 0x00000017  0x76D5        876             1/0/0
IS-IS Level-2 Link State Database:
LSPID                   LSP Seq Num  LSP Checksum  LSP Holdtime    ATT/P/OL
A.00-00                 * 0x00000018  0xB74F        881             0/0/0
0000.0000.000B.00-00    0x0000001A  0xB561        872             0/0/0
0000.0000.000B.01-00    0x00000016  0x6045        1095            0/0/0
C.00-00                 0x0000001E  0x6267        869             0/0/0
C.01-00                 0x00000002  0xF25F        958             0/0/0
0000.0000.000E.00-00    0x00000018  0x010A        858             0/0/0
0000.0000.000D.00-00    0x0000001A  0x413C        985             0/0/0
0000.0000.000D.04-00    0x00000017  0xFCA0        1006            0/0/0
```

Table 10-6 explains the meaning of the fields in the output. Note that both Level 1 and Level 2 databases are shown because the router is running the default configuration of Level 1-2 routing. All the LSP information is contained in these databases, including the LSPs generated by the router itself. An asterisk marks these entries in the output.

Table 10-6 *Explanation of the* **show isis database** *Command Output*

Field	Description
LSPID	The LSPID indicates the transmitting router. The system ID is followed by two octets. If the first octet has a value greater than 0x00, this indicates that the ID is the DIS. The last octet is the Fragment bit. If the value is 0x00, the entire LSP was carried in one LSP. Otherwise it indicates this PDU is the nth fragment of the LSP.
LSP Seq Num	Sequence number for the LSP. This allows routers to determine whether they have received the latest information from the source and ensures the integrity of the link-state database.
LSP Checksum	Checksum of the entire LSP packet.
LSP Holdtime	Amount of time the LSP remains valid (in seconds). An LSP holdtime of 0 indicates that this LSP was purged and is being removed from the link-state database.
ATT	The LSP indicates that this router is a Level 2 router with a path out of the area. Level 1 routers use the presence of this bit to identify the closest Level 1-2 router to send their out-of-area data to.
P	Partition repair capability. Not supported by Cisco.
OL	The Overload bit indicates that the router has an incomplete database because of memory overload and is therefore not used for transit data.

The show isis database detail Command

The **show isis database detail** command shows the complete LSP and the values for the individual fields. The command has the same syntax as the **show isis database** command in the preceding section.

Example 10-12 shows output for the **show isis database detail** command. The example shows, for each LSP, the area and the IP address of the transmitting interface and the metric cost to the IP routes it knows. The default metric is a cost of 10; therefore, a metric of 20 indicates a prefix is two hops away.

Example 10-12   *Output for the* **show isis database detail** *Command*

```
RouterA#show isis database detail

 IS-IS Level-1 Link State Database:
LSPID                    LSP Seq Num    LSP Checksum    LSP Holdtime    ATT/P/OL
A.00-00                * 0x00000017      0x76D5            873             1/0/0
  Area Address: 49.0001
  NLPID:        0xCC
  Hostname:A
  IP Address:   140.100.32.1
  Metric: 10        IP 140.100.96.0 255.255.255.0
  Metric: 10        IP 140.100.64.0 255.255.255.0
  Metric: 10        IP 140.100.32.0 255.255.255.0
  Metric: 10        IS A.01
 IS-IS Level-2 Link State Database:
LSPID                    LSP Seq Num    LSP Checksum    LSP Holdtime    ATT/P/OL
A.00-00                * 0x00000018      0xB74F            877             0/0/0
  Area Address: 49.0001
  NLPID:        0xCC
  Hostname: A
  IP Address:   140.100.32.1
  Metric: 10        IS 0000.0000.000B.00
  Metric: 10        IS C.00
  Metric: 10        IS 0000.0000.000D.04
  Metric: 10        IP 140.100.96.0 255.255.255.0
  Metric: 10        IP 140.100.64.0 255.255.255.0
  Metric: 10        IP 140.100.32.0 255.255.255.0
0000.0000.000B.00-00   0x0000001A      0xB561            868             0/0/0
  Area Address: 49.0002
  NLPID:        0xCC
  IP Address:   140.100.16.2
  Metric: 10        IS 0000.0000.000B.01
  Metric: 10        IS A.00
  Metric: 10        IS C.00
  Metric: 10        IP 140.100.104.0 255.255.255.0
  Metric: 20        IP 140.100.105.0 255.255.255.0
  Metric: 20        IP 140.100.106.0 255.255.255.0
  Metric: 20        IP 140.100.107.0 255.255.255.0
  Metric: 10        IP 140.100.32.0 255.255.255.0
  Metric: 10        IP 140.100.16.0 255.255.255.0
0000.0000.000B.01-00   0x00000016      0x6045           1089             0/0/0
  Metric: 0         IS 0000.0000.000B.00
  Metric: 0         IS 0000.0000.000E.00
C.00-00                0x0000001E      0x6267            863             0/0/0
  Area Address: 49.0003
  NLPID:        0xCC
  Hostname: C
  IP Address:   140.100.100.1
```

Example 10-12 *Output for the* **show isis database detail** *Command (Continued)*

```
  Metric: 10        IS C.02
  Metric: 10        IS A.00
  Metric: 10        IS 0000.0000.000B.00
  Metric: 10        IP 140.100.100.0 255.255.255.0
  Metric: 10        IP 140.100.64.0 255.255.255.0
  Metric: 10        IP 140.100.16.0 255.255.255.0
C.01-00                 0x00000002    0xF25F        951          0/0/0
  Metric: 0         IS C.00
0x00000018              0x010A        850          0/0/0
  Area Address: 49.0002
  0000.0000.000E.00-00   NLPID:       0xCC
  IP Address:   140.100.105.1
  Metric: 10        IS 0000.0000.000B.01
  Metric: 10        IP 140.100.104.0 255.255.255.0
  Metric: 10        IP 140.100.105.0 255.255.255.0
  Metric: 10        IP 140.100.106.0 255.255.255.0
  Metric: 10        IP 140.100.107.0 255.255.255.0
  Metric: 20        IP 140.100.32.0 255.255.255.0
  Metric: 20        IP 140.100.16.0 255.255.255.0
0000.0000.000D.00-00    0x0000001A    0x413C        976          0/0/0
  Area Address: 49.0003
  NLPID:        0xCC
  IP Address:   140.100.97.1
  Metric: 10        IS 0000.0000.000D.04
  Metric: 10        IP 140.100.96.0 255.255.255.0
  Metric: 10        IP 140.100.97.0 255.255.255.0
  Metric: 10        IP 140.100.98.0 255.255.255.0
  Metric: 10        IP 140.100.99.0 255.255.255.0
0000.0000.000D.04-00    0x00000017    0xFCA0        996          0/0/0
  Metric: 0         IS 0000.0000.000D.00
  Metric: 0         IS A.00
```

Table 10-7 explains the meaning of the fields in the output.

Table 10-7 *Explanation of the* **show isis database detail** *Command Output*

Field	Description
Area Address	Area addresses that may be reached from this router. Level 1 LSPs describe the area addresses configured manually on the originating router. Level 2 LSPs describe the area addresses for the area to which this route belongs.
Metric	The cost of the outbound interface between the originating router and the advertised neighbor, or the metric of the compound cost between the advertising router and the advertised destination.

Troubleshooting the Integrated IS-IS Operation

Unfortunately, even after careful planning, configurations can fail to work and the most scrutinized networks can break down. The **show** commands are essential for hunting down problems. The following commands are useful for troubleshooting Integrated IS-IS:

■ The **show isis spf-log** command

■ The **debug** commands

The following sections describe these commands in greater detail.

The show isis spf-log Command

The **show isis spf-log** command explains a great deal about the SPF calculations on the router. It reveals the events that triggered SPF for the last 20 occurrences.

To display how often, and why, the router has run a full SPF calculation, use the **show isis spf-log** EXEC command.

Example 10-13 shows output for the **show isis spf-log** command. The example shows that Router A sent an LSP because it had set the ATT bit, and later it generated a new LSP when new adjacencies came online. This output shows the healthy workings of an IS-IS network, but the command is very useful if the network appears unstable, with routes appearing and disappearing.

Example 10-13 *Output for the* **show isis spf-log** *Command*

```
RouterA#show isis spf-log

  Level 1 SPF log
  When    Duration  Nodes  Count    Last trigger LSP     Triggers
04:23:24      0       1      1                    A.00-00   TLVCODE
04:08:46      0       1      1                              PERIODIC
03:53:46      0       1      1                              PERIODIC
03:38:46      0       1      1                              PERIODIC
03:23:46      0       1      1                              PERIODIC
03:08:46      0       1      1                              PERIODIC
02:53:46      0       1      1                              PERIODIC
02:38:46      0       1      1                              PERIODIC
02:23:46      0       1      1                              PERIODIC
02:08:46      0       1      1                              PERIODIC
01:53:46      0       1      1                              PERIODIC
01:38:46      0       1      1                              PERIODIC
01:23:46      0       1      1                              PERIODIC
01:08:46      0       1      1                              PERIODIC
00:53:46      0       1      1                              PERIODIC
00:38:47      0       1      1                              PERIODIC
00:23:47      0       1      1                              PERIODIC
```

Example 10-13 *Output for the* **show isis spf-log** *Command (Continued)*

```
00:15:14       0      1      2                A.00-00  ATTACHFLAG LSPHEADER
00:08:46       0      1      1                         PERIODIC


   Level 2 SPF log
   When   Duration  Nodes  Count   First trigger LSP  Triggers
03:53:48       0      1      1                         PERIODIC
03:38:48       0      1      1                         PERIODIC
03:23:48       0      1      1                         PERIODIC
03:08:48       0      1      1                         PERIODIC
02:53:48       0      1      1                         PERIODIC
02:38:48       0      1      1                         PERIODIC
02:23:48       0      1      1                         PERIODIC
02:08:48       0      1      1                         PERIODIC
01:53:48       0      1      1                         PERIODIC
01:38:48       0      1      1                         PERIODIC
01:23:48       0      1      1                         PERIODIC
01:08:48       0      1      1                         PERIODIC
00:53:48       0      1      1                         PERIODIC
00:38:48       0      1      1                         PERIODIC
00:23:48       0      1      1                         PERIODIC
00:15:22       0      3      5                A.00-00  NEWADJ LSPHEADER TLVCONTENT
00:08:48       0      3      1                         PERIODIC
00:05:44       4      4      4                A.00-00  NEWADJ TLVCONTENT
00:05:38       4      7      5 0000.0000.000B.00-00    LSPHEADER TLVCONTENT
```

Table 10-8 explains the fields in Example 10-13.

Table 10-8 *Explanation of the* **show isis spf-log** *Command Output*

Field	Description
When	The amount of time since a full SPF calculation occurred (hh:mm:ss). The last 19 occurrences are shown.
Duration	Milliseconds it took to complete this SPF run (elapsed time as opposed to CPU time).
Nodes	Number of routers and pseudonodes (LANs) calculated in the SPF run.
Count	Number of events (such as new LSPs) that occurred while the router was waiting before running full SPF. The router waits five seconds after the first triggered LSP to ensure that all the information is received.
Last Trigger LSP	Whenever a full SPF calculation is triggered by the arrival of a new LSP, the ID of the LSP is stored. The LSPID can indicate where to start troubleshooting for any routing instability in an area. If multiple LSPs are causing an SPF run, only the LSPID of the last received LSP is remembered.
Trigger	A list of all events that triggered a full SPF calculation.

The debug Commands

The **debug** command is a helpful troubleshooting tool, but it does have certain disadvantages, of which you must be aware. The **debug** command is the highest process priority and can steal CPU time from other processes. It is capable of consuming all the resources on the router, thus becoming the problem instead of helping to solve the problem. It is important to turn on **debug** just for the specific task to be monitored and to turn it off as soon as the data has been gathered. The **no** form of this command disables debugging output. You should direct the output to a log file, because each character sent to the console creates a processor interrupt.

Table 10-9 lists options available for monitoring IS-IS.

Table 10-9 *The **debug** Command Options for Integrated IS-IS*

Command Option	Description
debug isis adjacencies-packets	Displays information on all adjacency-related activity, including • Hello packets (sent and received) • Any changes in the state of an adjacency in Integrated IS-IS
debug isis spf-statistics	Displays statistical information about building routes between routers. Using the statistical information provided, one can determine how long it takes to place a Level 1 IS or Level 2 IS on the shortest path tree (SPT) using the IS-IS protocol.
debug isis update-packets	Displays SNPs (CSNPs and PSNPs) and LSPs that are detected by the router.

Foundation Summary

The Foundation Summary provides a convenient review of many key concepts in this chapter. If you are already comfortable with the topics in this chapter, this summary might help you recall a few details. If you just read this chapter, this review should help solidify some key facts. If you are doing your final prep before the exam, the following lists and tables are a convenient way to review the day before the exam.

Table 10-10 summarizes the commands covered in this chapter.

Table 10-10 *Summary of Commands*

Command	Function
Router(config)#**router isis**	Starts IS-IS on the router
Router(config-router)#**net** *network-address*	Defines the NET address
Router(config-router)#**is-type level-1|level-2**	Defines the router as Level 1 or Level 2
Router(config-router)#**summary-address** *address mask*	Enables you to summarize the networks manually
Router(config-if)#**frame-relay map ip** *destination address DLCI* **broadcast**	Maps the Frame Relay DLCI to the destination IP address
Router#**show clns neighbor detail**	Displays information drawn from the neighbor table
Router#**show clns interface**	Displays information about IS-IS Hello and timers
Router#**show isis database**	Shows the link-state database
Router#**show isis spf-log**	Shows why and how often the SPF algorithm was recalculated

Table 10-11 shows the debug commands discussed in this chapter.

Table 10-11 *The* **debug** *Commands for IS-IS*

Command Option	Description
debug isis adjacencies-packets	Displays information on all adjacency-related activity.
debug isis spf-statistics	Displays statistical information about building routes between routers. Using the statistical information provided, one can determine how long it takes to place a Level 1 IS or Level 2 IS on the shortest path tree (SPT) using the IS-IS protocol.
debug isis update-packets	Displays SNPs (CSNPs and PSNPs) and LSPs that are detected by the router.

Q&A

The questions and scenarios in this book are designed to be challenging and to make sure that you know the answer. Rather than allowing you to derive the answers from clues hidden inside the questions themselves, the questions challenge your understanding and recall of the subject.

You can find the answers to these questions in Appendix A. For more practice with exam-like question formats, use the exam engine on the CD-ROM.

1. What command is used to configure the Integrated IS-IS router process?

2. What is the default routing level on a Cisco router?

3. What command is used to configure Integrated IS-IS routing on the interface?

4. How is the NET address configured on the router?

5. What command is used to show the state of adjacencies on the router?

6. What command identifies the designated intermediate system router for your LAN?

7. Explain briefly what **show isis database** reveals.

8. What command reveals the trigger for the last SPF calculation on the router?

9. For Frame Relay, when would you configure the map command with the broadcast parameter?

10. Which command is used to display all update packets that are both received and sent by a router?

11. Which command shows the LSPs in detail?

12. How would you ensure that an adjacency has been established?

13. What are the steps required for a basic configuration in IS-IS?

14. Give the commands required to summarize the networks 10.10.0.0 through to 10.10.255.0 into another area of IS-IS.

15. Which command verifies the circuit type and the metric?

16. For which WAN topology is a point-to-point configuration recommended?

17. Why is it necessary to map CLNS to the DLCI to support IS-IS?

18. In the **show clns** interface command, it is possible to identify the DIS on a multiaccess link. Which field in the output screen of this command would show the DIS for the segment?

Scenarios

The following scenarios and questions are designed to draw together the content of the chapter and to exercise your understanding of the concepts. There is not necessarily a right answer. The thought process and practice in manipulating the concepts are the goals of this section. The answers to the scenario questions are found at the end of this chapter.

Scenario 10-1

The ISP Flying Data has recently converted from OSPF to Integrated IS-IS. The migration was relatively painless. The company uses the private network 10.0.0.0 for IP and the private ISO addressing with AFI 49. They created a hierarchical addressing structure. Figure 10-7 illustrates this addressing scheme.

Figure 10-7 *Diagram for Scenario 10-1*

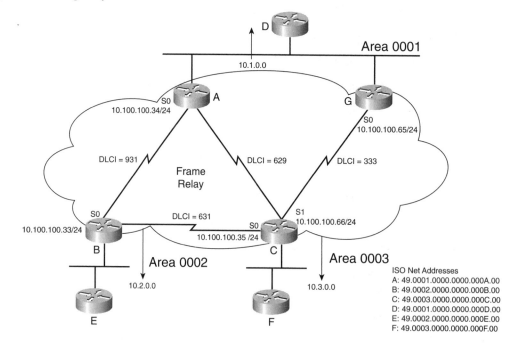

The addressing of the network was a large project, with all the pitfalls that accompany such a major exercise. The network is now stable, and it is time to configure the WAN connections using multipoint Frame Relay, as follows:

1. Issue the commands that will allow Router A to use IS-IS routing across the NBMA cloud as a broadcast medium. Refer to Figure 10-7 for the addressing scheme.

2. The WAN is Frame Relay, and Router G has a point-to-point link with Router C. Issue the commands that configure Router C's link for IS-IS as a point-to-point link.

3. To reduce bandwidth consumption and to hide some network detail, summarization has been suggested. Issue the commands for Router A that will summarize the networks with a prefix of /16 across the WAN.

Scenario 10-2

Given the configuration of IS-IS in Example 10-14, perform the tasks and answer the questions listed. The WAN has light user traffic and has a fully meshed configuration, as shown in Figure 10-8.

Figure 10-8 *Diagram for Scenario 10-2*

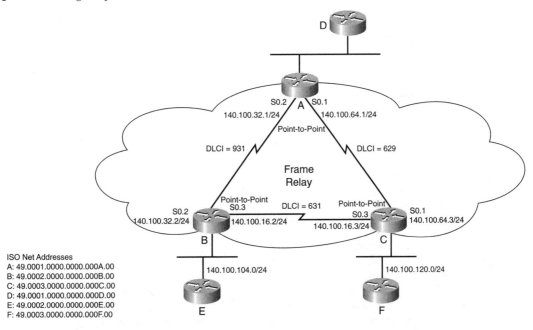

ISO Net Addresses
A: 49.0001.0000.0000.000A.00
B: 49.0002.0000.0000.000B.00
C: 49.0003.0000.0000.000C.00
D: 49.0001.0000.0000.000D.00
E: 49.0002.0000.0000.000E.00
F: 49.0003.0000.0000.000F.00

Example 10-14 *Router B's Configuration File*

```
RouterB#show running config
...
hostname B
!
clns routing
!
Interface Ethernet0
```

continues

Example 10-14 *Router B's Configuration File (Continued)*

```
 ip address 140.100.104.1 255.255.255.0
 ip router isis
!
Interface Serial0
 no ip address
 encapsulation frame-relay
 clockrate 56000
!
Interface Serial0.2 point-to-point
 ip address 140.100.32.2 255.255.255.0
 ip router isis
 frame-relay interface-dlci 931
!
Interface Serial0.3 point-to-point
 ip address 140.100.16.2 255.255.255.0
 ip router isis
 frame-relay interface-dlci 631
!
router isis
 net 49.0002.0000.0000.000b.00
B# show clns interface
Ethernet0 is up, line protocol is up
  Checksums enabled, MTU 1497, Encapsulation SAP
  ERPDUs enabled, min. interval 10 msec.
  RDPDUs enabled, min. interval 100 msec., Addr Mask enabled
  Congestion Experienced bit set at 4 packets
  CLNS fast switching enabled
  CLNS SSE switching disabled
  DEC compatibility mode OFF for this interface
  Next ESH/ISH in 15 seconds
  Routing Protocol: IS-IS
    Circuit Type: level-1-2
    Interface number 0x0, local circuit ID 0x1
    Level-1 Metric: 10, Priority: 64, Circuit ID: 0000.0000.000B.01
    Number of active level-1 adjacencies: 1
    Level-2 Metric: 10, Priority: 64, Circuit ID: 0000.0000.000B.01
    Number of active level-2 adjacencies: 1
    Next IS-IS LAN Level-1 Hello in 678 milliseconds
    Next IS-IS LAN Level-2 Hello in 1 seconds
Serial0 is up, line protocol is up
  CLNS protocol processing disabled
Serial0.1 is up, line protocol is up
  CLNS protocol processing disabled
Serial0.2 is up, line protocol is up
  Checksums enabled, MTU 1500, Encapsulation FRAME-RELAY
  ERPDUs enabled, min. interval 10 msec.
  RDPDUs enabled, min. interval 100 msec., Addr Mask enabled
```

Example 10-14 *Router B's Configuration File (Continued)*

```
    Congestion Experienced bit set at 4 packets
    CLNS fast switching disabled
    CLNS SSE switching disabled
    DEC compatibility mode OFF for this interface
    Next ESH/ISH in 43 seconds
    Routing Protocol: IS-IS
      Circuit Type: level-1-2
      Interface number 0x2, local circuit ID 0x101
      Level-1 Metric: 10, Priority: 64, Circuit ID: 0000.0000.000B.01
      Number of active level-1 adjacencies: 0
      Level-2 Metric: 10, Priority: 64, Circuit ID: 0000.0000.000B.01
      Number of active level-2 adjacencies: 1
      Next IS-IS Hello in 2 seconds
Serial0.3 is up, line protocol is up
  Checksums enabled, MTU 1500, Encapsulation FRAME-RELAY
  ERPDUs enabled, min. interval 10 msec.
  RDPDUs enabled, min. interval 100 msec., Addr Mask enabled
  Congestion Experienced bit set at 4 packets
  CLNS fast switching disabled
  CLNS SSE switching disabled
  DEC compatibility mode OFF for this interface
  Next ESH/ISH in 11 seconds
  Routing Protocol: IS-IS
    Circuit Type: level-1-2
    Interface number 0x1, local circuit ID 0x100
    Level-1 Metric: 10, Priority: 64, Circuit ID: 0000.0000.000C.01
    Number of active level-1 adjacencies: 0
    Level-2 Metric: 10, Priority: 64, Circuit ID: 0000.0000.000B.00
    Number of active level-2 adjacencies: 1
Next IS-IS Hello in 3 seconds
```

1. Identify the DIS on the Ethernet segment. How was this information apparent?

2. If Router A died, what would the effect be on the network?

3. Is summarization possible only on the routers entering the WAN cloud, or is it possible on the networks not shown in the figure, but on the other side of the routers? Give reasons for your answers.

Scenario Answers

The answers provided in this section are not necessarily the only possible answers to the questions. The questions are designed to test your knowledge and to give practical exercise in certain key areas. This section is intended to test and exercise skills and concepts detailed in the body of this chapter.

If your answer is different, ask yourself whether it follows the tenets explained in the answers provided. Your answer is correct not if it matches the solution provided in the book, but rather if it has included the principles of design laid out in the chapter.

If you do not get the correct answer, refer back to the text and review the subject tested. Be certain to also review your notes on the question to ensure that you understand the principles of the subject.

Scenario 10-1 Answers

1. *Issue the commands that will allow Router A to use Integrated IS-IS routing across the NBMA cloud as if the cloud were a broadcast medium. Refer to Figure 10-7 for the addressing scheme.*

   The serial configuration in Example 10-15 shows the configuration of IS-IS across the Frame Relay cloud, using the broadcast technology and LAN Hellos. The **frame-relay map ip** command maps the IP destination address to the outgoing DLCI and defines the interface as a broadcast interface.

   The **frame-relay map clns** command maps to the CLNS process on the destination router. Without the second command, no routes appear in the IP routing table because CLNS does not receive the frames to populate the IP routing table. Remember that these are IP routes carried in the IS-IS routing protocol.

Example 10-15   *Configuration for Router A*

```
hostname A
!
Interface Ethernet0
 ip address 10.1.128.1 255.255.255.0
 ip router isis
 isis circuit-type level-1
 Interface Serial0
 ip address 10.100.100.34 255.255.255.0
 ip router isis
 encapsulation frame-relay
 frame-relay map clns 629 broadcast
```

Example 10-15 *Configuration for Router A (Continued)*

```
 frame-relay map clns 931 broadcast
 frame-relay map ip 10.100.100.33 931 broadcast
 frame-relay map ip 10.100.100.35 629 broadcast
 isis circuit-type level-2-only
!
router isis
```

2. *The WAN is a Frame Relay cloud, and Router G has a point-to-point link with Router C. Issue the commands for Router C that configure the link for Integrated IS-IS as a point-to-point link.*

The configuration file in Example 10-16 shows the configuration of IS-IS across the Frame Relay cloud, using the point-to point technology and point-to-point Hellos. Because the link is point-to-point, there is no need to configure **frame-relay map** commands (there is no choice of destination to define). The point-to-point link is just a pipe that goes to one destination. As shown in the configuration, it is only necessary to configure the interface as point-to-point, start Frame Relay, and define the DLCI. In addition to configuring Frame Relay, you must start the IS-IS process for the interface.

Example 10-16 *Configuration for Router C*

```
hostname C
!
Interface Serial0
 no ip address
 encapsulation frame-relay
!
Interface Serial0.1 point-to-point
 ip address 10.100.100.66 255.255.255.0
 ip router isis
 frame-relay interface-dlci 333
!
Interface Serial1
 ip address 10.100.100.35 255.255.255.0
 ip router isis
 encapsulation frame-relay
 frame-relay map clns 629 broadcast
 frame-relay map clns 631 broadcast
 frame-relay map ip 10.100.100.33 631 broadcast
 frame-relay map ip 10.100.100.34 629 broadcast
 isis circuit-type level-2-only
!
router isis
 net 49.0003.0000.0000.000c.00
```

3. *To reduce bandwidth consumption and to hide some network detail, summarization has been suggested as a solution over the WAN links. Issue the commands for Router A that will summarize the networks behind this router with a prefix of /16 across the WAN.*

The IS-IS routing protocol configuration in Example 10-17 shows the **summary-address** command that is used to hide the routes within area 0001 from the other areas. This configuration is possible on Router A because it sits on the boundary between areas. Summarizing routes reduces the network resources required by the network.

Example 10-17 *Configuration for Router A*

```
hostname A
!
Interface Ethernet0
 ip address 10.1.128.1 255.255.255.0
 ip router isis
 isis circuit-type level-1
!
Interface Serial0
 ip address 10.100.100.34 255.255.255.0
 ip router isis
 encapsulation frame-relay
 frame-relay map clns 629 broadcast
 frame-relay map clns 931 broadcast
 frame-relay map ip 10.100.100.33 931 broadcast
 frame-relay map ip 10.100.100.35 629 broadcast
 isis circuit-type level-2-only
!
router isis
 summary-address 10.1.0.0 255.255.0.0
 net 49.0001.0000.0000.000a.00
```

Scenario 10-2 Answers

1. *Identify the DIS on the Ethernet segment. How was this information apparent?*

On examining the show interface output screen in Example 10-18, you can see the circuit ID is 0000.0000.000B.01. This is the system ID of the pseudonode, as is apparent because the last octet has a nonzero value. The system ID of the pseudonode is the system ID of the DIS plus the nonzero octet. Therefore, the DIS is 49.0002.0000.0000.000B.00.

Example 10-18 *Identifying the DIS in Scenario 10-2*

```
Router B
B# show clns interface
Ethernet0 is up, line protocol is up
  Checksums enabled, MTU 1497, Encapsulation SAP
  ERPDUs enabled, min. interval 10 msec.
```

Example 10-18 *Identifying the DIS in Scenario 10-2 (Continued)*

```
RDPDUs enabled, min. interval 100 msec., Addr Mask enabled
Congestion Experienced bit set at 4 packets
CLNS fast switching enabled
CLNS SSE switching disabled
DEC compatibility mode OFF for this interface
Next ESH/ISH in 15 seconds
Routing Protocol: IS-IS
    Circuit Type: level-1-2
    Interface number 0x0, local circuit ID 0x1
    Level-1 Metric: 10, Priority: 64, Circuit ID: 0000.0000.000B.01
    Number of active level-1 adjacencies: 1
    Level-2 Metric: 10, Priority: 64, Circuit ID: 0000.0000.000B.01
    Number of active level-2 adjacencies: 1
    Next IS-IS LAN Level-1 Hello in 678 milliseconds
    Next IS-IS LAN Level-2 Hello in 1 seconds
```

2. *If Router A died, what would the effect be on the network?*

If Router A died, Routers B and C would not be able to communicate with Router A or with Router D. However, Routers B and C would be able to communicate with each other. The network behind Router A would function, but it would be isolated from the others.

The neighbor tables would fail to hear the Hellos from Router A, and Routers B and C would time out all routes that they had heard from this router. Routers behind Router A would time out Router A from the neighbor table. All the former neighbors of Router A would send LSPs. The LSPs from Router A would be purged from all the databases, new LSPs would flood the network, and the SPF algorithm would be run. Router A and the network behind it would be annexed from the larger network of Routers B and C.

3. *Is summarization possible only on the routers entering the WAN cloud, or is it possible on the networks not shown in the figure, but on the other side of the routers? Give reasons for your answers.*

Summarization is only possible on the Level 1-2 routers, acting in a similar way to an OSPF ABR, and then only if the addressing scheme allows for it to be implemented. The Level 1-2 router would summarize the routes and inject them into the Level 2 network.

Part V covers the following Cisco BSCI exam topics related to implementing Cisco IOS routing features:

- Describe, configure, or verify route redistribution between IP routing IGPs (e.g., route-maps, default routes, etc.).

- Describe, configure, or verify route filtering (i.e., distribute-lists and passive interfaces).

- Describe and configure DHCP services (e.g., Server, Client, IP helper address, etc.).

This list reflects the exam topics posted on Cisco.com at the publication time of this book.

Part V: Cisco IOS Routing Features

This chapter covers the following topics:

- **Understanding Redistribution Fundamentals**—Describes reasons why multiple protocols may exist within an organization and introduces the basics of redistribution.

- **Understanding the Routing Decisions that Affect Redistribution**—Describes routing metrics, path selection, and potential problems associated with redistribution.

- **Controlling Routing Updates During Redistribution**—Describes the methods to control the routing information sent between routers during redistribution.

- **Configuring Redistribution**—Describes the steps involved in setting up redistribution.

- **Controlling Routing Updates with Filtering**—Describes the use of distribute lists.

- **Verifying, Maintaining, and Troubleshooting the Redistribution and Filtering Implementation**—Focuses on the **traceroute** and extended **ping** commands.

Implementing Redistribution and Controlling Routing Updates

The topics in this chapter deal with the traffic generated by routing updates in terms of both the network resources that they use and the information contained within them. The chapter covers two different but related areas, redistribution and filtering. The network overhead involved in routing updates has already been dealt with in other chapters; it keeps recurring as a theme because all network traffic directly influences the network's capability to scale or to grow.

The information propagated through the network is complex when dealing with one routing protocol. When multiple protocols have to share information (through redistribution) so that the larger network can see every route available within the autonomous system (AS), the information flow must be controlled and closely managed with filtering and other solutions.

This chapter deals with the need for redistribution, which increases the network overhead, and filtering, which is used to reduce overhead. The chapter first explains the design issues that might affect the configuration, and then provides configuration examples of route redistribution and filtering.

"Do I Know This Already?" Quiz

The purpose of the "Do I Know This Already?" quiz is to help you decide what parts of this chapter to use. If you already intend to read the entire chapter, you do not necessarily need to answer these questions now.

The 16-question quiz, derived from the major sections in the "Foundation Topics" portion of the chapter, helps you determine how to spend your limited study time.

Table 11-1 outlines the major topics discussed in this chapter and the "Do I Know This Already?" quiz questions that correspond to those topics.

> **CAUTION**   The goal of self-assessment is to gauge your mastery of the topics in this chapter. If you do not know the answer to a question or are only partially sure of the answer, you should mark this question wrong for purposes of the self-assessment. Giving yourself credit for an answer you correctly guess skews your self-assessment results and might provide you with a false sense of security.

Table 11-1 *"Do I Know This Already?" Foundation Topics Section-to-Question Mapping*

Foundation Topics Section	Questions Covered in This Section	Score
Understanding Redistribution Fundamentals	1–3	
Understanding the Routing Decisions That Affect Redistribution	4–7	
Controlling Routing Updates During Redistribution	8–9	
Configuring Redistribution	10–11	
Controlling Routing Updates with Filtering	12–14	
Verifying, Maintaining, and Troubleshooting the Redistribution and Filtering Implementation	15–16	
Total Score		

1. Which of the following are reasons to run multiple routing protocols?

   a. Applications requiring UNIX

   b. Smaller routing domains speed up convergence

   c. Transitioning from one routing protocol to another

   d. Smaller routing domains ensure a more stable network

2. EIGRP automatically redistributes into which routing protocols?

   a. IGRP running the same AS number

   b. IGRP with any process ID

   c. EIGRP running the same AS number

   d. EIGRP with any process ID

3. How many IP routing tables can be held on a router within a typical organization?

   a. One

   b. One per routing protocol

   c. Four

   d. Six

4. The problems experienced as a result of multiple routing processes and their redistribution include which of the following?

    a. Suboptimal path

    b. Loss of hello packets

    c. Routing loops

    d. Continuous LSA propagation

5. Which command is used to configure the administrative distance?

    a. **administrative distance**

    b. **distance**

    c. **ip default-distance**

    d. **ip administrative distance**

6. What action is taken if no seed or default metric is configured for OSPF when redistributing EIGRP?

    a. The route is not entered into the routing table.

    b. The route is entered with a cost of 0.

    c. The route is read into OSPF with a cost of 20 (type E2).

    d. The route is entered with a cost of 20 (type 1).

7. What techniques can be employed to avoid redistribution problems?

    a. Distribute lists

    b. Change administrative distance

    c. Ensure the default metric is set to 0

    d. Redistribute on all border routers in both directions

8. Which of the following may be necessary to control the routing updates?

    a. Security

    b. Prevention of routing loops

    c. Scaling the network

    d. Preserving the metric

9. Which of the following is a complex access list that permits conditional programming?

    a. distribute list

    b. passive interface

    c. route map

    d. filter list

10. Which command is used to establish the default or seed metric for EIGRP?

    a. **default-metric 5**

    b. **metric** *bandwidth delay reliability loading mtu*

    c. **default-metric** *bandwidth delay reliability loading mtu* **eigrp**

    d. **default-metric** *bandwidth delay reliability loading mtu*

11. What is the default metric type value for routes redistributed into OSPF?

    a. 1

    b. 2

    c. 3

    d. 4

12. What is the purpose of distribute lists?

    a. Determine the administrative distance of a distributed routing protocol

    b. Identify which interfaces will send updates

    c. Determine which networks are sent in updates

    d. Determine which networks are accepted into the routing table

13. Where are distribute lists defined?

    a. At the interface

    b. Under the routing process

    c. At the router level

    d. At the executive prompt

14. All the following statements are true; which of the following actions is taken first?

    a. Do not advertise the route if it is matched by a **deny** statement.

    b. If no match is found in the distribute list, the implicit **deny any** at the end of the access list will cause the update to be dropped.

    c. If a filter is present, the router examines the access list to see if there is a match on any of the networks in the routing update.

    d. Advertise the route if matched by a **permit** statement.

15. Which commands could be used to verify and troubleshoot a network that is redistributed?

    a. **show ip protocol**

    b. **show ip route**

    c. **show ip route** *routing-protocol*

    d. **show redistributed**

16. Which of the following commands is not useful for tracking redistribution problems?

    a. **show ip protocol**

    b. **show ip route**

    c. **show ip ospf database**

    d. **show ip eigrp neighbors**

    e. **show ip interface brief**

The answers to this quiz are found in Appendix A, "Answers to Chapter 'Do I Know This Already?' Quizzes and Q&A Sections." The suggested choices for your next step are as follows:

- **9 or less overall score**—Read the entire chapter. This includes the "Foundation Topics," "Foundation Summary," "Q&A," and "Scenarios" sections.

- **10–13 overall score**—Begin with the "Foundation Summary" section, and then go to the "Q&A" and "Scenarios" sections. If you have trouble with these exercises, read the appropriate sections in "Foundation Topics."

- **14–16 overall score**—If you want more review on these topics, skip to the "Foundation Summary" section, and then go to the "Q&A" and "Scenarios" sections at the end of the chapter. Otherwise, move to the next chapter.

Foundation Topics

Understanding Redistribution Fundamentals

Routing protocols have distinct advantages and disadvantages in different situations. A protocol that is supported on old equipment (such as RIP) might not support fast classless operation needed in the core of the network (such as OSPF, IS-IS, or EIGRP). Most organizations use the most appropriate routing protocol in different parts of their network. Organizations running multiple routing protocols need to pass networks learned by one protocol into another. This process is called *redistribution*.

Redistribution should not be thought of as a quick and easy solution. Redistribution is complex. It is crucial that you understand the operation of the processes and how this affects your network. This chapter focuses on the implementation of redistribution.

Each routing protocol within an AS can be thought of as a routing domain. Routes redistributed into a routing domain are termed *external routes*, while native routes are called *internal routes*.

The metric is the main method of route selection within a routing protocol. Therefore, it is necessary to define a default seed metric for the networks accepted from other routing protocols.

In Figure 11-1, the routing table for Router B has entries from RIP and OSPF. Router C is connected using EIGRP, but the protocol is only running on the link connecting B and C and therefore does not propagate non-EIGRP routes. You can see that the RIP updates sent out the interfaces do not include networks from OSPF. There are no entries for EIGRP.

Notice that Router C has only connected routes. Although EIGRP has been configured, Router C need only propagate its connected routes via EIGRP and use a default route pointing to Router B.

Redistribution can occur only between processes routing the same routed protocol. IPv4 routes can be passed from OSPF to EIGRP to RIP. IPv6 paths can be communicated from RIPng to OSPFv3.

Figure 11-1 *Routing Updates Without Using Redistribution*

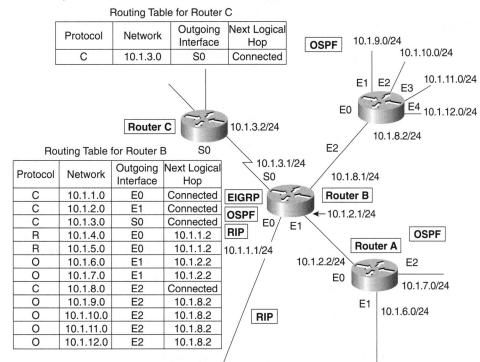

Key to Protocol: O = OSPF R = RIP C = Connected

Routing Table for Router C

Protocol	Network	Outgoing Interface	Next Logical Hop
C	10.1.3.0	S0	Connected

Routing Table for Router B

Protocol	Network	Outgoing Interface	Next Logical Hop
C	10.1.1.0	E0	Connected
C	10.1.2.0	E1	Connected
C	10.1.3.0	S0	Connected
R	10.1.4.0	E0	10.1.1.2
R	10.1.5.0	E0	10.1.1.2
O	10.1.6.0	E1	10.1.2.2
O	10.1.7.0	E1	10.1.2.2
C	10.1.8.0	E2	Connected
O	10.1.9.0	E2	10.1.8.2
O	10.1.10.0	E2	10.1.8.2
O	10.1.11.0	E2	10.1.8.2
O	10.1.12.0	E2	10.1.8.2

Routing Table for Router A

Protocol	Network	Outgoing Interface	Next Logical Hop
C	10.1.2.0	E0	Connected
C	10.1.6.0	E1	Connected
C	10.1.7.0	E2	Connected
O	10.1.8.0	E0	10.1.2.1
O	10.1.9.0	E0	10.1.2.1
O	10.1.10.0	E0	10.1.2.1
O	10.1.11.0	E0	10.1.2.1
O	10.1.12.0	E0	10.1.2.1

Table 11-2 explains the subtleties of redistribution.

Table 11-2 *Redistribution Between Routing Protocols*

Routing Protocol	Redistribution Policy
Static	Requires manual redistribution into other routing protocols.
Connected	Unless included in the network command for the routing process, requires manual redistribution.
RIP	Requires manual redistribution.
EIGRP	Will automatically redistribute between IGRP and EIGRP if the autonomous system number is the same. Otherwise, it requires manual redistribution.
OSPF	Requires manual redistribution between different OSPF process IDs and routing protocols.
IS-IS	Requires manual redistribution between different routing protocols.
BGP	Requires manual redistribution between different routing protocols.

Figure 11-2 illustrates redistribution within an organization.

The main reasons for having multiple protocols within an organization are as follows:

- The organization is transitioning from one routing protocol to another.

- The company wants to transition from multiple routing protocols to a single routing protocol.

- Often after a merger or a takeover, it takes planning, strategy, and careful analysis to determine the best overall design for the network.

- There are (political) ideological differences among the different network administrators, which currently have not been resolved.

- In a very large environment, the various domains might have different requirements, making a single solution inefficient. A clear example is in the case of a large multinational corporation, where EIGRP is the protocol used at the access and distribution layers, but BGP is the protocol connecting the core.

Figure 11-2 *Autonomous Systems Within an Organization*

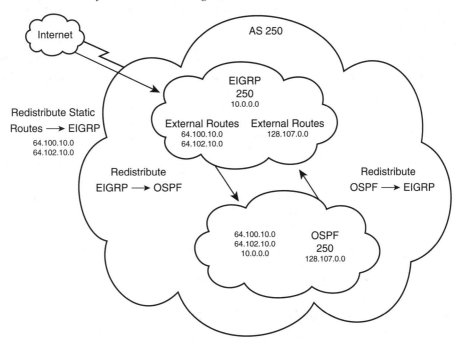

Understanding the Routing Decisions That Affect Redistribution

Redistribution is the answer to running multiple routing protocols within your network while maintaining one cohesive network. However, before you embark on this strategy, you must carefully consider the problems that might arise. You need to briefly consider the routing protocol operation—in particular, how a path is selected to go into the routing table.

Routing Metrics and Redistribution

There are many routing protocols for IP, and each uses a different metric. If two protocols want to share information through redistribution, the configuration must deal with this difference in metrics.

In redistribution, a receiving routing protocol has no point of reference for the metric; for example, RIP would be baffled by a metric of 786. Furthermore, there is no way to algorithmically compare metrics from different protocols. Instead, when routes are accepted into a new protocol, the receiving process must have a starting point, or *seed metric*, in order to calculate the metric for the routing protocol.

The seed metric is assigned to all the routes received into a process through redistribution. The metric is incremented from that point on as the networks propagate throughout the new routing domain.

There are defaults for the seed metrics; however, depending on the routing protocol, the default might prevent the route from entering the routing table. The seed metrics are defined in Table 11-3.

Table 11-3 *Default Seed Metrics*

IP Routing Protocol	Default Seed Metric	Action
EIGRP	Infinity	No routes entered into the routing table
IS-IS	0	Routes entered into the routing table
OSPF	20 (type 2), but routes from BGP are given a metric of 1 (type 2)	Routes entered into the routing table
BGP	MED is given the IGP metric value	Routes entered into the routing table

Path Selection Between Routing Protocols

This section discusses path selection between routing protocols. If the protocols have paths to the same remote destination network, the routing process must decide which path to enter into the routing table. Because the metrics differ between the protocols, selection is based on an arbitrary *administrative distance*. Remember that routers prefer paths with lower administrative distance.

It is important to consider the following rules when redistributing between IP routing protocols:

- If more than one routing protocol is running on a router, the routing table process will place the route with the best administrative distance into the routing table.

- Routing protocols can only redistribute routes they know. Thus, if RIP is being redistributed into EIGRP, the routing table must have an entry for the RIP network.

- When a route is redistributed, it inherits the default administrative distance of the new routing protocol.

- Redistributed routes are called external. External routes in EIGRP are given a different (higher) AD, while OSPF tracks the route as external and prefers internal routes.

Potential Problems with Redistribution

Redistribution is not optimal. The simpler and more straightforward the design, the better managed and more stable the network, which means fewer errors and faster convergence.

A hierarchical IP addressing scheme designed to allow continued network growth, combined with a single IP routing protocol that has the scope to support growth, results in a strong, reliable, and fast network. However, it is rare to find a network of any size that runs only one IP routing protocol. When multiple protocols are running, it is necessary to redistribute.

The problems that can arise from redistribution are typically difficult to troubleshoot because the symptoms often appear at some distance from the configuration error. The problems experienced as a result of multiple routing processes and their redistribution include the following:

- Routing loops because routers send routing information received from one autonomous system back into the same autonomous system.

- Suboptimal routing decisions are made because of the difference in routing metrics.

- The convergence time increases because of the different technologies involved. If the routing protocols converge at different rates, this might result in timeouts and the temporary loss of networks.

- The decision-making process and the information sent within the protocols might be incompatible and not easily exchanged, leading to errors and complex configuration.

The following sections describe how to avoid these potential problems.

Avoiding Routing Loops When Redistributing

Routing loops occur when a routing protocol redistributes routes into another protocol and then receives the same routes back—a process called *route feedback*. Because the metric is reset through redistribution, the routing protocol could see the redistributed path as more attractive. The potential for confusion is enormous, as shown in Figure 11-3; routes distributed from OSPF to EIGRP are distributed back to EIGRP at two redistribution points, causing the routing tables of the respective routers to continuously rotate between alternate primary paths for the redistributed routes.

Figure 11-3 *How Route Feedback Can Cause Routing Loops*

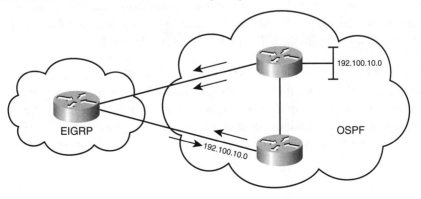

This problem is solved by the following configurations:

- Changing the metric

- Changing the administrative distance

- Using default routes

- Using passive interfaces with static routes

- Using distribute lists

These configurations are discussed in the section of this chapter titled "Configuring Redistribution."

Restricting (to some level) the information sent across various domains is often necessary to manage the complexity of these networks and to reduce the possibility of routing loops. This is done via filtering, using access lists.

Consider the problem by looking at the example in Figure 11-4, remembering that administrative distance is considered without any reference to the metrics. Imagine for a moment that Router A is running RIP and advertising network 190.10.10.0 to both Routers B and E. When Router B receives the RIP update, it redistributes the network 190.10.10.0 into OSPF and advertises it to Router C, which advertises the network to Router D. Eventually Router E receives an OSPF update from D, reporting a network 190.10.10.0 with the path D, C, B, A. However, Router E has a direct path to Router A via RIP; this would be the preferable path. In this instance, the administrative distance works against the network. Because OSPF has an administrative distance of 110 and RIP has an administrative distance of 120, the path placed in the routing table is the one advertised by OSPF via D, C, B and A.

If EIGRP is running on Routers B, C, D, and E, there should be no problems. When RIP redistributes into EIGRP on Router B and the update is propagated to Router E, the routing table should select the route to 190.10.10.0 via Router A. The reason for this is that when network 190.10.10.0 is redistributed into EIGRP, it is flagged as an external route. Thus, it has the administrative distance of 170 and is discarded in favor of the RIP administrative distance of 120. The routing table contains the RIP path to the network 190.10.10.0.

When EIGRP then redistributes into RIP at Routers B and E, the routing table, having no EIGRP entry for the network 190.10.10.0, cannot redistribute this network back into the RIP process. Theoretically, a routing loop is avoided. However, in practice, this might not be the case, as it is dependent on when the routing updates come into the routing process and the inherent stability of the network. For these reasons, you should be careful with bidirectional redistribution.

Figure 11-4 *Path Selection Using Administrative Distance*

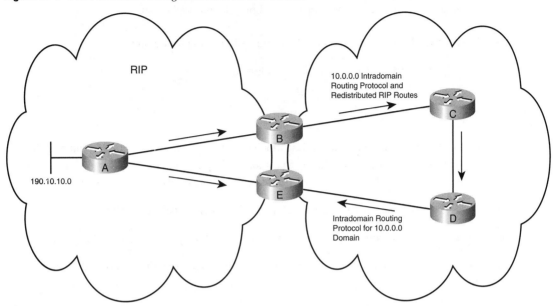

Remember that although you can change the defaults for administrative distance, you should take care when subverting the natural path selection, and any manual configuration must be done with careful reference to the network design of the organization and its traffic flow. To change the administrative distance of a routing protocol, use the following command:

```
Router(config-router)# distance weight [network wildcard-mask]
```

For a static route, use the following command:

```
Router(config)# ip route network [mask] {address | interface} [distance]
```

There are additional commands to change specific types of routes on a per-protocol basis. For example, it is possible to change the administrative distance of internal or external EIGRP or OSPF routes. The administrative distance reflects the preferred choice.

Avoiding Suboptimal Routing Decisions When Redistributing

Routing loops are only one problem that can result from redistributing routes between routing protocols. Suboptimal routing is another problem occasionally created by redistribution. For example, the administrative distance selects the suboptimal path when a directly connected network is designed as a backup link. Although this is a problem of administrative distance as opposed to redistribution, it is important to ensure that the suboptimal path is not propagated into the new routing protocol.

When designing your network, keep the following guidelines in mind when redistributing between routing protocols to avoid routing loops and suboptimal path selection:

- Have a sound knowledge and clear documentation of the following:

    — The network topology (physical and logical)

    — The routing protocol domains

    — The traffic flow

- Do not overlap routing protocols. It is much easier if the different protocols can be clearly delineated into separate domains, with routers acting in a function similar to area border routers (ABRs) in OSPF. This is often referred to as the *core and edge protocols*.

- Identify the boundary routers on which redistribution is to be configured.

- Determine which protocol is the core protocol and which protocol is the edge protocol.

- Determine the direction of redistribution; that is, into which routing protocol the routes are to be distributed.

- If two-way redistribution cannot be avoided, use the mechanisms in the following list:

    — Manually configuring the metric

    — Manually configuring the administrative distance

    — Using distribution access lists

Avoiding Problems with Network Convergence When Redistributing

A major concern is the computation of the routing table and how long it takes the network to converge. Although EIGRP is renowned for its speed in convergence, RIP is fairly slow. Sharing network information between the two might cause problems.

For example, the network converges at the speed of the slower protocol. At some point, this will create timeouts and possibly routing loops. Adjusting the timers might solve the problems, but any routing protocol configuration must be done with a sound knowledge of the entire network and of the routers that need to be configured. Timers typically require every router in the network to be configured to the same value.

Exchange of Routing Protocol-Specific Parameters

The decision-making process and the information sent within the protocols might be incompatible and not easily exchanged, leading to errors and complex configuration. Each routing protocol maintains parameters specific to that protocol—including route metrics. Part of the function of route redistribution is to manage the transformation of these parameters between routing protocols in a meaningful way.

For example, redistributing into OSPF requires translating all the parameters of the redistributed routing protocol into the OSPF cost metric. This is very limiting when converting from a protocol such as EIGRP which has five parameters (bandwidth, load, reliability, delay, and MTU) when redistributing *into* EIGRP, so a judicious decision must be made by the network engineer as to how to best convert EIGRP routes with their associated parameters into OSPF routes with the cost parameter. If the inter-protocol mappings are ill-conceived, the routing process of the *receiving* protocol will be adversely affected. Several illustrative examples are provided in this chapter, demonstrating the principle of route parameter mappings.

Controlling Routing Updates During Redistribution

Controlling routing updates is useful for many reasons:

- To hide some networks from the rest of the organization (security)

- To prevent routing loops

- To control network overhead

Various methods enable you to control the routing information sent between routers during redistribution. These methods include the following:

- Passive interfaces

- Static routes

- Default routes

- The null interface

- Distribute lists

- Route maps

The next sections describe each method in more detail.

Passive Interfaces

A *passive interface* does not participate in the routing process. In RIP, the process listens but will not send updates on a passive interface. In OSPF and EIGRP, the process does not send hellos, and therefore no neighbor relationship can form.

Interfaces that participate in the routing process are controlled by the interface configuration. The configuration instructs the routing process via the **network** command as to which interfaces to use. The **passive interface** command is useful to disable a routing protocol on a per-interface basis; this command can simplify the network administration and prevent routing loops.

Static Routes

A *static route* is a route that is manually configured. It takes precedence over routes learned by a routing process because it has a lower default administrative distance.

Static routes are not practical in a large network because the table cannot dynamically learn of changes in the network topology. In small environments or in stub networks, however, this is an excellent solution. Instead of redistributing the entire routing tables between the protocols, static routes are defined and redistributed. This is useful if you need to provide more information than a default route. The routing protocols have the information they need while you maintain careful control over the design and data flow. Again, this is a typical scenario for a BGP and an IGP to exchange information.

The reasons for static routing are summarized as follows:

- If there is only one path, then there is no need for the complication and overhead of a routing protocol.

- If there are two autonomous systems that do not need to exchange the entire routing table, but simply need to know about a few routes.

- To change the mask of the network. For example, as seen in BGP, you can statically define a supernet and redistribute the static route into the BGP process.

- To redistribute from a routing protocol that understands variable-length subnet mask (VLSM) to one that does not.

Default Routes

A default route is a "route of last resort." The default route (0.0.0.0 mask 0.0.0.0) is the least specific path and the router will always choose more specific paths. If there are no other matching entries in the routing table, the default route is used.

Default routes reduce overhead and complexity, and can remove loops, particularly when they are used instead of redistribution between routing protocols. One routing protocol can use a default route to the other routing protocol's domain; a typical example is an IGP pointing a default route into the BGP domain.

Another occasion for configuring a default route would be for a stub network to connect to the larger network.

Default and static routes are shown in Figure 11-5.

Figure 11-5 *The Use of Default and Static Routes*

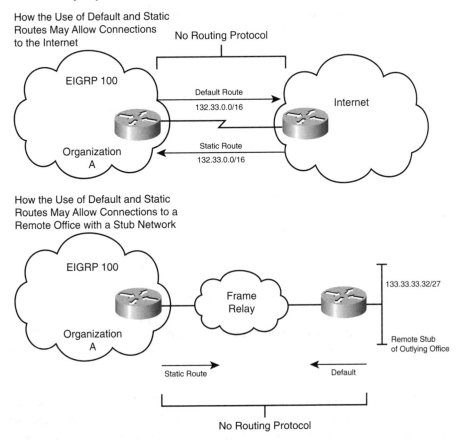

How the Use of Default and Static
Routes May Allow Connections
to the Internet

No Routing Protocol

EIGRP 100

Default Route
132.33.0.0/16

Internet

Organization
A

Static Route
132.33.0.0/16

How the Use of Default and Static
Routes May Allow Connections to a
Remote Office with a Stub Network

EIGRP 100

Frame
Relay

133.33.33.32/27

Organization
A

Remote Stub
of Outlying Office

Static Route

Default

No Routing Protocol

The Null Interface

A *null interface* is a virtual interface that could also be called a *bit bucket*. All traffic destined for the remote network is routed into a black hole. This is used either to discard routes by destination in a rudimentary filtering system or to redistribute between classless and classful routing protocols.

The null interface is a convenient place to point summarized links, as shown in Chapter 14, "BGP Concepts." Null interfaces are also used automatically by EIGRP to drop packets within a summarized network when the specific destination network does not appear in the routing table.

Distribute Lists

Distribute lists are access lists applied to the routing process, determining which networks are accepted into the routing table or sent in updates. When communicating to another routing process through redistribution, it is important to control the information sent into the other process. This control is for security, overhead, the prevention of routing loops, and management reasons. Access lists used in conjunction with careful network design afford the greatest control of the traffic flow within the network. You learn more about distribute lists in the section, "Controlling Routing Updates with Filtering," later in this chapter.

Route Maps

Route maps are complex access lists that permit conditional programming. Distribute lists are access lists filtering routing updates, whereas route maps use match criteria to match traffic as desired and a set function to alter parameters within the routing protocol packets. The ultimate effect of distribute lists can essentially be reproduced by a route map; that is, distribute lists are easier to implement but do not permit nearly as much granularity.

If a packet or route matches the criteria defined in a match statement, changes defined in the **set** command are performed on the packet or route in question. These are used in redistribution in the same way as distribute lists, but allow a greater level of sophistication in the criteria stated.

Figure 11-6 shows the options for controlling routing updates in a large and complex network.

In Figure 11-6, Router A has a distribute list that is denying the propagation of the network 140.100.32.0 out of E3, which is the network connected to E2. Network 140.100.32.0 might have some security reasons for not being seen by the networks connected to Router B. This network could be a test or an R&D project for the department connecting to Router B, and connectivity would confuse the situation.

A default route is configured to send packets out interface S0. A static route is configured to send packets out interface S1. Interface S0 provides a path to the Internet, and the static routes are configured by the ISP. This allows them to connect to the ISP without having to receive dynamic routing, which could be huge.

The organization has a default route, which is used when there is not a specific route to a destination.

On S1, the router's interface is configured with static routes so that the router at the other end does not need to run a routing protocol. The router at the other end has a default route configured, suggesting that this is a stub network. This ensures that Router C has a simple configuration with few demands on the router.

Figure 11-6 *Controlling Routing Updates*

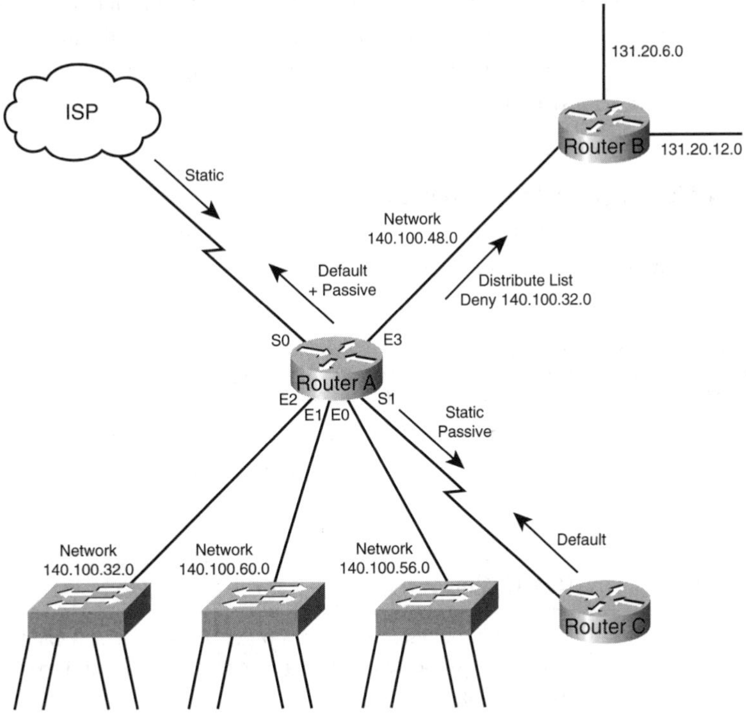

The concepts of redistribution are detailed in the following section with configuration examples.

Configuring Redistribution

Redistribution configuration is specific to the routing protocol itself. Before you contemplate implementation, reference the configuration guides from Cisco.

All protocols require the following steps for redistribution:

Step 1   Configure redistribution.

Step 2   Define the default metric of redistributed routes.

The commands for redistribution are configured as subcommands to the routing process. The **redistribute** command identifies the routing protocol from which the updates are to be accepted. The command identifies the source of the updates.

These commands, discussed in detail in the next sections, constitute the basic steps in the implementation of redistribution. Depending on the design of your network, additional configuration might be needed. The configuration of administrative distance, passive interfaces, and static and default routes are provided in the section "Configuration Commands to Control Routing Updates in Redistribution" later in this chapter.

Redistribution Configuration Syntax

To configure redistribution between routing protocols, the following command syntax is used under the routing protocol that receives the routes:

```
Router(config-router)# redistribute protocol [process-id] {level-1 | level-1-2 | level-2}
[metric metric-value] [metric-type type-value]
[match {internal | external 1 | external 2}] [tag tag-value]
[route-map map-tag] [weight weight] [subnets]
```

The command is very complex because it shows all the parameters for all the different protocols. For an explanation of the command parameters, refer to Table 11-4.

Table 11-4 *Parameters of the Command for Redistribution*

Command	Description
protocol	This is the routing protocol that provides the routes. It can be one of the following: **connected, bgp, eigrp, egp, igrp, isis, iso-igrp, mobile, ospf, static,** or **rip**.
process-id	For BGP, EGP, EIGRP, or IGRP, this is an autonomous system number. For OSPF, this is an OSPF process ID. RIPv1 and v2 do not use either.
level-1	For IS-IS, Level 1 routes are redistributed into other IP routing protocols independent of L2 routes.
level-1-2	For IS-IS, both Level 1 and Level 2 routes are redistributed into other IP routing protocols.
level-2	For IS-IS, Level 2 routes are redistributed into other IP routing protocols independently.
metric *metric-value*	This optional parameter is used to specify the metric for the redistributed route. When redistributing into protocols other than OSPF, if this value is not specified and no value is specified using the **default-metric** router configuration command, routes have a metric of infinity and are not used.
metric-type *type-value*	This is an optional OSPF parameter that specifies the external link type. This can be **1** for type 1 external routes, or **2** for type 2 external routes. The default is 2. Refer to Chapter 7, "Using OSPF Across Multiple Areas," and Chapter 8, "OSPF Advanced Topics," for details on OSPF external route types.

Table 11-4 *Parameters of the Command for Redistribution (Continued)*

Command	Description
match	This is an optional OSPF parameter that specifies the criteria by which OSPF routes are redistributed into other routing domains. It can be **internal**—Redistribute routes that are internal to a specific autonomous system. **external 1**—Redistribute routes that are external (imported into OSPF) as a type 1 external route. **external 2**—Redistribute routes that are external to OSPF but that are imported into OSPF as a type 2 external route.
tag *tag-value*	(Optional) The tag-value is a 32-bit decimal value attached to each external route. It can be used by EIGRP and IS-IS, but is not used by the OSPF protocol. Tags can be used to communicate information between autonomous system boundary routers. If no value is specified, then the remote autonomous system number is used for routes from BGP and EGP; for other protocols, zero (0) is used.
route-map	(Optional) This instructs the redistribution process that a route map must be referenced to filter the routes imported from the source routing protocol to the current routing protocol. If not specified, no filtering is performed.
map-tag	This is the optional identifier of a configured route map to filter the routes imported from the source routing protocol to the current routing protocol. You learn more about route maps in Chapter 12, "Controlling Redistribution with Route Maps."
weight *weight*	This option sets the BGP weight attribute when redistributing into BGP. This is an integer between 0 and 65,535.
subnets	When redistributing into OSPF, this imports routes with the entire VLSM prefix. It is important to use this when importing into OSPF.

Configuring the Default Metric

The default metric can be configured in two ways:

■ The **redistribute** command permits the assignment of the metric to the redistributed routing protocol specified in this command.

■ Use the **default-metric** command to assign a metric to all redistributed routes from all routing protocols.

If both the **redistribute** command and **default-metric** commands are used within a single routing process, the metric assigned by the **redistribute** command takes precedence. A **default-metric** command should be used if multiple routing protocols are being redistributed, because some routing protocols will not redistribute routes from other routing protocols without a specific metric assigned by the **redistribute** command.

Example 11-1 shows the metric included in the **redistribute** command.

Example 11-1 *Including the Metric in the **redistribute** Command*

```
Router(config)# router eigrp 100
Router(config-router)# redistribute rip metric 10000 100 255 1 1500
Router(config-router)# network 140.100.0.0
```

This configuration shows the following:

■ The use of the **redistribute** command

■ The routing process from which the routes are being accepted

■ The metric parameter, allowing the configuration of the EIGRP to state the new metric that the old RIP networks will use while traversing the EIGRP network

Configuring the Default Metric for OSPF, IS-IS, RIP, or BGP

It is possible to redistribute the routing protocol and then, with a separate command, to state the default metric. There is no advantage to handling metric assignment within the **redistribute** command or separately.

IS-IS cannot define a default metric. The metric must be stated when redistributing. If no metric is stated, the default (0 cost) is entered and the route discarded.

To configure the default metric for OSPF, RIP, or BGP, use the following command syntax:

```
Router(config-router)# default-metric number
```

The default-metric command is used in Example 11-2.

Example 11-2 *Configuring the Default Metric for Static and OSPF Routes Received by RIP*

```
Router(config)# router rip
Router(config-router)# redistribute static
Router(config-router)# redistribute ospf 25
Router(config-router)# default-metric 2
```

In Example 11-2, the default metric is set to 2. Generally you should set the metric high enough so that external routes are not as interesting as internal routes. If your network is five hops wide, consider a metric of 6 or more. Assigning a default metric helps prevent routing loops.

Configuring the Default Metric for EIGRP

To configure the default metric for EIGRP, use the following command syntax:

```
Router(config-router)# default-metric bandwidth delay reliability loading mtu
```

Typically, you should take the values shown on one of the outgoing interfaces of the router being configured by issuing the following EXEC command:

```
Router# show interface
```

The significance of the metric values is shown in Table 11-5.

Table 11-5 *The Parameters of the **default-metric** Command*

Command Parameter	Description
bandwidth	The bandwidth seen on the route to the destination, in kilobits per second (kbps).
delay	Delay is a constant for different interface types. This value is the cumulative delay experienced on the route and is presented in tens of microseconds.
reliability	The probability of a successful transmission given the history of this interface. The value is not used. It is expressed as a number from 0 to 255, where 255 indicates that the route is perfectly stable and available.
loading	A number range of 0 to 255, where 255 indicates that the line is 100 percent loaded. This parameter is not used either and is, therefore, set to one.
mtu	The maximum packet size that can travel through the network. This parameter is not used and is usually just set to 1500.

Example 11-3 shows the configuration of the default metric when redistributing between routing protocols.

Example 11-3 *Configuring the Default Metric for EIGRP*

```
Router(config)# router eigrp 100
Router(config-router)# redistribute rip
Router(config-router)# redistribute ospf 10
Router(config-router)# default-metric 10000 100 255 1 1500
Router(config-router)# network 140.100.0.0
```

In Example 11-3, EIGRP assigns the same seed metric to networks from both RIP and OSPF. Imagine the situation in which OSPF and RIP have been running. The decision to transition the network to EIGRP has been made. The network designed for EIGRP will run in the core, with the edge routers running redistribution. RIP has been included in the design map to accommodate the UNIX systems running *routed*, which is the routing process for UNIX systems.

The default, or seed, metric used is compound metric used by EIGRP. However, RIP and OSPF would supply a number for hop count and cost, respectively. (Refer to Example 11-2.) This design requires careful consideration and filtering of routing updates because it can result in route feedback, as shown in Figure 11-7.

Figure 11-7 *Configuring the Default Metric*

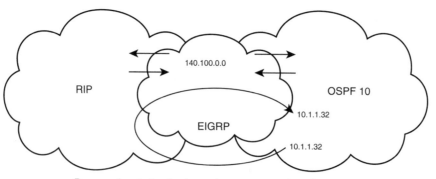

Beware of route feedback causing poor network performance.

In Figure 11-7, EIGRP redistributes the network 10.1.1.32 from OSPF throughout its domain. At the other end of the domain, EIGRP is redistributed into RIP. The network is now known by all routers, whatever their routing protocol preference. However, if another router on the border between the EIGRP domain and the RIP domain is redistributing, it will hear the RIP update for 10.1.1.32 and redistribute all its networks into EIGRP, including the network originating from OSPF. The end result of this scenario will be suboptimal routing, depending on the exact topology.

Configuring the Administrative Distance

As shown in this chapter, it is important to ensure that routes redistributed into another routing protocol are assigned an appropriate metric. On the other hand, it is equally important to consider the need to control the choice that the routing process makes when presented with multiple routes to the same destination from different routing protocols; in this case, the administrative distance determines which routing protocol is used in the routing table. The metric is only relevant within the route selection process of a given routing protocol.

To ensure the optimal path is chosen, it is sometimes necessary to change the administrative distance. The command structure is somewhat protocol-dependent, in that EIGRP requires separate internal and external distances. The following command syntax is used for EIGRP:

```
Router(config)# distance eigrp internal-distance external-distance
```

The **distance** command, as used to configure the EIGRP administrative distance, is explained in Table 11-6.

Table 11-6 *Configuring Administrative Distance for EIGRP*

Command	Description
internal-distance	Administrative distance for EIGRP internal routes. These are routes learned from another router within the same AS.
external-distance	Administrative distance for EIGRP external routes. These are redistributed routes, such as OSPF.

To configure the administrative distance for the other IP protocols, the following command syntax is used:

```
Router(config-router)# distance weight [address mask] [access-list-number | name] [ip]
```

The **distance** command to configure the administrative distance for other IP protocols is explained in Table 11-7.

Table 11-7 *Configuring Administrative Distance for Other IP Protocols*

Command	Description
weight	Administrative distance, an integer from 10 to 255, where 255 indicates that the route is unreachable. The values 0 to 9 are reserved for internal use.
address	Optional IP address. Assigns the administrative distance to networks matching the IP address.
mask	Optional wildcard mask for IP address. A bit set to 1 in the mask has the corresponding bit in the address value ignored.
*access-list-number	name*	Optional number or name of standard access list to be applied to the incoming routing updates. Assigns administrative distance to matching or permitted networks.
ip	Optional. Specifies IP-derived routes for Intermediate System-to-Intermediate System (IS-IS).

Configuration Commands to Control Routing Updates in Redistribution

As explained in the section "Controlling Routing Updates During Redistribution," it is necessary to control the flow of updates between the routing protocol as well as throughout the autonomous system. The following sections consider the implementation of passive interfaces, static routes, and default routes.

Configuring the Passive Interface

The passive interface is used for routing protocols that automatically send updates through every interface with an address that is included in the **network** command. If an interface does not connect to another router, it is a waste of time to send updates.

The command reduces spending limited resources without compromising the integrity of the router. The router processes all routes received on an interface. It is also useful for suppressing unwanted neighbors and preventing accidental misconfiguration.

The command syntax to configure a passive interface, where *type* and *number* indicate the interface to be made, is as follows:

```
Router(config-router)# passive-interface type number
```

Note that the **passive-interface default** command configures all interfaces as passive interfaces.

Configuring Static Routes

The following shows the syntax for configuring the static route:

```
Router(config)# ip route prefix mask {address|interface} [distance] [tag tag]
   [permanent]
```

This defines the path by stating the next-hop router to which to send the traffic. This configuration can be used only if the network address for the next-hop router is in the routing table. If the static route needs to be advertised to other routers, it should be redistributed.

Table 11-8 explains the options available in the static route command.

Table 11-8 *Explanation of the IP Route Options*

Command	Description
prefix	The route prefix for the destination.
mask	The prefix mask for the destination.
address	The IP address of the next-hop router.
interface	The interface used to get to the network.
distance	Optional administrative distance to assign to this route.
tag *tag*	Optional value that can be used as a match value in route maps.
permanent	Specification that the route will not be removed even if the interface associated with the route goes down.

Use static routes pointing to the outgoing interface only on point-to-point interfaces. Static routes configured on multipoint or multiaccess interfaces need a next-hop address. On point-to-point interfaces, the information is sent to the only other device on the network.

Example 11-4 (and Figure 11-8) illustrate the use of a static route and the **passive-interface** command. Additional configuration is included to place the commands in context.

Example 11-4 *The Use of Static Routing and Passive Interfaces*

```
Router(config)# Router A
RouterA(config)# username RouterB password Shhh
RouterA(config)# dialer-list 1 protocol ip permit
RouterA(config)# interface bri 0
RouterA(config-if)# encapsulation ppp
RouterA(config-if)# ip addr 10.1.2.1 255.255.255.0
RouterA(config-if)# ppp authentication chap
RouterA(config-if)# dialer map ip 10.1.2.2 broadcast name RouterB 1222555222201
RouterA(config-if)# dialer-group 1
RouterA(config)# interface ethernet 0
RouterA(config-if)# ip address 10.1.1.1 255.255.255.0
RouterA(config)# ip route 10.1.3.0 255.255.255.0 10.1.2.2
RouterA(config)# router eigrp 1
RouterA(config-router)# network 10.0.0.0
RouterA(config-router)# passive-interface Bri0
```

In this example, the link between Router A and Router B is raised when Router A sees interesting traffic try to exit the serial interface. *Interesting traffic* is traffic that is permitted in a preconfigured access list. In this example, all IP traffic is considered interesting. This example is valid for occasional access, except for the few additional ISDN parameters that need to be added. Figure 11-8 illustrates the use of both static routes and passive interfaces.

Figure 11-8 *The Use of Static Routes Across a Dialup Link*

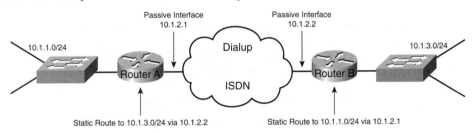

Note: No routing protocol is running across the ISDN cloud.

In this example, you see that EIGRP updates do not flow across the dialup line because the interface pointing into the ISDN cloud is configured as a passive interface. The same configuration has been applied to Router B so that no updates raise the WAN link.

Neither Router A nor Router B knows of the networks on the other side of the WAN, so static routes must be configured.

Configuring Default Routes

In larger networks, there might be many static routes to be configured. Not only is this a chore for the administrator, but it also requires vigilance so that changes in the routing table can be reconfigured. It might be that turning on a routing protocol is advised, or alternatively, you can configure a specialized static route, called a *static default route*.

The following is a static default route pointed out serial 0:

```
Router(config)# ip route 0.0.0.0 0.0.0.0 serial 0
```

The default routes can be propagated through the network dynamically or they can be configured into the individual routers.

When default information is being passed along through a dynamic routing protocol, no further configuration is required. In the case of RIP version 1, for example, there can be only one default route—network 0.0.0.0.

It is common practice to redistribute static routes at edge routers to propagate desired routes without the burden of unnecessarily exchanging all dynamic routes with a neighbor router.

Redistribution Case Studies

The following examples are case studies that pull together the concepts you learned about redistribution. Redistribution involves complex design and configuration considerations. Therefore, it is best to see the various problems and solutions illustrated in context.

This section presents three examples:

- Route redistribution without redundant paths between different routing protocols.

- Route redistribution with redundant paths between different routing protocols. The example also covers resolving the path selection problems that result in redistributed networks.

- The use of a default network in a redistributed environment.

Example 1: Route Redistribution Without Redundant Paths

See Figure 11-9 for this example of route redistribution without redundant paths between different routing protocols.

Figure 11-9 *Simple Redistribution Between RIP and EIGRP*

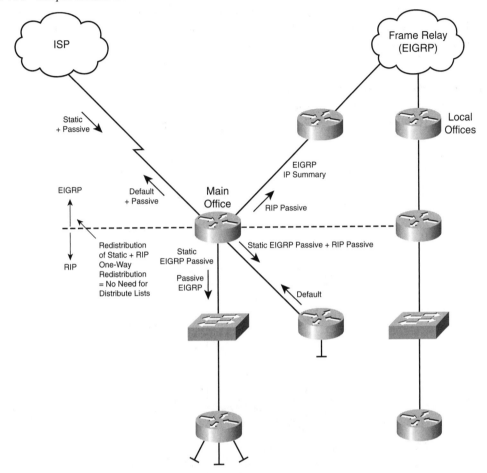

Figure 11-9 shows local offices connecting to the main office via Frame Relay. Each office has a point-to-point permanent virtual circuit (PVC) to a router in the main office.

EIGRP is being run through the Frame Relay cloud to reduce network overhead. There is no need for a routing protocol to be run on the LAN segments.

RIP is being run at the main office. This is to allow the corporate UNIX servers running *routed* to have an understanding of the network. *routed* listens only to RIP updates. Redistribution allows the servers to know about the EIGRP networks.

If the EIGRP networks need to know about each other, the RIP networks would need to be redistributed into the EIGRP environment. This is unlikely because the servers are centrally held at the main office, and there will be little lateral traffic flow. The configuration shown in

Figure 11-9 is simple because there are no redundant links. The Frame Relay cloud uses point-to-point PVCs. In the future, the company might want to add redundancy by meshing the Frame Relay cloud and consolidating the three core routers into one large router. Currently, the company has a simple and low-cost solution using existing equipment.

Example 2: Route Redistribution with Redundant Paths

This example covers route redistribution with redundant paths between different routing protocols and resolving path selection problems that result in redistributed networks.

In Figure 11-10, Router A is connected to networks 140.100.1.0, 140.100.2.0, and 140.100.3.0. Using RIP, network 140.100.1.0 is advertised to Router B, 140.100.3.0 is advertised to Router C, and network 140.100.2.0 is advertised to both Routers A and B.

Figure 11-10 *Choosing the Optimal Path, Through Administrative Distance, When Redistribution Is Using Redundant Paths*

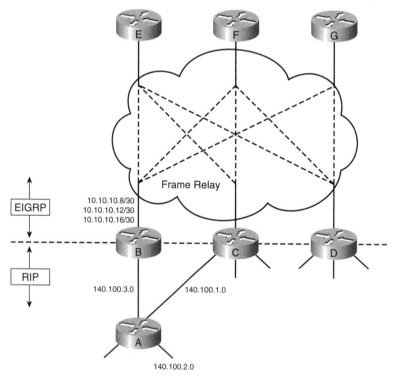

The routing table of Router A will show the information presented in Table 11-9.

Table 11-9 *Router A Routing Table Information*

Routing Protocol	Network/Subnet	Next Logical Hop	Metric
Connected	140.100.1.0/24	Connected E0	0
Connected	140.100.2.0/24	Connected E1	0
Connected	140.100.3.0/24	Connected E2	0
RIP	10.10.10.8/30	140.100.3.2	1 hop
RIP	10.10.10.12/30	140.100.3.2	1 hop
RIP	10.10.10.16/30	140.100.3.2	1 hop
RIP	10.10.10.20/30	140.100.3.2	1 hop
RIP	10.10.10.24/30	140.100.3.2	1 hop
RIP	10.10.10.28/30	140.100.3.2	1 hop
RIP	10.10.10.32/30	140.100.3.2	1 hop
RIP	193.144.6.0/24	140.100.3.2	1 hop
RIP	193.144.7.0/24	140.100.3.2	1 hop
RIP	193.144.8.0/24	140.100.3.2	1 hop

The routing table of Router B shows the information presented in Table 11-10.

Table 11-10 *Router B Routing Table Information*

Routing Protocol	Network/Subnet	Next Logical Hop	Metric
RIP	140.100.1.0/24	140.100.3.1	1 hop
RIP	140.100.2.0/24	140.100.3.1	1 hop
Connected	140.100.3.0/24	Connected E0	0
Connected	10.10.10.8/30	Connected S0	0
Connected	10.10.10.12/30	Connected S0	0
Connected	10.10.10.16/30	Connected S0	0

continues

Table 11-10 *Router B Routing Table Information (Continued)*

Routing Protocol	Network/Subnet	Next Logical Hop	Metric
EIGRP	10.10.10.20/30	10.10.10.9	2221056
EIGRP	10.10.10.24/30	10.10.10.9	2221056
EIGRP	10.10.10.28/30	10.10.10.13	2221056
EIGRP	10.10.10.32/30	10.10.10.13	2221056
EIGRP	193.144.6.0/24	10.10.10.9	2221056
EIGRP	193.144.7.0/24	10.10.10.13	2221056
EIGRP	193.144.8.0/24	10.10.10.17	2221056

Note that the routing table for Router A sees all the subnets for network 10.0.0.0 with a mask of 255.255.255.252 or /30. However, because RIP version 1 does not pass the network mark in updates and Router A is not connected to network 10.0.0.0, RIP version 2 must be the protocol in play between Router A and Router B.

The routing table sees all the paths as unique, so it is clear which paths are accessible through RIP or EIGRP. Even after redistribution, the routing table does not change; the confusion occurs after the propagation of the EIGRP updates through the network.

EIGRP updates are sent to all the routers in the domain, and Routers E, F, and G have no confusion. Depending on the timing of the updates and convergence, however, Router C might be confused. Routers E, F, and G have sent information on how to get to the networks 140.100.1.0 and 140.100.2.0. Router C also receives information from Router A. Sending the data traffic to Router A is obviously the optimum path; however, because EIGRP has a significantly better administrative distance, the EIGRP route is placed in the routing table as having the best path. Based on the assumption that the Frame Relay PVCs all have the same bandwidth, the routing table sees all three paths and distributes the traffic evenly among them.

Example 11-5 shows how to configure Routers B, C, and D to change the administrative distance to favor RIP for the LANs within its domain. The networks 140.100.1.0 and 140.100.2.0 are given an administrative distance of 200 in accordance with the access list. This ensures that the RIP path will be favored if it is available.

Example 11-5 *Changing the Administrative Distance to Favor RIP*

```
Router(config)# router rip
Router(config-router)# network 140.100.0.0
Router(config-router)# passive interface S0.1
Router(config-router)# redistribute eigrp 100 metric 3
```

Example 11-5 *Changing the Administrative Distance to Favor RIP (Continued)*

```
Router(config)# router eigrp 100
Router(config-router)# network 140.100.0.0
Router(config-router)# passive interface E0
Router(config-router)# default-metric 10000 100 255 1 1500
Router(config-router)# distance 200 0.0.0.0 255.255.255.255 3
Router(config)# access-list 3 permit 140.100.1.0
Router(config)# access-list 3 permit 140.100.2.0
```

The **distance** command sets the administrative distance for the EIGRP 100 process. It changes the distance from 90 to 200, which makes the routes that RIP offers more favorable because RIP has an administrative distance of 120.

The use of 0.0.0.0 with a wildcard mask of 255.255.255.255 is a placeholder. It indicates that although the command allows for a network to be specified so that the administrative distance can be applied selectively to that network, in this configuration, no network has been selected. The command has been applied to all networks. You do want the administrative distance to be altered on two networks, however. This granularity cannot be stated in the **distance** command; therefore, an access list is used.

In the example, the number 3 at the end of the command line points to the access list that carries that number as an identifier. By permitting networks 140.100.1.0 and 140.100.2.0, the access list is identifying the networks to which the **distance** command is to be applied.

Example 3: A Default Network in a Redistributed Environment

The use of the default network simplifies the configuration of a redistributed network by allowing the redistribution to be one-way. This significantly reduces the possibility of feedback of networks into the originating domain. The configuration for this example is inset within Figure 11-11 because the configuration of more than one router is shown.

Figure 11-11 *The Use of a Default Network in a Redistributed Network to Resolve Problems with Path Selection*

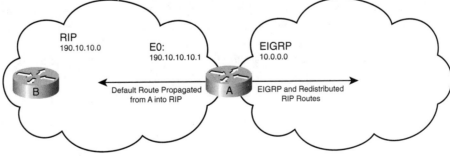
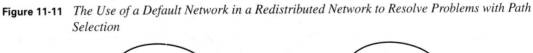

In this design, every router and, therefore, workstation within the RIP domain sees its own internal networks, but all other networks are accessed via the default route. Example 11-6 shows the configuration for Router B.

Example 11-6 *Router B Configuration*

```
RouterB(config)# router rip
RouterB(config-router)# network 190.10.10.0
```

Router A redistributes between RIP and EIGRP, with the RIP domain acting as a stub network. The default route is configured as a static route on Router A, redistributed into RIP, and propagated throughout the RIP domain. The internal RIP-only routers must be configured to accept a default route with a destination network because it is only reachable via a route default.

The configuration for Router A is shown in Example 11-7.

Example 11-7 *Router A Configuration*

```
RouterA(config)# router eigrp 100
RouterA(config-router)# redistribute rip
RouterA(config-router)# default-metric 10000 100 255 1 1500
RouterA(config-router)# network 10.0.0.0
RouterA(config)# router rip
RouterA(config-router)# network 190.10.10.0
RouterA(config-router)# default-metric 3
RouterA(config-router)# redistribute static
RouterA(config)# ip route 0.0.0.0 0.0.0.0 10.10.10.1
```

The redistribution on Router A can now be one-way. EIGRP needs to know all the networks in the RIP domain, but RIP, when configured with a default route, needs no understanding of the outside world. The RIP domain works in a similar fashion as a stub network in OSPF.

Controlling Routing Updates with Filtering

Despite all the mechanisms for controlling and reducing the routing updates on your network, it is sometimes necessary to wield greater and more flexible power. This comes in the form of access lists, which when applied to routing updates are referred to as *distribute lists*.

The logic used in the distribute list is similar to that of an access list. The process follows:

1. The router receives a routing update or is about to send a routing update about one or more networks.

2. The router looks at the appropriate interface involved with the action to check for filtering.

3. If a filter is present, the router examines the access list to see if there is a match on any of the networks in the routing update.

4. If there is no filter on the interface, the routing update is sent directly to the routing process as normal.

5. If there is a filter, the route entry is processed according to the distribute list: advertise the route if matched by a permit statement or do not advertise if it is matched by a deny statement.

6. If no match is found in the distribute list, the implicit deny any at the end of the access list will cause the update to be dropped.

Routing updates can be filtered per routing protocol by defining an access list and applying it to a routing protocol. There are some limitations to distribute lists when applied to OSPF—the inbound list prevents routes entering the routing table but does not prevent link-state packets from being propagated. Distribute lists are judiciously used with OSPF at the ABR or ASBR.

When creating a routing filter or distribute list, take the following steps:

Step 1   Identify the network addresses to be filtered and create an access list.
Permit the networks you want to have advertised.

Step 2   Determine whether you are filtering routing updates coming into the router
or updates to be propagated to other routers.

Step 3   Assign the access list using the **distribute-list** command.

Use the following command syntax to configure the distribute list to filter incoming updates:

```
Router(config-router)# distribute-list {access-list-number | name} in [type number]
```

Table 11-11 explains the options of the **distribute-list in** command.

Table 11-11 *Explanation of the* **distribute-list in** *Command Options*

Command	Description
*access-list-number	name*	Gives the standard access list number or name
in	Applies the access list to incoming routing updates
type *number*	Gives the optional interface type and number from which updates will be filtered

Use the following command syntax to configure the distribute list to filter outgoing updates:

```
Router(config-router)# distribute-list {access-list-number | name} out
[interface-name | routing-process | autonomous-system-number]
```

Table 11-12 explains the options of the **distribute-list out** command.

Table 11-12 *Explanation of the* **distribute-list out** *Command Options*

Command	Description
*access-list-number	name*	Gives the standard access list number or name
out	Applies the access list to outgoing routing updates
interface-name	Gives the optional interface name out of which updates will be filtered
routing-process	Gives the optional name of the routing process, or the keyword static or connected, from which updates will be filtered
autonomous-system-number	Gives the optional autonomous system number of routing process

Verifying, Maintaining, and Troubleshooting the Redistribution and Filtering Implementation

The key to maintaining and redistribution within your network is to have a clear understanding of the network topology from both a physical and a logical perspective. The traffic flows—the peaks and lows in the traffic volume—are also important in truly understanding the connectivity issues within the network. From this vantage point, it is possible to interpret the output presented by the various tools available.

Most of the appropriate commands in tracking redistribution problems were examined earlier in this book. They include the following:

- **show ip protocol**

- **show ip route**

- **show ip route** *routing-protocol*

- **show ip eigrp neighbors**

- **show ip ospf database**

In addition to these commands, the **traceroute** and extended **ping** commands are also very useful.

The traceroute Command

The **traceroute** command may be invoked from user mode, whereas the extended **traceroute** is only available from privileged mode. This shows the routers a packet has passed through to reach its destination.

The extended **traceroute** test is called by entering the command without any destination. This results in the utility asking a series of questions, allowing you to change the defaults.

The Extended ping Command

To check host may be invoked from user mode, whereas the extended **trace** reachability and network connectivity, use the **ping** Privileged EXEC command. The extended **ping** and extended **traceroute** utilities are called by entering the commands without any destination. This results in the utilities asking a series of questions, allowing you to change the defaults.

Using traceroute and Extended ping

You can use **traceroute** to determine the path taken, as well as to identify where there is a problem in the network. Where the **traceroute** utility fails indicates a good starting point for troubleshooting a complex network.

The extended **ping** command is very useful in that it announces every interface that it traverses if the record option is selected. The nine hop maximum of the record route option for extended **ping** is a real limitation, though.

It is also possible to specify a source address in the **traceroute** or **ping** commands (as long as it is an interface on the router). This can be useful for testing certain types of access lists, route maps, and so on. Otherwise, the route will choose the source address of its own interface closest to the destination. It is also useful for testing network reachability from the far end.

These commands are generic to TCP/IP troubleshooting.

Foundation Summary

The Foundation Summary provides a convenient review of many key concepts in this chapter. If you are already comfortable with the topics in this chapter, this summary might help you recall a few details. If you just read this chapter, this review should help solidify some key facts. If you are doing your final prep before the exam, the following lists and tables are a convenient way to review the day before the exam.

Various methods enable you to control the routing information sent between routers. These methods include the following:

- Passive interfaces

- Default route

- Static routes

- The null interface

- Distribute lists

- Route maps

Table 11-13 shows the requirements of automatic redistribution between routing protocols.

Table 11-13 *Redistribution Between Routing Protocols*

Routing Protocol	Redistribution Policy
Static	Requires manual redistribution.
Connected	Unless in the network command for the routing process, requires manual redistribution.
RIP	Requires manual redistribution.
EIGRP	Will automatically redistribute between IGRP and EIGRP if the AS number is the same. Otherwise, requires manual redistribution.
OSPF	Requires manual redistribution between different OSPF process IDs and routing protocols.

The following list explains the logic used in a distribute list:

1. The router receives a routing update or is about to send a routing update about one or more networks.

2. The router looks at the appropriate interface involved with the action to check for filtering.

3. If a filter is present, the router examines the access list to see if there is a match on any of the networks in the routing update.

4. If there is no filter on the interface, the routing update is sent directly to the routing process, as normal.

5. If there is a filter, the route entry is processed according to the distribute list: advertise the route if matched by a permit statement or do not advertise if it is matched by a deny statement.

6. If no match is found in the distribute list, the implicit deny any at the end of the access list will cause the update to be dropped.

Q&A

The questions and scenarios in this book are designed to be challenging and to make sure that you know the answer. Rather than allowing you to derive the answers from clues hidden inside the questions themselves, the questions challenge your understanding and recall of the subject.

You can find the answers to these questions in Appendix A. For more practice with exam-like question formats, use the exam engine on the CD-ROM.

1. State two of the methods that Cisco recommends for controlling routing protocol traffic.

2. State two instances when you do *not* want routing information propagated.

3. In what instance will EIGRP automatically redistribute?

4. Which command is used to view the administrative distance of a route in the routing table?

5. When is redistribution required?

6. Why does Cisco recommend that you do not overlap routing protocols?

7. What is the metric used for in a routing protocol?

8. Give two reasons for using multiple routing protocols.

9. State one possible problem that you might experience with redistribution, and explain why it is a problem.

10. What command is used to configure an outbound route filter? What part of the configuration does it go in (global, interface, line, routing protocol, and so on)?

11. What is a passive interface?

12. What is the purpose of administrative distance?

13. What is the concern of redistributing into a redundant path?

14. Why is it necessary to configure a seed metric when redistributing between routing protocols?

15. Which command is used to modify the administrative distance of a route?

Scenario

The following scenarios and questions are designed to draw together the content of the chapter and to exercise your understanding of the concepts. There is not necessarily a "right" answer. The thought process and practice in manipulating the concepts are the goals of this section. The answers to the scenario questions are found at the end of this chapter.

Scenario 11-1

A large hospital has several sites in the city. Although the sites connect to a centralized patient and administration database, the hospital has fought for local autonomy based on the specialization of the sites and the fact that each is its own business unit. An IT group manages the central administration and oversees the other sites. The chief information officer (CIO) who ran this group and the overall network has left because of political wrangling. The new CIO, recently appointed, is attempting to sort out the mess.

This new CIO has the agreement of the other hospital sites that there should be one routing protocol, as opposed to the four that are currently running. In turn, he has agreed to implement filtering to improve the network performance, grant some basic security, and indulge some turf wars.

The first step to creating a single routing protocol network is to redistribute the protocols so that the network can see all the available routes. Unfortunately, the routing protocols are aware of multiple path destinations. Therefore, the implementation must be done not only with consideration to preventing routing loops, but also with optimal path selection.

Figure 11-12 shows the network topology for the hospital.

Using Figure 11-12 as a reference, complete the following exercises.

1. Issue the configuration commands for the RIP network to be redistributed on Router A into EIGRP.

2. On Router A, ensure that the interfaces running EIGRP do not have RIP updates generated through them or that the RIP interfaces do not have EIGRP updates running through them.

3. The sites running EIGRP are running different autonomous system numbers. How would you implement a transition to both sites running EIGRP using the same autonomous system number?

4. The OSPF redistribution into RIP has been implemented, but users are complaining about delays. State the first step that you would take to verify the configuration.

5. The CIO has been asked to submit a transition plan to the board of trustees that includes a reasoned explanation for the need for redistribution. What should it look like?

Figure 11-12 *Topology for the Scenario 11-1 Network*

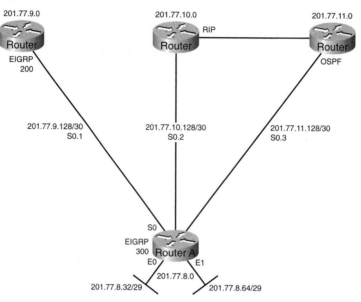

Scenario Answers

The answers provided in this section are not necessarily the only possible answers to the questions. The questions are designed to test your knowledge and to give practical exercise in certain key areas. This section is intended to test and to exercise skills and concepts detailed in the body of this chapter.

If your answer is different, ask yourself whether it follows the tenets explained in the answers provided. Your answer is correct not if it matches the solution provided in the book, but rather if it has included the principles of design laid out in the chapter.

In this way, the testing provided in these scenarios is deeper: It examines not only your knowledge, but also your understanding and ability to apply that knowledge to problems.

If you do not get the correct answer, refer to the text and review the subject tested. Be certain to also review your notes on the question to ensure that you understand the principles of the subject.

Scenario 11-1 Answers

1. *Issue the configuration commands for the RIP network to be redistributed on Router A into EIGRP.*

   ```
   Router(config)# router eigrp 300
   Router(config-router)# network 210.77.8.0
   Router(config-router)# redistribute rip
   Router(config-router)# default-metric 10000 100 255 1 1500
   ```

2. *On Router A, ensure that the interfaces running EIGRP do not have RIP updates generated through them or that the RIP interfaces do not have EIGRP updates running through them.*

   Strictly speaking, the **passive-interface** command on s0.2 is not required because the interface address is different from that stated in the **network** command. The same is true for RIP. To ensure this:

   ```
   Router(config)# router eigrp 300
   Router(config-router)# network 210.77.8.0
   Router(config-router)# redistribute rip
   Router(config-router)# default-metric 10000 100 255 1 1500
   Router(config-router)# passive-interface s0.2
   Router(config)# router rip
   Router(config-router)# network 201.77.10.0
   Router(config-router)# passive-interface s0.1
   Router(config-router)# passive-interface s0.3
   Router(config-router)# passive-interface e0
   Router(config-router)# passive-interface e1
   ```

3. *The sites running EIGRP are running different autonomous system numbers. How would you implement a transition to both sites running EIGRP using the same autonomous system number?*

   There are several ways to transition from different autonomous systems to one autonomous system so that EIGRP 200 and 300 automatically redistribute:

   — Configure redistribution at both sites and, in a controlled manner during downtime, switch all the routers in the EIGRP sites to the same autonomous system. Because the prevailing routing protocol is to be EIGRP, it makes sense to combine the two EIGRP domains.

   — Configure EIGRP with autonomous system 200 on all routers at the EIGRP sites. Increase the AD of EIGRP 200 to be 200 so that none of the routes is acceptable to the routing process. Then, during downtime on the systems, cut over to the EIGRP 200 process by changing its administrative distance back to 90. The beauty of this plan is that everything can be put in place before the cutover; if problems are experienced, it is equally easy to reverse the command to return to the IGRP configuration.

4. *The OSPF redistribution into RIP has been implemented, but users are complaining about delays. State the first step that you would take to verify the configuration.*

   The first step is to issue the following commands, possibly on both the OSPF and RIP routers:

   — **show ip route**: To ensure that each routing process sees the appropriate paths. A routing loop might be visible here.

   — **extended ping**: To see the path that is taken to the remote locations. A routing loop could be detected.

   — **show ip protocols**: To see how RIP and OSPF are being redistributed, what the default metrics are, and whether there are any distribute lists impeding the flow of updates.

   — **show ip ospf database**: To ensure that all the routes are in place.

   — **show ip ospf neighbor**: To ensure that OSPF can still see the adjacent routers.

5. *The CIO has been asked to submit a transition plan to the board of trustees that includes a reasoned explanation for the need for redistribution. What should it look like?*

   The transition plan should include the following:

   — The transition would happen at the main site where the centralized records and databases are maintained. This site must be the most stable because it serves the other sites.

   — The next step would be to review the addressing scheme to ensure that it was hierarchical and could support summarization and VLSM.

— Because the non-Cisco Systems equipment for RIP and OSPF machines might not support EIGRP, a careful assessment should be done, and plans should be made to upgrade the equipment as necessary.

— Configure redistribution in the network to ensure full connectivity throughout the campuses.

— When redistribution is in place, centralization of resources and maintenance of the data and network can be implemented, granting a full exchange of information throughout the hospital to harness the power of the information available.

This chapter covers the following topics:

- **Understanding Route Maps**—Describes what route maps are and how to formulate them.

- **Configuring Route Maps**—Describes how to configure route maps.

- **Monitoring the Configuration of Route Maps and Redistribution**—Describes the commands used to monitor and troubleshoot route maps.

CHAPTER 12

Controlling Redistribution with Route Maps

The topics in this chapter deal with controlling routing traffic with route maps, which are similar to, but more sophisticated than, access lists. This is an advanced topic that deals with programming the router to match criteria against assigned lists and to perform tasks based on the result of the match.

The chapter deals with why route maps are needed and how they work. This chapter also provides the configuration syntax with working examples.

"Do I Know This Already?" Quiz

The purpose of the "Do I Know This Already?" quiz is to help you decide what parts of this chapter to use. If you already intend to read the entire chapter, you do not necessarily need to answer these questions now.

The 10-question quiz, derived from the major sections in the "Foundation Topics" portion of the chapter, helps you determine how to spend your limited study time.

Table 12-1 outlines the major topics discussed in this chapter and the "Do I Know This Already?" quiz questions that correspond to those topics.

Table 12-1   *"Do I Know This Already?" Foundation Topics Section-to-Question Mapping*

Foundation Topics Section	Questions Covered in This Section	Score
Understanding Route Maps	1–5	
Configuring Route Maps	6–8	
Monitoring the Configuration of Route Maps and Redistribution	9–10	
Total Score		

> **CAUTION**   The goal of self-assessment is to gauge your mastery of the topics in this chapter. If you do not know the answer to a question or are only partially sure of the answer, you should mark this question wrong for purposes of the self-assessment. Giving yourself credit for an answer you correctly guess skews your self-assessment results and might provide you with a false sense of security.

1. How are route maps more sophisticated than access lists?

   a. Access lists can change the destination address of the outbound data packet.

   b. Route maps take less CPU because of streamlined processing.

   c. Access lists either exclude or include, whereas route maps can change characteristics of the path.

   d. Access lists can only be applied on inbound updates.

2. Route maps can be used for which of the following applications?

   a. NAT

   b. BGP

   c. OSPF Summarization

   d. Redistribution

3. Which of the following best describes a **match** statement?

   a. The means by which a route is modified

   b. A list of selection criteria

   c. The method of discarding unwanted packets

   d. A list of network prefixes

4. Which of the following best describes a **set** statement?

   a. The method used to determine the best metric

   b. The means of selecting a CoS

   c. A list of conditions to apply to chosen routes

   d. The means of changing routes that are matched

5. Many **match** statements can be used in a route map. How many **match** statements must be matched for the **set** to be applied?

   a. At least one

   b. All the criteria

   c. None of them

   d. At least 50 percent of the criteria

6. When using route maps for redistribution when a statement is configured to deny and there is a match, what action will be taken by the route map?

   a. The packet is dropped.

   b. The route is not redistributed.

   c. An ICMP packet is sent to the sender.

   d. The packet is sent to the normal routing process.

7. How is a route map for redistribution initiated?

   a. The **route-map** command

   b. Under the incoming interface

   c. The redistribution command

   d. As a global configuration command

8. The following route map configuration has what effect on OSPF routes redistributed into EIGRP?

```
router eigrp 1
 redistribute ospf 1 route-map ospf-to-eigrp
 default-metric 20000 2000 255 1 1500
 !
route-map ospf-to-eigrp deny 10
 match tag 6
 match route-type external type-2
 !
route-map ospf-to-eigrp permit 20
 match ip address prefix-list pfx
 set metric 40000 1000 255 1 1500
 !
route-map ospf-to-eigrp permit 30
 set tag 8
 !
```

   a. Routes with a tag of 6 are redistributed unchanged.

   b. Routes matching prefix-list pfx are forward with EIGRP metric 20000 2000 255 1 1500.

   c. Routes without a tag of 6 and not matching prefix-list pfx have their tag set to 8.

   d. All routes are redistributed.

9. Which command is useful for validating the path to the destination with a specified packet size?

   a. Extended **ping**

   b. **show ip protocol**

   c. **show ip route**

   d. **show redistribution**

10. Which command is used to show the configured route maps?

    a. **show ip route-map**

    b. **show route-map**

    c. **show ip map**

    d. **show ip policy**

The answers to this quiz are found in Appendix A, "Answers to Chapter 'Do I Know This Already?' Quizzes and Q&A Sections." The suggested choices for your next step are as follows:

- **6 or less overall score**—Read the entire chapter. This includes the "Foundation Topics," "Foundation Summary," and "Q&A" sections.

- **7–8 overall score**—Begin with the "Foundation Summary" section, and then go to the "Q&A" section. If you have trouble with these exercises, read the appropriate sections in "Foundation Topics."

- **9–10 overall score**—If you want more review on these topics, skip to the "Foundation Summary" section, and then go to the "Q&A" section. Otherwise, move to the next chapter.

Foundation Topics

Understanding Route Maps

Route maps are pattern-matching tools that can be used to change packet headers or the way packets route. Route maps are often called "access lists on steroids" because they are similar to access lists, but much more powerful. In fact, route maps are a flexible tool that you can use in a variety of situations. Example uses of route maps include

- **Controlling redistribution**—Route maps can permit or deny routes and can change metrics.

- **Defining policies in policy-based routing (PBR)**—PBR is created using route maps and allows complex routing decisions to be implemented on more sophisticated criteria.

- **To add granularity in the configuration of Network Address Translation (NAT)**—Traditional NAT is limited to "static" translations, but NAT using route maps can make arbitrary translations. For instance, an internal server might be translated to one public address when conversing with a business partner and to a different address when speaking to the Internet.

- **To implement BGP PBR**—BGP, at its core, is a way to communicate network policy. Route maps are a common way of defining that policy, and several examples are given in Part VI, "BGP."

The next sections describe the characteristics of route maps and provide a route map example.

Route Map Characteristics

Route maps and access lists are similar because they are both processed "top down" and action is taken (permit or deny) on the first match. Route maps can do more than just permit or deny, however. For example, route maps can change the next-hop and metric in the IP header. In fact, the list of attributes that route maps can affect is very long. This chapter discusses some of these capabilities in context as different situations are considered.

The characteristics of route maps are summarized in the following list:

- A collection of route map statements with the same name is considered one route map (like an ACL).

- Route maps are processed top down until a match is found (like an ACL).

- Each route map statement has zero or more match conditions. A statement without a match applies to all traffic (like the *any* option in an access list). Traffic that is not a match is not changed, but is considered by the next statement. Two logical considerations for route map formulation are

- — A single match statement can contain multiple conditions. If any one condition is true then a match is made; this is a logical OR.

- — If there are multiple match statements, all must be considered true for the route map statement to be considered matched. This is a logical AND.

■ Each route map statement has zero or more **set** statements. **set** statements define an action to be taken. The parameters of the **set** statement apply if all the match criteria are met.

■ Each route map statement has permit or deny permission. Traffic that matches a permit is affected by the route map. Traffic that matches a deny, or does not find a match in the list, is not affected by the route map.

■ Traffic that is not explicitly permitted is implicitly denied.

■ Within a route map, each route map statement has a sequence number and can be edited individually.

Using route maps is very common in any network with redistribution of routing protocols. However, route maps should be used with caution because they can cause traffic to forward in ways you may not have fully considered—creating routing loops, for example.

Pseudo-code Example

Before going too far, it can be useful to see an example of a route map. Example 12-1 shows how a route map might be applied to cupcakes. Although this is not a real route map, it is intended to demonstrate the flow of the tool.

Example 12-1 *Route-Map Logic*

```
route-map cupcakes permit 10
     match lemon-flavored
     match poppy-seed
     set add lemon-butter-frosting
Route-map cupcakes deny 20
     match granola
route-map cupcakes permit 30
     match walnuts baked-today
     set melted-chocolate-frosting
Route-map cupcakes permit 40
     set vanilla-frosting
```

Notice the following facts relating to Example 12-1:

■ All route maps with the same name are part of a list. In this example, the list name is *cupcakes*.

- Route maps are organized by sequence number (10, 20, or 30 in the example).

- Each route map statement has zero or more match conditions:

  — Statement 10 has two match statements. Both must be true for the set to apply.

  — Statement 20 only applies to cupcakes that match *granola*. Denied packets are not considered (in the case of route redistribution, the denied routes are not redistributed).

  — Statement 30 has two match conditions in the same statement. Either can be true for the set to apply.

  — Statement 40 has no match statements, so it applies to all cupcakes.

- Each route map statement has zero or more set statements:

  — Statements 10, 30, and 40 apply frosting.

  — Statement 20 has no set statement, so only the permit/deny action is taken.

- Traffic that matches a permit is affected by the route map, traffic that matches a deny, or does not find a match in the list, is not affected by the route map:

  — Statement 20 prevents matches from being affected by the list, so anything matching will not be frosted.

  — Because of the *permit any* logic of statement 40, all traffic will find a match.

Example 12-1 could be written in pseudo-code as

    If (*a* and *b*) then set *x*
    Else if *c* then stop
    Else if (d or e) then set y
    Else set z

In plain text, Example 12-1 translates into

    If the cupcake is lemon or poppy-seed, then apply lemon-butter frosting. If not, then if the
    cupcake is granola, do not frost. If none of the above apply, then if the cupcake has walnuts or
    is freshly baked, then coat it with melted chocolate. Otherwise, just put vanilla frosting on it.

Configuring Route Maps

This section deals with the implementation and configuration of route maps.

The **route-map** command is shown here:

```
Router(config)# route-map map-tag [{permit | deny} sequence-number]
```

Entering **no route-map** *map-tag* by itself will delete the entire route map.

Table 12-2 describes the syntax options available for the **route-map** command.

Table 12-2 *The* **route-map** *Command Options*

Command	Description
map-tag	The name of the route map.
**permit	deny**	If the match criteria are met for this route map and **permit** is specified, the packet is forwarded as defined by the set actions. If the match criteria are not met and **permit** is specified, the next statement with the same map tag is tested. If no match criteria are specified, all packets match. If no **set** statement is specified, matching packets are permitted unchanged.
sequence-number	Sequence number indicates processing order. If sequence is not specified, statements are automatically ordered in multiples of ten.

The strength of route maps lies in their ability to change the route in some way. A common manipulation is changing the metric.

The following commands are summarized here into groups: the **match** commands that can be configured for redistribution, and the **set** commands that can be applied if the route matches the criteria stated.

The match Commands for Redistribution with Route-Maps

The **match** commands used in redistribution are summarized in Table 12-3. These **match** commands are used to determine whether the route is to be redistributed.

Table 12-3 *The* **match** *Commands Used in Redistribution*

Command	Description
match interface (IP)	Distributes routes with the next-hop out one of the interfaces specified. Matches any routes that have their next hop out of one of the listed interfaces.
match ip address [*access-list-number*	*name*]	Matches an access list.
match ip next-hop	Matches routes that have a particular next hop router address.
match ip route-source	Redistributes routes that have been advertised from the address specified.
match metric	Redistributes routes with the metric specified.
match route-type (IP)	Redistributes routes of the specified type.
match tag	Redistributes routes in the routing table that match the specified tags.

NOTE   A route is not redistributed unless it is matched under a permit entry in the route map. The command **match ip address** is often used to match criteria in establishing policy-based routing; access lists referenced by this command are used to specify the addressing of the packets to be affected.

The set Commands for Redistributing with Route-Maps

The following **set** commands are used after the **match** criteria have been satisfied. Whereas the **match** parameter determines whether the route will be redistributed, the **set** parameter determines how the route is to be redistributed.

The **set** command is

```
Router(config-route-map)# set {criteria}
```

The **set** commands used in redistribution are summarized in Table 12-4.

Table 12-4   *The set Commands Used in Redistribution*

Command	Description
set level {**level-1**	**level-2**	**level-1-2**	**stub-area**	**backbone**}	Used by IS-IS to determine the level of router to which the process should import routes. Also used by OSPF to state the type of area router to which routes should be imported.
set metric (BGP, OSPF, RIP)	Sets the metric value for a routing protocol.
set metric-type {*internal*	*external*	*type-1*	*type-2*}	Sets the metric type for the destination routing protocol.
set tag *tag-value*	Sets a tag value for the destination routing protocol.

Once configured, the route map must be called into service using the following redistribution statement:

```
Router(config-router)# redistribute protocol [process-id] [route-map map-tag]
```

map-tag is the name of the route map to use for redistribution, and must match a map tag specified by a **route-map** command.

Example 12-2 is very simple, but it illustrates the functionality of the route map. Study the example in reference to Figure 12-1.

Example 12-2   *Route-Map to Distribute RIPv2 into OSPF*

```
Router(config)# router ospf 25
Router(config-router)# redistribute rip route-map rip-routes
-
Router(config)# route-map rip-routes permit 10
Router(config-route-map)# match metric 1
Router(config-route-map)# set metric 3000
                                                              continues
```

Example 12-2 *Route-Map to Distribute RIPv2 into OSPF (Continued)*

```
Router(config-route-map)# set metric-type type-1
Router(config-route-map)# set tag 1
Router(config)# route-map rip-routes permit 20
Router(config-route-map)# match metric 2
Router(config-route-map)# set metric 4000
Router(config-route-map)# set metric-type type-1
Router(config-route-map)# set tag 2
Router(config)# route-map rip-routes permit 30
Router(config-route-map)# set metric 32000
```

Figure 12-1 *Route Map to Distribute RIPv2 into OSPF*

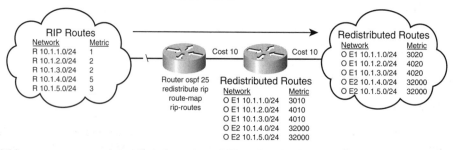

This route map examines all updates from RIP and redistributes RIP routes into OSPF. Routes with a hop count of 1 will have a tag of 2768 and an OSPF cost of 3000 (and type-1 means it will continue to grow). Routes with a hop count of 2 will have a tag of 2768 and an OSPF external type-1 cost of 4000. All other routes will have a static cost of 32,000 and no tag.

The tag is useful for matching routes during redistribution, when the routes change from one routing domain to another—for example, from RIPv2 to OSPF. The routes are tagged at the point at which they are redistributed into another protocol. Although the routing protocols ignore tags, they are passed between the different domains during redistribution. Later, the tags could be used to match routes redistributed from this router.

Monitoring the Configuration of Route Maps and Redistribution

Most of the appropriate commands in tracking route maps are the same as those illustrated in Chapter 11. The commands used to test connectivity throughout the network include the following:

- **show ip protocol**

- **show ip route**

- **show ip route** *routing-protocol*

- **show ip eigrp neighbors**

- **show ip ospf database**

- **show route-map**

In addition to these commands, **traceroute** and extended **ping** are also very useful.

Foundation Summary

The Foundation Summary provides a convenient review of many key concepts in this chapter. If you are already comfortable with the topics in this chapter, this summary might help you recall a few details. If you just read this chapter, this review should help solidify some key facts. If you are doing your final prep before the exam, the following lists and tables are a convenient way to review the day before the exam.

The following list summarizes the characteristics of route maps:

- A collection of route map statements with the same name is considered one route map (like an ACL).

- Route maps are processed top down until a match is found (like an ACL).

- Each route map statement has zero or more match conditions. A statement without a match applies to all traffic (like an access-list *any*). Traffic that is not a match is not changed, but is considered by the next statement.

  — A single match statement can contain multiple conditions. If any one condition is true then a match is made; this is a logical OR.

  — If there are multiple match statements, all must be considered true for the route map statement to be considered matched. This is a logical AND.

- Each route map statement has zero or more set statements. Set statements define an action to be taken.

- Each route map statement has permit or deny permission. Traffic that matches a permit is affected by the route map, traffic that matches a deny, or does not find a match in the list, is not affected by the route map.

- Traffic that is not explicitly permitted is implicitly denied.

- Within a route map, each route map statement has a sequence number and can be edited individually.

The following list characterizes the operation of route map statements:

- The route map statements used for routing can be marked as **permit** or **deny**.

- The **set** commands will be applied only if the statement is marked as **permit** and the packet meets the match criteria.

- The statements in a route map correspond to the lines of an access list. Specifying the match conditions in a route map is similar to specifying the source and destination addresses and masks in an access list.

- The statements in the route map are compared to the route or packet to see if there is a match. The statements are examined in order starting at the top, like in an access list. The single **match** statement can contain multiple conditions. At least one condition in the **match** statement must be true. This is a logical OR.

- A route map statement can contain multiple **match** statements. All **match** statements in the route map statement must be considered true for the route map statement to be considered matched. This is a logical AND.

The **route-map** command syntax is shown here:

```
Router(config)# route-map map-tag [{permit | deny} sequence-number]
```

Q&A

The questions and scenarios in this book are designed to be challenging and to make sure that you know the answer. Rather than allowing you to derive the answers from clues hidden inside the questions themselves, the questions challenge your understanding and recall of the subject.

You can find the answers to these questions in Appendix A. For more practice with exam-like question formats, use the exam engine on the CD-ROM.

1. Explain the command **match ip address** {*access-list-number* | *name*} [*access-list number* | *name*].

2. How are matching routes modified in a route map?

3. Explain briefly the difference between the **match** and **set** commands.

4. What is the purpose of the sequence number in a route map?

5. What logic is used if there are multiple match statements in the route map?

6. Configuring route maps is complex, and it is easy to confuse the logic by which they work. State one of the things you should be aware of when configuring a route map.

This chapter covers the following topics:

- **Understanding DHCP**—Describes the process of allocating IP addresses with DHCP.

- **DHCP Roles**—Defines the server, relay, and client used by DHCP.

- **Troubleshooting DHCP**—Lays out a seven-step process for troubleshooting DHCP.

CHAPTER 13

Dynamic Host Control Protocol

This chapter is about using IPv4 DHCP (the Dynamic Host Control Protocol) with Cisco IOS. Cisco IOS devices may act as DHCP servers, relays, or clients, and this chapter deals with each case. This chapter also provides the configuration syntax with working examples.

"Do I Know This Already?" Quiz

The purpose of the "Do I Know This Already?" quiz is to help you decide what parts of this chapter to use. If you already intend to read the entire chapter, you do not necessarily need to answer these questions now.

The 11-question quiz, derived from the major sections in the "Foundation Topics" portion of the chapter, helps you determine how to spend your limited study time.

Table 13-1 outlines the major topics discussed in this chapter and the "Do I Know This Already?" quiz questions that correspond to those topics.

Table 13-1 *"Do I Know This Already?" Foundation Topics Section-to-Question Mapping*

Foundation Topics Section	Questions Covered in This Section	Score
Understanding DHCP	1–2	
DHCP Roles	3–10	
Troubleshooting DHCP	11	
Total Score		

CAUTION   The goal of self-assessment is to gauge your mastery of the topics in this chapter. If you do not know the answer to a question or are only partially sure of the answer, you should mark this question wrong for purposes of the self-assessment. Giving yourself credit for an answer you correctly guess skews your self-assessment results and might provide you with a false sense of security.

1. List the following actions in order: A-Acknowledgement, B-Discover, C-Offer, and D-Request.

   a. ABCD

   b. BADC

   c. CABD

   d. BCDA

2. DHCP is a descendant of what protocol?

   a. BootP

   b. RARP

   c. GARP

   d. SDLC

3. Which of the following are roles a device can assume in DHCP?

   a. Server

   b. Designee

   c. Relay Agent

   d. Client

   e. Communicating Peer

4. Given the following configuration, users are not able to communicate through the router. What should be changed to fix the configuration?

   ```
   interface f0/1
        ip address 192.168.1.1 255.255.255.0
   interface f0/0
        ip address 172.16.15.1 255.255.255.0
   ip dhcp pool exp_pool
        network 192.168.15.0 255.255.255.0
   ```

   a. Illegal IP address

   b. Pool name is not valid

   c. Pool is not applied

   d. No default gateway in DHCP

   e. Illegal/inappropriate mask

5. What is the default lease time for an IOS DHCP server?

    a. 1 day

    b. 2 days

    c. 3 days

    d. 4 days

6. How do you configure an IOS device as a DHCP client?

    a. **service dhcp**

    b. **ip address dhcp**

    c. Match IP address to network

    d. **ipconfig/renew**

7. Which command is used to configure DHCP relay agents?

    a. **ip helper-address**

    b. **ip address dhcp**

    c. **ip dhcp relay-agent**

    d. **service dhcp relay-agent**

8. Which of the following ports are forwarded by UDP by default?

    a. UDP 51

    b. UDP 666

    c. UDP 500

    d. UDP 67

9. Which command is used to add a UDP port that should have broadcasts relayed through DHCP?

    a. **ip helper-address**

    b. **ip address dhcp**

    c. **ip dhcp relay-agent**

    d. **ip forward-protocol udp**

10. Which UDP broadcasts are automatically forwarded by an IOS DHCP relay?

    a. NTP (port 37)

    b. DNS (port 53)

    c. TFTP (port 69)

    d. TACACS (port 49)

    e. NetBIOS name service (port 137)

    f. NetBIOS datagram service (port 138)

11. What command generates the following output?

    ```
    IP address    Hardware address    Lease expiration       Type
    172.16.1.11   00a0.9802.32de      Feb 01 1998 12:00 AM   Automatic
    ```

    a. **show ip dhcp conflict**

    b. **show ip dhcp pool**

    c. **show ip dhcp binding**

    d. **dhow ip dhcp database**

The answers to this quiz are found in Appendix A, "Answers to Chapter 'Do I Know This Already?' Quizzes and Q&A Sections." The suggested choices for your next step are as follows:

■ **7 or less overall score**—Read the entire chapter. This includes the "Foundation Topics," "Foundation Summary," and "Q&A" sections.

■ **8–9 overall score**—Begin with the "Foundation Summary" section, and then go to the "Q&A" section at the end of the chapter. If you have trouble with these exercises, read the appropriate sections in "Foundation Topics."

■ **10–11 overall score**—If you want more review on these topics, skip to the "Foundation Summary" section, and then go to the "Q&A" section. Otherwise, move to the next chapter.

Foundation Topics

Understanding DHCP

DHCP, a descendant of BootP, allows a server to automatically provision IPv4 addresses and configuration information to clients as they boot.

There are two principal advantages to DHCP, and they are big ones. First, DHCP makes it easier to administer an IP network. Without DHCP, administrators would have to manually assign and track addresses and this is—at best—laborious and error-prone. Second, DHCP allows clients to temporarily use IP addresses and thus make better use of IP address space. DSL customers of an ISP, for example, only need IP addresses when they are currently online.

With DHCP, the following process takes place:

1. Clients broadcast asking for IP configuration information and servers respond with address, mask, gateway, and other information. Specifically, new clients broadcast a DHCP DISCOVER message.

2. Each server on the network responds with an OFFER. It is not uncommon—particularly in enterprise settings—to have redundant DHCP servers, so the user could get two or more responses. The OFFER contains an IP address, mask, gateway, lease time, and possibly option codes.

3. The client considers its offers and picks one. Different implementations pick in different ways; Windows XP will take a previous address if offered, other operating systems will take the first OFFER. The client sends back a REQUEST that basically says "if this IP is still available, I would like it."

4. The server responds with an ACK to indicate that it has recorded the assignment.

5. Finally, the client will send an ARP request for its new address. If anyone else responds, the client knows it has been assigned an address that is already in use and the client starts the DHCP process again. This process is called a gratuitous ARP.

> **NOTE** Many client operating systems use something called Automatic Private IP Addressing. This process assigns an IP address, even in the absence of a DHCP server. If a DISCOVER message is not answered, the client picks a random 16-bit number and prepends it with 169.254. It performs a gratuitous ARP and assigns that address to itself.
>
> The idea of Automatic Private IP Addressing is that two travelers could link their devices quickly and easily. For instance, two train commuters could play a game on the way to the city. They configure DHCP on their laptops and use Automatic Private IP Addressing on the train and get a different IP in the office.
>
> If you see a 169.254.x.x address, it means that the DHCP server is not reachable. The PC will not work because there is not a router to or from that IP. Troubleshoot this by finding out why the PC cannot see the DHCP server.

DHCP Roles

There are at least two devices involved in any DHCP setup—a DHCP server and a DHCP client. There are often additional devices in the network between the client and server, called *DHCP relays*. The following sections describe the function and configuration of each of these DHCP roles.

Acting as a DHCP Server

The following steps configure an IOS device as a DHCP server:

Step 1   Create a pool of addresses to assign to clients. The syntax for this command is

```
Router(config)# ip dhcp pool name
```

Step 2   Assign a network to the pool:

```
Router(config-dhcp)# network network/mask
```

Step 3   Tell the client how long it can keep the address—this is called the *lease period*. Most DHCP implementations use a three-day lease, but IOS defaults to one day:

```
Router(config-dhcp)# lease days
```

Step 4   Identify the DNS server:

```
Router(config-dhcp)# dns-server address
```

Step 5   Finally, identify the default gateway:

```
Router(config-dhcp)# default-router ip-address
```

Addresses are always assigned on the interface that has an IP address in the same subnet as the pool. Example 13-1 shows this configuration in context.

Example 13-1 *DHCP*

```
Router(config)# interface fastethernet 0/1
Router(config-if)# ip address 172.16.1.1 255.255.255.0
Router(config)# ip dhcp pool 1
Router(config-dhcp)# network 172.16.1.0 /24
Router(config-dhcp)# default-router 172.16.1.1
Router(config-dhcp)# lease 3
Router(config-dhcp)# dns-server 172.16.77.100
```

Some IOS devices receive an IP address on one interface and assign IP addresses on another. In these instances, DHCP may import the options and parameters from one interface and pass them to the other interface. The command to do so is

```
Router(config-dhcp)# import all
```

Using **import all** can reduce the headache of setting up DHCP in remote offices. The router, once it is onsite, can determine the local DNS and options.

There are a variety of commands to manage an IOS DHCP server. The additional commands are listed in Table 13-2.

Table 13-2 *Descriptions of DHCP Server Commands*

Command	Description
service dhcp	Enables DHCP server (on by default)
ip dhcp database	Configures a database agent
no ip dhcp conflict logging	Disables logging of conflicts
ip dhcp excluded-address *start-ip end-ip*	Lists addresses that should be excluded from the pool
domain-name *domain*	Default DNS assignment

Acting as a DHCP Relay

Normally, routers do not forward broadcast. There are a few times when an exception to this rule would be useful. IP assignment, for instance, would be easier if you did not have to deploy a DHCP server on every segment. If routers passed broadcasts, a central server could take care of remote locations.

Cisco IOS allows routers to forward broadcasts through the **ip helper-address** command. When configured, a router will forward broadcasts to select UDP ports to predetermined remote locations. A router configured to forward DHCP requests is called a DHCP relay. DHCP relays forward requests and set the gateway to the local router.

To use helper-address, enter the following command in interface configuration mode:

```
Router(config-if)# ip helper-address address
```

When first configured, helper-address supports eight UDP ports. Broadcasts to these eight ports are forwarded to the remote address specified by the command. The ports are

- NTP (UDP 37)

- TACACS (UDP 49)

- DNS (UDP 53)

- DHCP (UDP 67 and 68)

- TFTP (UDP 69)

- NetBIOS name service (UDP 137)

- NetBIOS datagram service (UDP 138)

Additional ports may be added using the command **ip forward-protocol udp** *port*. For example, if UDP 5000 should be forwarded and TFTP should not, the commands would be

```
Router(config)# interface fastethernet0/0
Router(config-if)# ip helper-address 172.16.5.100
Router(config-if)# exit
Router(config)# ip forward-protocol udp 5000
Router(config)# no ip forward-protocol udp 69
```

The **ip dhcp relay information option** command, used on a DHCP relay, enables the system to insert a DHCP relay agent information option (also called option 82) in forwarded BOOTREQUEST messages to a DHCP server. The DHCP server can then use this information to assign the correct subnet.

Acting as a DHCP Client

Setting an IOS device to be a DHCP client is easy. The command is supplied in interface configuration mode. Instead of supplying an IP and mask, the IP address command is used to specify DHCP:

```
Router(config)# interface fastethernet0/0
Router(config-if)# ip address dhcp
```

This is a quick and painless way to get remote offices and SOHO users up and running.

Troubleshooting DHCP

The most obvious way to troubleshoot DHCP installations is to type **show run** and compare the output to this book. This approach, however, can fail due to a lack of details. A more robust way to troubleshoot is to examine the process step-by-step as assignments are made.

Before discussing troubleshooting, we need to rule out some issues. We assume, in this section, that the PC has been shown to have a connection to the network, and the DHCP server is turned on.

Troubleshooting is best approached by following a pre-existing model, such as the OSI model, as follows:

Step 1   Start by verifying that the PC is not getting an IP address. Verify that the PC and server are each attached to the network.

Step 2   Make sure that DHCP is set up and that the client is attached to the network and capable of sending traffic.

Step 3   Examine the DHCP database. To see the database, try **show ip dhcp database**.

Step 4   To view more detailed information about the DHCP configuration, use the command **show ip dhcp server statistics**.

Step 5   Use **show ip dhcp binding** and **clear binding**. To display address bindings on the DHCP server, use the **show ip dhcp binding** command. To delete an automatic address binding from the DHCP server database, use the **clear ip dhcp binding** command.

Step 6   To enable DHCP server debugging, use the **debug ip dhcp server events** and the **debug ip dhcp server packets** commands.

Step 7   Check access control lists to ensure that DHCP messages are not being blocked by ACLs.

Foundation Summary

The Foundation Summary provides a convenient review of many key concepts in this chapter. If you are already comfortable with the topics in this chapter, this summary might help you recall a few details. If you just read this chapter, this review should help solidify some key facts. If you are doing your final prep before the exam, the following lists and tables are a convenient way to review the day before the exam.

A five-step process is used by DHCP to allocate IP addresses:

1. Clients broadcast with DISCOVER messages.

2. Servers respond with OFFER messages.

3. Clients REQUEST addresses.

4. Servers respond with ACKS to indicate the assignment is recorded.

5. Clients send ARP requests to see if their new addresses are in use.

There are three DHCP roles: server, relay, and client. The server is configured as follows:

Step 1 Create a pool of addresses to assign to clients:

```
Router(config)# ip dhcp pool name
```

Step 2 Assign a network to the pool:

```
Router(config-dhcp)# network network/mask
```

Step 3 Specify the lease with default of one day:

```
Router(config-dhcp)# lease days
```

Step 4 Identify the DNS server:

```
Router(config-dhcp)# dns-server address
```

Step 5 Identify the default gateway:

```
Router(config-dhcp)# default-router ip-address
```

Use the following commands to configure DHCP relay:

- **ip helper-address** *address*

- **forward-protocol udp** *port*

An IOS device is configured as a DHCP client with the interface command **ip address dhcp**.

The **show ip dhcp bindings** command displays the active DHCP bindings.

Q&A

The questions and scenarios in this book are designed to be challenging and to make sure that you know the answer. Rather than allowing you to derive the answers from clues hidden inside the questions themselves, the questions challenge your understanding and recall of the subject.

You can find the answers to these questions in Appendix A. For more practice with exam-like question formats, use the exam engine on the CD-ROM.

1. Discuss the expected DHCP traffic flow.

2. List the commands necessary to configure a DHCP Server on an IOS device.

3. List the commands necessary to configure a DHCP client on an IOS device.

4. List the command necessary to configure a DHCP Relay Server on an IOS device.

5. What applications are supported by default by DHCP Relay?

6. What are the three DHCP roles?

7. What command will forward UDP broadcasts to port 5000?

8. What are the five steps to configuring a DHCP server?

9. What interface command is used on a Cisco router to configure it as a DHCP client?

10. What command is used to view the DHCP bindings on a DHCP server?

Part VI covers the following Cisco BSCI exam topics related to implementing BGP for enterprise ISP connectivity:

- Describe the functions and operations of BGP.

- Configure or verify BGP operation in a non-transit AS (e.g., authentication).

- Configure BGP path selection (i.e., Local Preference, AS Path, Weight, or MED attributes).

This list reflects the exam topics posted on Cisco.com at the publication time of this book.

Part VI: BGP

This chapter covers the following topics:

- **Introduction to BGP**—Describes where and when to use BGP, as well as some basic BGP operations.

- **Connecting to the Internet with BGP**—Describes multihoming and load sharing.

- **Synchronization**—Describes what synchronization is and when to use it.

- **BGP States**—Describes the five neighbor states for BGP.

CHAPTER 14

BGP Concepts

This chapter details Border Gateway Protocol version 4 (BGP-4, referred to throughout this book as BGP). This chapter deals with the basic concepts and configuration commands of BGP, which are covered in greater complexity in Chapter 15, "BGP Neighbors." This chapter builds on your understanding of routing within large enterprise networks. This chapter introduces external BGP (eBGP) and familiarizes you with the necessary terms and concepts.

This chapter deals with how BGP works theoretically. Implementing and managing a BGP network is described in Chapter 15.

"Do I Know This Already?" Quiz

The purpose of the "Do I Know This Already?" quiz is to help you decide what parts of this chapter to use. If you already intend to read the entire chapter, you do not necessarily need to answer these questions now.

The 11-question quiz, derived from the major sections in the "Foundation Topics" portion of the chapter, helps you determine how to spend your limited study time.

Table 14-1 outlines the major topics discussed in this chapter and the "Do I Know This Already?" quiz questions that correspond to those topics.

Table 14-1   *"Do I Know This Already?" Foundation Topics Section-to-Question Mapping*

Foundation Topics Section	Questions Covered in This Section	Score
Introduction to BGP	1–5	
Connecting to the Internet with BGP	6–7	
Synchronization	8–9	
BGP States	10–11	
Total Score		

> **CAUTION** The goal of self-assessment is to gauge your mastery of the topics in this chapter. If you do not know the answer to a question or are only partially sure of the answer, you should mark this question wrong for purposes of the self-assessment. Giving yourself credit for an answer you correctly guess skews your self-assessment results and might provide you with a false sense of security.

1. Which of the following are key features of BGP?

   a. Periodic keepalives

   b. Periodic updates

   c. Poison reverse

   d. Triggered updates

2. Which of the following best describes the routers that utilize eBGP to communicate with each other?

   a. Routers within an autonomous system

   b. Routers in different countries

   c. Routers in different autonomous systems

   d. Routers running different IGPs

3. What is the transport protocol for BGP?

   a. BGP runs directly on top of the data link layer

   b. IP

   c. UDP

   d. TCP

4. When are full routing updates sent in BGP?

   a. At the beginning of each established session

   b. Whenever a fault is seen on the link

   c. Every 30 minutes

   d. At the startup of the BGP process

5. Which of the following are BGP message types?

   a. Updates

   b. Keepalives

   c. ACK

   d. Notification

6. Place the BGP connection strategies in order from lowest to highest, in terms of memory and bandwidth requirements.

   a. Accept only default routes from all providers

   b. Accept some routes plus a default route from all providers

   c. Accept full routing updates from all providers

7. Place the BGP connection strategies in order from lowest to highest, in terms of likelihood to take the best path.

   a. Accept only default routes from all providers

   b. Accept some routes plus a default route from all providers

   c. Accept full routing updates from all providers

8. The synchronization rule is best described by which of the following?

   a. Do not use or advertise a route until the route is learned from a BGP peer.

   b. Wait until a CONFIRM message is received before using routes from BGP neighbors.

   c. Do not use or internally advertise a route until the route is learned from a source other than BGP.

   d. Do not use or advertise routes marked PARTIAL.

9. Which of the following are benefits of enabling BGP synchronization?

   a. It prevents traffic from being forwarded to unreachable destinations.

   b. It reduces unnecessary traffic.

   c. It ensures consistency within the autonomous system.

   d. It ensures access to a complete set of Internet routes.

10. Place the BGP states in order, from startup to peering.

   a. Open Sent

   b. Idle

   c. Established

   d. Open Confirm

   e. Connect

11. Ideally, the output of the **show ip bgp neighbors** command will display what?

   a. Open

   b. Active

   c. Established

   d. Idle

The answers to the "Do I Know This Already?" quiz are found in Appendix A, "Answers to Chapter 'Do I Know This Already?' Quizzes and Q&A Sections." The suggested choices for your next step are as follows:

- **7 or less overall score**—Read the entire chapter. This includes the "Foundation Topics," "Foundation Summary," and "Q&A" sections.

- **8 or 9 overall score**—Begin with the "Foundation Summary" section, and then go to the "Q&A" section at the end of the chapter. If you have trouble with these exercises, read the appropriate sections in "Foundation Topics."

- **10 or 11 overall score**—If you want more review on these topics, skip to the "Foundation Summary" section, and then go to the "Q&A" section. Otherwise, move on to the next chapter.

Foundation Topics

Introduction to BGP

This section presents the basics of BGP and when it is appropriate, introduces some terminology, and explains the ways you might use BGP to connect to the Internet. Complexities within BGP are then layered over this description in succeeding chapters.

The Context for BGP

BGP is a modern routing protocol designed to scale to the largest networks and create stable routes between organizations. BGP supports variable-length subnet mask (VLSM), classless interdomain routing (CIDR), and summarization.

BGP is an extremely complex protocol used throughout the Internet and within multinational organizations. Its main purpose is to connect very large networks or autonomous systems. Large organizations use BGP as the glue between divisions; for example, a conglomerate might use it between lines-of-business or the military might use BGP to communicate between the Army, the Navy, and the Air Force. BGP is also used on the Internet to connect organizations to one another.

BGP is the only routing protocol in use today that supports interdomain routing. The equipment and networks controlled by an organization are called an *autonomous system (AS)*. Autonomous means independent, and when you use BGP you cannot force another organization to route traffic nor can they force routing decisions on you.

BGP Route Stability

Another key point about BGP is that BGP wants the network to be quiet. Whereas IGPs want the latest information and are constantly adjusting routes based on new information, BGP is designed to prefer routes that are stable and not constantly re-advertised. Also, BGP configurations normally require complex policy decisions. Thus, given this complexity coupled with the extreme size of the BGP routing table (often hundreds of thousands of routes), it is not surprising that constantly adjusting routes could overwhelm BGP.

BGP Operation Basics

BGP associates networks with autonomous systems. Other Internet routers then send traffic to your network toward your AS. When that traffic arrives at your edge BGP routers, it is typically the job of an IGP (such as EIGRP or OSPF) to find the best internal path.

BGP is a path-vector routing protocol. Routes are tracked in terms of the AS they pass through, and routers avoid loops by rejecting routes that have already passed through their AS. The idea of path-vector loop detection is illustrated in Figure 14-1.

Figure 14-1 *BGP Loop Detection Using AS-Path*

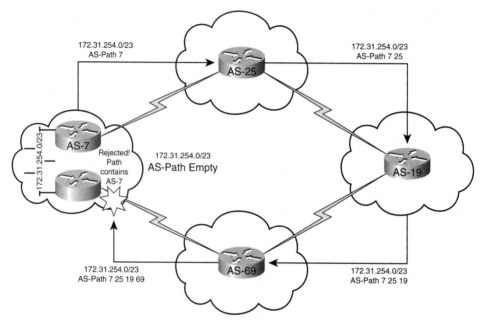

BGP neighbors are called *peers*; peers are not discovered promiscuously but must be predefined.

There are four BGP message types used in peer relationship building and maintenance:

- Open
- Keepalive
- Update
- Notification

When a BGP process starts, it creates and maintains connections between peers on TCP 179, using BGP Open messages. These sessions are maintained by periodic keepalive messages, and peer information is kept in a separate neighbor table. If a peer is reset, it sends a notification message to indicate that it is closing the relationship.

When neighborship is first established, BGP routers exchange their complete routing tables using update messages. Subsequently, routing updates are only sent when something changes.

For example, an update might be sent to reflect a new network that has become available or to remove a route that has been withdrawn.

BGP Record Keeping

Routing with BGP involves three tables:

■   Neighbor table

■   BGP table

■   IP Routing table

BGP routes are maintained in a separate BGP table and the best BGP routes are passed on to the IP routing table.

BGP does not have a "metric" in the same manner as the other protocols that have been discussed. Instead, BGP has a ten-step process for selecting routes that looks at a variety of properties. The complexity of the path selection process, explored in Chapter 16, is one of BGP's great strengths. In addition, BGP supports tools (such as route maps and distribute lists) that allow administrators to manipulate traffic flow based on BGP attributes.

BGP and Hierarchy

Other routing protocols are designed to work in highly summarized, hierarchically organized networks. Organizations are not organized hierarchically (for instance, there is no hierarchical relationship between the UN, General Electric, and the Australia Zoo), so BGP has to work with whatever topology it is given. However, BGP still benefits from summarization for the same reasons as other protocols: smaller and fewer routing updates, less memory and processor utilization in making routing decisions, and less processor utilization maintaining the routing table. Thus an optimized BGP network will be highly summarized, although not necessarily hierarchical. Remember that BGP, by nature, provides a summary of key routes identifying paths between autonomous systems; because the collection of autonomous systems is loosely organized, it follows that BGP networks reflect that (lack of) organization.

BGP can be implemented in between networks and within a network. Remember, as shown in Figure 14-1, that BGP detects loops by seeing its AS in the path. The local AS is added to the path when it is advertised externally. When BGP is used internally, there is no way to use AS-path to detect loops and thus there are some special rules to prevent self-inflicted wounds. Because internal routing with BGP is a special case, we differentiate between the expected use of BGP, external BGP (eBGP), and internal BGP (iBGP). External BGP is used between autonomous systems and iBGP is used within an AS.

When to Use BGP

Because of its complexity and specialization for exterior functions, BGP is best in some specific cases:

■ BGP is the only routing protocol that can connect your organization to multiple autonomous systems. For instance, sometimes multiple Internet links are used for redundancy and route optimization purposes.

■ BGP should be considered if you need to implement a routing policy that is only possible with BGP, for instance, to control the link to your ISP.

■ Finally, BGP is a must if your organization acts as a transit AS and connects other AS together. An ISP is an example of a transit AS.

On the contrary, BGP is probably not needed unless the preceding circumstances applies. If your routing requirements can be met in a simpler way, for instance with a default route, then do not encumber yourself with the monetary, financial, and intellectual overhead of BGP. And above all, do not use BGP if your router has insufficient processor or memory resources or if you are not absolutely sure of the potential effects of your BGP configuration.

Connecting to the Internet with BGP

As an exterior routing protocol, BGP is used to connect to the Internet and to route traffic within the Internet. You must ensure that the amount of traffic and routes does not overwhelm your network.

The following sections deal with two important design considerations: the need for redundant links into the Internet, called *multihoming*, and the need to decide how much routing information to receive from the Internet.

Redundant Connections to the Internet—Multihoming

To most modern organizations, losing Internet connectivity is akin to losing dial tone on phones. The Internet carries an enormous amount of traffic and use of the Internet continues to expand for individuals, finance, business, and commerce. It is therefore incumbent on network administrators to address the organization's needs for constant connectivity.

Smart administrators evaluate their Internet connections and try to address the most likely sources of failure. Redundant connections are a common way of addressing requirements for constant Internet service.

Redundant Internet connectivity is referred to as *multihoming*. The idea of multihoming is that failures at one link or ISP can cause a failover to a second link and ISP. When both links are functioning, this arrangement also increases capacity and improves performance. BGP load sharing between multiple links to distinct autonomous systems is possible via policy configurations.

Multihoming might involve more than one connection to the same ISP or connections to separate ISPs. Connecting to more than one ISP creates some issues you should carefully consider:

- You need to verify that your IP addresses are advertised correctly by your provider. One way to do this is to visit a "looking glass" site, which is an Internet site where you can see how your network is advertised through BGP.

- If routes that you advertise, or external routes you depend on, are advertised in different forms (for instance, a /24 instead of two /25 routes), remember that the more specific route will always be preferred regardless of BGP attributes.

- If you are connected to two different providers, your AS could become a transit AS between the ISPs. This is generally undesirable, even for most ISPs, because this results in supporting traffic from multiple remote autonomous systems through your AS, where both the source and destination of the traffic is outside of your AS.

Generally, the ISP is capable of dealing with these issues and will preconfigure their network to protect you. Of course, mistakes do happen and you should not trust that the provider has correctly configured their side. It is also important that you include both ISPs in your plan to multihome so that they can make necessary adjustments.

Receiving Routing Information from the Internet

When connecting to the Internet, some planning is necessary to decide what updates are to be sent to and received from the outside world.

There are three main approaches to connecting to the Internet:

- Accept only default routes from all providers

- Accept some routes plus a default route from all providers

- Accept full routing updates from all providers

Table 14-2 summarizes the different approaches to obtaining routing information from the Internet.

Table 14-2 *Receiving Routing Updates from Multiple ISPs*

Routes Accepted	Memory and CPU	Path Selection
Default routes from each ISP	Low	Route to the nearest BGP router.
Some routes plus default from ISPs	Medium	Take the router receiving specific path if offered; otherwise, route to the nearest BGP router.
All routes from ISPs	High	Always take the most direct path.

The easiest way to connect to the Internet is to take default routes from all providers. This provides your company with a backup path if one provider fails. Because you are only receiving one route, the processor and memory utilization is quite low. The tradeoff, however, is that sometimes traffic will take an indirect path because your router does not have all the information necessary to choose a shorter route—in fact, traffic will generally route to whichever edge router is closest. As an example of when this trade-off is appropriate, imagine that your company only connects to the Internet for e-mail and business research. In this case, some inefficient routing is not important and a complex BGP setup might be difficult to support anyway.

Skipping the second case, for a moment, consider the opposite approach. Taking all routes from all providers guarantees best-case routing, but the tradeoff is high memory and CPU utilization. As of this writing, the Internet BGP routing table has 197,866 routes and continues to grow steadily. The table consumes about 200 MB of memory. Synchronization of the table and receiving updates consumes processor cycles and network capacity. If your company is a service provider then it is important to have best-paths to all endpoints. Service providers would also have routers capable of supporting such large tables, high speed connections, and experienced engineers.

As is often the case in life, the middle road is attractive and fits many situations. Cherry-picking a limited set of routes to receive, plus a default, allows you to have as large or as small a table as you need. Traffic going to specific destinations known by the router will always take the best path, but even the traffic to unusual destinations will take the default path and be okay. As an example, imagine that your company has a handful of major customers and suppliers. For these customers, it is important to optimize routing, but other traffic can take the default routes.

Choosing between these options is an important decision, but not a permanent decision. In general, conservatively taking only the portion of the BGP table that is required is a good starting point. As your needs grow, you can work with your service provider to receive a larger and larger portion.

Synchronization

The BGP synchronization requirement states that before iBGP can propagate a route, the route must be known from another source. That is to say, the route must be learned from an IGP. This synchronization is to ensure that a router really knows how to get to the locations it advertises.

If you have a transit autonomous system with only the edge routers running iBGP, you are relying on the IGP to carry the traffic between the iBGP routers. It is therefore important for the IGP to have the information in its routing table to fulfill this task. The synchronization rule is beneficial for the following reasons:

■ It prevents traffic from being forwarded to unreachable destinations.

■ It reduces unnecessary traffic.

■ It ensures consistency within the autonomous system.

The synchronization rule is on by default and is turned off on some occasions. (Just remember that the synchronization requirement exists for a reason!) It might be useful to turn off synchronization for the following reasons:

■ All the routers in the AS are running BGP.

■ All the BGP routers inside the AS are meshed.

■ When the AS is not a transit autonomous system.

To turn off synchronization, use the following command:

```
Router(config-router)# no synchronization
```

Turning off synchronization allows routers to advertise routes into BGP before the IGP has a copy of the route in its routing table.

BGP States

BGP cycles through five states as it runs:

■ **Idle**—Searching for neighbors

■ **Connect**—TCP three-way handshake complete with neighbor

■ **Open Sent**—BGP Open message has been sent

■ **Open Confirm**—Response received

■ **Established**—BGP neighborship is established

BGP starts each neighbor in idle, and evolves through Connect, Open Sent, and Open Confirm quickly (these are all displayed as "active") and ends in Established. The Established state indicates that both routers agree that all peering requirements are met. The easiest way to check this is to use the **show ip bgp neighbors** command. Look at the third line in Example 14-1.

Example 14-1 *Show IP BGP Neighbors*

```
Router# show ip bgp neighbors
BGP neighbor is 10.1.1.1, remote AS 100, external link
  BGP version 4, remote router ID 172.31.2.3
  BGP state = Established, up for 00:19:10
!output omitted
```

Remember: Established is good, anything else is bad.

If a neighbor does not progress from "idle," look for a next-hop address that cannot be reached.

If the neighbor stays "active," the neighbor is not responding as expected, so look for things that affect this reply. For instance, the peering address or AS may be incorrect, the neighbor may be misconfigured, or authentication may be misconfigured.

Foundation Summary

The Foundation Summary provides a convenient review of many key concepts in this chapter. If you are already comfortable with the topics in this chapter, this summary might help you recall a few details. If you just read this chapter, this review should help solidify some key facts. If you are doing your final prep before the exam, the following lists and tables are a convenient way to review the day before the exam.

The key features of BGP include the following:

- BGP is an enhanced path vector protocol that supports VLSM, CIDR, and summarization.

- BGP creates and maintains connections between peers, using the destination TCP port 179 and keepalives, respectively.

- BGP path attributes allow granularity in path selection.

- BGP has its own table. BGP routes appearing in the routing table are judiciously selected from the BGP table.

Table 14-3 summarizes the different approaches to obtaining routing information from the Internet.

Table 14-3 *Receiving Routing Updates from Multiple ISPs*

Routes Accepted	Memory and CPU	Path Selection
Default routes from each ISP	Low	Route to the nearest BGP router.
Some routes plus default from ISPs	Medium	Take the router receiving specific path if offered; otherwise, route to nearest BGP router.
All routes from ISPs	High	Always take the most direct path.

BGP cycles through five states as it runs:

- **Idle**—Searching for neighbors

- **Connect**—TCP three-way handshake complete with neighbor

- **Open Sent**—BGP Open message has been sent

- **Open Confirm**—Response received

- **Established**—BGP neighborship is established

Q&A

The questions and scenarios in this book are designed to be challenging and to make sure that you know the answer. Rather than allowing you to derive the answers from clues hidden inside the questions themselves, the questions challenge your understanding and recall of the subject.

You can find the answers to these questions in Appendix A. For more practice with exam-like question formats, use the exam engine on the CD-ROM.

1. State three situations in which you should not use BGP to connect to the Internet.

2. What type of routing protocol is BGP classified as, and what does this mean?

3. Your company wants to connect to the Internet redundantly, but does not depend on the Internet for business functions. What is the simplest way to run BGP and meet the needs of the business?

4. What is the synchronization requirement?

5. List the BGP states, in transition order.

6. List the three tables maintained by BGP.

7. What state should the **show ip bgp neighbors** output display if the neighbor relationship is working correctly?

8. When multihoming with BGP to a single provider, load balancing is possible. What is the term for the policy-based configuration that can be used for a similar result when multihoming with BGP to more than one provider?

9. What is the most common implementation synchronization of BGP in an AS?

10. What type of routing protocol is BGP?

This chapter covers the following topics:

- **Basic BGP Configuration Commands**— Describes the commands for forming BGP neighbor relationships and advertising networks.

- **Managing and Verifying the BGP Configuration**—Describes the common BGP commands used to view the status of BGP neighbor relationships and the routes learned through these relationships.

- **Resetting Neighbors**—Describes the methods for resetting BGP neighbor relationships.

CHAPTER 15

BGP Neighbors

This chapter details the basic configuration of BGP: how to configure iBGP and eBGP neighbor relationships, how to advertise routes, and how to summarize routes. You also learn how to display the status of BGP neighbor relationships, the routes learned via BGP neighbor relationships, and how to reset BGP neighbor relationships. Once you master the content of this chapter, the remaining topics in BGP consist of advanced methods for performing policy routing.

"Do I Know This Already?" Quiz

The purpose of the "Do I Know This Already?" quiz is to help you decide what parts of this chapter to use. If you already intend to read the entire chapter, you do not necessarily need to answer these questions now.

The 11-question quiz, derived from the major sections in the "Foundation Topics" portion of the chapter, helps you determine how to spend your limited study time.

Table 15-1 outlines the major topics discussed in this chapter and the "Do I Know This Already?" quiz questions that correspond to those topics.

Table 15-1   *"Do I Know This Already?" Foundation Topics Section-to-Question Mapping*

Foundation Topics Section	Questions Covered in This Section	Score
Basic BGP Configuration Commands	1–6	
Managing and Verifying the BGP Configuration	7–8	
Resetting Neighbors	9–11	
Total Score		

> **CAUTION** The goal of self-assessment is to gauge your mastery of the topics in this chapter. If you do not know the answer to a question or are only partially sure of the answer, you should mark this question wrong for purposes of the self-assessment. Giving yourself credit for an answer you correctly guess skews your self-assessment results and might provide you with a false sense of security.

1. What is the purpose of the **network** command?

   a. To advertise the stated network

   b. To identify the interfaces to run BGP

   c. To forward stated networks

   d. To create neighbors within these networks

2. What is the purpose of the **neighbor** command?

   a. Forces the path to be chosen

   b. Identifies the next hop router and sends LSAs and hellos

   c. States the address and autonomous system of the neighbor with whom to peer

   d. States the neighbor that might be considered as feasible paths

3. Which command enables the BGP process?

   a. **router bgp remote** autonomous-system-number

   b. **router bgp** *process-id*

   c. **ip routing bgp**

   d. **router bgp** *autonomous-system-number*

4. Which IP is used for the source address of BGP traffic in the absence of the command **update-source**?

   a. 0.0.0.0

   b. Derived from the AS

   c. Router ID

   d. Output interface

5. BGP next hop is (by default) set to which of the following?

    a. The first router in the AS

    b. Your BGP neighbor

    c. The first router in the advertising AS

    d. The local router

6. How can you tell which neighbors are iBGP?

    a. The remote AS is zero

    b. Check the list of local AS

    c. The local AS is the same as the remote AS

    d. **show ip bgp neighbor**

7. Which command is used to show the BGP connections between peers?

    a. **show ip bgp connections**

    b. **show ip bgp neighbor**

    c. **show ip bgp sessions**

    d. **show ip bgp topology**

8. Which command is used to show the number of prefixes learned from a BGP neighbor?

    a. **show ip bgp connections**

    b. **show ip bgp sessions**

    c. **show ip bgp topology**

    d. **show ip bgp summary**

9. What is the purpose of the command **clear ip bgp ***?

    a. To disconnect all sessions

    b. To clear the BGP routing table

    c. To end an administrative session

    d. To clear all IGP entries from the routing table

10.   Which of the following techniques can be entered at both ends of a BGP connection to resend BGP updates so that routing policy may be reapplied?

    a. Rebooting the local router

    b. clear ip bgp *

    c. clear ip bgp * soft in

    d. clear ip bgp * soft out

11.   Which technique allows policies to be reapplied without destroying the existing peering?

    a. Rebooting the local router

    b. clear ip bgp *

    c. clear ip bgp * soft in

    d. clear ip bgp * soft out

The answers to the "Do I Know This Already?" quiz are found in Appendix A, "Answers to Chapter 'Do I Know This Already?' Quizzes and Q&A Sections." The suggested choices for your next step are as follows:

- **7 or less overall score**—Read the entire chapter. This includes the "Foundation Topics," "Foundation Summary," "Q&A," and "Scenarios" sections.

- **8 or 9 overall score**—Begin with the "Foundation Summary" section, and then go to the "Q&A" and "Scenarios" sections at the end of the chapter. If you have trouble with these exercises, read the appropriate sections in "Foundation Topics."

- **10 or 11 overall score**—If you want more review on these topics, skip to the "Foundation Summary" section, and then go to the "Q&A" and "Scenarios" sections. Otherwise, move on to the next chapter.

Foundation Topics

Basic BGP Configuration Commands

BGP is designed to connect to neighboring autonomous systems. To do so, you must enable BGP, identify your AS, and identify your neighbors and their AS. Configurations also include commands to define the networks being advertised.

This section describes the generic commands used to implement BGP. Later sections then build on this basic configuration to discuss more complex topics.

Enabling BGP

Just like the other routing protocols, BGP is enabled with the **router** command. This same command is used to identify the AS of this router. The syntax is

```
Router(config)# router bgp autonomous-system-number
```

Identifying Neighbors and Defining Peer Groups

BGP does not promiscuously attach to other routers—neighbors must be predefined. The **neighbor** command is used to identify each neighbor and its AS. If the neighbor AS is the same as this router's AS, this is an iBGP connection. If the AS is different, this is an external neighbor. After the neighbor is defined, further neighbor commands are used to describe the policy used to filter routes to the neighbor.

```
Router(config-router)# neighbor ip-address remote-as autonomous-system-number
```

Listing a series of neighbors and the associated policies could be tedious. Large blocks of configuration lines are hard to read and debug. The concept of a peer group helps solve these problems.

A peer group is a group of neighbors that share the same update policy. Routers are listed as members of the peer group and then policy is associated with the peer group. The group policy is applied to each neighbor, although it can be customized for individual partners.

Peer groups not only reduce the configuration; they also ease the overhead on the router. If each neighbor is configured individually then the BGP update process has to run separately for each neighbor. If multiple neighbors are configured as a group, the update process can run once and then send the same update to all members of the group. Because of this, all members of the group must be either internal or external.

The **neighbor** *peer-group-name* command is used to create the peer group and to associate the peers with an AS. Once the peer group has been defined, members are defined using the **neighbor peer-group** command.

```
Router(config-router)# neighbor peer-group-name peer-group
Router(config-router)# neighbor ip-address | peer-group-name remote-as autonomous-
  system-number
Router(config-router)# neighbor ip-address peer-group peer-group-name
```

In Example 15-1, a router has been configured with three neighbors.

Example 15-1 *Basic Configuration of Neighbors*

```
Router(config)# router bgp 100
Router(config-router)# neighbor 10.255.255.202 remote-as 100
Router(config-router)# neighbor 10.255.255.203 remote-as 100
Router(config-router)# neighbor 10.255.255.204 remote-as 100
```

Example 15-2 shows the same configuration using a peer group.

Example 15-2 *Basic Configuration of a Peer Group*

```
Router(config)# router bgp 100
Router(config-router)# neighbor MyAS peer-group
Router(config-router)# neighbor 10.255.255.202 peer-group MyAS
Router(config-router)# neighbor 10.255.255.203 peer-group MyAS
Router(config-router)# neighbor 10.255.255.204 peer-group MyAS
Router(config-router)# neighbor MyAS remote-as 100
```

The **neighbor** command can also be used to disable a peer. Administratively shutting down a peer is done during maintenance to prevent "flapping" (to prevent the router from annoying its neighbors by oscillating between up and down).

```
Router(config-router)# neighbor ip-address | peer-group-name shutdown
```

Figure 15-1 shows the topology for the forthcoming Example 15-3.

Example 15-3 shows the basic configuration commands required to make eBGP operate between autonomous systems. In Example 15-3, Router A in AS100 connects to routers in AS100, AS200, AS300, AS400, and AS500.

Figure 15-1 *Topology for Example 15-3*

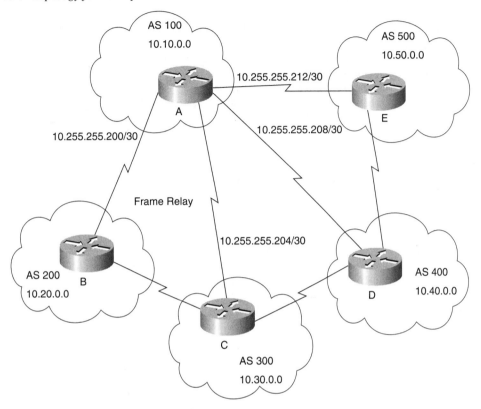

Example 15-3 *Basic Configuration of eBGP on Router A*

```
Router A

Router(config)# interface Serial0.1
Router(config-int)# ip address 10.255.255.201 255.255.255.252
!
Router(config)# interface Serial0.2
Router(config-int)# ip address 10.255.255.205 255.255.255.252
!
Router(config)# interface Serial0.3
Router(config-int)# ip address 10.255.255.209 255.255.255.252
!
                                                              continues
```

Example 15-3 *Basic Configuration of eBGP on Router A (Continued)*

```
Router(config)# interface Serial0.4
Router(config-int)# ip address 10.255.255.213 255.255.255.252
!
Router(config)# router bgp 100
Router(config-router)# neighbor 10.255.255.202 remote-as 200
Router(config-router)# neighbor 10.255.255.206 remote-as 300
Router(config-router)# neighbor 10.255.255.210 remote-as 400
Router(config-router)# neighbor 10.255.255.214 remote-as 500
```

Source IP Address

Internal neighbors do not have to be directly attached. Typically, an IGP is responsible for routing within the AS so that BGP speakers can reach each other from across the AS.

In Figure 15-2, Router A has three IP addresses. When peering to A, B could choose to peer to the directly connected IP (172.25.1.1); however, if the associated link goes down, the interface no longer responds to that address. Even though there continues to be a path from B to A through C, B cannot reach the peering address and A is unavailable.

Figure 15-2 *Internal Peering*

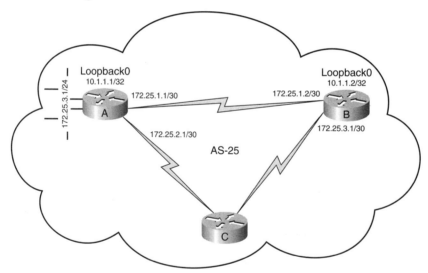

Peering to a loopback address helps to prevent this conundrum. If Router B peers to the loopback interface (10.1.1.1) then it is unaffected by the status of the top link. However, it is important that the routers advertise the loopback networks used in this fashion with the IGP.

A second problem is that, when BGP traffic is created, the source IP is the output interface. On Router B, traffic from B to A would normally follow the direct path and be sourced from 172.25.1.2, but when that link fails, traffic will be sourced from the other interface (172.25.3.1). Since the new source address does not match the peer address configured on Router A, the connection will be refused.

To truly allow for redundant paths, the source address must always be what the neighbor expects. This can be accomplished with the **neighbor update-source** command:

```
Router(config-router)# neighbor ip-address | peer-group-name update-source interface
```

Example 15-4 shows an example configuration for Routers A and B. Both routers peer to their neighbors' loopback and source traffic from their own loopback, allowing for redundancy.

Example 15-4 *Allowing for Redundant Peering Paths*

```
Router A
RouterA(config)# router bgp 25
RouterA(config-router)# neighbor 10.1.1.2 remote-as 25
RouterA(config-router)# neighbor 10.1.1.2 update-source loopback0

Router B
RouterB(config)# router bgp 25
RouterB(config-router)# neighbor 10.1.1.1 remote-as 25
RouterB(config-router)# neighbor 10.1.1.1 update-source loopback0
```

External neighbors do not have the benefit of a routing protocol to learn peering addresses and so are usually directly attached. eBGP packets also have a TTL of 1, which prevents them from traveling more than one hop. It is possible to use a similar redundancy technique externally—however, the following two conditions must be met:

- There must be a route to the peering address.

- The TTL must be set to an appropriate number of hops.

To change the default TTL of external connections, use the command **neighbor ebgp-multihop**:

```
Router(config-router)# neighbor ip-address | peer-group-name ebgp-multihop hops
```

Forcing the Next-Hop Address

A BGP next hop is the point of entry into an AS. Typically, the next hop will be the address of the edge router, but there are some cases where it makes sense to change this. For instance, routes received from external neighbors will be advertised with external next-hop IP addresses. Internal neighbors might not recognize this as a valid address. The **next-hop-self** command allows a router to substitute its internal address so that internal neighbors understand how to reach the next-hop address. The next-hop attribute is discussed further in the attributes section of this chapter.

The syntax of the command is as follows:

```
Router(config-router)# neighbor {ip-address | peer-group} next-hop-self
```

Defining the Networks to Be Advertised

The **network** command determines the networks that are originated by this router. This is a different use of the **network** command than you are accustomed to configuring with EIGRP, OSPF, and RIP. This command does not identify the interfaces on which to run BGP; it states the networks that are available within the AS. Multiple **network** commands may be used as needed. The **mask** portion is used because BGP can handle subnetting and supernetting. The command syntax is

```
Router(config-router)# network network-number mask network-mask
```

Aggregating Routes

To aggregate (summarize) routes within the BGP domain, use the following command from router configuration mode:

```
Router(config-router)# aggregate-address ip-address mask [summary-only] [as-set]
```

If the parameter **summary-only** is used, then the specific routes are suppressed and the summary route is the only one propagated. Sending only the summary is the usual usage. If the parameter **as-set** is used, then all the autonomous systems that have been traversed will be recorded as a set in the update message.

> **NOTE**   Before the **aggregate-address** command, routes were summarized by using a network statement and a static route. The network statement defined the route and then a static route to *null0* met the synchronization requirement and prevented routing loops.
>
> The following configuration illustrates the older method for advertising an aggregate address:
>
> ```
> Router(config)# router bgp 10
> Router(config-router)# network 10.0.0.0 255.255.254.0
> Router(config)# ip route 10.0.0.0 255.255.254.0 null0
> ```
>
> This set of commands is equivalent to **aggregate-address 10.0.0.0 255.255.254.0; aggregate-address** improves on the older method because it allows for easy summarization, allows for easy filtering of subnets, and is easier to read in a configuration.

Example 15-5 is a BGP configuration using the **aggregate-address** command with the summarization parameter. In this example, routes with a prefix longer than /16 are summarized. In this way, the route 10.10.35.8/29 is not seen in BGP updates because it is summarized into the 10.20.0.0/16 advertisement. Any route that does not summarize into those specified in the example is listed individually. Summarization reduces the overhead on the network and simplifies system administration.

Example 15-5   *The* **aggregate-address** *Command with the Summarization Parameter*

```
Router A
Router(config)# interface Serial0
Router(config-int)# ip address 10.255.255.201 255.255.255.224
Router(config)# router bgp 100
Router(config-router)# network 10.10.35.8 255.255.255.252
Router(config-router)# network 10.10.27.0 255.255.255.0
Router(config-router)# network 10.10.100.0 255.255.2550.0
Router(config-router)# aggregate-address 10.10.0.0 255.255.0.0 summary-only
Router(config-router)# neighbor 10.255.255.202 remote-as 200
Router(config-router)# neighbor 10.255.255.202 next-hop-self
Router(config-router)# neighbor 10.255.255.206 remote-as 300
Router(config-router)# neighbor 10.255.255.206 next-hop-self
```

Authentication

Authentication is extremely important with BGP—some providers even require authentication. Without authentication, Internet routing would be exposed to poisoning or misdirection that could allow attackers to insert themselves into a path or prevent communication.

BGP authentication involves agreeing to a key (password) and is accomplished by sending an MD5 hash of the key with every BGP packet. Authentication is easy to setup; simply associate a password with a neighbor:

```
Router(config-router)# neighbor ip-address password password
```

For example, authenticating neighbor 10.1.1.1 using a password of b8k6m3w1 follows:

```
Router(config-router)# neighbor 10.1.1.1 password b8k6m3w1
```

Managing and Verifying the BGP Configuration

The **show** commands for BGP are comprehensive and give clear information about the BGP sessions and routing options. These informative commands were introduced in the previous chapter. Their functions are as follows:

- **show ip bgp**—Displays the BGP routing table.

- **show ip bgp summary**—Displays the status of all BGP sessions, as well as the number of prefixes learned per session.

- **show ip bgp neighbors**—Displays information about the TCP connections to neighbors, such as the number of each type of BGP message sent and received with each neighbor. When the connection is established, the neighbors can exchange updates.

- **show processes cpu**—Displays active processes and is used to identify any process that is using excessive resources.

Another command that helps to troubleshoot any implementation and should be considered in the BGP configuration is the **debug** command. An entire book in the IOS documentation set is devoted to this command. For BGP, **debug** is a very useful command. It is shown here with all the possible options:

```
Router# debug ip bgp [dampening | events | keepalives | updates]
```

This command displays live information of events as they occur. The options available display dampening information, events, keepalives to maintain the TCP session with the peer, and routing updates as they are sent or received. *Route dampening* is a mechanism to minimize the instability caused by route flapping. By counting the number of times the identified route fails and applying a penalty to the route for each flap, BGP can ignore ill-behaved routes and use only the well-behaved.

Resetting Neighbors

After configuration changes in BGP, it is sometimes necessary to do a "hard reset" and disconnect the TCP session between neighbors. This can be forced with the following command:

```
Router(config-router)# clear ip bgp {* | address}[soft [in | out]]
```

This command disconnects the session between the neighbors and reestablishes it using the new configuration that has been entered. BGP only exchanges routes when neighbor relationships are established, so if neighbors change policies—for example, to implement new distribute lists—resetting is the only way to propagate the changes without cycling the power.

There are several problems with a hard reset, however:

- Hard resets take a long time to complete and interrupt routing in the interim.

- Hard resets count as a flap and could cause peers to disassociate themselves.

- Hard resets force a full set of routing updates and could generate a lot of traffic.

Soft resets have the same effect as "hard resets" but do not interrupt routing or cause a flap. Soft resets can be done inbound or outbound. An outbound soft reset looks like this:

```
Router(config-router)# clear ip bgp {* | address} soft out
```

An outbound soft reset tells the local router to resend its entire BGP table to this neighbor, but to do so without tearing down the TCP session between them. Changes to outbound route filtering can be passed to neighbors this way.

There are times, however, when you want your neighbor to softly resend their advertisement. Of course, you cannot force an "autonomous" neighbor to do anything. You could call the provider and ask, but this can be difficult or impossible.

Soft inbound resets allow you to simulate receiving an update. First, your router must have an unprocessed copy of the neighbor update. The **soft-reconfiguration-inbound** command must be preset for the neighbor, as shown in the following syntax. Since this causes your router to remember two copies of the advertisement (the before and after processing versions), this consumes much more memory.

```
Router(config-router)# neighbor ip-address soft-reconfiguration inbound
```

Assuming that the capability is available, you may replay a previously recorded advertisement—for example, to force a neighbor advertisement through new filters—using the command:

```
Router(config-router)# clear ip bgp ip-address soft in
```

Using the **soft** option (with or without any additional keywords) initiates a soft reset and does not tear down the session.

At this point, you have seen the array of BGP commands used most frequently in BGP implementations. This completes the exploration of the more commonly used BGP commands. Chapter 16 delves into greater depth with more specific formulations of BGP implementations.

Foundation Summary

The Foundation Summary provides a convenient review of many key concepts in this chapter. If you are already comfortable with the topics in this chapter, this summary might help you recall a few details. If you just read this chapter, this review should help solidify some key facts. If you are doing your final prep before the exam, the following lists and tables are a convenient way to review the day before the exam.

The key features of BGP include the following:

- iBGP neighbors are normally set up using loopback networks and external neighbors are normally set up using connected physical interfaces.

- BGP neighbors can be configured directly or by using peer groups.

Table 15-2 summarizes the commands covered in this chapter.

Table 15-2 *Summary of BGP Commands*

Command	Function
router bgp *autonomous-system-number*	Starts the BGP routing process.
network *network-number* **mask** *network-mask*	Identifies the networks to be advertised by the BGP process.
neighbor {*ip-address* | *peer-group-name*} **remote-as** *autonomous-system-number*	Identifies the neighbor with whom the router is synchronizing its routing table and activates a TCP session with the neighbor. It also configures the **remote-as** option for a peer group.
neighbor {*ip-address* | *peer-group-name*} **next-hop-self**	Used to force the router to use its own IP address as the next hop when advertising to neighbors.
aggregate-address *ip-address mask* [**summary-only**] [**as-set**]	Used to create an aggregate address. The **summary-only** option advertises the summary, and the **as-set** option lists the autonomous system numbers that the more specific routes have traversed.
debug ip bgp [**dampening** | **events** | **keepalives** | **updates**]	Enables you to be very specific about the BGP **debug** parameters.

Table 15-2 *Summary of BGP Commands (Continued)*

Command	Function
clear ip bgp {* | *address*} [**soft** [**in** | **out**]]	Resets the session between the neighbors and reestablishes it with the new configuration that has been entered. The soft option does not tear down the sessions, but it resends the updates. The **in** and **out** options allow the configuration of inbound or outbound soft updates. The default is for both.
show ip bgp [**summary** | **neighbors**]	Shows the BGP connections. A network can be specified to retrieve information on the lone network. The **summary** option will give the status of the BGP connections. The **neighbors** option gives both TCP and BGP connections.

Q&A

The questions and scenarios in this book are designed to be challenging and to make sure that you know the answer. Rather than allowing you to derive the answers from clues hidden inside the questions themselves, the questions challenge your understanding and recall of the subject.

You can find the answers to these questions in Appendix A. For more practice with exam-like question formats, use the exam engine on the CD-ROM.

1.   What does the command **clear ip bgp *** achieve, and why should it be used cautiously?

2.   Explain the use of the command **neighbor 10.10.10.10 remote-as 250**.

3.   State four message types of BGP.

4.   Give two reasons why BGP peer groups are useful.

5.   What is the difference between a peer and a neighbor?

6.   In BGP, describe the purpose of the **network** command.

7.   Explain the command **neighbor** {*ip-address* | *peer-group-name*} **next-hop-self**.

Scenarios

The following scenarios and questions are designed to draw together the content of the chapter and to exercise your understanding of the concepts. There is not necessarily a right answer. The thought process and practice in manipulating the concepts are the goals of this section. The answers to the scenario questions are found at the end of this chapter.

Scenario 15-1

The company Humugos is waiting for the consultant to configure the network. The requirement is to give each country in which Humugos operates its own autonomous system number. The countries will be connected via eBGP and will use leased lines. The autonomous system numbers are private because the connection to the Internet is dealt with by an ISP at each local site. For the first phase of the switchover, EIGRP is removed from the connections between the countries, and the BGP configuration needs to be implemented to ensure a smooth transition. The intention is for each country to have the same configuration to ease management and troubleshooting.

1. Using the diagram in Figure 15-3 as a reference, issue the commands that need to be configured at each country or autonomous system. The private autonomous system numbers range from 64,512 to 65,535.

   Figure 15-3 has been simplified and does not contain all the autonomous systems that Humugos network engineers must take into consideration.

2. What commands would indicate that there was a problem of scaling?

Figure 15-3 *Diagram for Scenario 15-1*

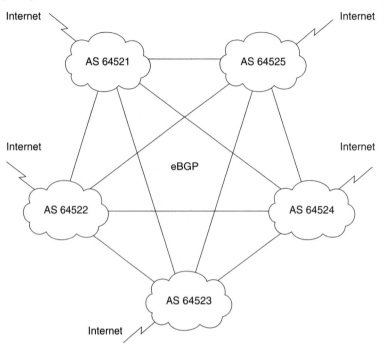

Scenario 15-2

A small company called Insolvent, Inc., has a main office in Chicago and satellite offices on the west coast of the United States. The company has recently changed its routing protocol to OSPF.

Insolvent has a connection to the Internet from each site, over which it does all its business. The link is a fractional T1 at the satellite offices and a full T1 at the main office. The network administrator at the main office is responsible for the corporate network and is currently trying to recruit staff to manage the local networks. The network administrator was advised at a technical seminar that BGP is what is needed to connect to the Internet. Figure 15-4 shows the network.

1. Given the description of the company and with reference to Figure 15-4, do you agree that BGP is a requirement for this network? Give reasons for your answer.

2. What alternatives are available?

3. Give the alternative configuration commands for the satellite site to connect to the Internet.

4. What commands would show that the link is up and operational?

Figure 15-4 *Diagram for Scenario 15-2*

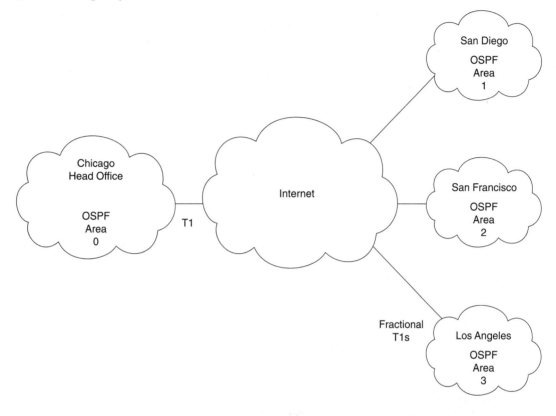

Scenario 15-3

Review the output in Example 15-6, and answer the following questions.

Example 15-6 *Scenario 15-3 Output*

```
FARADAY-gw# show ip bgp neighbor
BGP neighbor is 155.94.83.1,  remote AS 2914, external link
 Index 1, Offset 0, Mask 0x2
  BGP version 4, remote router ID 129.250.116.16
  BGP state = Established, table version = 457046, up for 1w5d
  Last read 00:00:20, hold time is 180, keepalive interval is 60 seconds
  Minimum time between advertisement runs is 30 seconds
  Received 890723 messages, 0 notifications, 0 in queue
  Sent 36999 messages, 0 notifications, 0 in queue
  Inbound path policy configured
  Outbound path policy configured
```
                                                                    continues

Example 15-6 *Scenario 15-3 Output (Continued)*

```
Continues
  Outgoing update AS path filter list is 1
  Route map for incoming advertisements is limit-verioverdi
  Connections established 3; dropped 2
  Last reset 1w5d, due to : User reset request
  No. of prefix received 11031
 No. of prefix received 11031
Connection state is ESTAB, I/O status: 1, unread input bytes: 0
Local host: 155.94.83.2, Local port: 11036
Foreign host: 155.94.83.1, Foreign port: 179
Enqueued packets for retransmit: 0, input: 0  mis-ordered: 0 (0 bytes)
Event Timers (current time is 0x845DFA38):
Timer          Starts    Wakeups         Next
Retrans        18473        11            0x0
TimeWait           0         0            0x0
AckHold        86009     50293            0x0
SendWnd            0         0            0x0
KeepAlive          0         0            0x0
GiveUp             0         0            0x0
PmtuAger           0         0            0x0
DeadWait           0         0            0x0
iss:  829352113 snduna:  829702916  sndnxt:  829702916    sndwnd:  16004
irs:  625978143 rcvnxt:  652708970  rcvwnd:         16342 delrcvwnd:    42
SRTT: 300 ms, RTTO: 607 ms, RTV: 3 ms, KRTT: 0 ms
minRTT: 4 ms, maxRTT: 764 ms, ACK hold: 300 ms
Flags: higher precedence, nagle
Datagrams (max data segment is 536 bytes):
Rcvd: 122915 (out of order: 0), with data: 105023, total data bytes: 26731112
Sent: 109195 (retransmit: 11), with data: 18461, total data bytes: 350802
!
!
BGP neighbor is 144.39.228.49,  remote AS 701, external link
 Index 2, Offset 0, Mask 0x4
  BGP version 4, remote router ID 144.39.3.104
  BGP state = Established, table version = 457055, up for 2w0d
  Last read 00:00:08, hold time is 180, keepalive interval is 60 seconds
  Minimum time between advertisement runs is 30 seconds
  Received 50265 messages, 0 notifications, 0 in queue
  Sent 37016 messages, 0 notifications, 0 in queue
  Inbound path policy configured
  Outbound path policy configured
  Outgoing update AS path filter list is 1
  Route map for incoming advertisements is limit-uunetmemenet
  Connections established 2; dropped 1
  Last reset 2w0d, due to : Peer closing down the session
  No. of prefix received 1635
Connection state is ESTAB, I/O status: 1, unread input bytes: 0
```

Example 15-6 *Scenario 15-3 Output (Continued)*

```
Local host: 144.39.228.50, Local port: 179
Foreign host: 144.39.228.49, Foreign port: 11013
Enqueued packets for retransmit: 0, input: 0  mis-ordered: 0 (0 bytes)
Event Timers (current time is 0x845F16B8):
Timer          Starts     Wakeups             Next
Retrans         20357          4              0x0
TimeWait            0          0              0x0
AckHold         29701      26058              0x0
SendWnd             0          0              0x0
KeepAlive           0          0              0x0
GiveUp              0          0              0x0
PmtuAger            0          0              0x0
DeadWait            0          0              0x0
iss: 3360945234  snduna: 3361331966  sndnxt: 3361331966     sndwnd:  15890
irs: 2976917809  rcvnxt: 2977685910  rcvwnd:      15072  delrcvwnd:   1312
SRTT: 306 ms, RTTO: 642 ms, RTV: 15 ms, KRTT: 0 ms
minRTT: 4 ms, maxRTT: 908 ms, ACK hold: 300 ms
Flags: passive open, nagle, gen tcbs
Datagrams (max data segment is 1460 bytes):
Rcvd: 48675 (out of order: 0), with data: 29705, total data bytes: 768119
Sent: 46955 (retransmit: 4), with data: 20353, total data bytes: 386750
```

1. How many sessions are active?

2. What is the state of the sessions, and what do the states mean?

Scenario Answers

The answers provided in this section are not necessarily the only possible answers to the questions. The questions are designed to test your knowledge and to give practical exercise in certain key areas. This section is intended to test and exercise skills and concepts detailed in the body of this chapter.

If your answer is different, ask yourself whether it follows the tenets explained in the answers provided. Your answer is correct not if it matches the solution provided in the book, but rather if it has included the principles of design laid out in the chapter.

In this way, the testing provided in these scenarios is deeper: It examines not only your knowledge, but also your understanding and ability to apply that knowledge to problems.

If you do not get the correct answer, refer back to the text and review the subject tested. Be certain to also review your notes on the question to ensure that you understand the principles of the subject.

Scenario 15-1 Answers

1. *Using the diagram in Figure 15-3 as a reference, issue the commands that need to be configured at each country or autonomous system.*

   The commands configured at each country or autonomous system would be the same structurally, although the details, such as the IP addresses and the autonomous system numbers, would change.

Example 15-7 shows the configuration of the autonomous system 64522, which is the San Francisco router. It has been assigned network 10.2.0.0.

Example 15-7   *Scenario 15-1 Configuration*

```
Router(config)#
router bgp 64522
no auto-summary
neighbor 10.1.100.1 remote-as 64521
neighbor 10.3.100.1 remote-as 64523
neighbor 10.4.100.1 remote-as 64524
neighbor 10.5.100.1 remote-as 64525
neighbor 10.6.100.1 remote-as 64526
neighbor 10.7.100.1 remote-as 64527
neighbor 10.8.100.1 remote-as 64528
neighbor 10.9.100.1 remote-as 64529
neighbor 10.10.100.1 remote-as 64530
!neighbor commands omitted for brevity
neighbor 10.250.100.1 remote-as 64750
network 10.2.0.0
```

The protocol has had the neighbors in each autonomous system defined with their next-hop IP address and the number of the autonomous system to which they are connecting. The **no auto-summary** command is used to ensure that the subnets of network 10.0.0.0 are advertised; otherwise, each subnet would need to be defined as a **network** command.

2. *What commands would indicate that there was a problem of scaling?*

The **show ip bgp**, **show ip bgp summary**, and **show ip route** commands would indicate whether there is a scaling issue.

Scenario 15-2 Answers

1. *Given the description of the company and with reference to Figure 15-4, do you agree that BGP is a requirement for this network? Give reasons for your answer.*

Because the company is small and has only a single connection per site to the Internet, it would be too complex to configure and maintain BGP when there are simply not enough resources. The bandwidth is inadequate for the task, and the administrative expertise is already overstretched. It would be far better to configure one or two static/default routes to the Internet and to redistribute these routes into the IGP running within the autonomous system.

2. *What alternatives are available?*

   The only real alternative is the one already mentioned: to configure a default route into the Internet from every location and to redistribute this default route into the IGP for the autonomous system.

3. *Give the alternative configuration commands for the satellite site to connect to Internet.*

   Each site would have the same configuration structure, although the details might differ:

   ```
   ip route 0.0.0.0 0.0.0.0 155.94.83.1
   router ospf 100
   network 207.111.9.0 0.0.0.255 area 0
   default-information originate always
   ```

   The first line configures the default route. The second line turns on the OSPF process 100. The third line identifies which interfaces are participating in OSPF and what area they are in. The fourth line propagates the default route into the network, whether or not the advertising router has a path to the network.

4. *What commands would show that the link is up and operational?*

   The commands to prove that the link is up and operational are the **show ip route** command and the **ping** and **traceroute** commands. Refer to the Cisco web site or the ICND course for more details on these commands.

Scenario 15-3 Answers

1. *How many sessions are active?*

   There are two active sessions. In reading the large amount of information on the **show ip bgp neighbor** command, there is a line at the beginning of each session identifying the neighboring peer. The lines in this output screen are as follows:

   ```
   BGP neighbor is 155.94.83.1,   remote AS 2914, external link
   BGP neighbor is 144.39.228.49,  remote AS 701, external link
   ```

2. *What is the state of the sessions, and what do the states indicate?*

   ```
   BGP state = Established, table version = 457046, up for 1w5d
   BGP state = Established, table version = 457055, up for 2w0d
   ```

   Both the peers have established sessions. This means that they have a TCP session between them. They are now in a position to exchange routing tables and to synchronize their databases. The rest of the line indicates how many times the table has been updated and how long the session has been maintained. In this example, the first peer has had a session with the local router for one week and five days, while the second peer has been up for exactly two weeks.

There are three autonomous systems in this configuration. The first peer belongs to autonomous system 2914, and the second belongs to 701. Because both of these neighbors that belong to their autonomous systems have an external BGP session, there must be a third autonomous system, within which the local router resides.

```
BGP neighbor is 155.94.83.1,   remote AS 2914, external link
BGP neighbor is 144.39.228.49,  remote AS 701, external link
```

This chapter covers the following topics:

- **BGP Attributes**—Describes the BGP attributes used for determining BGP behavior.

- **Controlling BGP Path Selection**—Describes explains how to configure BGP attributes on Cisco routers.

- **Verifying the Configuration of Attributes**—Describes Cisco IOS commands to display output related to BGP attributes.

CHAPTER 16

Controlling BGP Route Selection

The topics in this chapter describe the values and process used in BGP path selection and build on the basic configuration of BGP described in the previous chapter. In this discussion of advanced BGP topics, explanation of the technology is coupled with configuration examples so that your conceptual understanding of BGP is reinforced by concrete implementation examples.

"Do I Know This Already?" Quiz

The purpose of the "Do I Know This Already?" quiz is to help you decide what parts of this chapter to use. If you already intend to read the entire chapter, you do not necessarily need to answer these questions now.

The 14-question quiz, derived from the major sections in the "Foundation Topics" portion of the chapter, helps you determine how to spend your limited study time.

Table 16-1 outlines the major topics discussed in this chapter and the "Do I Know This Already?" quiz questions that correspond to those topics.

Table 16-1 *"Do I Know This Already?" Foundation Topics Section-to-Question Mapping*

Foundation Topics Section	Questions Covered in This Section	Score
BGP Attributes	1–5	
Controlling BGP Path Selection	6–12	
Verifying the Configuration of Attributes	13–14	
Total Score		

CAUTION The goal of self-assessment is to gauge your mastery of the topics in this chapter. If you do not know the answer to a question or are only partially sure of the answer, you should mark this question wrong for purposes of the self-assessment. Giving yourself credit for an answer you correctly guess skews your self-assessment results and might provide you with a false sense of security.

1. Well-known mandatory attributes are described as which of the following?

    a. Must be included in updates

    b. Must be supported

    c. Stripped if not recognized

    d. Marked partial if not recognized

2. Optional nontransitive attributes are described as which of the following?

    a. Must be included in updates

    b. Must be supported

    c. Stripped if not recognized

    d. Marked partial if not recognized

3. Which BGP attributes are used in BGP path selection?

    a. AS-Path

    b. Atomic Aggregate

    c. Community

    d. Next Hop

    e. Origin

4. A route has an AS-Path of 7 25 19 69. What can you learn from reading this path?

    a. The local AS is 7.

    b. The origin AS is 69.

    c. There is a loop.

    d. 7 is the origin.

5. Place the following attributes in the order that BGP evaluates them to select a best path: AS-Path, Local Preference, MED, Weight.

    a. AS-Path, Local-Preference, MED, Weight.

    b. Local-Preference, AS-Path, Weight, MED.

    c. AS-Path, MED, Weight, Local-Preference.

    d. Weight, Local-Preference, AS-Path, MED.

6. Give the command that would change the weight attribute for the path to the peer 192.10.5.3.

   a. set weight 192.10.5.3 48

   b. neighbor 192.10.5.3 weight 48

   c. set attribute weight 48

   d. ip bgp neighbor 192.10.0.0 remote-as 300 weight 48

7. Which of the following statements are true about the BGP weight attribute?

   a. Default value is zero

   b. BGP prefers the lowest value

   c. It is proprietary

   d. Only used within an AS

8. Which of the following statements about the BGP local-preference attribute are true?

   a. Default value is zero

   b. BGP prefers the highest value

   c. It is proprietary

   d. Only used outside an AS

9. Which of the following statements describes MED?

   a. Default value is 1

   b. Only applies to external neighbors

   c. BGP prefers higher values

   d. It is a "strong" attribute

10. Consider the following route map. What will be the local-preference for 192.168.26.0/24?

```
access-list 39 permit 192.168.24.0 0.0.3.255
access-list 32 permit 192.168.26.0 0.0.0.255
route-map test permit 10
        match ip address 39
        match ip address 32
        set ip local preference 150
route-map test permit 20
        match ip address 39 32
        set ip local preference 200
```

   a. 0

   b. 100

   c. 150

   d. 200

11. Consider the route map from the previous question. What will be the local-preference for 192.168.25.0/24?

    a. 0

    b. 100

    c. 150

    d. 200

12. Consider the route map from the previous question. What will be the local-preference for 192.168.20.0/24?

    a. 0

    b. 100

    c. 150

    d. 200

13. In the command **show ip bgp**, the "i" origin code is placed at the end of a line in the BGP table. It can be which of the following values?

    a. Entry originated from IGP and was advertised with a network router configuration command.

    b. Entry originated from an EGP.

    c. Origin of the path is not clear. Usually, this is a router that is redistributed into BGP from an IGP.

    d. The IP address of the originating router.

14. Which command shows the local preference and weight attribute values?

    a. **show bgp attributes**

    b. **show ip bgp**

    c. **show ip bgp path**

    d. **show ip bgp attributes**

The answers to the "Do I Know This Already?" quiz are found in Appendix A, "Answers to Chapter 'Do I Know This Already?' Quizzes and Q&A Sections." The suggested choices for your next step are as follows:

- **10 or less overall score**—Read the entire chapter. This includes the "Foundation Topics," "Foundation Summary," "Q&A," and "Scenarios" sections.

- **11 to 12 overall score**—Begin with the "Foundation Summary" section, and then go to the "Q&A" and "Scenarios" sections at the end of the chapter. If you have trouble with these exercises, read the appropriate sections in "Foundation Topics."

- **13 or 14 overall score**—If you want more review on these topics, skip to the "Foundation Summary" section, and then go to the "Q&A" section and "Scenarios" sections at the end of the chapter. Otherwise, move on to the next chapter.

Foundation Topics

BGP Attributes

Routes learned via BGP have associated properties that are used to determine the best route to a destination when multiple paths exist to a particular destination. These properties are referred to as BGP *attributes*; designing robust networks requires an understanding of how BGP attributes influence route selection. This chapter describes the attributes that BGP uses in the route selection process.

Table 16-2 lists the attributes supported by Cisco IOS.

Table 16-2   *BGP Attributes*

Attribute Name	Category	Description
Aggregator	Optional, transitive	Router ID and AS of router that summarized. Not used in path selection.
AS_Path	Well-known, mandatory	List of AS route has passed through. Prefer shortest path.
Atomic aggregate	Well-known, discretionary	Summary includes multiple AS. Not used in path selection.
Cluster ID	Optional, nontransitive	Originating cluster. Not used in path selection.
Community	Optional, transitive	Route tag. Not used in path selection.
Local preference	Well-known, discretionary	Metric for external paths, for internal neighbors. Prefer highest.
Multiple Exit Discriminator (MED)	Optional, nontransitive	Informs external peers which path to take into the autonomous system. Prefer lowest.
Next Hop	Well-known, mandatory	External peer in neighboring AS. Not used in path selection.
Origin	Well-known, mandatory	Lowest origin type preferred: (i)IGP is lower than (e)EGP, and EGP is lower than (?)incomplete.
Originator ID	Optional, nontransitive	Identifies Route Reflector. Not used in path selection.
Weight	Optional, not communicated to peers	Administrative Cisco attribute. Prefer highest.

It is possible for BGP to receive multiple advertisements for the same route from multiple sources. BGP selects only one path as the best path. When the path is selected, BGP puts the selected path in the IP routing table and propagates the path to its neighbors. Table 16-3 displays the complete path selection process, summarizing the descriptions in this section.

Table 16-3 *BGP Path Selection*

Order	Preference	Description
0. Synchronized	TRUE	Use only routes that meet the synchronization requirement
1. Weight	Highest	Administrative override
2. Local Preference	Highest	Used internally to pick path out of AS
3. Self originated	TRUE	Used to prefer paths originated on this router
4. AS-Path	Shortest	Minimize AS-hops
5. Origin	i<?	Prefer stability
6. MED	Lowest	Used external to come in
7. External	EBGP<IBGP	External path preferred over internal path
8. IGP cost	Lowest	Look for more information
9. EBGP Peering	Oldest	Prefer stability
10. RID	Lowest	Choose one with lowest BGP router ID

Looking at Table 16-3, it seems that there is a lot to know about BGP. This is an accurate impression. Unfortunately, this is one case where you simply have to memorize content; you must memorize Table 16-3. Notice that the first two steps (after synchronization) prefer higher values, the third step is true or false, and the remaining steps prefer lower values.

In general, with BGP, the three most important concepts to master are

- Synchronization rule

- BGP Split Horizon

- BGP Path Selection

Controlling BGP Path Selection

The path selection criteria gives BGP a reasonable idea about the best way to route traffic in the Internet, but there are still times when an administrator has a more complete understanding of requirements than the router. In those cases, each BGP attribute may be tuned until the desired routing is achieved.

There are many methods to influence path selection, but the route maps are by far the most common technique for implementing policy routing. You can use the route map technique described in this section for any attribute, but this section describes only the weight and local preference attributes.

Using the Weight Attribute

The Cisco proprietary weight attribute selects the exit interface when there are multiple paths to the same destination. The higher the weight value, the better the path. Weight is local to the router and the attribute is not propagated to other routers. To configure the weight attribute, use the following command:

```
Router(config-router)# neighbor {ip-address | peer-group-name} weight weight
```

Remember that weight can be a value from 0 to 65,535. The default weight is 0, unless this router sources the route (in which case the weight defaults to 32,768).

Figure 16-1 illustrates the use of the weight attribute, and Example 16-1 shows how the path through San Francisco is chosen. As you can see, the weight has been set on Chicago, making it prefer the path through San Francisco no matter which network it is trying to reach. The best path to 130.16.0.0 is through New York, but the path chosen will be through San Francisco.

Example 16-1 *Sample Configuration to Illustrate Tuning the Weight Attribute*

```
Chicago(config)# router bgp 100
Chicago(config-router)# bgp log-neighbor-changes
Chicago(config-router)# neighbor 167.55.191.3 remote-as 100
Chicago(config-router)# neighbor 167.55.199.2 remote-as 100
Chicago(config-router)# neighbor 167.55.199.2 weight 200
```

Remember that weight is a very powerful attribute—weight is considered before any other value and trumps all other settings.

Using the Local-Preference Attribute

The local preference is equally easy to configure. You can set it on either a default or a per-prefix basis. The syntax for the default command is

```
Router(config-router)# bgp default local-preference value
```

Figure 16-1 *The Weight Attribute and Selecting a Path*

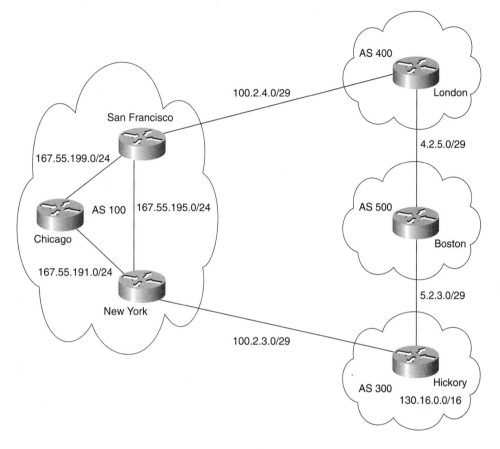

Local preference has a range from 0 to 4,294,967,295; higher values are preferred in selecting routes. The default is 100.

Example 16-2 is based on Figure 16-2. The local preference, set in the San Francisco router to 200, is propagated in the updates to all its peers. Likewise, the local preference of 100 set in the New York router is propagated to its peers. When Chicago has to decide on a path to the network 130.16.0.0, the highest local preference attribute dictates the San Francisco router as the exit point from the autonomous system.

Figure 16-2 *Using Local Preference to Select a Path*

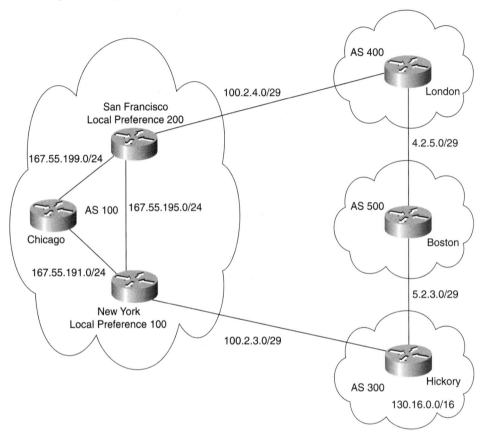

Example 16-2 *Sample Configuration Illustrating Local Preference*

```
SanFrancisco(config)# router bgp 100
!
SanFrancisco(config-router)# bgp default local-preference 200
SanFrancisco(config-router)# aggregate-address 167.55.0.0 255.255.0.0 summary-only
SanFrancisco(config-router)# neighbor 100.2.4.4 remote-as 400
SanFrancisco(config-router)# neighbor 100.2.4.4 default-originate
!
SanFrancisco(config-router)# neighbor 167.55.195.3 remote-as 100
SanFrancisco(config-router)# neighbor 167.55.199.1 remote-as 100

NewYork(config)# router bgp 100
!
NewYork(config-router)# bgp default local-preference 100
NewYork(config-router)# network 167.55.0.0
```

Example 16-2 *Sample Configuration Illustrating Local Preference (Continued)*

```
NewYork(config-router)# aggregate-address 167.55.0.0 255.255.0.0 summary-only
NewYork(config-router)# neighbor 100.2.3.2 remote-as 300
NewYork(config-router)# neighbor 167.55.191.1 remote-as 100
NewYork(config-router)# neighbor 167.55.195.2 remote-as 100
```

Local preference can also be set per prefix. Although several methods exist to filter or modify routes using BGP, route maps is the only technique we explore. To use a route map to change BGP parameters, apply the route map to the peer using the neighbor command.

```
Router(config-router)# neighbor {IP | peer group} route-map route-map name {in|out}
```

Example 16-3 shows a route map applied to routes received from a peer. Routes are compared to an access list and permitted routes have a local preference set to 500. Route map line 20 does not include a **match** command and so matches all routes, meaning that routes denied by the access list have a local preference set to 50.

Example 16-3 *Local Preference Set for Specific Prefixes*

```
Hickory(config)# router bgp 100
Hickory(config-router)# neighbor 10.5.5.25 remote-as 100
Hickory(config-router)# neighbor 10.5.5.25 route-map example_LP in
Hickory(config-router)# exit
Hickory(config)# access-list 5 permit 10.1.1.0 0.0.0.255
Hickory(config)# route-map example_LP permit 10
Hickory(config-rmap)# match ip address 5
Hickory(config-rmap)# set ip local-preference 500
Hickory(config)# route-map example_LP permit 20
Hickory(config-rmap)# set ip local-preference 50
```

Using the MED Attribute

Multi-exit discriminator (MED) is advertised to external neighbors to try to influence path selection into an AS. For instance, consider a case where there are redundant links to an ISP and you want traffic to flow across the higher bandwidth path. Weight or LP could be used to control how local routers send traffic out of the AS, but external neighbors do not receive this information. A lower MED could be set on one path, indicating to your neighbors that they should reply on this circuit.

MED is often called a weak attribute, because MED is only considered after weight, local preference, AS-path length, and origin. MED is an optional, nontransitive attribute—lower MED is preferred. The default MED is 0. The syntax for setting MED on all routes is

```
Router(config-router)# default-metric value
```

Example 16-4 shows a route map applied to routes advertised to a peer. Advertised routes are first compared to an access list and permitted routes have a metric set to 500. Route map line 20 does not include a **match** command and so matches all routes, meaning that routes denied by the access list have a metric of 5000.

Example 16-4 *MED Set for Specific Prefixes*

```
Hickory(config)# router bgp 100
Hickory(config-router)# neighbor 10.6.6.36 remote-as 200
Hickory(config-router)# neighbor 10.6.6.36 route-map med_rm out
Hickory(config-router)# exit
Hickory(config)# access-list 5 permit 10.1.1.0 0.0.0.255
Hickory(config)# route-map med_rm permit 10
Hickory(config-rmap)# match ip address 5
Hickory(config-rmap)# set metric 500
Hickory(config)# route-map med_rm permit 20
Hickory(config-rmap)# set metric 5000
```

Verifying the Configuration of Attributes

It is always important to be able to check your work, particularly when that work defines an entire organization's method of connecting to the Internet.

The **show ip bgp** command shows attribute values and status. It is a good command to verify configuration changes and manage the traffic flow to and from the autonomous system.

Example 16-5 shows how BGP is running before the configuration in Example 16-2. The next hop is to 100.2.3.2, which is in autonomous system 300 because the traffic would be routed via New York. Note that in Example 16-3, the local preference on Chicago has been set by the BGP process to be 100 by default.

Example 16-5 *The* **show ip bgp** *Command Example for Chicago Before Attributes Are Set*

```
Chicago# show ip bgp
BGP table version is 22, local router ID is 192.168.0.231
Status codes: s suppressed, d damped, h history, * valid, > best, i - internal,
              r RIB-failure
Origin codes: i - IGP, e - EGP, ? ñ incomplete

   Network          Next Hop          Metric LocPrf Weight Path
*>i4.0.0.0          100.2.4.4              0    100      0 400 I
*>i5.0.0.0          100.2.3.2              0    100      0 300 I
*>i100.2.3.0/29     100.2.3.2              0    100      0 300 I
*>i100.2.4.0/29     100.2.4.4              0    100      0 400 I
*>i130.16.0.0       100.2.3.2              0    100      0 300 I
r>i167.55.0.0       167.55.191.3      281600    100      0 I
Chicago#
```

Example 16-6 occurs after a weight is set to 200 for the neighbor 167.55.199.5, which is San Francisco. This forces the longest path to be taken to 130.16.0.0 via San Francisco.

Example 16-6 *The* **show ip bgp** *Command Example Showing the Use of the Weight Attribute*

```
Chicago# show ip bgp
BGP table version is 8, local router ID is 192.168.0.231
Status codes: s suppressed, d damped, h history, * valid, > best, i - internal,
              r RIB-failure
Origin codes: i - IGP, e - EGP, ? - incomplete

   Network          Next Hop          Metric LocPrf Weight Path
*>i4.0.0.0          100.2.4.4              0    100    200 400 i
*>i5.0.0.0          100.2.3.2              0    100      0 300 i
*>i100.2.3.0/29     100.2.3.2              0    100      0 300 i
*>i100.2.4.0/29     100.2.4.4              0    100    200 400 i
*>i130.16.0.0       100.2.4.4                   100    200 400 500 300 i
* i                 100.2.3.2              0    100      0 300 i
r>i167.55.0.0       167.55.191.3      281600    100      0 i
Chicago#
```

Table 16-4 describes significant fields shown in Examples 16-3 and 16-4. The large metric values in these examples derive from the respective IGPs.

Table 16-4 *Explanation of Output from the* **show ip bgp** *Command*

Field	Description
BGP table version	Internal table version number. This is incremented whenever the table changes.
local router ID	The IP address that is used as a BGP ID.
status codes	Status is displayed at the beginning of each line. It will be one of the following values: s—suppressed. *—valid. >—best entry to use for that network. i—learned via an iBGP session. d—dampened.

continues

Table 16-4 *Explanation of Output from the* **show ip bgp** *Command (Continued)*

Field	Description
Origin	The origin code is placed at the end of each AS-path. It can be one of the following values: i—advertised with a BGP network command. e—originated from an EGP. ?—redistributed into BGP from an IGP.
Network	A destination prefix.
Next hop	IP address of the first external neighbor along the path. An entry of 0.0.0.0 indicates that the route is self-originated.
Metric	If shown, this is the value of the metric between autonomous systems. This field is frequently not used.
LocPrf	Local preference values as set on the routers with interfaces to other autonomous systems. It defines how preferable that router is as a transit point out of the autonomous system. The default value is 100.
Weight	Weight of the route, determining which path the router will choose. It is proprietary to Cisco and is an attribute local to the router.
Path	Autonomous system paths to the destination network. There can be one entry in this field for each autonomous system in the path.

Foundation Summary

The Foundation Summary provides a convenient review of many key concepts in this chapter. If you are already comfortable with the topics in this chapter, this summary might help you recall a few details. If you just read this chapter, this review should help solidify some key facts. If you are doing your final prep before the exam, the following lists and tables are a convenient way to review the day before the exam.

Table 16-5 lists the attributes supported by IOS.

Table 16-5   *BGP Attributes*

Attribute Name	Category	Description
Aggregator	Optional, transitive	Router ID and AS of router that summarized. Not used in path selection.
AS_Path	Well-known, mandatory	List of AS route has passed through. Prefer shortest path.
Atomic aggregate	Well-known, discretionary	Summary includes multiple AS. Not used in path selection.
Cluster ID	Optional, nontransitive	Originating cluster. Not used in path selection.
Community	Optional, transitive	Route tag. Not used in path selection.
Local preference	Well-known, discretionary	Metric for external paths, for internal neighbors. Prefer highest.
Multiple Exit Discriminator (MED)	Optional, nontransitive	Informs external peers which path to take into the autonomous system. Prefer lowest.
Next Hop	Well-known, mandatory	External peer in neighboring AS. Not used in path selection.
Origin	Well-known, mandatory	Prefer BGP routes (i) over EGP (e) over redistributed (?).
Originator ID	Optional, nontransitive	Identifies Route Reflector. Not used in path selection.
Weight	Optional, not communicated to peers	Administrative Cisco attribute. Prefer highest.

The complete path selection process, summarizing the descriptions in this section, is displayed in Table 16-6.

Table 16-6 *BGP Path Selection*

Order	Preference	Description
0. Synchronized	TRUE	Use only routes that meet the synchronization requirement
1. Weight	Highest	Administrative override
2. Local Preference	Highest	Used internally to pick path out of AS
3. Self originated	TRUE	Used to prefer paths originated on this router
4. AS-Path	Shortest	Minimize AS-hops
5. Origin	i<?	Prefer stability
6. MED	Lowest	Used external to come in
7. External	EBGP<IBGP	Hot potato routing
8. IGP cost	Lowest	Look for more information
9. EBGP Peering	Oldest	Prefer stability
10. RID	Lowest	External path preferred over internal path

Q&A

The questions and scenarios in this book are designed to be challenging and to make sure that you know the answer. Rather than allowing you to derive the answers from clues hidden inside the questions themselves, the questions challenge your understanding and recall of the subject.

You can find the answers to these questions in Appendix A. For more practice with exam-like question formats, use the exam engine on the CD-ROM.

1. List at least five different examples of BGP attributes.

2. Describe the weight attribute in terms of default value and the routers it affects.

3. Describe the local-preference attribute in terms of default value and the routers it affects.

4. Describe the AS-path attribute in terms of default value and the routers it affects.

5. Describe the origin attribute in terms of default value and the routers it affects.

6. Describe the MED attribute in terms of default value and the routers it affects.

7. How would you set a weight for a given router?

8. How would you set a default local-preference for all routes on a given router?

9. Write a route-map to change the MED of only 192.168.25.0/24.

10. List the BGP path selection process, in order, and describe the preference (higher or lower) for each step.

Scenarios

The following scenarios and questions are designed to draw together the content of the chapter and to exercise your understanding of the concepts. There is not necessarily a right answer. The thought process and practice in manipulating the concepts are the goals of this section. The answers to the scenario questions are found at the end of this chapter.

Scenario 16-1

The company Humugos has successfully implemented iBGP in each country in which it operates, using eBGP to connect the autonomous systems. The company now wants to change the way it connects to the Internet. Currently, it has one connection into the Internet per autonomous system. Figure 16-3 provides the diagram for the network in this scenario.

Figure 16-3 *Diagram for Scenario 16-1*

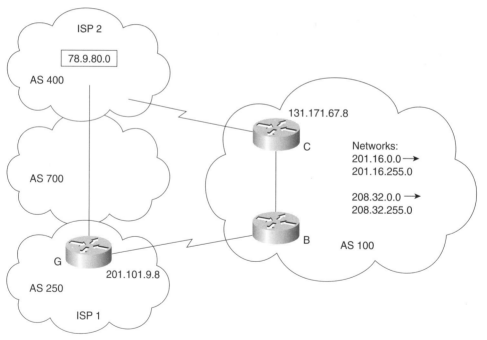

1. Give reasons to support Humugos's desire to have multiple connections to the Internet.

2. Using Figure 16-3, issue the configuration commands that would allow Router B to select the path to network 78.9.80.0 via Router G when connecting to the Internet. Use the local-preference attribute to select the path.

Scenario Answers

The answers provided in this section are not necessarily the only possible answers to the questions. The questions are designed to test your knowledge and to give practical exercise in certain key areas. This section is intended to test and exercise skills and concepts detailed in the body of this chapter.

If your answer is different, ask yourself whether it follows the tenets explained in the answers provided. Your answer is correct not if it matches the solution provided in the book, but rather if it has included the principles of design laid out in the chapter.

In this way, the testing provided in these scenarios is deeper: It examines not only your knowledge, but also your understanding and ability to apply that knowledge to problems.

If you do not get the correct answer, refer back to the text and review the subject tested. Be certain to also review your notes on the question to ensure that you understand the principles of the subject.

Scenario 16-1 Answers

1. *Give reasons to support Humugos's desire to have multiple connections to the Internet.*

    Multiple connections to the Internet would not only provide redundancy, but could also be configured to load balance traffic into the Internet. If load balancing is not an option because the multiple connections are to different ISPs, traffic management could still be enforced by using each link for different purposes. Tuning the attributes and configuring prefix lists would do this very effectively.

2. *Using Figure 16-3, issue the configuration commands that would allow Router B to select the path to network 78.9.80.0 via Router G when connecting to the Internet. Use the local preference attribute to select the path.*

    Given the design of the network, the path to network 78.9.80.0 has a longer AS_Path through Router G. Tuning the local preference to select this path means altering the selection that it would naturally have taken. The configuration commands are as follows:

    ```
    Router B(config)# router bgp 100
    network 167.55.0.0 mask 255.255.0.0
    neighbor 131.171.67.8 remote-as 100
    neighbor 201.101.9.8 remote-as 250
    bgp default local-preference 250
    ```

    Remember that the higher the preference, the more likely the selection.

Part VII covers the following Cisco BSCI exam topics related to implementing multicast forwarding:

- Describe IP Multicast (e.g., Layer 3 to Layer 2 mapping, IGMP, etc.).
- Describe, configure, or verify IP multicast routing (i.e., PIM Sparse-Dense Mode).

This list reflects the exam topics posted on Cisco.com at the publication time of this book.

Part VII: Multicasting

This chapter covers the following topics:

- **IP Styles of Addressing**—Explains the different delivery mechanisms that may be specified by an IP address (unicast, broadcast, or multicast).

- **Multicast Addressing**—Describes a multicast IP address and the process used to convert a multicast IP to a multicast MAC address.

- **Current Multicast Usage**—Lists some of the ways that multicasts are used and some of the problems that limit the use of multicasting.

CHAPTER 17

What Is Multicasting?

Multicast traffic is typically sent by one source and received by a group of recipients that might be spread throughout a network and that might change over time. Examples of multicast traffic include video streams for instruction or entertainment, certain audio conference calls, and one-to-many PC file-imaging applications.

This chapter outlines the differences between unicast, broadcast, and multicast packet types. It then describes multicast addressing, including multicast IP and multicast MAC addresses. You then learn about how today's applications use multicasting and the related challenges that you need to be aware of.

"Do I Know This Already?" Quiz

The purpose of the "Do I Know This Already?" quiz is to help you decide which parts of this chapter to use. If you already intend to read the entire chapter, you do not necessarily need to answer these questions.

The 10-question quiz, derived from the major sections in the "Foundation Topics" portion of the chapter, helps you determine how to spend your limited study time.

Table 17-1 outlines the major topics discussed in this chapter and the corresponding quiz questions.

Table 17-1 *"Do I Know This Already?" Foundation Topics Section-to-Question Mapping*

Foundation Topics Section	Questions Covered in This Section	Score
IP Styles of Addressing	1–3	
Multicast Addressing	4–8	
Current Multicast Usage	9–10	
Total Score		

CAUTION   The goal of self-assessment is to gauge your mastery of the topics in this chapter. If you do not know the answer to a question or are only partially sure of the answer, you should mark the question wrong for purposes of the self-assessment. Giving yourself credit for an answer you correctly guessed skews your results and might provide you with a false sense of security.

1. Which of the following describes a difference between broadcasts and multicasts?

   a. Multicasts are one-to-many.

   b. Multicasts are unidirectional.

   c. Multicasts are routable.

   d. Multicasts are used by RIPv1.

2. Multicasting is efficient in terms of processor resources for which of the following reasons?

   a. Multicasts can be ignored by the network card.

   b. Multicasts have a specific set of IP addresses.

   c. Multicasts are not routable.

   d. Multicasts do not support TCP.

3. How do Layer 2 switches treat multicast traffic by default?

   a. Discard it

   b. ARP for the MAC

   c. Ignore it

   d. Flood it

4. Which one of the following is a multicast address?

   a. 128.224.1.1

   b. 172.17.224.1

   c. 225.17.1.1

   d. 242.17.1.1

5. 224.1.2.3 corresponds to which of the following MAC addresses?

    a. 0102.0300.0000

    b. 0100.5e01.0203

    c. e000.0001.0203

    d. 1000.5e01.0203

6. How many unique multicast IP addresses can correspond to one multicast MAC address?

    a. 1

    b. 2

    c. 8

    d. 32

7. Which one of the following multicast addresses does not share a multicast MAC address?

    a. 225.145.1.1

    b. 227.17.1.1

    c. 235.17.1.1

    d. 237.117.1.1

8. Which of the following is the OUI for multicast MAC addresses?

    a. 015E00

    b. 01005E

    c. 00015E

    d. 5E0100

9. Which of the following is not a capability of UDP multicast?

    a. Packet ordering

    b. Retransmission

    c. Limiting receivers

    d. Dynamic membership

10. Multicasting supports applications that communicate

   a. one-to-one

   b. one-to-many

   c. many-to-many

   d. many-to-one

You can find the answers to the "Do I Know This Already?" quiz in Appendix A, "Answers to Chapter 'Do I Know This Already?' Quizzes and Q&A Sections." The suggested choices for your next step are as follows:

■ **7 or less overall score**—Read the entire chapter. This includes the "Foundation Topics," "Foundation Summary," and "Q&A" sections.

■ **8 or 9**—Begin with the "Foundation Summary" section and then go to the "Q&A" section at the end of the chapter. If you have trouble with these exercises, read the appropriate sections in "Foundation Topics."

■ **10**—If you want more review on these topics, skip to the "Foundation Summary" section and then go to the "Q&A" section at the end of the chapter. Otherwise, move to the next chapter.

Foundation Topics

IP Styles of Addressing

An IP network—and therefore the hardware that makes up the network—supports three types of packets:

- **Unicast**—Packets that are sent from one source address to a single destination host address.

- **Broadcast**—Packets sent to a broadcast destination address.

- **Multicast**—Packets sent to a special group-based destination address.

The following sections describe each packet type in more detail.

Unicasts

Unicasts are packets sent to a specific destination address. When transmitting the same information to a group, unicasts require retransmitting the same information to each individual, which eats up network capacity.

Unicasts are forwarded by a router or Layer 3 switch by finding the destination IP address in its routing table. A Layer 2 switch relies on the destination's MAC address. Unicast forwarding is turned on by default, and is the type of routing familiar to you already.

Broadcasts

Broadcasts are one way to communicate the exact same information to a group. Broadcasts are single transmissions that are received and acted upon by all devices.

Broadcasts can be used to communicate to all devices. For example, some routing protocols use broadcasts to distribute routing information. Rather than requiring a series of unicast transmissions, a single packet can reach all parties.

Broadcasts are also useful when a destination address is unknown. An example of the use of broadcasts is device startup: DHCP uses broadcasts to assign unicast addresses.

Network cards are programmed to listen to all traffic; they are programmed to ignore most frames, but to recognize frames destined for the local MAC address or the broadcast MAC and to copy those frames to the CPU.

The problem with broadcasts is that they must be processed by the CPU. For instance, a PC receiving a RIP advertisement will process the packet enough to understand that it is not interested. That effort leeches computing cycles away from other processes.

Another way to understand this broadcast issue is to consider an example from real life. Have you ever worked or visited an office where anyone could page over the intercom? Regardless of how important a conversation or project is, everyone must stop and listen to every page. Conversations are interrupted and folks look at each other and say "Was that for me?" This can be annoying, distracting, and reduce everyone's ability to concentrate. Broadcasts create a similar annoyance for network systems.

Ethernet broadcasts are sent to the reserved MAC address FFFF.FFFF.FFFF. Layer 2 switches flood broadcasts out all ports in the same VLAN. IP broadcasts use the reserved destination IP 255.255.255.255. Routers do not forward broadcasts by default.

Multicasts

Multicast addresses are "group" addresses. An IP device joins a group by recognizing group IP addresses and reprogramming its network interface card (NIC) to copy traffic destined for the group MAC. Because a multicast goes to a different MAC, some hosts will pay attention to it and others will ignore it. For example, EIGRP uses 224.0.0.10 and the corresponding MAC 0100.5E00.000A. Routers pay attention to this traffic, but your PC can safely ignore it.

Because multicasts allow the NIC to discriminate at the data-link layer, less time is spent processing traffic. For this reason, multicasts are conservative in terms of both bandwidth and processing.

Multicast traffic is generally unidirectional. Because many hosts are receiving the same data, it makes little sense to allow one of the hosts to send packets back toward the source over the multicast mechanism. Instead, a receiving host can send return traffic to the source as a unicast. Multicast traffic is also sent in a best-effort connectionless format. UDP (connectionless) is commonly used, whereas TCP (connection-oriented) is not.

Hosts that want to receive data from a multicast source can join or leave a multicast group dynamically (by enabling the group MAC on their NIC). In addition, a host can decide to become a member of more than one multicast group at any time. The principal network task is then to figure out how to deliver multicast traffic to the group members without disturbing other uninterested hosts.

Multicast traffic is only processed by hosts that are programmed to receive it. A router does not forward IP-multicast packets by default unless some form of multicast routing is enabled. By default, Layer 2 switches flood Ethernet multicasts to all ports on the destination VLAN.

Video over IP Scenario

Figure 17-1 shows a company topology. The CIO wants to address the team via video-over-IP and asks everyone to attend the video briefing. Notice that the Ethernet links are Fast Ethernet (100 Mbps) and that the WAN link is a DS3 (about 45 Mbps). Users A, B, C, and E wish to attend the online briefing, but user D does not.

Figure 17-1 *Network Topology*

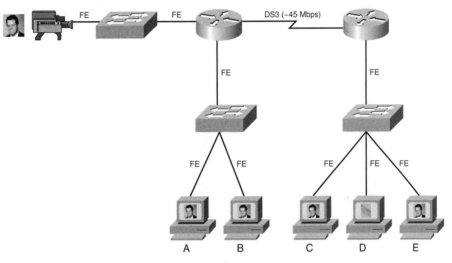

What would happen if the video were distributed using unicast? First, if the video stream were 1-Mbps, each additional user would require a 1-Mbps path to the source. The fast Ethernet links would limit the number of clients to no more than 100 and the DS3 would limit the clients at the remote site to 45 (and inefficiencies in the network would prevent even that many). Figure 17-2 charts this function of clients versus capacity.

Of course, while those 100 users are listening to the CIO, all possible network capacity is consumed and other users are left unable to use the network. Figure 17-3 shows that individual unicast streams would be required for each user watching the CIO. Although only five users are shown, no more than 55 users at headquarters and 45 users at the remote site could be supported.

Figure 17-2 *Utilization Versus Clients*

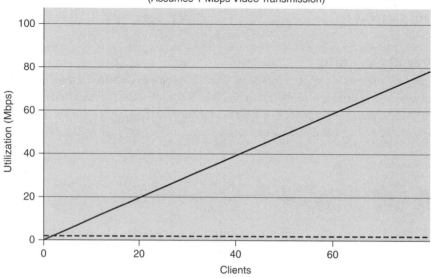

Figure 17-3 *Unicast Video Traffic*

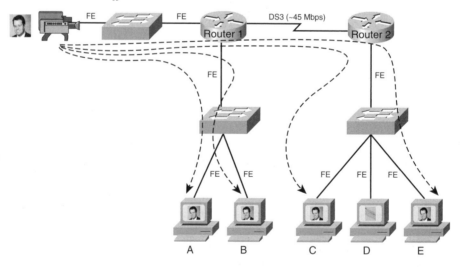

When they recognize the problem, the administrators of this imaginary network try to distribute the video using broadcasts. What happens? Nothing—routers do not forward broadcasts (as shown in Figure 17-4).

Even inside a LAN, broadcasts are problematic. Broadcasting inside a LAN does allow one transmission to reach everyone, but now even those devices that are not intended recipients must slog through a megabit per second of video broadcast, burdening their processors.

Figure 17-4   *Broadcast Video Traffic*

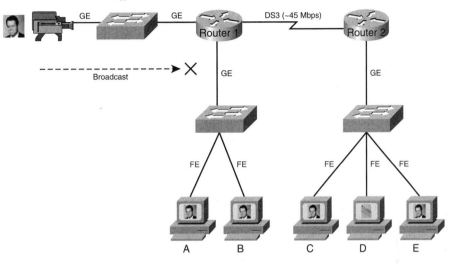

Multicasting solves this problem. A single multicast stream may be distributed to all users, conserving capacity. Multicasts are routable, and users that do not wish to see the CIO may ignore the video without penalty (processor penalty, anyway).

Exactly what occurs with user D? In the worst-case scenario, user D receives the multicast traffic but the NIC ignores it. In the best-case scenario, the switch is smart enough to filter the multicast (using either IGMP snooping or CGMP). Figure 17-5 shows the video being distributed with multicasts.

Figure 17-5   *Multicast Video Traffic on a LAN*

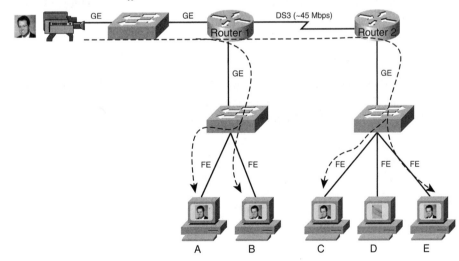

Multicast Addressing

As discussed in the previous section, end systems and intermediate devices must have a way to distinguish multicast traffic from unicasts or broadcasts.

At Layer 3, this is done by reserving Class D IP addresses (224.0.0.0 through 239.255.255.255) for multicasting. Network devices can quickly distinguish multicast IP addresses by looking at the first four bits, which are always 1110. Ethernet devices similarly have a range of addresses set aside for multicasts. The low-order bit in the first byte of a MAC address is a unicast/multicast bit, and setting it indicates the frame is a multicast. Beyond this single bit, IP multicasts are mapped to a specific range of MAC addresses to aid hosts in discriminating between multicasts.

Multicast MAC Addressing

At Layer 2, systems recognize multicast traffic because each multicast IP address is mapped to a 48-bit MAC address. The first 24 bits of that MAC address (the organizationally unique identifier or OUI) always begin with 0100.5e and the 25th bit is always 0. The lower 23 bits of the multicast MAC address are copied from the far right 23 bits of the multicast IP address.

Figure 17-6 shows the address-mapping concept. Only the lower 23 bits of the address are copied from IP to MAC (or vice versa). The high-order prefixes of both IP and MAC addresses are fixed, predictable values.

Notice that 5 bits of the IP address are *not* transferred into the MAC address. This creates the possibility of a multicast MAC address not being entirely unique. There are 32 (5-bits worth) different multicast IP addresses that all could correspond to a single multicast MAC address.

This situation is demonstrated in Figure 17-7, showing that the NIC would be unable to distinguish traffic for 234.64.3.5, 225.192.3.5, and 227.64.3.5. The diagram displays the binary for the three IP addresses. The bottom row shows the corresponding multicast MAC address (the black boxes show digits from the IP multicast MAC prefix that are always the same). However, the network card would be able to distinguish traffic for 230.177.3.5 from the other addresses.

Figure 17-6 *Multicast IP to MAC Calculation*

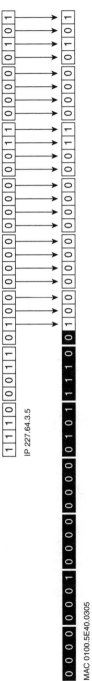

Figure 17-7 *Multicast IP to MAC Collisions*

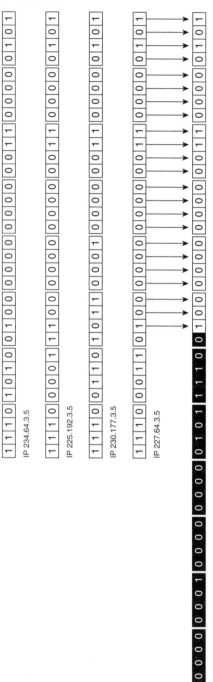

Because of this ambiguity, a multicast host faces a small problem when it receives an Ethernet frame destined for a multicast MAC address. This single MAC address could correspond to 32 different multicast IP addresses. Therefore, the host must receive and examine every frame that includes the MAC address it is interested in, regardless of which IP address the frame is traveling toward.

The host then examines the destination IP address in the packet header to verify that the more specific IP multicast address is a desired multicast group. If not, the packet is discarded.

NOTE   Because of the overlap in IP-to-MAC mapping, it is most efficient to use Multicast IP addresses that do not overlap.

Multicast IP Addressing

In addition to the Class D multicast address space, some IP multicast addresses have been reserved for particular uses, such as the following:

- **Link-local addresses (224.0.0.0/24)**—Used on a local segment (TTL=1) only. Routers do not forward these packets because of TTL. These are known as fixed-group addresses because they are well-known and predefined. Examples are given in the following table:

Address	Destination
224.0.0.1	All hosts
224.0.0.5	All OSPF routers
224.0.0.6	All OSPF DRs
224.0.0.9	All RIPv2 routers
224.0.0.10	All EIGRP routers

- **Source-specific multicast (232.0.0.0/8)**—An extension of multicasting wherein hosts only receive traffic from a particular server instead of from any server using a multicast channel.

- **GLOP (233.0.0.0/8)**—Allocates 256 multicast IP addresses to each registered autonomous system (AS). The 16-bit AS number is used for the middle-two octets, so that AS 1000 has 233.3.232.0/24.

- **Administratively scoped addresses (239.0.0.0/8)**—This space can be used in private multicast domains, much like the private IP address ranges from RFC 1918. These addresses are not supposed to be routed between domains; this way, they can be reused.

  Within the administratively scoped addresses, 239.252.0.0/14 is reserved for site-local multicast and the rest of 239.192.0.0/10 is reserved for organization-local scope.

- **Globally scoped addresses (224.0.1.0–231.255.255.255 and 234.0.0.0–238.255.255.255)**—These addresses can be used by any entity and can be routed across an organization or the Internet. They must be unique and globally significant, and therefore are usually temporarily assigned (think of this range as neither local nor private; it is the rest of the multicast range).

Current Multicast Use

This section describes how today's applications use multicasting and the related challenges that you need to be aware of.

Multicast Applications

Multicasting is used in many applications. For example, PC imaging software typically allows image distribution through multicast. In this scenario, a server is loaded with an image and each client is booted with a special disk that sets them to receive the multicast. Schools, for instance, might use this to image a lab in one step. Music-on-hold in IP Telephony systems is another example of the use of multicast in modern networks.

Another common use of multicasting is in "shared whiteboard" applications where many users edit a common workspace. Finally, it is very common to use multicasting for resource discovery; for instance, the routing processes RIPv2, OSPF, and EIGRP discover neighbors using multicasts.

Applications may therefore be one-to-many (imaging), many-to-many (whiteboarding), or many-to-one (routing).

Multicast Issues

There are downsides to multicasting that must be recognized. Because multicast traffic is generally UDP, it lacks windowing functions, packet ordering, and capability for retransmission. It also lacks the ability to allow some users to receive multicasts while preventing others on the segment (although there are ways to block multicasts at the router).

These challenges can be met creatively at the protocol level. For multimedia traffic, ordering is handled by the Real Time Protocol (RTP). Security could be addressed by encrypting the traffic using IPSec.

Foundation Summary

The Foundation Summary provides a convenient review of many key concepts in this chapter. If you are already comfortable with the topics in this chapter, this summary might help you recall a few details. If you just read this chapter, this review should help solidify some key facts. If you are doing your final prep before the exam, the following lists and tables are a convenient way to review the day before the exam.

IP supports three transmission modes:

■   Unicast (1:1)

■   Broadcast (1:all others)

■   Multicast (1:some others)

IP multicast addresses have been reserved for particular uses, as follows:

■   IP multicast addresses range is 224.0.0.0/4.

■   Link-local addresses are 224.0.0.0/24.

■   Source-specific multicast is 232.0.0.0/8.

■   GLOP uses 233.0.0.0/8.

■   Administratively scoped addresses are 239.0.0.0/8.

Multicast MAC addressing has the following characteristics:

■   Multicast OUI is 0100.5e.

■   25th bit is always 0.

■   Last 23 bits are mapped from IP address.

Q&A

The questions and scenarios in this book are designed to be challenging and to make sure that you know the answer. Rather than allowing you to derive the answers from clues hidden inside the questions themselves, the questions challenge your understanding and recall of the subject.

You can find the answers to these questions in Appendix A. For more practice with exam-like question formats, use the exam engine on the CD-ROM.

1. List the three types of IP routing identified by the IP address.

2. By default, how does a router handle a broadcast?

3. By default, what does a router do with multicast packets?

4. By default, what does a Layer 2 switch do with a multicast packet?

5. What high-order bit combination signals that an IP address is used for multicast?

6. Since the IP-to-MAC multicast address mapping is somewhat ambiguous, how can a frame be forwarded to the correct destination group?

7. What IP multicast address range is set aside for use only on the local network segment?

8. What class D address range is reserved for private use?

9. In terms of distributing multimedia traffic, what is the advantage of multicast over unicast?

10. What are the advantages of multicast over broadcast for distributing multimedia traffic?

This chapter covers the following topics:

- **Data Link Layer Support for Multicast**—Describes three methods to send multicasts to ports where the traffic is wanted and to hide multicasts from other hosts.

- **Understanding IGMP**—Describes the features of IGMPv1, IGMPv2, and IGMPv3 and how to determine which IGMP version is running on a router.

- **Configuring IGMP**—Describes enabling IGMP groups and configuring IGMP snooping.

CHAPTER 18

IGMP

Because not everyone on a network wants to receive the traffic from a multicast source, routers must have some means of forwarding traffic to only the destinations that want to receive it. This chapter covers IP multicast and some of the protocols used to forward multicast packets. You will learn the basic features and operation of IGMP and how to configure IGMP groups and IGMP snooping.

"Do I Know This Already?" Quiz

The purpose of the "Do I Know This Already?" quiz is to help you decide which parts of this chapter to use. If you already intend to read the entire chapter, you do not necessarily need to answer these questions.

The 11-question quiz, derived from the major sections in the "Foundation Topics" portion of the chapter, helps you determine how to spend your limited study time.

Table 18-1 outlines the major topics discussed in this chapter and the corresponding quiz questions.

Table 18-1 *"Do I Know This Already?" Foundation Topics Section-to-Question Mapping*

Foundation Topics Section	Questions Covered in This Section	Score
Data Link Layer Support for Multicast	1–4	
Understanding IGMP	5–8	
Configuring IGMP	9–11	
Total Score		

CAUTION   The goal of self-assessment is to gauge your mastery of the topics in this chapter. If you do not know the answer to a question or are only partially sure of the answer, you should mark the question wrong for purposes of the self-assessment. Giving yourself credit for an answer you correctly guessed skews your results and might provide you with a false sense of security.

1. Layer 2 switches build a MAC table by observing which of the following?

    a. Source address and port

    b. Destination address and port

    c. Source VLAN

    d. Broadcast address and VLAN

2. IGMP stands for which of the following?

    a. Internal Group Multicast Protocol

    b. IP Group Management Protocol

    c. IP Group Maintenance Protocol

    d. Internet Group Membership Protocol

3. Which of the following is *not* a method of associating multicasts with ports?

    a. IGMP snooping

    b. CGMP

    c. CGMP snooping

    d. Static MAC Entries

4. Which of the following are differences between IGMP Snooping and CGMP?

    a. CGMP learns subscribing MAC addresses by passive listening.

    b. CGMP learns subscribing MAC addresses from the router.

    c. IGMP snooping is Cisco proprietary.

    d. IGMP snooping requires layer 3 processing.

5. What is the primary issue with IGMP version 1?

    a. Join and leave vacancy

    b. Join and leave latency

    c. It is proprietary

    d. It requires a BSR

6. Which of the following are advantages of IGMP v2 over IGMPv1?

    a. Group-specific queries

    b. Group Joins

    c. Group Leaves

    d. Source Filtering

7. IGMPv1 does not have a mechanism to allow a host to leave a group when it is no longer interested in the content of that group. Which of the following is an advantage of IGMPv3 over version 2?

    a. Group-specific queries

    b. Joins

    c. Leaves

    d. Source Filtering

8. What command displays the current IGMP version used on a port?

    a. **show ip igmp interface**

    b. **show igmp port**

    c. **show ip igmp-snooping**

    d. **show multicast router**

9. What command is used to manually join a router to a group?

    a. **ip igmp interface**

    b. **ip multicast-group**

    c. **ip igmp join-group**

    d. **igmp join-group**

10. How do you turn on IGMP Snooping?

    a. **igmp-snooping**

    b. **ip igmp snooping**

    c. **igmp interface**

    d. **no ip cgmp**

11. Which of the following commands displays the multicast groups used?

    a. ip igmp snooping

    b. show multicast group

    c. show multicast router

    d. show igmp interface

You can find the answers to the "Do I Know This Already?" quiz in Appendix A, "Answers to Chapter 'Do I Know This Already?' Quizzes and Q&A Sections." The suggested choices for your next step are as follows:

- **8 or less overall score**—Read the entire chapter. This includes the "Foundation Topics," "Foundation Summary," and "Q&A" sections.

- **9 or 10 overall score**—Begin with the "Foundation Summary" section and then go to the "Q&A" section at the end of the chapter. If you have trouble with these exercises, read the appropriate sections in "Foundation Topics."

- **11 overall score**—If you want more review on these topics, skip to the "Foundation Summary" section and then go to the "Q&A" section at the end of the chapter. Otherwise, move to the next chapter.

Foundation Topics

Data Link Layer Support for Multicast

Layer 2 switches build a table of MAC addresses and the ports that lead to them. Switches learn about MAC addresses and associated ports by looking at the source MAC address on received traffic. To cope with startup, frames to unknown MAC addresses are flooded out all ports within the broadcast domain when the MAC is empty. Unintended recipients simply note that the destination is not their MAC address and ignore the traffic.

This system works fine for broadcasts. A broadcast address is never a source address and is therefore not in the MAC table. Broadcasts are therefore flooded.

Multicasts also qualify as "unknown" because multicast addresses only show up as the destination address. Switches flood multicasts and it is up to the individual PC to sort out the frames in which it is interested.

Multicasts to an uninterested device waste bandwidth. To compound the situation, unsophisticated network cards may not be able to discriminate between interesting and uninteresting frames and involve the processor in those decisions. This eats into the available processor cycles on the device and slows down other processes.

There are three methods of optimizing Cisco switches to handle this situation. All three work to limit multicasts to ports where the traffic is wanted and to hide multicasts from other hosts:

- Static MAC table entries (creating manual MAC entries)

- Cisco Group Management Protocol (CGMP)

- IGMP Snooping

Creating manual MAC entries is the most easily understood of these methods, but it cannot react dynamically to changes. This method also involves touching a lot of switches to make a change and the workload becomes immense as the network grows. Therefore, manually creating MAC entries is not the recommended approach.

CGMP is a Cisco-proprietary solution. CGMP is a protocol that runs between switches and routers. When routers receive IGMP messages, they pass the MAC of the requestor and the multicast group requested on to the switch. The switch then cross-references the requestor with its MAC table and enables the multicast group for a port.

Another method of accomplishing the same result is to enable the switch to recognize requests for multicast traffic that use the Internet Group Management Protocol (IGMP). This is called *IGMP snooping* and it allows the switch to understand the requested multicast group and the port of the requestor. This could create a processing burden for the switch, but modern Cisco routers support snooping in hardware.

Understanding IGMP

Before routers can forward multicast traffic, they must first understand where clients are located. IGMP is the protocol used by clients to identify themselves to the router and request multicast service.

To receive multicast traffic from a source, recipients join a common multicast group (identified by a multicast IP address). A host joins a group by sending a request to its local router. The request is accomplished through the Internet Group Management Protocol (IGMP). IGMPv1 is defined in RFC 1112; its successors, IGMPv2 and IGMPv3, are defined in RFC 2236 and RFC 3376, respectively.

IGMPv1

To join a multicast group, a host dynamically sends a *Membership Report* IGMP message to its local router. This message tells the router which multicast address (group) the host is joining. The multicast address is used as the destination IP address and is the group address listed in the message. Multicast routers must intercept all multicast packets to receive the membership reports and add hosts to the appropriate groups.

Every 60 seconds, one router (the *querier*) on each network segment sends a query to the all-hosts address (224.0.0.1) to see if there is at least one host still interested in receiving the multicast group. Only one host needs to respond to maintain the forwarding. Interested hosts respond with a membership report (if another host has not already reported).

> **NOTE**   Notice that the querier sends its invitations to a multicast group address, 224.0.0.1. Does this mean that every host on a network must first join the 224.0.0.1 group? Actually, every host is inherently a member of this group, without a formal IGMP exchange. That is why it is called the "all-hosts" address.

Hosts can join multicast groups at any time. However, IGMPv1 does not have a mechanism to allow a host to leave a group when it is no longer interested in the content of that group. Instead, routers "age out" a multicast group if no membership reports are received for three consecutive query intervals. This means that multicast traffic is still sent onto a segment up to 3 minutes after all group members have stopped listening.

A router does not keep a complete membership list for each multicast group that is active. Instead, it needs to record only which multicast groups are active on which interfaces. Whether 1 host or 100 hosts on a network segment are members of a group, the router still needs to send only one copy of a multicast packet onto that segment.

IGMPv2

IGMP version 2 (RFC 2236) enhances the IGMP feature set. This section describes those improvements and briefly explains IGMPv2 operation.

IGMPv2 Features

IGMPv2 includes four significant improvements:

- Queries can be sent as *general queries* to the all-hosts address (as in IGMPv1) or *group-specific queries*, which are sent only to members of a specific group.

- Hosts can now leave a group dynamically.

- Querier election.

- Query-interval response time.

When a host decides to leave a group it has joined, it sends a *Leave Group* message to the all-routers address (224.0.0.2). All routers on the local segment take note, and the querier router responds with a group-specific query message (sent to the group address), asking if others are still interested in receiving that group. Interested hosts must reply with a membership report, or the querier assumes there is no need to continue forwarding the group on that segment.

> **NOTE**   Because IGMPv1 routers cannot understand IGMPv2, if an IGMPv1 router is present on a segment, all routers must run IGMPv1. In this way, IGMPv2 is backward-compatible.
>
> On interfaces where PIM is configured, IGMPv2 is enabled by default. PIM is covered in the next section. To change the IGMP version, you can use the following interface-configuration command:
>
> ```
> Switch(config-if)# ip igmp version  {1 | 2 | 3}
> ```

IGMPv2 also adds a querier election mechanism. In version 1, election was handled by the routing protocol. In version 2, all routers start as queriers and transition to non-queriers if they hear another querier with a higher IP address.

The final significant change in IGMPv2 is that version 2 adds a query-interval response time. A query now includes a field to tell members how long they have to respond, which should prevent a rush to respond.

IGMPv2 Operation

Members may join a multicast group at any time by producing an unsolicited report sent to the desired multicast address. Attached routers simply track whether there is at least one client interested in a group. To see the current membership records of a router, use the command **show ip igmp group**, as shown in Example 18-1.

Example 18-1 *The* **show ip igmp group** *command*

```
Router#  show ip igmp group
IGMP Connected Group Membership
Group Address  Interface        Uptime      Expires      Last Reporter
227.100.100.1  FastEthernet0/0  0d0h28m     00:02:19     192.168.0.105
```

From the output shown in Example 18-1, you can see that 227.100.100.1 has been active on fastethernet0/0 for 28 minutes. The group will expire if a membership report is not received in a little over two minutes. The last device to send a report was 192.168.0.105.

In IGMPv1, hosts leave the group passively; they just stop responding to membership queries. Eventually the router will get the message. The problem is that in the interim—between when a host no longer needs the traffic and the router recognizes that it no longer needs to forward the traffic—network capacity is absorbed with sending unneeded multicasts.

In IGMPv2, hosts leave explicitly by sending a Leave message. The last reporter field from **show ip igmp group** is significant for leave operations. If a device other than the last reporter sends a leave message, the router assumes that at least one user is still present. If the last reporter sends a Leave, the router sends a Membership Query. In this way, leave latency is reduced.

IGMPv3

IGMPv3 (RFC 3376) builds on IGMPv2 and adds support for multicast source filtering. With source filtering, a recipient host can request membership in a multicast group and also supply a list of IP addresses representing multicast sources from which it will accept traffic.

A router running IGMPv3 can coexist with routers running older versions. To do this, the router must degrade itself to the highest common IGMP version in each multicast group.

> **NOTE**   IGMPv3 is primarily used for source-specific multicast (SSM). SSM is based on PIM sparse mode, with a separate source-distribution tree for each source that is used within each group. IGMPv3 is discussed here in less detail than the previous versions, because SSM is beyond the scope of the BSCI course and exam.

Determining the Current IGMP Version

The best way to look at the IGMP parameters used by a router is to use the command **show ip igmp interface**, as shown in Example 18-2.

Example 18-2   *The* **show ip igmp interface** *Command*

```
router>show ip igmp interface fastethernet0/0
 FastEthernet0/0 is up, line protocol is up
 Internet address is 192.168.0.1, subnet mask is 255.255.255.0
 IGMP is enabled on interface
 Current IGMP version is 2
 CGMP is disabled on interface
 IGMP query interval is 60 seconds
 IGMP querier timeout is 120 seconds
 IGMP max query response time is 10 seconds
 Inbound IGMP access group is not set
 Multicast routing is enabled on interface
 Multicast TTL threshold is 0
 Multicast designated router (DR) is 192.168.0.1 (this system)
 IGMP querying router is 192.168.0.1 (this system)
 Multicast groups joined: 224.0.1.40 227.100.100.1
```

In this example, the current IGMP version is version 2.

Configuring IGMP

As described in the previous section, the Internet Group Management Protocol (IGMP) is used to allow end systems to request the multicast traffic that they desire from the local router. Without IGMP, your router would not understand which channels were desired. This section describes enabling IGMP groups and configuring IGMP snooping.

IGMP Groups

IGMP is used to identify multicast groups that the clients require. When troubleshooting multicast, you need to verify that IGMP is enabled on the client-facing interfaces and that users are subscribing to groups.

The **show ip igmp interface** command shows the status of IGMP on a given interface.

In Example 18-3, notice that the router supports IGMP version 2. Details about timers, activity, and groups joined can also be seen from this command.

Example 18-3 *The* **show ip igmp interface** *Output*

```
Stewart#show ip igmp interface e0
Ethernet0 is up, line protocol is up
  Internet address is 172.16.24.1/29
  IGMP is enabled on interface
  Current IGMP version is 2
  CGMP is disabled on interface
  IGMP query interval is 60 seconds
  IGMP querier timeout is 120 seconds
  IGMP max query response time is 10 seconds
  Last member query response interval is 1000 ms
  Inbound IGMP access group is not set
  IGMP activity: 3 joins, 0 leaves
  Multicast routing is enabled on interface
  Multicast TTL threshold is 0
  Multicast designated router (DR) is 172.16.24.1 (this system)
  IGMP querying router is 172.16.24.1 (this system)
  Multicast groups joined: 224.0.1.40
```

Use **show ip igmp groups** to provide specifics about the active groups. In Example 18-4, three groups have been active for about a half hour.

Example 18-4 *The* **show ip igmp groups** *Output*

```
Stewart#show ip igmp groups
IGMP Connected Group Membership
Group Address     Interface        Uptime    Expires    Last Reporter
239.255.255.250   Ethernet0        00:33:05  00:02:59   192.168.0.102
235.80.68.83      Ethernet0        00:33:08  00:02:44   192.168.0.1
224.0.1.40        Ethernet0        00:33:14  never      172.16.24.1
```

> **NOTE**   To join a router to a group, use the command **ip igmp join-group**—for instance, **ip igmp join-group 227.0.0.1**. This can be useful for troubleshooting the group. Since the router responds to ping, ICMP echo-requests sent to the group will result in a reply from the router. The multicast version of ping is called *mping*.
>
> The **ip igmp static-group** command allows a router to be statically joined to a group. This is useful if you use a group to support a common application. Imagine that your company uses 227.0.0.1 as a multicast group for an internal application—using static joins on every router cuts out the processing of joins and leaves, removes the need for queries, and allows the router to fast switch the traffic.
>
> Just to be clear—neither of these commands are commonly used. Joining a router to a group forces the router to process a lot of traffic that it cannot use, such as video captures. However, joining a group can be useful in troubleshooting a new multicast network. In a similar vein, static joins are useful if all traffic uses a well-known address. Multicast traffic tends to be fairly unpredictable, however, so this is not a solution for most networks.

IGMP Snooping

IGMP snooping allows a switch to identify end systems that request multicast traffic and limit forwarding of a multicast address to specific ports. IGMP snooping is enabled by default, and can be manually enabled by the command **ip igmp snooping**. You can use the **show multicast group** and **show multicast router** commands to display the learned groups and associated router ports.

Example 18-5 shows these commands applied to a working switch. Notice that **show ip igmp snooping** goes through the IGMP settings, that **show multicast router** shows that port 1/1 is active, and that **show multicast group** shows two groups active.

Example 18-5 *Multicast **show** Commands*

```
Stewart-Switch#show ip igmp snooping vlan 6
vlan 6
----------
 IGMP snooping is globally enabled
 IGMP snooping TCN solicit query is globally disabled
 IGMP snooping global TCN flood query count is 2
 IGMP snooping is enabled on this Vlan
 IGMP snooping immediate-leave is disabled on this Vlan
 IGMP snooping mrouter learn mode is pim-dvmrp on this Vlan
 IGMP snooping source only learning age timer is 10
```

continues

Example 18-5 *Multicast* **show** *Commands (Continued)*

```
 IGMP snooping is running in IGMP_ONLY mode on this Vlan
 IGMP snooping report suppression is enabled on this Vlan
Stewart-Switch# show multicast router igmp
Port      Vlan
--------- ---------------
1/1       6


Total Number of Entries = 1
'*' - Configured
'+' - RGMP-capable

Stewart-Switch> show multicast group igmp

VLAN  Dest MAC/Route Des  [CoS]  Destination Ports or VCs / [Protocol Type]
----  ------------------------------------------------------------------
6     01-00-5e-00-01-28          1/1
6     01-00-5e-01-02-03          1/1-2

Total Number of Entries = 2
```

Foundation Summary

The Foundation Summary provides a convenient review of many key concepts in this chapter. If you are already comfortable with the topics in this chapter, this summary might help you recall a few details. If you just read this chapter, this review should help solidify some key facts. If you are doing your final prep before the exam, the following lists and tables are a convenient way to review the day before the exam.

Hosts use IGMP to communicate to a router to join a multicast group. The following are key points about IGMPv1:

■ The host sends a *Membership Report* that includes group address to join group.

■ Users lack the ability to leave a group dynamically.

■ The querier router sends a query to 224.0.0.1 every 60 seconds to check for members.

■ Only one host needs to respond with a *membership report* to maintain the forwarding.

■ Hosts can join multicast groups at any time.

■ Querier election is handled by the routing protocol.

■ Routers age out a multicast group if no membership reports are received for three consecutive query intervals.

The following are key points about IGMPv2:

■ IGMPv2 is backward compatible.

■ The version is changed with the command

```
Router(config-if)# ip igmp version  {1 | 2 | 3}
```

■ Queries can be sent as *general queries* to the all-hosts address (like v1) or *group-specific queries*.

■ Hosts can leave a group dynamically using a *Leave Group* message. The querier responds with a group-specific query asking if any other members remain.

■ Querier election occurs—all routers start as queriers and transition to non-queriers if they hear another querier with a higher IP address.

■ It has a query-interval response time—queries include a field to tell members how long they have to respond.

■ Current membership records can be displayed with the command

```
Router#  show ip igmp group
```

■ The last reporter field from **show ip igmp group** is significant for leave operations.

The following are key components of IGMPv3:

■ Added support for multicast source filtering

■ Backward-compatibility with v2 and v1

■ The following command to see IGMP parameters (including version):

```
show ip igmp interface
```

Switch support for multicasting is important. The following are key points:

■ Switches associate MAC addresses with ports using the source-addresses of sent traffic.

■ Frames to unknown MAC addresses are flooded out all ports.

■ Multicast addresses are only used as the destination address. Switches flood multicasts.

The three ways to forward multicast specifically are

■ **Static MAC table entries**—Labor intensive and not scalable.

■ **CGMP**—Cisco proprietary. Routers receive IGMP and pass CGMP to the switch with the MAC of the requestor and the multicast group requested.

■ **IGMP snooping**—Enables switch to recognize IGMP and act on it.

Q&A

The questions and scenarios in this book are designed to be challenging and to make sure that you know the answer. Rather than allowing you to derive the answers from clues hidden inside the questions themselves, the questions challenge your understanding and recall of the subject.

You can find the answers to these questions in Appendix A. For more practice with exam-like question formats, use the exam engine on the CD-ROM.

1. What is the function of an IGMP querier?

2. What change from IGMPv1 to IGMPv2 affects leave latency?

3. What change is found in IGMPv3 compared to IGMP version 2?

4. How do routers communicate in a mixed-version IGMP environment?

5. Describe the function of CGMP.

6. Describe the function of IGMP snooping.

7. How is querier election handled in IGMPv2?

8. What command is used to see the current IGMP membership information?

9. What capability is added in IGMPv3?

10. What command shows IGMP parameters and the current IGMP version running on an interface?

This chapter covers the following topics:

- **The Central Multicast Problem**— Describes the key issue with multicasting— identifying sources.

- **Routing Multicast Traffic**—Describes multicast routing protocols.

- **Enabling PIM Sparse-Dense Mode**— Describes the commands necessary to implement multicasting.

CHAPTER 19

Configuring Multicast

When configuring multicast routing, the trick is not remembering a large set of commands, but understanding how those simple commands and your environment are supported by the router. The first section of this chapter deals with finding the multicast server. The second section describes how multicast routing and routing protocols work, and the third section covers the required commands to create an IP multicast network.

"Do I Know This Already?" Quiz

The purpose of the "Do I Know This Already?" quiz is to help you to decide what parts of this chapter to use. If you already intend to read the entire chapter, you do not necessarily need to answer these questions now.

The 14-question quiz, derived from the major sections in the "Foundation Topics" portion of the chapter, helps you determine how to spend your limited study time.

Table 19-1 outlines the major topics discussed in this chapter and the "Do I Know This Already?"quiz questions that correspond to those topics.

Table 19-1 *"Do I Know This Already?" Foundation Topics Section-to-Question Mapping*

Foundation Topics Section	Questions Covered in This Section	Score
The Central Multicast Problem	1	
Routing Multicast Traffic	2–8	
Enabling PIM Sparse-Dense Mode	9–14	
Total Score		

CAUTION The goal of self-assessment is to gauge your mastery of the topics in this chapter. If you do not know the answer to a question or are only partially sure of the answer, you should mark this question wrong for purposes of the self-assessment. Giving yourself credit for an answer you correctly guess skews your self-assessment results and might provide you with a false sense of security.

1. What common engineering problem must be solved by all multicast implementations?

    a. Identifying multicast servers

    b. Preventing multicast storms

    c. Preventing multicast loops

    d. Multicast TTL

2. Which of the following multicast routing protocols is fully supported on Cisco routers?

    a. Center-Based Trees

    b. Core-Based Trees

    c. DVMRP

    d. Multicast OSPF

    e. PIM

3. If a multicast group has recipients on every subnet, which of the PIM modes should be used?

    a. Dense mode

    b. Sparse mode

    c. Sparse-compress mode

    d. Flood mode

4. Which type of tree structure is built for sparse-mode multicast routing?

    a. Spanning tree

    b. Sparse tree

    c. Shared tree

    d. Simple tree

5. What router maintains the RP-to-group correlation for Auto-RP in PIMv1?

    a. RP agent

    b. PIM root

    c. Mapping agent

    d. RP discovery server

6. Rendezvous points are configured with an access list. What is the purpose of this list?

   a. Restricting users that use the RP

   b. Restricting routers that use the RP

   c. Restricting source addresses that use the RP

   d. Limiting multicast IP addresses that use the RP

7. What router advertises candidate RP routers in PIMv2?

   a. Auto-RP

   b. Mapping agent

   c. Bootstrap router

   d. PIM root

8. TTL is used by multicast for what purpose?

   a. Preventing loops

   b. Limiting scope

   c. Determining path

   d. Determining hops

9. Which command is used to enable multicast routing on an IOS device?

   a. (config)#**ip multicast-routing**

   b. (config-if)#**multicast address** {*ip-address*}

   c. (config-if)#**ip pim** {**dense-mode** | **sparse-dense-mode** | **sparse-mode**}

   d. (config)#**ip pim send-rp-announce** {**interface** *type*} {**scope** *ttl*} {**group-list** acl}

   e. (config)#**ip pim send-rp-discovery** {**interface** *type*} {**scope** *ttl*}

10. Which command enables a multicast routing protocol on an IOS device?

   a. (config)#**ip multicast routing**

   b. (config-if)#**multicast address** {*IP-address*}

   c. (config-if)#**ip pim** {**dense-mode** | **sparse-dense-mode** | **sparse-mode**}

   d. (config)#**ip pim send-rp-announce** {**interface** *type*} **scope** {**ttl**} **group-list** {**acl**}

   e. (config)#**ip pim send-rp-discovery** {**interface** *type*} **scope** {**ttl**}

11. Which command causes an IOS device to volunteer itself as an RP?

    a. (config)#**ip multicast routing**

    b. (config-if)#**multicast address** {*IP-address*}

    c. (config-if)#**ip pim** {**dense-mode** | **sparse-dense-mode** | **sparse-mode**}

    d. (config)#**ip pim send-rp-announce** {**interface** *type*} {**scope** *ttl*} {**group-list** *acl*}

    e. (config)#**ip pim send-rp-discovery** {**interface** *type*} **scope** {*ttl*}

12. Which command displays the multicast IP routing table?

    a. **show ip mroute**

    b. **show ip pim interface**

    c. **show ip pim neighbors**

    d. **show ip pim rp**

    e. **show ip rpf**

13. Which command displays information about rendezvous points?

    a. **show ip mroute**

    b. **show ip pim interface**

    c. **show ip pim neighbors**

    d. **show ip pim rp**

    e. **show ip rpf**

14. Which command utilizes the unicast IP routing table to calculate the interface on which traffic from a source should arrive?

    a. **show ip mroute**

    b. **show ip pim interface**

    c. **show ip pim neighbors**

    d. **show ip pim rp**

    e. **show ip rpf**

The answers to the "Do I Know This Already?" quiz are found in Appendix A, "Answers to Chapter 'Do I Know This Already?' Quizzes and Q&A Sections." The suggested choices for your next step are as follows:

- **10 or less overall score**—Read the entire chapter. This includes the "Foundation Topics," "Foundation Summary," and "Q&A" sections.

- **11 or 12 overall score**—Begin with the "Foundation Summary" section and then go to the "Q&A" section at the end of the chapter. If you have trouble with these exercises, read the appropriate sections in "Foundation Topics."

- **13 or 14 overall score**—If you want more review on these topics, skip to the "Foundation Summary" section and then go to the "Q&A" section at the end of the chapter. Otherwise, move to the next chapter.

Foundation Topics

The Central Multicast Problem

Multicasting works very well, but there is one problem that haunts it. Although a PC subscribes to a channel, it still needs to discover the servers producing traffic on that channel. It should be easy to notice the traffic if the server is local, but not if the server is remote.

This chapter centers on this problem. Multicast traffic routes, but routes are built from users back toward servers. Your PC has to somehow know the address of the server.

There are many ways to publish server contact information. The simplest way is to send a link in e-mail. There is also an application called Session Directory (SD) that distributes exactly this kind of information. With SD, servers announce themselves using SDP (session description protocol) via a well-known multicast group (224.2.127.254). SD is used within Cisco IP/TV to distribute multicast servers and session descriptions.

This chapter explores ways that the PC may dynamically alert the router that it is looking for a multicast channel and ways that the router may search out servers producing traffic on that channel. Instead of discovering a server, a client may simply be told where the server is located.

Routing Multicast Traffic

IP multicast traffic must be routed, but with a different logic than that employed in unicast IP. Unicast IP packets are destined for a single interface (even if multiple paths exist), whereas multicast IP packets can have many destination interfaces, depending upon where the recipients are located.

Several multicast routing protocols are available, including Multicast OSPF (MOSPF), Distance Vector Multicast Routing Protocol (DVMRP), Center-Based Trees, Core-Based Trees, and Protocol Independent Multicast (PIM). Cisco routers do not support Center- or Core-Based Trees and support DVMRP only enough to redistribute routes. The only MOSPF command used in IOS is one to turn off an annoying error message that comes from receiving MOSPF. Therefore, this section focuses exclusively on PIM.

This section describes some of the facilities used to support multicast routing, such as RPF, multicast trees, and PIM operation. The following section builds on this by showing the commands required to implement these technologies.

Reverse Path Forwarding

Routers perform an RPF test on every multicast packet they receive. *Reverse Path Forwarding (RPF)* checks to make sure traffic always flows away from the root of the tree—from the source toward the recipients.

As a packet is received on a router interface, the source IP address is determined. An RPF check is used to verify that the packet *arrived* on the same interface that would be used if the router were to send traffic *toward* the source. If this is true, the packet is traveling out the branches of the tree, away from the source. If it is not true, the path is redundant or someone else has injected the packet on an unexpected interface, headed back down the branches of the tree toward the source.

To perform the RPF test, the PIM router looks up the source address in its unicast routing table. This is the *reverse* of normal packet forwarding, which looks up the destination address. If the next-hop interface used to reach the source address also matches the interface where the packet was received, the packet can be forwarded toward the multicast recipients. If not, the packet is discarded.

Multicast Trees

The routers in a network must determine a forwarding path to get multicast packets from the source to each of the recipients. Think of the network as a tree structure. At the root of the tree is the source, blindly sending IP packets to a multicast address. The source is not aware of lists of hosts or recipients that are members of a multicast group. Instead, it depends upon multicast routers and switches to handle the actual multicast packet delivery.

Each router along the way sits at a branch or fork in the tree. Routers learn which branches of the tree are home to multicast group recipients. Traffic is only forwarded on interfaces that have interested receivers.

This tree structure is somewhat similar to a spanning-tree topology because it has a root at one end and recipients at the other end. They differ, though, in that a spanning tree must connect the root to all end nodes, whereas the multicast tree does not necessarily have to do so. One way they are similar is that both are loop free—the multicast needs to be loop free so that none of the multicast traffic gets fed back into the tree.

Multicast routes are written as (S,G) for source and group. If 192.168.0.1 is transmitting on 227.182.150.159, the route would look like (192.168.0.1, 227.182.150.159). Multicast traffic is distributed by moving the traffic away from the source, along the RPF paths. The complete set of RPF paths can be thought of as a brachiating structure—a distribution tree—and this structure becomes the basis for multicast routing protocols.

Distribution Trees

The paths used in multicast routing are called *distribution trees* and there are two types: shared and source-rooted.

Shared trees define a common set of links over which all multicast traffic flows. Shared trees are interesting because they are pre-calculated and are efficient in terms of router resources. Shared trees can also be rooted at rendezvous points (RP). For each group, shared trees have one (*, G) route (all sources within the group route the same way).

Source-based trees take the shortest path from the source to the receiver, which is to say each source has a separate set of routes associated with it. Because there are many more paths to consider and hold in memory, source-based trees are more complicated but more efficient in terms of bandwidth.

Dense and Sparse Multicast Routing Protocols

Multicast routing protocols are also described as either sparse or dense. A dense multicast routing protocol assumes that all hosts on all links are interested in the traffic and so floods multicasts out all paths, only to have some paths ask not to receive the traffic. This could succinctly be described as "bush out, prune back." Sparse multicast routing protocols assume that no one wants the traffic until they ask for it.

Dense-mode protocols work better in LANs, where bandwidth is plentiful. Sparse-mode protocols work better in WANs, where conserving bandwidth is critical.

PIM

Protocol Independent Multicast (PIM) is a routing protocol that can be used for forwarding multicast traffic between IP subnets or network segments. PIM operates independently of any particular IP routing protocol. Therefore, PIM makes use of the IP unicast routing table and does not keep a separate multicast routing table. (The unicast-routing table is itself routing protocol–independent because one or more routing protocols can be used to populate a single table.)

PIM can operate in two modes, depending on the density of the recipients in a multicast group. Additionally, Cisco has developed a third, hybrid mode. The PIM modes are

- PIM dense mode

- PIM sparse mode

- PIM sparse-dense mode

In addition, two versions of the PIM protocol can be used in a network: PIM version 1 and PIM version 2. By default, PIM version 2 is used on a router interface.

PIM Dense Mode

PIM routers can be configured for *dense mode* (also called *PIM-DM*) if it is safe to assume that a multicast group's recipients are located on every subnet. In other words, the multicast group is densely populated across the network.

The multicast tree is built by first allowing a flood of traffic from the source to every dense-mode router in the network. The tree is grown from the root toward the leaves. For a brief time, unnecessary traffic is allowed. As each router receives traffic for the group, it must decide whether it already has active recipients wanting to receive the data. If so, the router can remain quiet and let the flow continue.

If no hosts have registered (via IGMP) for the multicast group with the router, the router sends a *Prune* message to the source. That branch of the tree is then pruned off so that the unnecessary traffic does not continue. The resulting tree is called a *source tree* or a *source-distribution tree* because it is unique from the source to the receivers.

Figure 19-1 shows the flood-then-prune operation of dense mode. The tree is built by a wave of join requests moving through all dense-mode multilayer switches. Then the switches that have no interested hosts request to be pruned from the tree.

Figure 19-1 *PIM Dense Mode Constructs a Multicast Tree*

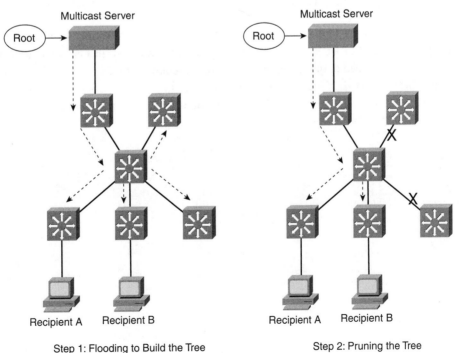

Step 1: Flooding to Build the Tree   Step 2: Pruning the Tree

PIM-DM routers become aware of their neighbors by exchanging hello messages. This neighbor information is first used to build the tree to all neighbors and then to prune branches.

If a multicast flow has begun and the tree has been built and then pruned, the tree exists only where active group members are located. After that, if a new host registers for the group, the branch of the network where it is located can be added or *grafted* back onto the tree.

PIM Sparse Mode

PIM *sparse mode* (also called *PIM-SM*) takes a different approach: The multicast tree is not extended to a router unless a host there has already joined the group. The multicast tree is built by beginning with the group members at the end leaf nodes and extending back toward a central root point. The tree is grown in reverse, from the leaves toward the root.

Sparse mode also works on the idea of a shared tree structure, where the root is not necessarily the multicast source. Instead, the root is a PIM-SM router that is centrally located in the network. This root router is called the *rendezvous point (RP)*.

The tree from the RP to the group members is actually a subset of the tree that could be drawn from the source to the group members. Subsequently, if a multicast source anywhere in the network can register for group membership with the RP, the tree can be completed. Because of this, the sparse-mode tree is a shared tree.

As a recipient joins a multicast group via IGMP, the local router forwards the membership report toward the RP at the root of the tree. Each router along the way adds that branch to the shared tree. Pruning is performed only when a group member is removed from the group. This process is shown in Figure 19-2. Notice that it consists of only one step: Only routers with active group members join the tree. The routers that did not join the group are not pruned because they never became a part of the tree in the first place.

Figure 19-2   *PIM Sparse Mode Constructs a Multicast Tree*

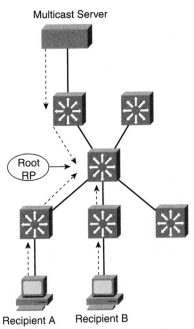

Step 1: Members join the group
to build a tree.

Once PIM-SM routers start receiving traffic from a source (and learn the source IP address), they switch over to a shortest-path tree rooted at the multicast server.

Figure 19-3 illustrates the resulting tree structures for both PIM dense mode and PIM sparse mode, along with the multicast data flow. Notice that both PIM modes have constructed identical tree structures, yielding the same multicast traffic flow patterns.

Figure 19-3 *Identical Results from PIM Dense and Sparse Modes*

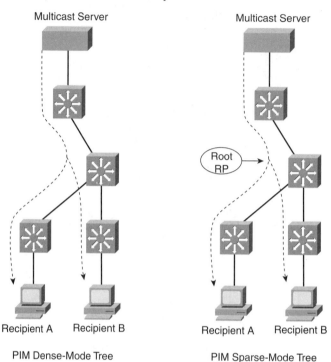

PIM Sparse-Dense Mode

PIM has the potential to support both dense and sparse modes because they can exist on different multicast groups in a network and even on the same router interface. Cisco offers the hybrid *sparse-dense* mode, allowing a PIM router to use sparse or dense mode on a per-group basis. If a group has an RP defined, sparse mode is used; otherwise, dense mode is used.

Sparse-dense mode is important because it solves the central multicast problem—discovering servers—in a simple and elegant way. Dense mode is used to flood RP discovery and announcement messages, which then allow the client to find the RP and use the RP to find the server.

PIM Version 1

For routers using the first version of PIM, RPs can be configured manually or by the more dynamic *auto-RP* process.

You can limit the range of multicast groups supported by the RP with the use of an access list. The **override** keyword causes this RP to be preferred over any that is automatically determined. Because the RP does not advertise itself, its address and function must be defined on *every* router in the PIM domain, including the RP itself. This makes future changes in the RP location difficult to carry out because every router must be reconfigured with the new RP address.

Cisco also provides a proprietary means of automatically informing PIM-SM routers of the appropriate RP for a group. This is known as *Auto-RP*. This is done by identifying a centrally located and well-connected router to function as the *mapping agent*. The mapping agent learns of all candidate RPs that are announced over the *Cisco-RP-Announce* multicast address 224.0.1.39 (by definition, all PIM-SM routers automatically must join 224.0.1.39).

The mapping agent sends RP-to-group mapping information to all PIM routers over the *Cisco-RP-Discovery* multicast address 224.0.1.40. The Time To Live (TTL) value is sent in these messages to limit the scope of the mapping. This limits how many router-hops away the information will reach and still be valid.

You then must explicitly define each candidate RP router. When a router knows it can be an RP, it begins sending announcements to the mapping agent.

The interface must be given because it corresponds to the advertised RP address and identifies where the mapping agent can be found. The scope of the announcement is limited by the number of router hops (TTL). The router can also advertise itself as a candidate RP for the multicast groups permitted in the **group-list** access list. By adding the **interval** keyword, the announcements will be sent at an interval of *seconds*.

PIM Version 2

The second version of PIM also includes a dynamic RP-to-group mapping advertisement mechanism. This is known as the *bootstrap router method* and is standards based.

PIMv2 is similar to the Cisco auto-RP method. First, a *bootstrap router (BSR)* is identified; this router learns about RP candidates for a group and advertises them to PIM routers. You need to configure only the BSR and candidate RPs; all other PIM routers learn of the appropriate RP from the BSR.

Enabling PIM Sparse-Dense Mode

This section describes the steps involved in setting up multicast networking and configuring PIM. Once completed, you can view and troubleshoot the operating conditions with several **show** commands, as described in this section.

Setting Up Multicast Networking

There are three steps to setting up IP multicast routing on a Cisco router:

Step 1   Enable multicast routing.

Step 2   Turn on PIM in appropriate mode on selected interfaces.

Step 3   Set up rendezvous points (RPs).

The following sections describe each step in greater detail.

Enabling Multicast Routing

Multicast routing is not supported on Cisco routers by default. Use the following command to enable multicast routing in global configuration mode:

```
Router(config)#ip multicast-routing
```

Turning on PIM

Starting PIM on an interface automatically starts IGMP. PIM is enabled at the interface level, so the first step is to analyze your network and understand which router interfaces should support PIM. Once identified, activate PIM in interface-configuration mode, as shown in the following syntax. PIM runs in three modes: sparse, dense, and sparse-dense.

```
Router(config-if)#ip pim {dense-mode | sparse-dense-mode | sparse-mode}
```

To change the PIM version, you can use the following interface-configuration command:

```
Router(config-if)# ip pim version {1 | 2}
```

Configuring RPs

The final step is to configure RPs. To manually identify an RP, use the following global configuration command:

```
Router(config)# ip pim rp-address ip-address [access-list] [override]
```

Alternatively, RPs can be dynamically determined using Auto-RP. With Auto-RP, some routers need to volunteer to be RPs, while others need to advertise the RPs. Auto-RP identifies a centrally located and well-connected router to function as the *mapping agent*. The mapping agent learns of all candidate RPs that are announced over the *Cisco-RP-Announce* multicast address 224.0.1.39 (by definition, all PIM-SM routers automatically must join 224.0.1.39), compiles a list of which routers are RP for which groups, and advertises the list to client routers on 224.0.1.40. To define a router as a mapping agent, use the following global configuration command:

```
Router(config)# ip pim send-rp-discovery scope ttl
```

Again, the interface is used to determine an IP address to advertise from and is typically a loopback. TTL is still used to limit the scope of advertisement.

Configure a router as a candidate RP with the following global configuration command:

```
Router(config)# ip pim send-rp-announce type mod/num scope ttl [group-list
    access- list] [interval seconds]
```

When configured, the router announces itself as a possible RP for the multicast range described by the access list. The announcement is sent using Auto-RP to 224.0.1.39. The interface is mapped to an IP address to specify how clients can reach the RP, so it is often a loopback. The TTL field is a security measure, which prevents propagation of RP offers into untrusted neighboring systems.

Alternatively, PIMv2 supports a bootstrap router (BSR). Define a BSR using the following global configuration command:

```
Router(config)# ip pim bsr-candidate type mod/num hash-mask-length [priority]
```

The interface specified determines the BSR address. RP selection for a group is based on a hashing function. The length of the hash mask controls the number of consecutive multicast groups that hash to the same RP.

Next, you must identify each of the candidate RP routers. Configure each RP with the following global configuration command:

```
Router(config)# ip pim rp-candidate type mod/num ttl [group-list access-list]
```

Finally, by default, the bootstrap messages permeate the entire PIM domain. You can limit the scope of the advertisements by defining PIMv2 border routers, which will not forward the bootstrap messages any farther. Use the following global configuration command:

```
Router(config)# ip pim border
```

Verifying Routes

Where **show ip mroute** shows the unicast table, the command to show a multicast routing table is

```
router#show ip mroute [group-address] [summary] [count][active kpbs]
```

The **summary** option displays each route on one line. The **count** option shows statistics. The **active** option filters the display to show only active sources. Example 19-1 shows this command used to display a particular route in the table.

Example 19-1 *The* **show ip mroute** *Output*

```
Router#show ip mroute 227.100.100.100
IP Multicast Routing Table
Flags: D - Dense, S - Sparse, C - Connected, L - Local, P - Pruned
       R - RP-bit set, F - Register flag, T - SPT-bit set, J - Join SPT
Timers: Uptime/Expires
Interface state: Interface, Next-Hop, State/Mode

(*, 227.100.100.100), 00:01:50/00:02:59, RP 172.16.3.1, flags: SPF
  Incoming interface: Tunnel35, RPF nbr 172.16.1.20, Mroute
  Outgoing interface list: Null

(170.100.1.1/32, 227.100.100.100), 00:01:50/00:01:09, flags: PFT
  Incoming interface: Ethernet0, RPF nbr 0.0.0.0, Registering
Outgoing interface list: Null
```

Notice the routes that are not source-specific (meaning routes to an RP) are (*,G). Routes to the source are listed as (S,G). This example shows how an entry evolves from (*,G) to (S,G).

Verifying Neighbors

If there is an issue building a multicast routing table, a good place to start troubleshooting is to verify that PIM sees its neighbors.

Use the **show ip pim interface** command to look at settings on the interfaces, as shown in Example 19-2. This command shows the assigned (unicast) IP address; the interface name; the PIM version (1 or 2) and mode (dense, sparse, or sparse-dense); number of neighbors; frequency of queries; and the designed querier.

Example 19-2 *The* **show ip pim interface** *Output*

```
Stewart#show ip pim interface

Address          Interface     Version/Mode  Nbr   Query   DR
Count    Intvl
192.168.0.1      Ethernet0     v2/S            1     30     192.168.0.10
```

The **show ip pim neighbor** command shows a list of neighbors, with much of the same information shown in **show ip pim interface**. See Example 19-3.

Example 19-3 *The **show ip pim neighbor** Command Output*

```
Router#show ip pim neighbor
PIM Neighbor Table
Neighbor Address      Interface      Uptime      Expires    Ver    Mode
192.168.0.10          Ethernet0      00:01:37    00:01:05   v2     Sparse
```

Verifying Rendezvous Points

Even when PIM routing is in place, RPs must be configured correctly to find traffic sources. The command **show ip pim rp** allows you to inspect the configured RPs and look at the mappings that have been applied. The full command is

```
Router(config)#show ip pim rp [group-name | group-address | mapping]
```

Using **show ip pim rp**, without further modifiers, displays RPs for active groups. If the command is modified with the group name, then only the RPs for the selected group are shown. The **show ip pim rp mappings** command maps multicast IP addresses to RPs, as shown in Example 19-4.

Example 19-4 *The **show ip pim rp** and **show ip pim rp mappings** Output*

```
Router#show ip pim rp
Group: 227.1.1.1, RP: 192.168.5.1, uptime 00:00:20, expires never

Router#show ip pim rp mapping
PIM Group-to-RP Mappings
…
Group(s): 224.0.0.0/4, Static
RP: 192.168.5.1
```

Verifying Multicast Routing

Because multicast routes away from a source, it is important to understand the reverse-path. The **show ip rpf** command allows you to inspect reverse-path forwarding information for your traffic, as shown in Example 19-5.

Example 19-5 *The* **show ip rpf** *Output*

```
Router#show ip rpf 172.16.0.1
RPF information for ? (172.16.0.1)
  RPF interface: Serial0
  RPF neighbor: ? (172.16.5.2)
  RPF route/mask: 172.16.0.0/24
  RPF type: unicast (ospf 1)
  RPF recursion count: 0
Doing distance-preferred lookups across tables
```

Foundation Summary

The Foundation Summary provides a convenient review of many key concepts in this chapter. If you are already comfortable with the topics in this chapter, this summary might help you recall a few details. If you just read this chapter, this review should help solidify some key facts. If you are doing your final prep before the exam, the following lists and tables are a convenient way to review the day before the exam.

Multicast routing protocols include the following. Note that Cisco fully supports only PIM.

- Multicast OSPF (MOSPF)

- Distance Vector Multicast Routing Protocol (DVMRP)

- Center-Based Trees

- Core-Based Trees

- Protocol Independent Multicast (PIM)

RPF checks to ensure traffic flows away from the root.

The two types of distribution trees are

- Shared

- Source-rooted

Multicast routing protocols are described as either sparse or dense:

- A dense multicast routing protocol assumes that all hosts on all links are interested in the traffic and so floods multicasts out all paths, only to have some paths ask not to receive the traffic (also called "bush out, prune back").

- Sparse multicast routing protocols assume that no one wants the traffic until they ask for it.

The PIM modes are as follows:

- **PIM dense mode**—Assumes that a multicast group's recipients are located on every subnet.

- **PIM sparse mode**—The multicast tree is not extended to a router unless a host there already has joined the group.

- **PIM sparse-dense mode**—Cisco hybrid that allows a PIM router to use sparse or dense mode on a per-group basis. If a group has an RP defined, sparse mode is used; otherwise, dense mode is used.

The PIM versions are

- **PIMv1**—Uses auto-RP

- **PIMv2**—Uses bootstrap routers

The three steps to set up IP multicast routing on a Cisco router are as follows:

Step 1   Enable multicast routing with the following command:

```
Router(config)#ip multicast-routing
```

Step 2   Turn on PIM in appropriate mode on selected interfaces:

```
Router(config-if)#ip pim {dense-mode | sparse-dense-mode | sparse-mode}
```

Step 3   Set up RPs:

```
Router(config)#ip pim send-rp-announce {interface type} {scope ttl} {group-
   list acl}
Router(config)#ip pim send-rp-discovery {interface type} scope {ttl}
```

The principal commands used to understand a multicast configuration are shown in Table 19-2.

Table 19-2 *Multicast* **show** *Commands*

Command	Description
show ip mroute [group-address] [summary] [count][active kpbs]	Shows multicast routing tables
show ip pim interface	Shows settings on the interfaces
show ip pim neighbor	Shows a list of neighbors
**show ip pim rp [group-name	group-address	mapping]**	Allows you to inspect the configured RPs
show ip pim rp	Displays RPs for active groups
show ip pim rp mappings	Maps multicast IP addresses to RPs
show ip rpf	Allows you to inspect reverse path forwarding information for your traffic

Q&A

The questions and scenarios in this book are designed to be challenging and to make sure that you know the answer. Rather than allowing you to derive the answers from clues hidden inside the questions themselves, the questions challenge your understanding and recall of the subject.

You can find the answers to these questions in Appendix A. For more practice with exam-like question formats, use the exam engine on the CD-ROM.

1. What is RPF?

2. What is PIM?

3. What is PIM Dense Mode?

4. What is PIM Sparse Mode?

5. Describe the PIM Sparse-Dense Mode.

6. What is Auto-RP?

7. Describe the function of the BSR.

8. When is a BSR used, as opposed to auto-RP?

9. Describe the three steps to setting up multicast routing on a Cisco router.

10. A router has three interfaces (f0/0, s0/1, s0/2). The router should be configured to support multicast and to use PIM-SD and IGMP version 2 on all interfaces. List the multicast commands necessary.

11. Continuing from the previous question, the same router needs to be configured as a candidate RP for 227.0.0.0/8. List the commands necessary.

12. What is the difference between a (*,G) route and an (S,G) route?

Part VIII covers the following Cisco BSCI exam topics related to implementing IPv6:

- Describe IPv6 addressing operations.
- Describe IPv6 interoperation with IPv4.
- Describe, configure, or verify OSPF routing with IPv6 addressing.

This list reflects the exam topics posted on Cisco.com at the publication time of this book.

Part VIII: IPv6

This chapter covers the following topics:

- **Introduction to IPv6**—Discusses the need for IPv6's larger address space and the features of IPv6.

- **The IPv6 Packet Header**—Describes the fields in the IPv6 packet header.

- **IPv6 Addressing**—Explains how IPv6 addresses are represented, and describes the details of each type of IPv6 addresses.

- **IPv6 Address Assignment**—Describes how IPv6 addresses can be assigned to devices.

- **IPv6 Mobility**—Discusses how IPv6 allows mobile users to stay connected.

CHAPTER 20

Introduction to IPv6 and IPv6 Addressing

This chapter begins the discussion of Internet Protocol version 6 (IPv6) and focuses on understanding the features of IPv6, its packet header, and its addressing types and structure. The chapter concludes with a discussion of IPv6 address-assignment strategies and IPv6 mobility.

A well-designed IPv6 network looks similar to a well-designed Internet Protocol version 4 (IPv4) network. Of course there are differences in addressing, but the hierarchical design discussed in Chapter 1, "Network Design," continues to be preferred because it supports summarization, which is the key to scalability.

"Do I Know This Already?" Quiz

The purpose of the "Do I Know This Already?" quiz is to help you decide which parts of this chapter to use. If you already intend to read the entire chapter, you do not necessarily need to answer these questions.

The 12-question quiz, derived from the major sections in the "Foundation Topics" portion of the chapter, helps you determine how to spend your limited study time.

Table 20-1 outlines the major topics discussed in this chapter and the corresponding quiz questions.

Table 20-1 *"Do I Know This Already?" Foundation Topics Section-to-Question Mapping*

Foundation Topics Section	Questions Covered in This Section	Score
Introduction to IPv6	1	
The IPv6 Packet Header	2–4	
IPv6 Addressing	5–10	
IPv6 Address Assignment	11	
IPv6 Mobility	12	
Total Score		

> **CAUTION** The goal of self-assessment is to gauge your mastery of the topics in this chapter. If you do not know the answer to a question or are only partially sure of the answer, you should mark the question wrong for purposes of the self-assessment. Giving yourself credit for an answer you correctly guessed skews your results and might provide you with a false sense of security.

1. How long is an IPv6 address?

    a. 16 hexadecimal numbers

    b. 32 decimal numbers

    c. 128 bits

    d. 32 bits

2. For which field in the IPv4 header is there *not* a similar field in the IPv6 header?

    a. Version

    b. ToS

    c. TTL

    d. Checksum

3. How large is the basic IPv6 header (without any extensions)?

    a. 20 bytes

    b. 128 bits

    c. 320 bits

    d. 512 bits

4. Which of the following functions is implemented with extension headers?

    a. Fragmentation

    b. Flow labels

    c. TCP

    d. Checksum

5. Which of the following is a valid host unicast IPv6 address?

  a. 2001::240E::0AC0:3428:121C

  b. 2001:240E::0AC0:3428::

  c. 2001::0000::240E::0000::0000::0AC0::3428::121C

  d. 2001:0:240E::0AC0:3428:121C

6. What is the EUI-64 format interface identifier that corresponds to the MAC address 00-0C-27-A2-13-1B?

  a. C:27A2:131B

  b. 020C:27FF:FEA2:131B

  c. FEFE:C:27A2:131B

  d. 000C:27A2:131B:0000:0000

7. Which of the following is not supported by IPv6?

  a. Unicast

  b. Broadcast

  c. Multicast

  d. Anycast

8. An IPv6 enterprise will typically be assigned a prefix at which level?

  a. /3

  b. /8

  c. /16

  d. /48

9. A NIC has a MAC address of 00-0F-66-81-19-A3 and discovers a routing prefix of 2001:0:1:5::/64. Which IPv6 addresses are assigned to it?

  a. 2001::1:5:20F:66FF:FE81:19A3

  b. FE80::20F:66FF:FE81:19A3

  c. ::1

  d. FF02::1

10. IPv6 multicast addresses use which prefix?

   a. F000::/16

   b. FF00::/8

   c. 0::/8

   d. 4000::/8

11. Which two items does stateless autoconfiguration use?

   a. Multicast prefix

   b. Advertised prefix

   c. Advertised interface ID

   d. EUI-64 format interface ID

12. A mobile IPv6 binding is an association between which of the following?

   a. Home address

   b. Correspondent nodes

   c. Prefix

   d. Care-of address

The answers to the "Do I Know This Already?" quiz are found in Appendix A, "Answers to Chapter 'Do I Know This Already?' Quizzes and Q&A Sections." The suggested choices for your next step are as follows:

■ **8 or less overall score**—Read the entire chapter. This includes the "Foundation Topics," "Foundation Summary," "Q&A," and "Scenarios" sections.

■ **9 or 10 overall score**—Begin with the "Foundation Summary" section and then go to the "Q&A" and "Scenarios" sections at the end of the chapter. If you have trouble with these exercises, read the appropriate sections in "Foundation Topics."

■ **11 or 12 overall score**—If you want more review on these topics, skip to the "Foundation Summary" section and then go to the "Q&A" and "Scenarios" sections at the end of the chapter. Otherwise, move to the next chapter.

Foundation Topics

Introduction to IPv6

This section introduces the features of IPv6 and its need for a larger address space.

The Need for a Larger Address Space

IPv6 has been under development for many years—since the mid 1990s—and has variously been billed as the protocol that would expand the IP address space, bring mobile IP to maturity, or finally incorporate security at Layer 3. While these statements are all true, many of the capabilities of IPv6 have been back-ported to IPv4 over the years. However, IPv4 addresses are now scarce, and the main reason that the Internet will transition to IPv6 is that more addresses will be available.

One reason that IPv4 addresses are scarce is that they are not assigned efficiently. Class A addresses (/8) are too big for most organizations (supporting 16,777,214 host addresses) while Class C addresses (/24, supporting 254 host addresses) are too small to allow even small organizations to grow. As a result, most organizations request Class B addresses (/16, supporting 65,534 host addresses), but they use only a fraction of their assigned space.

Initially, every IP device required a unique public address. To forestall the day when the pool of public IPv4 addresses would be depleted, the Internet Engineering Task Force (IETF) adopted classless interdomain routing (CIDR), variable-length subnet mask (VLSM), classless routing, and Network Address Translation (NAT). CIDR and VLSM work together to allow greater flexibility in address assignment, while NAT hides clients and minimizes the need for public addresses.

Another reason for IPv4 address scarcity is that they have not been assigned evenly across the globe. Citizens and corporations in the United States—the home to the early Internet—were the primary benefactors of early assignments, and a large portion of new addresses continue to go to North America. Europe—next in line on the Internet—has the next largest portion of addresses, while Asia has an insufficient number of addresses relative to its population. Although the perception in the United States might be that IPv4 still has "elbow room," internationally— specifically in Asia—there is already a recognition of the need to move beyond IPv4.

Continuing with this idea that the Internet needs more IP addresses, consider that the world population is about 6.6 billion, of which about 1 billion are "online" already. Given the proliferation of IP-ready devices, many users will need more than one IP address simultaneously, especially as IP moves into consumer electronics such as home entertainment centers and phones. It is certainly beyond a doubt that IP usage will continue to accelerate.

This need for IP addresses could be mitigated somewhat by using NAT and temporary address allocation via Dynamic Host Configuration Protocol (DHCP), but having intermediate devices manipulate packets complicates design and troubleshooting, and interferes with end-to-end encryption and quality of service. The Internet is designed as a peer-to-peer network with dumb intermediate systems; because NAT works against that design, it is at best a necessary evil.

IPv6 Features

Probably the most noticeable feature of IPv6 is its larger, 128-bit addresses, making 2^{128} (or $3.4 * 10^{38}$) unique IPv6 addresses available. While it is reasonable to note that some IPv6 addresses are reserved for multicasting and other special functions, with 6.6 billion people in the world, there are approximately $5 * 10^{28}$ IPv6 addresses for each of us—hopefully enough for the foreseeable future!

NOTE The total number of IPv4 addresses is 2^{32} (or $4 * 10^9$); when reserved addresses are considered, approximately two billion ($2 * 10^9$) usable addresses remain.

IPv6 also includes a simplified packet header, which is described in detail in the next section. This simpler header can be processed more efficiently and provides a flexible extension mechanism for support of other features.

One of these features is mobility; mobile IP is an IETF standard that allows people with wireless devices to stay connected, transparently, as they move around. Mobile IPv6 is described in the "IPv6 Mobility" section later in this chapter.

Security—a hot topic these days—is built-in to IPv6. IP security (IPsec) is therefore available on every IPv6 device, and its use should make IPv6 networks more secure.

Because migration from the current IPv4 Internet to IPv6 will not happen overnight, clever ways are needed to manage the transition. As described in Chapter 21, "IPv6 Routing Protocols, Configuration, and Transitioning from IPv4," tunneling, dual stack, and translation are three ways this migration can be accomplished.

Taking into account all of the IPv6 features, the United States Congress has set 2008 as when the U.S. Department of Defense will have its systems IPv6-compatible, with other departments sure to follow. Meanwhile, Japan, China, and other countries—including some in the European Union—are moving to IPv6 now.

The IPv6 Packet Header

As mentioned earlier, although an expanded address space is the main reason that the Internet will transition to IPv6, IPv6 has many other features that reflect the experience gained over thirty years of using IPv4. These advanced features can be seen in the IPv6 packet header, illustrated in Figure 20-1, and by looking at what has changed from IPv4.

The fields in the IPv6 header are described as follows:

- **Version**—A 4-bit field, set to the number six for IPv6.

- **Traffic Class**—Also called priority. Similar to the type of service (ToS) field in IPv4, this 8-bit field describes relative priority and is used for quality of service (QoS).

- **Flow Label**—The 20-bit flow label allows traffic to be tagged so that it can be handled faster, on a per-flow basis; this field can also be used to associate flows with traffic classes.

- **Payload Length**—This 16-bit field is the length of the data in the packet.

- **Next Header**—Like the protocol field in the IPv4 header, this 8-bit field indicates how the fields after the IPv6 basic header should be interpreted. It could indicate that the following field is transmission control protocol (TCP) or user datagram protocol (UDP) transport layer information, or it could indicate that an extension header is present.

- **Hop Limit**—Similar to the time to live (TTL) field of IPv4, this 8-bit field is decremented by intermediate routers and, to prevent looping, the packet is discarded and a message is sent back to the source if this field reaches zero.

- **Source Address** and **Destination Address**—These 128-bit fields are the IPv6 source and destination addresses of the communicating devices.

- **Extension Headers**—Zero or more extension headers follow the basic IPv6 header (for example, before the transport layer data). The *next header* field within an extension header points to the next header in the chain. The extension headers (in their suggested order) could include:

  - **Hop-by-Hop options**—Options for intermediate routers along the path.

  - **Destination options**—Options for the end node (and intermediate routers if the routing header is also present).

  - **Routing**—Used to specify intermediate routers that the route must include; the effect is to force routing along an administratively defined path.

Figure 20-1 *IPv6 Header*

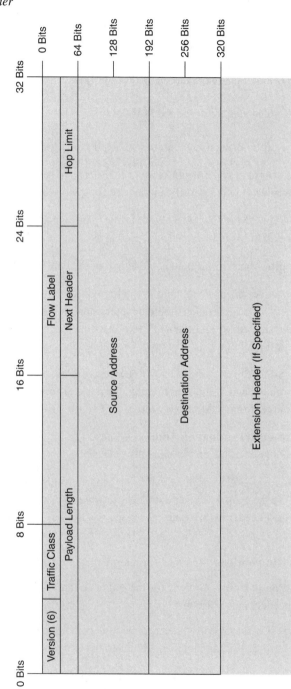

— **Fragment**—Used to divide packets that are too large for the maximum transmission unit (MTU) of a link along the path. This header replaces the fragmentation fields of the IPv4 packet header.

— **Authentication and Encapsulating Security Payload (ESP)**—Used by IPsec to provide packet authentication, integrity, and confidentiality. The authentication header (AH) and ESP header are identical in IPv4 and IPv6.

The IPv6 header is optimized for 32- and 64-bit processors, and the extension headers allow for expandability without forcing unused fields to be constantly transmitted.

What has changed between the IPv4 and IPv6 headers? The source and destination addresses are larger, of course. Three other changes are apparent: checksum, fragmentation, and the flow label. These changes are described in the following sections.

Checksum

In IPv4, each packet includes a header checksum. Since intermediate routers decrement the TTL, they also have to recalculate the checksum each time they handle a packet, resulting in more processing resources being used throughout the network. Since upper layer protocols perform a checksum anyway, the IPv6 header does not include a checksum field; this results in more efficient forwarding.

Fragmentation

There are two changes to the way fragmentation behaves in IPv6, as follows:

■ Fragmentation information has been moved to an extension header.

■ Intermediate routers no longer fragment packets. If fragmentation is required, it is performed by the source node, reducing the processing burden on the network.

A discovery process determines the optimum MTU to use during a given session. First, the source IPv6 device attempts to send a packet. If the device receives an Internet Control Message Protocol (ICMP) "packet too big" message, which includes the proper MTU size for the path, it retransmits the MTU discovery packet with the smaller MTU. This process is repeated until the device receives a response stating the discovery packet arrived at its final destination successfully. The source sets the resulting MTU as the MTU for the session, and caches its value. The MTU is based on destination address or flow label, or if source-based routing is performed, on source address. Devices perform the MTU discovery process every five minutes to see whether it has changed. If, for some reason, upper layers do not accept MTU change notifications from the IPv6 layer, IPv6 has a mechanism to fragment large packets; however, upper layers should avoid sending messages that require fragmentation.

Flow Label

The flow label field allows flows to be tagged as they enter the network so that similar traffic may be tagged and switched quickly along a path instead of being examined at each intermediate router. The flow label may also be associated with a particular QoS treatment.

IPv6 Addressing

This section explains how IPv6 addresses are represented, describes the types of addresses, and discusses the interface identifiers used in IPv6 addresses. The details of the various IPv6 address types are presented below.

Representing IPv6 Addresses

Instead of using the IPv4 dotted decimal format, IPv6's 128-bit addresses are represented in hexadecimal format, with colons between each of the eight 16-bit fields. Since each hexadecimal digit maps to four bits, each 16-bit field is four digits long. An example of an IPv6 address is 2001:0000:0001:0002:0000:0000:0000:ABCD. Fortunately, there are ways to shorten this representation—imagine trying to ping that address!

There are two ways that an IPv6 address may be represented in a more compact, human-readable, form. First, leading zeros in each 16-bit field may be omitted. Doing so changes the previous address to 2001:0:1:2:0:0:0:ABCD. Secondly, once, and only once, in an address, sequential zeros can be replaced with a pair of colons (::). Using this shortcut changes the example address to 2001:0:1:2::ABCD. Note that only one pair of colons can be used within an IPv6 address. This is because the number of missing 0s is calculated by separating the two parts of the address and filling in 0s, until there are a total of 128 bits. If an address had two :: notations, it would be impossible to determine the size of each block of 0s.

Types of IPv6 Addresses

IPv6 supports three types of addresses:

- **Unicast**—For sending to a single interface. The two currently defined types of unicast addresses are global-aggregatable unicast (also known as global unicast) and link-local unicast.

- **Multicast**—For sending to *all* of the interfaces in a group. An IPv6 multicast address identifies a set of interfaces on different devices.

- **Anycast**—For sending to the *nearest* interface in a group. An IPv6 anycast address also identifies a set of interfaces on different devices; however, a packet sent to an anycast address goes only to the nearest interface, as determined by the routing protocol in use. Therefore, all nodes with the same anycast address should provide the same service.

An interface can have several addresses, including a link-local address, any global unicast or anycast addresses assigned, a loopback address (::1/128), the all-nodes multicast addresses, solicited-nodes multicast addresses, and any other multicast addresses to which the node is assigned. In addition, routers must recognize the subnet-router anycast address and the all-routers multicast addresses. The details of these address types are provided later in this chapter.

> **NOTE**   All systems support the loopback address, ::1/128, representing an imaginary interface that a system may use to send traffic to itself. The loopback address is never used as a source IP address and routers should not forward traffic to or from the loopback address.

Multicast addresses are in the range FF00::/8. All other IPv6 addresses are in the IPv6 unicast address space; anycast addresses are allocated from this same address space.

Broadcast addresses do not exist in IPv6. Broadcasts can be thought of as a special case of multicasting, where every device is the intended recipient. In IPv4, sending a broadcast causes *all* devices to process the packet, even those that are not concerned with the contents. Using multicasts is much more efficient because the packets can be targeted to a subset of devices, such as routers running Open Shortest Path First (OSPF).

IPv6 Interface Identifiers

Interface identifiers (IDs) in IPv6 addresses are used to identify a unique interface on a link and are sometimes referred to as the "host portion" of the IPv6 address. Interface IDs must be unique on a link. They are always 64-bits long and can be dynamically created, based on the data-link layer address.

The specific data link layer type of the interface determines how the IPv6 interface IDs are dynamically created and how address resolution works. For Ethernet, the interface ID is based on the media access control (MAC) address of the interface, in a format called the extended universal identifier 64-bit (EUI-64) format. The EUI-64 format interface ID is derived from the 48-bit MAC address by inserting the hexadecimal number FFFE between the organizationally unique identifier (OUI) field (the upper three bytes) and the vendor code (the lower three bytes) of the MAC address. The seventh bit in the first byte of the resulting interface ID, corresponding to the Universal/Local (U/L) bit, is set to binary 1. Figure 20-2 illustrates this process.

The U/L bit indicates whether the interface ID is locally unique (on the link only) or universally (globally) unique; IDs derived from universally unique MAC addresses are assumed to be globally unique.

The eighth bit in the first byte of the interface ID is the individual/group (I/G) bit for managing multicast groups; it is not changed.

Figure 20-2 *Creating an EUI-64 Format Interface ID for IPv6 Addresses*

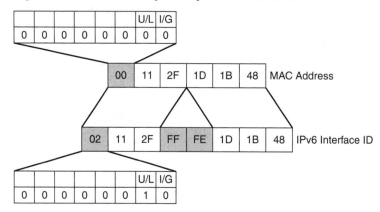

> **NOTE** On Ethernet, the first bit of the MAC address transmitted is the I/G bit, used for broadcast and multicast addresses. The second bit transmitted is the U/L bit, used to identify whether the MAC is assigned by the manufacturer (and therefore globally unique) or locally created. Since Ethernet transmits the low-order bit of each byte first, the U/L bit is the seventh bit of the address and I/G is eighth bit of the address.

IPv6 Unicast Addresses

This section describes the two types of IPv6 unicast addresses: global aggregatable and link-local.

> **NOTE** Older specifications mentioned two other types of IPv6 unicast addresses which have now been deprecated, in RFC 4291, *IP Version 6 Addressing Architecture*. These addresses are mentioned here for your information only.
>
> IPv4-compatible IPv6 addresses were made by concatenating 0::/96 and the IPv4 address. For instance, the IPv4 address 192.168.9.5 became 0::C0A8:0905, because 192.168.9.5 is C0A8:0905 in hexadecimal.
>
> Site-local addresses were similar to the IPv4 private addresses and were created by concatenating the prefix FEC0::/10 with a 54-bit subnet and a 64-bit interface ID.

IPv6 Global Aggregatable Unicast Addresses

As has been repeated several times in this book, scalability is an emergent property of summarization. This is just as true for IPv6 as for IPv4. As in IPv4, the far-left bits of IPv6 addresses indicate the routing prefix and may be summarized. Theoretically, there are 2^{64} IPv6 prefixes. If each prefix were stored in router memory using 256 bits (32 bytes), then the routing table would consume $5.9 * 10^{20}$ bytes! Therefore, addresses must be deployed hierarchically and summarized, or the number of networks could grow to be too large for routers to track.

Figure 20-3 shows the IPv6 global-aggregatable unicast address structure as described by RFC 3587, *IPv6 Global Unicast Address Format*. The IPv6 global unicast address is similar to the IPv4 global unicast address.

Figure 20-3   *IPv6 Global Aggregatable Unicast Address Structure*

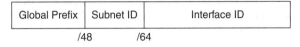
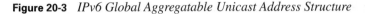

The first 48 bits of the IPv6 global unicast address are used for global routing at the Internet Service Provider (ISP) level. The next 16 bits are the subnet ID, allowing an enterprise to subdivide their network. The final 64 bits are the interface ID, typically in EUI-64 format.

The Internet Assigned Numbers Authority (IANA) is currently assigning addresses that start with the binary value 001, which is 2000::/3, for IPv6 global unicast addresses. This is one-eighth of the total IPv6 address space. The IANA is currently allocating address space in the 2001::/16 ranges to the registries. Registries typically have a /23 range, and allocate /32 ranges to ISPs.

For example, an ISP might assign 2001:0:1AB::/48 to an organization. In a network assigned subnet 5, the prefix would be 2001:0:1AB:5::/64. On a device with a MAC address 00-0F-66-81-19-A3, the EUI-64 format interface ID would be 020F:66FF:FE81:19A3. The complete IPv6 global unicast address of the device would therefore be 2001:0:1AB:5:20F:66FF:FE81:19A3.

> **NOTE**   In the now obsolete RFC 2374, *An IPv6 Aggregatable Global Unicast Address Format*, two other fields were included in the global prefix: the Top-Level Aggregator and the Next-Level Aggregator. Some early IPv6 networks may still use these fields, but they are no longer included in the latest RFC 3587, *IPv6 Aggregatable Global Unicast Address Format*.

IPv6 Link-Local Unicast Addresses

Link-local unicast addresses allow devices on the same local network to communicate, without requiring them to have global unicast addresses. Link-local addresses are used by routing and discovery protocols and are autoconfigured using the FE80::/10 prefix and the EUI-64 format interface ID, as shown in Figure 20-4.

Figure 20-4   *IPv6 Link-Local Address Structure*

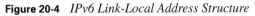

For example, on an interface with the MAC address 00-0F-66-81-19-A3, the link-local address would be FF80::020F:66FF:FE81:19A3.

> **NOTE**   RFC 4291 also specifies another unicast address, the IPv4-mapped IPv6 address, formed by concatenating 0::FFFF:0:0/96 with an IPv4 address. For instance, 10.0.0.1 becomes 0::FFFF:A00:1, because 10.0.0.1 is 0A00:0001 in hexadecimal. This address can be used by dual-stack hosts (those running both IPv4 and IPv6).

IPv6 Anycast Addresses

An IPv6 anycast address is a global unicast address that is assigned to two or more devices. Other devices route to the *closest* active device with the anycast address; the routing protocol metric determines which is closest.

Figure 20-5 shows an example network topology from which there are two connections to an ISP. Both border routers have been configured with the same IPv6 anycast address; the internal routers simply route the client to the closest one (Router A in this case). If Router A goes down, then Router B becomes the closest, and routing reconverges toward Router B. This technique automatically load-balances traffic toward the closest exit and provides redundancy in case an exit router goes down.

Figure 20-5   *Anycast Addresses Route Toward the Closest Active Device*

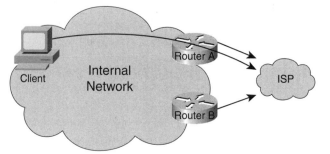

Anycast addresses are created by assigning the same unicast address to more than one device; there is no reserved address space for anycast. Nodes on which the address is assigned must be explicitly configured to use and know that the address is an anycast address.

All routers must support the *subnet-router anycast address* for the subnets on which they have interfaces. The subnet-router anycast address is the unicast address of the subnet with the interface ID (the host bits) set to zero. For example, a router with an IPv6 interface address 2001:0:1:5:20F:66FF:FE81:19A3 must support the anycast address 2001:0:1:5::. Packets sent to the subnet-router anycast address will be delivered to one router on the subnet.

IPv6 Multicast Addresses

A multicast address identifies a group of interfaces; traffic sent to the group goes to *all* of the interfaces. Interfaces can belong to many multicast groups simultaneously.

Each interface should recognize several multicast addresses, including the all-nodes multicast, the solicited-nodes multicast, and any other group addresses to which the node belongs. Routers should also recognize the all-routers multicast address. Figure 20-6 illustrates the format of an IPv6 multicast address.

Figure 20-6 *IPv6 Multicast Address*

8 bits	4 bits	4 bits	112 bits
1111 1111	Flag	Scope	Group ID

FF00::/8

As shown in Figure 20-6, all IPv6 multicast addresses start with the prefix FF00::/8. The next four bits are flags, which are described in the following list:

■ The first flag bit is currently undefined and always set to zero.

■ The second flag bit is known as the "R" bit; it is set to binary 1 if the multicast rendezvous point (RP) address is embedded in the multicast address (as defined in RFC 3956, *Embedding the Rendezvous Point (RP) Address in an IPv6 Multicast Address*). Chapter 19, "Configuring Multicast," describes RPs.

■ The third flag bit is known as the "P" bit; it is set to binary 1 if the multicast address is assigned based on the unicast prefix (as defined in RFC 3306, *Unicast-Prefix-based IPv6 Multicast Addresses*).

■ The fourth flag bit is known as the "T" bit; it is set to binary 0 if the address is permanently assigned or to binary 1 if the address is temporary (as defined in RFC 4291).

The four bits after the flags indicate the scope of the address, limiting how far the multicast may travel. IPv4 uses TTL as a crude way to accomplish this, but there are times when the distance allowed by TTL is too far in one direction and not far enough in another. The IPv6 multicast scope is flexible enough to limit the multicast to a link, to a site, or to an enterprise. The currently defined scope values, in hexadecimal, are as follows:

■ 1: interface-local scope; used for loopback transmission

■ 2: link-local scope; similar to unicast link-local scope

- 4: admin-local scope; must be administratively configured

- 5: site-local scope; spans a single site

- 8: organization-local scope; spans multiple sites belonging to an organization

- E: global scope

The multicast group ID is the lower 112 bits of the address.

All devices should recognize and respond to the all-nodes multicast addresses:

- FF01::1 is interface-local.

- FF02::1 is link-local.

Solicited-node multicast addresses are used in neighbor solicitation messages, and are sent on a local link by a device that wants to determine the data-link layer address of another device on the same local link, similar to the Address Resolution Protocol (ARP) in IPv4. A solicited-node multicast address is formed by starting with the prefix FF02::1:FF00:/104 and appending the last 24 bits of the corresponding unicast or anycast address of the device. Nodes are required to join the associated solicited-nodes group for each unicast and anycast address they support.

Routers should also recognize and respond to the all-routers multicast addresses:

- FF01::2 is an interface-local address.

- FF02::2 is a link-local address.

- FF05::2 is a site-local address.

Routers will also join other groups to support routing protocols; for example, OSPF version 3 (OSPFv3) uses FF02::5 and FF02::6, and Routing Information Protocol (RIP) new generation (RIPng) uses FF02::9.

IPv6 Address Assignment

IPv6 addresses may be manually assigned, or dynamically assigned through DHCP version 6 (DHCPv6) or stateless autoconfiguration. If an address is manually defined, take care to ensure it is unique.

Stateless Autoconfiguration

For stateless autoconfiguration, each router advertises network information (either periodically or upon a request from a host), including the 64-bit prefix, on each of its links. By listening for this advertisement, end-systems create a unique address by concatenating the prefix and the EUI-64 format interface ID. This process is referred to as *stateless* autoconfiguration because no device tracks the state of particular addresses.

End-systems request network information using a router solicitation message, and routers reply with a router advertisement message. A process called duplicate address detection (DAD) detects and avoids duplicate addresses.

This same feature can be used to renumber a network by changing the network information on only the routers. When the routers advertise the new prefix information, the end-systems autoconfigure themselves with the new network number.

DHCPv6 and Stateless DHCPv6

The abilities to control which devices get addresses and track the address assignments for auditing purposes are important issues that can be accomplished using DHCPv6. Ironically, privacy is another reason that DHCPv6 could be a good idea. Normally IPv6 addresses contain the MAC address, a unique ID that can be linked back to a specific system. DHCPv6 could be used to break the link between the MAC address and the Layer 3 address.

Stateless DHCPv6 is a method between stateless autoconfiguration and stateful DHCPv6; stateless DHCPv6 is also known as DHCP-lite and is defined in RFC 3736, *Stateless Dynamic Host Configuration Protocol (DHCP) Service for IPv6.*

IPv6 Mobility

The IPv6 mobility feature, defined in RFC 3775, *Mobility Support in IPv6*, allows users to stay connected while moving about the network.

An IPv6 mobile node has a *home address* on its home network and a *care-of address* on its current network. A node communicating with a mobile node is called a *correspondent node* of the mobile node. The association between the home address and the care-of address of a mobile node is known as a *binding.* When a mobile node roams away from its home network, it sends a binding update to its *home agent,* a router on its home network.

There are two ways that a mobile node and a correspondent node can communicate—via the home agent or directly.

In the first case, packets from the correspondent node are routed to the home agent and then tunneled to the mobile node. Packets to the correspondent node are tunneled from the mobile node to the home agent and then routed normally from the home network to the correspondent node.

In the second case, when the mobile node first receives a packet from the correspondent node, it sends a binding update to the correspondent node. Packets from the correspondent node can then be routed directly to the care-of address of the mobile node and all traffic flows directly between the correspondent node and the mobile node. Figure 20-7 illustrates an example of a mobile node that has moved from one network to another.

Figure 20-7 *IPv6 Mobility*

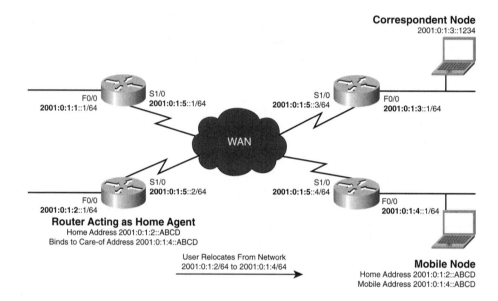

If the mobile node moves—and that is what being mobile is all about—it sends a binding update to its home agent and to all correspondent nodes.

Foundation Summary

The Foundation Summary provides a convenient review of many key concepts in this chapter. If you are already comfortable with the topics in this chapter, this summary might help you recall a few details. If you just read this chapter, this review should help solidify some key facts. If you are doing your final prep before the exam, the following lists, tables, and figures are a convenient way to review the day before the exam.

IPv6 provides many important capabilities, including

- 128-bit addresses, which considerably expands the address space, allowing all users in all countries to have sufficient addresses

- Improved support for Mobile IP

- Built-in security

- Techniques for transitioning from IPv4

- Built-in QoS support

- Easy autoconfiguration of end-stations

The US Department of Defense plans to have its systems IPv6-compatible by 2008, and many other countries have already started moving to IPv6.

Table 20-2 lists the IPv6 packet header fields, their length in bits, and their use, and indicates comparable IPv4 packet header fields.

Table 20-2 *IPv6 Packet Header Fields*

IPv6 Packet Header Field	No. of Bits	Use	Comparable IPv4 Header Field
Version	4	IP version	Version
Traffic class	8	Relative priority	ToS
Flow label	20	Tagging	(None)
Payload length	16	Length of data	Total length

continues

Table 20-2   *IPv6 Packet Header Fields (Continued)*

IPv6 Packet Header Field	No. of Bits	Use	Comparable IPv4 Header Field
Next header	8	Pointer to extension header or transport-layer header	Protocol
Hop limit	8	Prevent looping	TTL
Source address	128	Source of packet	Source address
Destination address	128	Destination of packet	Destination address
Extension headers	(Variable)	Transport layer or optional features	Transport layer header

Note that fragmentation has been moved to an extension header and is performed by the source node rather than by routers. The IPv4 packet header checksum has been removed.

IPv6 addresses are represented in hexadecimal, with colons between each of the eight 16-bit (4 hexadecimal digit) fields. Two ways to shorten an address are

- Omitting leading 0s within a field

- Once, and only once, within an address, replacing sequential zeros with a pair of colons (::)

IPv6 supports three types of addresses:

- **Unicast**—The two currently defined types of unicast addresses are global aggregatable unicast (also known as global unicast) and link-local unicast.

- **Multicast**—For sending to *all* of the interfaces in a group.

- **Anycast**—For sending to the *nearest* interface in a group.

IPv6 does not have broadcast addresses.

IPv6 interface IDs are always 64-bits long and can be dynamically created, based on the data-link layer address. For Ethernet, the interface ID is based on the MAC address of the interface, in an EUI-64 format. The process of creating an EUI-64 format interface ID is illustrated in Figure 20-8.

Figure 20-8 *Creating an EUI-64 Format Interface ID for IPv6 Addresses*

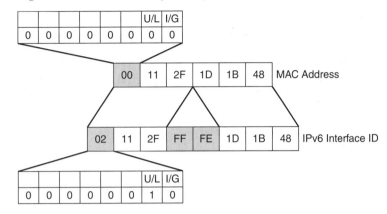

IPv6 hosts should support *at least* the following addresses:

■ Assigned global unicast and anycast addresses (2000::/3)

■ Link-local address (FE80::/10), autoconfigured

■ Loopback address (::1/128)

■ All-nodes multicast addresses (FF01::1 and FF02::1)

■ Solicited-nodes multicast addresses (FF02::1:FF00:/104 and appending the last 24 bits of the corresponding unicast or anycast address of the device)

■ Any other assigned multicast addresses (in the range FF00::/8)

Routers should additionally support at least the following:

■ Subnet-router anycast address (the unicast address of the subnet, with the interface ID—the host bits—set to zero)

■ All-routers multicast addresses (FF01::2, FF02::2, and FF05::2)

IPv6 addresses may be manually assigned, or dynamically assigned through DHCPv6 or stateless autoconfiguration.

An IPv6 mobile node has a home address on its home network and a care-of address on its current network. When a mobile node roams away from its home network, it sends a binding update to its home agent, a router on its home network, and to all correspondent nodes.

Q&A

The questions and scenarios in this book are designed to be challenging and to make sure that you know the answer. Rather than allowing you to derive the answers from clues hidden inside the questions themselves, the questions challenge your understanding and recall of the subject.

You can find the answers to these questions in Appendix A. For more practice with exam-like question formats, use the exam engine on the CD-ROM.

1. What are some of the benefits of IPv6?

2. Describe the fields in the IPv6 packet header.

3. What is an IPv6 extension header?

4. List some differences between the IPv4 header and the IPv6 header.

5. What is the shortest way to write the IPv6 address 2001:0000:240E:0000:0000:0AC0:3428:021C?

6. Why is IPv6 multicasting more efficient than IPv4 broadcasting?

7. A device has a MAC address 00-0C-0A-28-12-1C. What is its EUI-64 bit interface ID? How could this value be used?

8. List three ways that an IPv6 host can obtain an address.

9. How is an anycast address used in a network?

10. How is the scope of a multicast address specified?

11. Hosts may respond to many IPv6 addresses on each interface. List as many as you can.

12. Along with the addresses described in the previous question, routers must respond to additional IPv6 addresses on each interface. What are they?

13. How does IPv6 support renumbering?

14. How does IPv6 support mobility?

Scenarios

The following scenario and questions are designed to draw together the content of the chapter and exercise your understanding of the concepts. There is not necessarily one right answer. The thought process and practice in manipulating the concepts is the goal of this section. The answers to the scenario questions are found at the end of this chapter.

Scenario 20-1

Figure 20-9 illustrates your network diagram. Your ISP gives you an address range of 2001:1BE0:3A0::/48. The edge routers also have addresses assigned on the links through which they connect to the ISP; these addresses are in a different address space. Subnet your assigned IPv6 space for this network and be sure to support summarization.

Figure 20-9 *An IPv6 Network to Address*

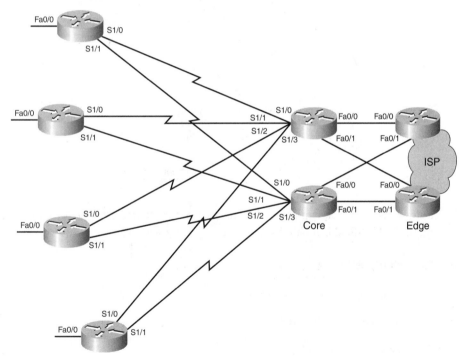

Scenario 20-1 Answers

Figure 20-10 shows one solution for IPv6 subnet assignment on each of the links in this network. (Of course, this problem could have been solved in many other ways.) All network prefixes use the ISP assigned address space 2001:1BE0:3A0::/48, with the subnet assignment (shown as hexadecimal numbers in boxes on the diagram) as the next 16 bits, resulting in a /64 prefix.

Figure 20-10 *One Solution to the IPv6 Network in Figure 20-9*

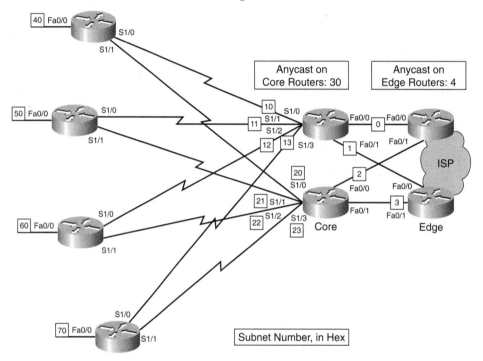

To illustrate the address assignments, the addresses of the interfaces on the top core router are as follows (the subnet field is highlighted):

- Fa0/0: 2001:1BE0:03A0:0000::1/64

- Fa0/1: 2001:1BE0:03A0:0001::1/64

- S1/0: 2001:1BE0:03A0:0010::1/64

- S1/1: 2001:1BE0:03A0:0011::1/64

- S1/2: 2001:1BE0:03A0:0012::1/64

■   S1/3: 2001:1BE0:03A0:0013::1/64

■   Anycast address on all serial interfaces: 2001:1BE0:03A0:0030::1/64

The addresses on the top internal router are as follows:

■   Fa0/0: 2001:1BE0:03A0:0040::1/64

■   S1/0: 2001:1BE0:03A0:0010::2/64

■   S1/1: 2001:1BE0:03A0:0020::2/64

Note the following points:

■   All network prefixes are derived from the ISP assigned address space 2001:1BE0:3A0::/48.

■   The two core routers have the same anycast address configured on their serial links (on subnet 0x0030), for routing redundancy.

■   The two edge routers have the same anycast address configured on all of their interfaces connected to the internal network (on subnet 0x0004); this can be used for routing redundancy.

■   Summarization is supported. For example, each of the two core routers could summarize the subnets via which they connect to the internal network. The top core router's summary route for its internal networks is 2001:1BE0:3A0:0010::/60, and the lower router's summary route for its internal networks is 2001:1BE0:3A0:0020::/60.

This chapter covers the following topics:

- **IPv6 Routing Overview**—Describes the various routing protocols that support IPv6.

- **Configuring and Verifying IPv6 and OSPFv3**—Provides the commands to configure and verify IPv6 and OSPFv3.

- **Transitioning from IPv4 to IPv6**—Discusses several transition mechanisms that may be used to move from an IPv4 network to an IPv6 network.

CHAPTER 21

IPv6 Routing Protocols, Configuration, and Transitioning from IPv4

The main theme of this book is routing. This chapter first describes how routing can be accomplished within an Internet Protocol (IP) version 6 (IPv6) network. Next, the chapter explores, in detail, configuring and verifying an IPv6 network with Open Shortest Path First (OSPF) version 3 (OSPFv3) routing. The final part of this chapter examines how a mixture of IP version 4 (IPv4) and IPv6 protocols will be handled, since there obviously will not be an "IPv6 Conversion Day" when all networks change from IPv4 to IPv6.

"Do I Know This Already?" Quiz

The purpose of the "Do I Know This Already?" quiz is to help you decide which parts of this chapter to use. If you already intend to read the entire chapter, you do not necessarily need to answer these questions.

The 10-question quiz, derived from the major sections in the "Foundation Topics" portion of the chapter, helps you determine how to spend your limited study time.

Table 21-1 outlines the major topics discussed in this chapter and the corresponding quiz questions.

Table 21-1 *"Do I Know This Already?" Foundation Topics Section-to-Question Mapping*

Foundation Topics Section	Questions Covered in This Section	Score
IPv6 Routing Overview	1–5	
Configuring and Verifying IPv6 and OSPFv3	6–8	
Transitioning from IPv4 to IPv6	9–10	
Total Score		

CAUTION   The goal of self-assessment is to gauge your mastery of the topics in this chapter. If you do not know the answer to a question or are only partially sure of the answer, you should mark the question wrong for purposes of the self-assessment. Giving yourself credit for an answer you correctly guessed skews your results and might provide you with a false sense of security.

1. Which of the following routing protocols support IPv6?

   a. RIPv2

   b. EIGRP for IPv6

   c. OSPFv3

   d. ODR

2. How is a default route represented in IPv6?

   a. 0/0

   b. 0:0:0:0:0:0:0:0/0

   c. ::/0

   d. 0::0/0

3. Which of the following is supported by OSPFv3 but not by OSPFv2?

   a. Multiple OSPF processes

   b. NBMA networks

   c. NSSAs

   d. 128-bit prefixes

4. Which multicast addresses are used by OSPFv3?

   a. 224.0.0.5 and 224.0.0.6

   b. FF02::5 and FF02::6

   c. FF:FF:FF:FF:FF:FF:FF

   d. FF::FFFF

5. Which of the following OSPFv3 LSAs carry IPv6 prefixes?

   a. Type 1

   b. Type 2

   c. Type 3

   d. Type 9

6. Which command is necessary to enable IPv6 routing on a Cisco router?

   a. **ipv6 address**

   b. **ipv6 unicast-routing**

   c. **ipv6 routing**

   d. None, IPv6 routing is enabled by default.

7. At which prompt is the command that specifies the OSPFv3 area configured?

   a. Router(config)#

   b. Router(config-router)#

   c. Router(config-rtr)#

   d. Router(config-if)#

8. Which command output displays OSPFv3 timers?

   a. **show ipv6 route**

   b. **show ipv6 ospf**

   c. **show ipv6 ospf database**

   d. **show ipv6 ospf database database-summary**

9. Dual stack is best described by which of the following statements?

   a. Running IPv4 and IPv6 at the same time

   b. Translating IPv4 traffic to IPv6

   c. Passing IPv6 through UDP

   d. Process interception

10. How is a 6-to-4 tunnel different than a manually configured tunnel?

    a. It uses NAT-PT.

    b. IPv6 addresses are embedded in IPv4 addresses.

    c. Automatic tunnel creation.

    d. It is not a dual-stack solution.

The answers to the "Do I Know This Already?" quiz are found in Appendix A, "Answers to Chapter 'Do I Know This Already?' Quizzes and Q&A Sections." Compare your score with the suggestions below to proceed:

- **7 or less overall score**—Read the entire chapter. This includes the "Foundation Topics," "Foundation Summary," "Q&A," and "Scenarios" sections.

- **8 or 9 overall score**—Begin with the "Foundation Summary" section and then go to the "Q&A" and "Scenarios" sections at the end of the chapter. If you have trouble with these exercises, read the appropriate sections in "Foundation Topics."

- **10 overall score**—If you want more review on these topics, skip to the "Foundation Summary" section and then go to the "Q&A" and "Scenarios" sections at the end of the chapter.

Foundation Topics

IPv6 Routing Overview

IPv6 uses updated versions of the same routing protocols that are available for IPv4. The various protocols work much the same as they do with IPv4, with some changes.

IPv6 routing can be accomplished with the following protocols:

- Static routes

- Routing Information Protocol (RIP) new generation (RIPng), defined in RFC 2080, *RIPng for IPv6*

- Enhanced Interior Gateway Routing Protocol (EIGRP) for IPv6

- Intermediate System-Intermediate System (IS-IS) for IPv6

- Multiprotocol Border Gateway Protocol Version 4 (MP-BGP4), defined in RFC 2545, *Use of BGP-4 Multiprotocol Extensions for IPv6 Inter-Domain Routing*, and RFC 2858, *Multiprotocol Extensions for BGP-4*

- OSPFv3, defined in RFC 2740, *OSPF for IPv6*

Choosing which of these to run involves considering the same trade-offs as with IPv4: RIPng, OSPFv3, and MP-BGP4 are well-supported standards; EIGRP for IPv6 is proprietary to Cisco; and IS-IS for IPv6 is seldom found in enterprise networks.

The following sections describe these protocols.

Static Routes

Like IPv4 static routes, static routes for IPv6 are easily configured. Default routes are represented by double colons with a prefix of zero (::/0). The command to configure an IPv6 static route is

```
Router(config)# ipv6 route ipv6-prefix/prefix-length {ipv6-address | interface-type
   interface-number [ipv6-address]} [administrative-distance] [administrative-
   multicast-distance | unicast | multicast] [next-hop-address] [tag tag]
```

RFC 2461, *Neighbor Discovery for IP Version 6 (IPv6)*, specifies that a router must be able to determine the link-local address of its neighboring routers. Thus, in static routes, the next-hop address must be configured as the link-local address of the neighboring router.

RIPng

RIPng for IPv6 is the next-generation IPv6 version of RIP, based on RIP version 2 (RIPv2). Like RIPv2, RIPng is a distance-vector routing protocol that uses hop count for the metric, has a maximum hop count of 15, and multicasts periodic updates every 30 seconds. RIPng uses a multicast address of FF02::9, the all-RIP-routers multicast group.

RIPng sends updates, using user datagram protocol (UDP) port 521, within IPv6 packets. These updates include an IPv6 prefix and an IPv6 next-hop address.

EIGRP for IPv6

EIGRP for IPv6 is based on EIGRP for IPv4. Like its predecessor, it is an advanced distance-vector routing protocol that uses a complex metric, reliable updates, and the Diffusing Update Algorithm (DUAL) algorithm for fast convergence. EIGRP for IPv6 is available in Cisco IOS 12.4(6)T and later.

IS-IS for IPv6

As discussed in Chapter 9, "Fundamentals of the Integrated IS-IS Protocol," IS-IS runs directly on the data-link layer and is independent of the Layer 3 protocol. Therefore, changing IS-IS to handle IPv6 only required creating a new protocol identifier and two new type length values (TLV)—IPv6 reachability and IPv6 interface address. IS-IS allows one routing update to contain routes from IPv4 and IPv6, resulting in a more efficient use of link capacity than other protocols, such as OSPF.

MP-BGP4 for IPv6

MP-BGP4 includes new extensions to BGP4 that allows it to carry reachability information for other protocols, such as IPv6 and multiprotocol label switching (MPLS); a new identifier is defined for IPv6. The NEXT_HOP attribute can include a global IPv6 unicast address and a link-local address. The NEXT_HOP and network layer reachability information (NLRI) attributes are expressed as IPv6 prefixes and addresses.

OSPFv3

This section details the similarities and differences between OSPFv3 and its predecessor— OSPF version 2 (OSPFv2)—and examines the types of OSPFv3 LSAs.

OSPFv2 and OSPFv3 Similarities

OSPFv3 shares many features with OSPFv2. OSPFv3 is a link-state routing protocol that uses the Dijkstra shortest path first (SPF) algorithm to select the best paths through the network. OSPFv3 routers are organized into areas, with all areas touching area 0 (the backbone area). OSPFv3 routers communicate with their neighbors using Hellos; exchange Link-State Advertisements (LSAs) and Database Descriptors (DBD); and run the SPF algorithm against the accumulated link-state database (LSDB).

OSPFv3 uses the same packet types as OSPFv2, forms neighbor relationships in the same way, and floods and ages LSAs identically. OSPFv3 supports nonbroadcast multiaccess (NBMA) topologies in the same way as OSPFv2: the RFC-compliant nonbroadcast mode and point-to-multipoint mode are supported, and Cisco IOS devices continue to support Cisco's three proprietary modes (point-to-point, broadcast, and point-to-multipoint nonbroadcast). Capabilities such as the various types of stub areas, including not-so-stubby areas (NSSA), and on-demand circuits are also supported.

NOTE Because it would be unproductive to repeat a detailed description of link-state theory or OSPF specifics, you may want to make sure you are familiar with Chapters 5 through 8 before proceeding with the rest of this section.

OSPFv2 and OSPFv3 Differences

OSPFv3 also differs from OSPFv2 in many ways. The most obvious is that OSPFv3 supports 128-bit prefixes.

OSPFv3 runs directly within IPv6 packets and can co-exist with OSPFv2. The two routing protocols do not exchange information or pay attention to each other in any way (this is referred to as "ships in the night" routing in some documentation, because packets from the two versions of OSPF pass each other without knowing of the other's existence, like ships passing in the night).

The OSPFv2 multicast addresses are 224.0.0.5 and 224.0.0.6; OSPFv3 uses the IPv6 multicast addresses FF02::5 (for all OSPF routers) and FF02::6 (for all designated routers [DR] and backup DRs [BDR]).

OSPFv3 IPv6 routers are expected to support many addresses per interface, including the link-local address, global unicast addresses, and multicast addresses, including the two addresses for OSPFv3.

OSPFv2 builds neighbor relationships about *subnets*, but the terms "network" or "subnet" imply a specific address space on an interface; in contrast, OSPFv3 is only concerned about its connection across a link to its neighbor. Thus, OSPFv3 terminology is discussed in terms of *links*, and an OSPFv3 router uses its link-local address as the source address of its advertisements—not its global unicast address. It uses the appropriate OSPFv3 IPv6 multicast address as the destination address.

The OSPFv3 packet header is 16 bytes, while the OSPFv2 packet header is 24 bytes. Figure 21-1 illustrates the OSPFv3 packet header.

Authentication is not built-in to OSPFv3; the authentication and authentication type fields in the OSPFv2 header do not appear in the OSPFv3 header. OSPFv3 instead relies on the underlying capabilities of IPv6 to provide authentication and encryption, using extension headers.

Figure 21-1 *OSPFv3 Packet Header*

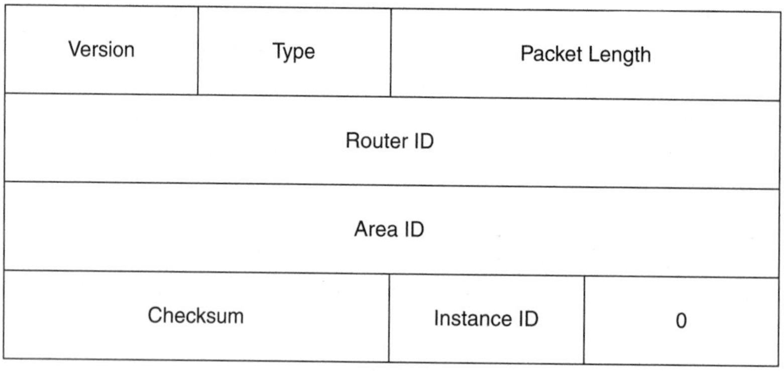

Version	Type	Packet Length	
Router ID			
Area ID			
Checksum		Instance ID	0

OSPFv2 can run multiple processes but can only run one copy of OSPF per link. The new instance ID field in the OSPFv3 header is used to differentiate OSPF processes; two instances need to have the same instance ID to communicate with each other. This allows multiple routing domains to communicate across the same link. Separate neighbor tables, link-state databases, and shortest-path trees are kept for each instance.

Perhaps surprisingly, the OSPFv3 router ID and area ID (and the link-state ID within an LSA) are still 32-bit numbers, and they are written in an IPv4-address dotted decimal format. In the same way that IS-IS requires a Connectionless Network Service (CLNS) address, OSPFv3 reveals its heritage in IPv4 by requiring a 32-bit number for its router ID. The OSPFv3 DR and BDR are identified by their router ID, not by their IP address, as they are identified in OSPFv2.

OSPFv3 LSA Types

OSPFv3 and OSPFv2 use a similar set of LSAs, with some differences. Table 21-2 lists the OSPFv3 LSAs, including the LSA function code, which indicates the function of the LSA.

Table 21-2 *OSPFv3 LSAs*

LSA Function Code	Name	Description
1	Router-LSA	Advertise router IDs within an area, from a router
2	Network-LSA	Advertise router IDs within an area, from a DR
3	Inter-Area-Prefix-LSA	Advertise prefixes from one area to another
4	Inter-Area-Router-LSA	Advertise location of an autonomous system boundary router (ASBR)
5	AS-External-LSA	Advertise routes redistributed into OSPF
6	Group-Membership LSA	Advertise multicast information

Table 21-2 *OSPFv3 LSAs (Continued)*

LSA Function Code	Name	Description
7	Type-7-LSA	Pass external routes through an NSSA
8	Link-LSA	Advertise a router's link-local address to directly attached neighbors and allow the local routers to share prefix and option information
9	Intra-Area-Prefix-LSA	Advertise prefixes associated with a router ID

NOTE The LSA link-state (LS) type is created by concatenating 0x200 with the LSA function code. For example, LSA function code 1 has an LS type 0x2001. However, because the 0x200 doesn't really add any new information, the LS function code typically is used when discussing LS types.

LSA types 1 and 2 no longer contain route prefixes; instead, they contain 32-bit IDs. Types 3 and 4 have been renamed but still fulfill the same functions as they do in OSPFv2. Types 8 and 9 are new LSAs in OSPFv3.

In OSPFv3, address prefixes are stored as *prefix*, *options*, and *prefix length*. Addresses are expressed as *prefix*, *prefix length*, a more flexible format than the OSPFv2 method of using *prefix* and *mask*.

OSPFv3 type 3 and type 9 LSAs carry all IPv6 prefix information; in OSPFv2, IPv4 prefix information is carried in router and network LSAs (type 1 and type 2).

LSAs are sourced from the link-local address of an interface and have an OSPFv3 IPv6 multicast address as the destination address.

Configuring and Verifying IPv6 and OSPFv3

This section describes how to configure and verify IPv6 and OSPFv3.

IPv6 Configuration

Before configuring any routing protocol, IPv6 support must be enabled on the router; it is turned off by default. The command to enable IPv6 is

```
Router(config)#ipv6 unicast-routing
```

Enable Cisco Express Forwarding (CEF) for IPv6 (CEFv6) using the following command:

```
Router(config)#ipv6 cef
```

CEFv6 is an advanced, Layer 3 IP-switching technology for forwarding IPv6 packets.

Next, configure interfaces with IPv6 unicast addresses, using the following command:

```
Router(config-if)#ipv6 address ipv6-address/prefix-length [eui-64]
```

The **eui-64** parameter causes the router to complete the lower order 64 bits of the address using an extended universal identifier 64-bit (EUI-64) format interface ID, as described in Chapter 20, "Introduction to IPv6 and IPv6 Addressing."

The IPv6 configuration for Router A in Figure 21-2 is shown in Example 21-1.

Figure 21-2 *Sample IPv6 Network*

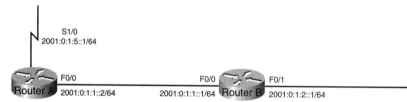

Example 21-1 *IPv6 Configuration of Router A in Figure 21-2*

```
RouterA#configure terminal
RouterA(config)#ipv6 unicast-routing
RouterA(config)#ipv6 cef
RouterA(config)#interface fastethernet0/0
RouterA(config-if)#description Local LAN
RouterA(config-if)#ipv6 address 2001:0:1:1::2/64
RouterA(config-if)#interface serial 1/0
RouterA(config-if)#description point-to-point connection to Internet
RouterA(config-if)#ipv6 address 2001:0:1:5::1/64
```

OSPFv3 Configuration

The two main configuration and troubleshooting differences between OSPFv2 and OSPFv3 are

- The inclusion of the **ipv6** keyword in OSPFv3 commands.

- The fact that interfaces are enabled for OSPFv3 in interface configuration mode instead of using the **network** command in router configuration mode, as is done for OSPFv2.

Assuming that IPv6 routing is enabled and IPv6 addresses are configured on the appropriate interfaces, the commands used to implement OSPFv3 are

```
Router(config)#ipv6 router ospf process-id
Router(config-rtr)#router-id 32-bit-router-id
Router(config-rtr)#area area-id range summary-range/prefix-length [advertise | not-
  advertise] [cost cost]
Router(config-rtr)#interface type number
Router(config-if)#ipv6 ospf process-id area area-id [instance instance-id]
Router(config-if)#ipv6 ospf priority priority
Router(config-if)#ipv6 ospf cost interface-cost
```

The router ID must be a 32-bit number in an IPv4-address dotted decimal format, and can be set to the value of an IPv4 address on the router. Priority works the same way it does for OSPFv2. Routers default to a priority of 1; a higher priority means a better chance of being elected DR or BDR, and 0 means that the router will not serve as a DR or BDR.

Cost also has not changed and is by default inversely proportional to the bandwidth of the interface. The default cost may be overridden with the **ipv6 ospf cost** command.

The **area range** command provides summarization, which is off by default in OSPFv3 as it is in OSPFv2. Scalability comes from summarization, and summarization comes from assigning addresses in a way that can be grouped, and from building a hierarchical network with natural points where summarization may be implemented. OSPFv3 allows redistribution of routes to and from other IPv6 routing protocols and allows route filtering in the same ways that OSPFv2 does.

> **NOTE**   For OSPFv3, the cost of the summarized route is the *highest* cost of the routes being summarized.

To help explain OSPFv3 configuration an example topology is shown in Figure 21-3. Both routers are area border routers (ABRs), and Router B has a loopback interface.

Figure 21-3   *A Simple OSPFv3 Network Topology*

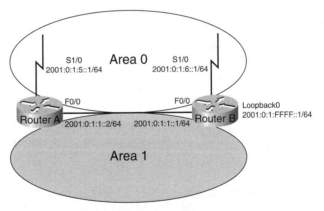

Example 21-2 shows a simple OSPFv3 configuration on Router A.

Example 21-2   *OSPFv3 Configuration on Router A in Figure 21-3*

```
RouterA#configure terminal
RouterA(config)#ipv6 unicast-routing
RouterA(config)#ipv6 cef
RouterA(config)#ipv6 router ospf 1
RouterA(config-rtr)#router-id 10.255.255.1
```

continues

Example 21-2 *OSPFv3 Configuration on Router A in Figure 21-3 (Continued)*

```
RouterA(config-rtr)#interface fastethernet0/0
RouterA(config-if)#description Local LAN
RouterA(config-if)#ipv6 address 2001:0:1:1::2/64
RouterA(config-if)#ipv6 ospf 1 area 1
RouterA(config-if)#ipv6 ospf cost 10
RouterA(config-if)#ipv6 ospf priority 20
RouterA(config-if)#interface serial 1/0
RouterA(config-if)#description multi-point line to Internet
RouterA(config-if)#ipv6 address 2001:0:1:5::1/64
RouterA(config-if)#ipv6 ospf 1 area 0
RouterA(config-if)#ipv6 ospf priority 20
```

Router B is configured similarly. The outputs of the **show** commands in the following section are from the routers in this same network.

Verifying IPv6 and OSPFv3 Configuration

This section illustrates some of the commands used to verify IPv6 and OSPFv3.

show ipv6 route, clear ipv6, and ping ipv6 Commands

Approach troubleshooting OSPFv3 the same way that you do for OSPFv2: Start by using the **show ipv6 route** command to verify whether the expected routes are being advertised. Assuming that a route is in the routing table, test reachability to it using the **ping** [**ipv6**] *ipv6-address* command.

> **NOTE** The **ipv6** keyword in the **ping** [**ipv6**] *ipv6-address* command is optional because if the Cisco IOS recognizes that the address is an IPv6 address it will perform an IPv6 ping.

The **clear ipv6 ospf** [*process-id*] {**process** | **force-spf** | **redistribution** | **counters** [**neighbor** [*neighbor-interface* | *neighbor-id*]]} command triggers SPF recalculation and repopulation of the routing table.

Example 21-3 provides the routing table on Router A in Figure 21-3. The address of Router B's loopback interface is in this routing table, learned from Router B via the Fast Ethernet 0/0 interface. Connectivity to the loopback interface is verified with a ping.

Example 21-3 *IPv6 Routing Table on Router A in Figure 21-3*

```
RouterA#show ipv6 route
IPv6 Routing Table - 6 entries
Codes: C - Connected, L - Local, S - Static, R - RIP, B - BGP
       U - Per-user Static route
       I1 - ISIS L1, I2 - ISIS L2, IA - ISIS interarea
       O - OSPF intra, OI - OSPF inter, OE1 - OSPF ext 1, OE2 - OSPF ext 2
```

Example 21-3 *IPv6 Routing Table on Router A in Figure 21-3 (Continued)*

```
C   2001:0:1:2::/64 [0/0]
      via ::, FastEthernet0/0
L   2001:0:1:2::2/128 [0/0]
      via ::, FastEthernet0/0
OI  2001:0:1:6::/64 [110/1010]
      via FE80::213:80FF:FE63:D676, FastEthernet0/0
O   2001:0:1:FFFF::1/128 [110/10]
      via FE80::213:80FF:FE63:D676, FastEthernet0/0
L   FE80::/10 [0/0]
      via ::, Null0
L   FF00::/8 [0/0]
      via ::, Null0
RouterA#ping ipv6 2001:0:1:FFFF::1

Type escape sequence to abort.
Sending 5, 100-byte ICMP Echos to 2001:0:1:FFFF::1, timeout is 2 seconds:
!!!!!
Success rate is 100 percent (5/5), round-trip min/avg/max = 1/2/4 ms
```

show ipv6 interface Command

The **show ipv6 interface** [**brief**] [*interface-type interface-number*] [**prefix**] command displays IPv6 information about an interface, as displayed in Example 21-4.

Example 21-4 **show ipv6 interface brief** *Command Output*

```
RouterA#show ipv6 interface brief
FastEthernet0/0            [up/up]
    FE80::213:80FF:FE63:D66E
    2001:0:1:1::2
Serial1/0                  [up/down]
    FE80::213:80FF:FE63:D66E
    2001:0:1:5::1
```

show ipv6 ospf interface Command

One common reason that OSPFv3 routes may not be propagated on an interface is that the interface is not enabled for OSPFv3. A quick way to check this, as well as to get interface-specific OSPFv3 information, is with the **show ipv6 ospf interface** command. Example 21-5 demonstrates this command. The highlighted lines indicate the link-local address, area ID, and router ID.

Example 21-5 *OSPFv3 Interface Troubleshooting*

```
RouterA#show ipv6 ospf interface fa0/0
FastEthernet0/0 is up, line protocol is up
  Link Local Address FE80::213:80FF:FE63:D66E, Interface ID 2
```

continues

Example 21-5 *OSPFv3 Interface Troubleshooting (Continued)*

```
Area 1, Process ID 1, Instance ID 0, Router ID 10.255.255.1
Network Type BROADCAST, Cost: 10
Transmit Delay is 1 sec, State BDR, Priority 20
Designated Router (ID) 10.255.255.2, local address FE80::213:80FF:FE63:D676
 Backup Designated router (ID) 10.255.255.1, local address FE80::213:80FF:FE63
D66E
 Timer intervals configured, Hello 10, Dead 40, Wait 40, Retransmit 5
   Hello due in 00:00:01
 Index 1/1/2, flood queue length 0
 Next 0x0(0)/0x0(0)/0x0(0)
 Last flood scan length is 1, maximum is 2
 Last flood scan time is 0 msec, maximum is 0 msec
 Neighbor Count is 1, Adjacent neighbor count is 1
   Adjacent with neighbor 10.255.255.2  (Designated Router)
 Suppress hello for 0 neighbor(s)
```

show ipv6 ospf Command

The **show ipv6 ospf** command allows you to verify the OSPFv3 router ID and timers, as well as other general routing protocol settings. Example 21-6 provides output of this command.

Example 21-6 *OSPFv3 Protocol Troubleshooting*

```
RouterA#show ipv6 ospf
 Routing Process "ospfv3 1" with ID 10.255.255.1
 SPF schedule delay 5 secs, Hold time between two SPFs 10 secs
 Minimum LSA interval 5 secs. Minimum LSA arrival 1 secs
 LSA group pacing timer 240 secs
 Interface flood pacing timer 33 msecs
 Retransmission pacing timer 66 msecs
 Number of external LSA 0. Checksum Sum 0x000000
 Number of areas in this router is 2. 2 normal 0 stub 0 nssa
    Area BACKBONE(0) (Inactive)
        Number of interfaces in this area is 1
        SPF algorithm executed 1 times
        Number of LSA 1. Checksum Sum 0x008A7A
        Number of DCbitless LSA 0
        Number of indication LSA 0
        Number of DoNotAge LSA 0
        Flood list length 0
    Area 1
        Number of interfaces in this area is 1
        SPF algorithm executed 9 times
        Area ranges are
          2001:0:1::/80 Passive Advertise
        Number of LSA 9. Checksum Sum 0x05CCFF
        Number of DCbitless LSA 0
        Number of indication LSA 0
        Number of DoNotAge LSA 0
        Flood list length 0
```

show ipv6 ospf neighbor Command

Another important step in troubleshooting OSPFv3 is to verify that neighbor relationships have been established with the appropriate directly connected routers, using the **show ipv6 ospf neighbor [detail]** command. Sample output of this command is shown in Example 21-7.

Example 21-7 *OSPFv3 Neighbor Troubleshooting*

```
RouterA#show ipv6 ospf neighbor detail
 Neighbor 10.255.255.2
    In the area 1 via interface FastEthernet0/0
    Neighbor: interface-id 2, link-local address FE80::213:80FF:FE63:D676
    Neighbor priority is 20, State is FULL, 6 state changes
    DR is 10.255.255.2 BDR is 10.255.255.1
    Options is 0x81EA8189
    Dead timer due in 00:00:31
    Neighbor is up for 00:03:28
    Index 1/1/1, retransmission queue length 0, number of retransmission 1
    First 0x0(0)/0x0(0)/0x0(0) Next 0x0(0)/0x0(0)/0x0(0)
    Last retransmission scan length is 2, maximum is 2
    Last retransmission scan time is 0 msec, maximum is 0 msec
```

show ipv6 ospf database Command

The OSPFv3 database may be displayed using the **show ipv6 ospf database** and **show ipv6 ospf database database-summary** commands. The first command shows a list of LSAs received that may be helpful in recognizing how routes are propagated, while the second command simply provides totals for the various types of LSAs. However, troubleshooting based on this output can be difficult. Outputs from both of these commands are shown in Example 21-8.

Example 21-8 *OSPFv3 Database*

```
RouterA#show ipv6 ospf database

            OSPFv3 Router with ID (10.255.255.1) (Process ID 1)

            Router Link States (Area 0)

ADV Router      Age        Seq#        Fragment ID  Link count  Bits
10.255.255.1    799        0x80000003  0            0           None

            Link (Type-8) Link States (Area 0)

ADV Router      Age        Seq#        Link ID      Interface

            Router Link States (Area 1)

ADV Router      Age        Seq#        Fragment ID  Link count  Bits
10.255.255.1    235        0x80000008  0            1           None
10.255.255.2    240        0x80000007  0            1           B
```

continues

Example 21-8 *OSPFv3 Database (Continued)*

```
                    Net Link States (Area 1)

ADV Router      Age       Seq#        Link ID   Rtr count
10.255.255.2    946       0x80000001  2         2

              Inter Area Prefix Link States (Area 1)

ADV Router      Age       Seq#        Prefix
10.255.255.2    977       0x80000001  2001:0:1:5::/64

              Link (Type-8) Link States (Area 1)

ADV Router      Age       Seq#        Link ID   Interface
10.255.255.1    247       0x80000004  2         Fa0/0
10.255.255.2    980       0x80000002  2         Fa0/0

              Intra Area Prefix Link States (Area 1)

ADV Router      Age       Seq#        Link ID   Ref-lstype   Ref-LSID
10.255.255.2    915       0x80000002  1002      0x2002       2

RouterA#show ipv6 ospf database database-summary

          OSPFv3 Router with ID (10.255.255.1) (Process ID 1)

Area 0 database summary
  LSA Type          Count   Delete   Maxage
  Router            1       0        0
  Network           0       0        0
  Link              0       0        0
  Prefix            0       0        0
  Inter-area Prefix 0       0        0
  Inter-area Router 0       0        0
  Type-7 External   0       0        0
  Subtotal          1       0        0

Area 1 database summary
  LSA Type          Count   Delete   Maxage
  Router            2       0        0
  Network           1       0        0
  Link              2       0        0
  Prefix            1       0        0
  Inter-area Prefix 1       0        0
  Inter-area Router 0       0        0
  Type-7 External   0       0        0
  Subtotal          7       0        0
```

Example 21-8 *OSPFv3 Database (Continued)*

```
Process 1 database summary
  LSA Type            Count    Delete    Maxage
  Router              3        0         0
  Network             1        0         0
  Link                2        0         0
  Prefix              1        0         0
  Inter-area Prefix   1        0         0
  Inter-area Router   0        0         0
  Type-7 External     0        0         0
  Type-5 Ext          0        0         0
Total                 8        0         0
```

Transitioning from IPv4 to IPv6

At this point, you might be thinking that IPv6 is exciting, that it represents the future of networking, and you want to deploy it today! Reality sets in when you realize that—although you are clearly a networker of the future—today's Internet still uses IPv4. How will you communicate with the websites and e-mail servers that your business depends on?

One great solution would be to have everyone change all of their systems to IPv6 on a single day—April 1 has been suggested. Since this seems an unlikely solution, this chapter ends with some ideas about managing the transition period which, as a practical matter, may stretch out for years. Success during the transition period means integrating IPv6 nodes into your network, allowing them to communicate to IPv4 nodes, and making the whole process transparent to users.

Several transition mechanisms have been proposed, including

- Dual stack

- Tunneling

- Translation

These transition mechanisms are described in the following sections.

Dual Stack

The dual-stack approach simply means to run IPv6 and IPv4 concurrently, with no communication between the two. Hosts and routers have both IPv4 and IPv6 addresses and use whichever is appropriate to reach a given resource. If a resource, such as a server, is reachable using either protocol, IPv6 should be used.

To implement dual stack on a Cisco router, simply enable IPv6 and configure IPv4 and IPv6 interface addresses, as demonstrated in Example 21-9.

Example 21-9   *Dual-Stack Configuration*

```
RouterA#configure terminal
RouterA(config)#ipv6 unicast-routing
RouterA(config)#ipv6 cef
RouterA(config)#interface fastethernet0/0
RouterA(config-if)#ip address 192.168.0.1 255.255.255.0
RouterA(config-if)#ipv6 address 2001:0:1:1::2/64
```

The dual-stack approach allows servers, clients, and applications to be gradually moved to the new protocol. Global experience with changing applications to support IPv6 has usually resulted in minimal impact on the applications. Furthermore, running two protocols concurrently is a well-known and tested approach to protocol transition that has been used in the past; for example, it was used by many organizations switching from Internetwork Packet Exchange (IPX) to IPv4 in the 1990s.

Tunneling

Dual stack works so long as the infrastructure supports both protocols, but in some cases the core of the network will only support IPv4. Until the core is upgraded, another technique is needed, such as tunneling between IPv6 "islands."

With tunneling, routers that straddle the IPv4 and IPv6 worlds encapsulate the IPv6 traffic inside IPv4 packets. The source of the IPv4 packet is the local router and the destination is the peer router at the other end of the tunnel. When the destination router receives the IPv4 packet, it decapsulates the external IPv4 header and forwards the enclosed IPv6 traffic.

Tunneling is effective, but decreases the maximum transmission unit (MTU) because of the 20 bytes consumed by the IPv4 header on the intermediate links. Tunneling can also be difficult to troubleshoot.

Four types of tunneling are described in this section: manual, 6-to-4, Teredo, and Intra-Site Automatic Tunnel Addressing Protocol (ISATAP).

Manual Tunnels

Configuring manual tunneling is not difficult, as shown in Example 21-10 for Router A in Figure 21-4.

Figure 21-4   *Manual Tunneling*

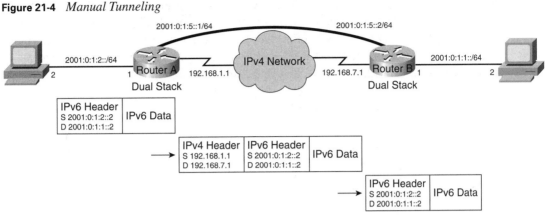

Example 21-10   *Manual Tunnel Configuration of Router A in Figure 21-4*

```
RouterA#configure terminal
RouterA(config)#interface tunnel0
RouterA(config-if)#ipv6 address 2001:0:1:5::1/64
RouterA(config-if)#tunnel source 192.168.1.1
RouterA(config-if)#tunnel destination 192.168.7.1
RouterA(config-if)#tunnel mode ipv6ip
```

The **tunnel mode ipv6ip** command specifies that the manual IPv6 tunnel has IPv6 as the passenger protocol and IPv4 as both the encapsulation and transport protocols.

> **NOTE**   The **show interface tunnel** command shows the details of the tunnel interface; the **clear counters tunnel** *interface-number* command clears the counters displayed in the **show interface tunnel** command.

Tunneling also works between a PC and a router. For instance, a dual-stack workstation can send tunneled traffic that is removed from the tunnel by the router it is communicating with.

IPv6-to-IPv4 (6-to-4) Tunnels

A 6-to-4 tunnel works similarly to a manual tunnel, except that the tunnel is set up automatically. 6-to-4 tunnels use IPv6 addresses that concatenate 2002::/16 with the 32-bit IPv4 address of the edge router, creating a 48-bit prefix.

An example of 6-to-4 tunneling is shown in Figure 21-5. The tunnel interface on Router A has an IPv6 prefix of 2002:C0A8:501::/48, where C0A8:501 is the hexadecimal equivalent of 192.168.5.1, the IPv4 address of its interface in the IPv4 network. The tunnel interface on Router B has an IPv6 prefix of 2002:C0A8:122::/48, where C0A8:122 is the hexadecimal equivalent of 192.168.1.34, the IPv4 address of its interface in the IPv4 network. Note that the prefixes are subnetted appropriately on each side of the tunnel and each router has a static route across the tunnel to the prefix of the other router. When Router A receives traffic with an IPv6 destination address of 2002:C0A8:122:1::2, the following occurs:

1. Router A extracts the IPv4 address from the IPv6 address. In this case, the IPv4 address is C0.A8.01.22, which in dotted decimal format is 192.168.1.34.

2. Router A encapsulates the IPv6 packet in an IPv4 packet with a destination address of 192.168.1.34; the packet is routed normally through the IPv4 network to Router B.

3. Router B receives the IPv4 packet, decapsulates the IPv6 packet, and routes it normally to its final IPv6 destination.

Figure 21-5 *6-to-4 Tunneling*

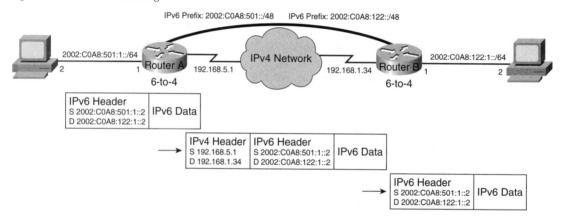

Teredo

Another type of tunnel is called Teredo (also known as *shipworm*). Teredo encapsulates IPv6 packets in IPv4/UDP segments and works similarly to other tunnels but with the added benefit of being able to traverse network address translation (NAT) devices and firewalls. Teredo is described in RFC 4380, *Teredo: Tunneling IPv6 over UDP through Network Address Translations (NAT)*.

ISATAP

ISATAP treats the IPv4 network as an NBMA network and allows an IPv4 private network to incrementally implement IPv6 without upgrading the network. ISATAP is documented in RFC 4214, *Intra-Site Automatic Tunnel Addressing Protocol (ISATAP)*.

Translation

The problem with tunneling, whether manually or automatically configured, is that it is a dual-stack solution. IPv6 clients must continue to support IPv4 to contact IPv4-only devices.

Translation is a different type of solution, allowing IPv6 devices to communicate with IPv4 devices, without requiring either to be dual stack.

Stateless IP/ICMP Translation (SIIT) translates IP header fields, and NAT Protocol Translation (NAT-PT) maps IPv6 addresses to IPv4 addresses. If IPv6 is used on the inside of a network and IPv4 is used on the outside, a NAT-PT device receives IPv6 traffic on its inside interface and replaces the IPv6 header with an IPv4 header before sending it to an outside interface. Reply traffic follows the mapping backwards, enabling two-way communication.

Good NAT implementations interpret application traffic and understand when IP information is included in the application data; NAT-PT inherits this capability. For example, DNS packets include IP addresses; therefore, NAT-PT must recognize DNS traffic and change the IPv4 addresses into IPv6 addresses, and vice-versa.

IPv4 and IPv6 routing domains can also be connected using application-level gateways (ALG) or proxies. A proxy intercepts traffic and converts between the two protocols; it can increase the transmission speed by responding to some requests using information in its cache. A separate ALG is required to support each protocol, so this method only solves specific types of translation problems.

Bump-in-the-API (BIA) and Bump-in-the-Stack (BIS) are NAT-PT implementations within a host. BIA/BIS intercepts system calls to IPv4 functions and dynamically responds with IPv6 information, allowing, for example, a server to be converted to IPv6 without rewriting applications. This approach will not work, however, for applications that embed IP addresses in the payload, such as the file transfer protocol (FTP).

Foundation Summary

The Foundation Summary provides a convenient review of many key concepts in this chapter. If you are already comfortable with the topics in this chapter, this summary might help you recall a few details. If you just read this chapter, this review should help solidify some key facts. If you are doing your final prep before the exam, the following lists, tables, and figures are a convenient way to review the day before the exam.

IPv6 supports the following routing methods:

- Static routes

- RIPng

- EIGRP for IPv6

- IS-IS for IPv6

- MP-BGP4

- OSPFv3

OSPFv3 shares the following features with OSPFv2:

- Link-state (uses SPF algorithm, areas, hellos, LSAs, DBDs, and LSDB)

- Packet types, method to form neighbor relationships, and NBMA topology support

- Stub area support

OSPFv3 is different from OSPFv2 in many ways, including the following:

- Has 128-bit prefix support and runs within IPv6 packets; however, still uses 32-bit router ID, area ID, and link-state ID

- Uses multicast addresses FF02::5 and FF02::6

- Uses *links* rather than *subnets*; uses link-local address as source address

- Has a 16-byte packet header; authentication not built-in, uses IPv6 extension headers instead

- Has support for multiple instances

OSPFv3 LSA types 1 and 2 no longer contain route prefixes, instead they contain 32-bit IDs. Types 3 and 4 have been renamed but still fulfill the same functions as they do in OSPFv2. Types 8 and 9 are new LSAs in OSPFv3.

Table 21-3 summarizes the IPv6 and OPSFv3 configuration commands covered in this chapter.

Table 21-3 *IPv6 and OSPFv3 Configuration Commands Covered in This Chapter*

Command	Function
Router(config)# **ipv6 route** *ipv6-prefix/prefix-length* { *ipv6-address* | *interface-type interface-number* [*ipv6-address*]} [*administrative-distance*] [*administrative-multicast-distance* | **unicast** | **multicast**] [*next-hop-address*] [**tag** tag]	Creates an IPv6 static route.
Router(config)#**ipv6 unicast-routing**	Enables IPv6.
Router(config)#**ipv6 cef**	Enables CEFv6.
Router(config-if)#**ipv6 address** *ipv6-prefix/ prefix-length* [**eui-64**]	Assigns an IPv6 address to an interface.
Router(config)#**ipv6 router ospf** *process-id*	Creates an OSPFv3 process.
Router(config-rtr)#**router-id** *32-bit-router-id*	Assigns a 32-bit router ID, in an IPv4-address dotted decimal format.
Router(config-rtr)#**area** *area-id* **range** *summary-range/prefix-length* [**advertise** | **not-advertise**] [**cost** *cost*]	Summarizes an area into another area.
Router(config-if)#**ipv6 ospf** *process-id* **area** *area-id* [**instance** *instance-id*]	Assigns an interface to an OSPFv3 area.
Router(config-if)#**ipv6 ospf priority** *priority*	Changes the OSPF priority from its default of 1.
Router(config-if)#**ipv6 ospf cost** *interface-cost*	Changes the OSPF default cost.

Table 21-4 summarizes the IPv6 and OPSFv3 verification commands covered in this chapter.

Table 21-4 *IPv6 and OSPFv3 Verification Commands Covered in This Chapter*

Command	Function
show ipv6 route	Displays the IPv6 routing table.
ping [ipv6] *ipv6-address*	Pings an IPv6 address.

continues

Table 21-4 *IPv6 and OSPFv3 Verification Commands Covered in This Chapter (Continued)*

Command	Function
clear ipv6 ospf [*process-id*] {**process** l **force-spf** l **redistribution** l **counters** [**neighbor** [*neighbor-interface* l *neighbor-id*]]}	Triggers SPF recalculation and repopulation of the routing table.
show ipv6 interface [**brief**] [*interface-type interface-number*] [**prefix**]	Displays IPv6 information about an interface.
show ipv6 ospf interface	Displays interface-specific OSPFv3 information.
show ipv6 ospf	Displays the OSPFv3 router ID and timers, as well as other general routing protocol settings.
show ipv6 ospf neighbor [**detail**]	Displays OSPFv3 neighbor information.
show ipv6 ospf database [**database-summary**]	Displays OSPFv3 database.

There are several transition mechanisms from IPv4 to IPv6:

- **Dual Stack**—Dual stack simply means to run IPv6 and IPv4 concurrently, with no communication between the two.

- **Tunneling**—With tunneling, routers that straddle the IPv4 and IPv6 worlds encapsulate the IPv6 traffic inside IPv4 packets. Four types of tunneling are described in this chapter: manual, 6-to-4, ISATAP, and Teredo.

- **Translation**—Translation allows IPv6 devices to communicate with IPv4 devices, without requiring either to be dual stack. SIIT translates IP header fields, and NAT-PT maps IPv6 addresses to IPv4 addresses.

Q&A

The questions and scenarios in this book are designed to be challenging and to make sure that you know the answer. Rather than allowing you to derive the answers from clues hidden inside the questions themselves, the questions challenge your understanding and recall of the subject.

You can find the answers to these questions in Appendix A. For more practice with exam-like question formats, use the exam engine on the CD-ROM.

1. List the IPv6 routing protocols.

2. What algorithm is used by OSPFv3 to determine routes?

3. What address is used as the source addresses in an OSPFv3 hello packet?

4. What are some of the differences between OSPFv2 and OSPFv3?

5. What is the difference between an OSPFv3 type 1 LSA and a type 9 LSA?

6. What is the default interface priority for OSPFv3?

7. A router has two interfaces. Write the configuration commands so that the IPv6 address on the Fast Ethernet 0/0 interface is 2001:0:1:1::2/64, the IPv6 address on the Serial 1/0 interface is 2001:0:1:5::1/64, the router ID is 10.255.255.1, and both interfaces are running OSPFv3 in area 1.

8. How is an OSPFv3 router ID configured?

9. How are OSPFv3 areas assigned?

10. Which command can be used to verify that two OSPFv3 neighbors see each other?

11. What are the mechanisms available for IPv4 to IPv6 transition?

12. A router has two interfaces. Write the commands required to configure the router to support dual stack using the following addresses:

   ■ Fast Ethernet 0/0 has addresses 2001:1:A:ABCD::1/64 and 192.168.0.1/24.

   ■ Fast Ethernet 0/1 has addresses 2001:1:A:FEDC::1/64 and 192.168.254.1/24.

13. What is the 6-to-4 prefix of a router with the IPv4 address 172.20.64.192?

14. What is NAT-PT and how does it differ from NAT?

Scenarios

The following scenario and questions are designed to draw together the content of the chapter and exercise your understanding of the concepts. There is not necessarily a right answer. The thought process and practice in manipulating the concepts is the goal of this section. The answers to the scenario questions are found at the end of this chapter.

Scenario 21-1

In Scenario 20-1, you assigned IPv6 addresses to a network. Figure 21-6 illustrates the network diagram and possible subnet assignments. In this scenario, provide the configuration commands to implement IPv6 and OSPFv3 in this network, using your address assignments.

Figure 21-6 *IPv6 Network Subnet Assignments*

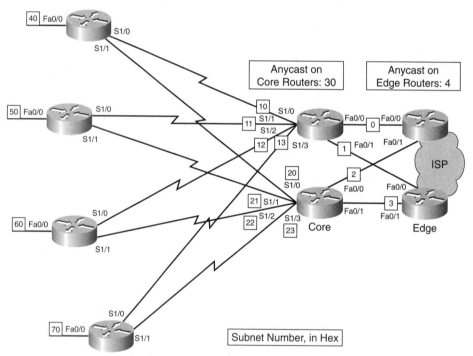

Scenario 21-1 Answers

Example 21-11 provides a sample configuration for the top core router, using the subnet assignments in Figure 21-6 (as explained in Chapter 20).

Example 21-11   *IPv6 Configuration of Top Core Router in Figure 21-6*

```
ipv6 unicast-routing
ipv6 cef
ipv6 router ospf 1
  router-id 10.255.255.1
interface serial 1/0
  ipv6 address 2001:1BE0:03A0:0010::1/64
  ipv6 address 2001:1BE0:03A0:0030::1/64 anycast
  ipv6 ospf 1 area 0
interface serial 1/1
  ipv6 address 2001:1BE0:03A0:0011::1/64
  ipv6 address 2001:1BE0:03A0:0030::1/64 anycast
  ipv6 ospf 1 area 0
interface serial 1/2
  ipv6 address 2001:1BE0:03A0:0012::1/64
  ipv6 address 2001:1BE0:03A0:0030::1/64 anycast
  ipv6 ospf 1 area 0
interface serial 1/3
  ipv6 address 2001:1BE0:03A0:0013::1/64
  ipv6 address 2001:1BE0:03A0:0030::1/64 anycast
  ipv6 ospf 1 area 0
interface fastethernet 0/0
  ipv6 address 2001:1BE0:03A0:0000::1/64
  ipv6 ospf 1 area 0
interface fastethernet 0/1
  ipv6 address 2001:1BE0:03A0:0001::1/64
  ipv6 ospf 1 area 0
```

Answers to Chapter "Do I Know This Already?" Quizzes and Q&A Sections

Chapter 1

"Do I Know This Already?"

1. B
2. B
3. B
4. C
5. B
6. A
7. D
8. A
9. C
10. D
11. C and D
12. B, C, D

Q&A

1. Access devices are responsible for attaching end systems to the network and assigning them to virtual LANs (VLAN).

   Distribution devices are Layer 3 switches and act as intermediate devices that route between VLANs and apply traffic policies such as firewalling and QoS decisions.

   Core devices, also known as the backbone, provide high-speed paths between distribution elements.

2. The enterprise campus features five sections:

    — Campus backbone (such as the core layer of the hierarchical model)

    — Building distribution

    — Building access

    — Management (overlaid resources to maintain the network)

    — Server farm (for enterprise services)

3. The enterprise campus specifically calls out and describes management. The server farm describes how enterprise servers are housed, where previously there was not a standard place to put servers.

4. The enterprise edge details the connections from the campus to the wide area.

    — E-commerce

    — Internet connectivity

    — Remote access (dial and VPN)

    — WAN (internal links)

5. $(7*6)/2 = 21$

6. 6

7. A network policy is implemented at the distribution level in the hierarchical design model.

8. The two have few differences. A server farm is a standard switch block, but servers are usually dual-homed to two access switches.

9. A "converged" network is a design that includes support for traditional data applications as well as newer voice and video uses.

10. IIN describes a vision of a network that integrates network and application functionality cooperatively and allows the network to be smart about how it handles traffic to minimize the footprint of applications.

    SONA is the use of IIN in an enterprise environment.

    AON is application-oriented networking (AON) blades that make the network "application aware."

11. SONA (Services-Oriented Network Architecture) is the application of the IIN ideas to Enterprise networks—those ideas being to develop a solid converged network foundation and then to build up application services on that. SONA breaks down the IIN functions into three layers:

    — Network Infrastructure, which describes a hierarchical converged network and the attached end-systems.

— Interactive Services, which allocates resources to applications.

— Application, which includes business policy and logic integration

12. OSPF, EIGRP, and IS-IS

13. Classful routing protocols communicate a prefix. The associated mask is assumed.

14. All three protocols are wholly acceptable; however, there are some small differences between them from a support perspective.

OSPF is a public standard, and is therefore supported on a wide variety of equipment. This protects against incompatibilities with legacy equipment or "vendor lock-in." On the other hand, OSPF networks are complicated to build and maintain.

IS-IS, like OSPF, is a public standard. IS-IS, however, is not as commonly supported and finding equipment and personnel to support it can be challenging. Also, because it is not as commonly used, development of IS-IS has stagnated and it is not as feature-rich as OSPF.

EIGRP is the easiest to configure of the three, doing many smart things automatically. EIGRP, however, is a Cisco proprietary protocol and using it locks you in to Cisco equipment.

Obviously, different organizations will weigh factors such as ease of use and public standards. The "best" protocol is the one that is most appropriate for a given situation.

Chapter 2

"Do I Know This Already?"

1. B

2. C

3. A

4. B

5. A

6. C

7. C

8. A

9. C

10. C

11. D

Q&A

1. 181 = 1011 0101

   202 = 1100 1010

   152 = 1001 1000

   109 = 0110 1101

2. 10101111 = 175

   10000001 = 129

   00111100 = 60

   01001001 = 73

3. 1100 0000 . 1010 1000 . 0000 0000 . 0000 0001

4. 12.150.146.181 is Class A, 150.159.216.202 is Class B, 209.209.158.152 is Class C, and 224.137.116.109 is Class D (Multicast)

5. A (255.0.0.0), B (255.255.0.0), C (255.255.255.0)

6. /24 includes 32–24 = 8 host bits. 28–2 = 254 host addresses.

   /27 has 5 host bits, for 30 host addresses

   /20 has 12 host bits, or 4094 host addresses.

7. 24.177.78.62/27 includes 24.177.78.33–63

   135.159.211.109/19 includes 135.159.192.1–135.159.223.254

   207.87.193.1/30 includes 207.87.193.1 and 2.

8. 192.168.160.0/21

9. 172.30.31.0/24, 172.30.32.0/22, 172.30.36.0/23, 172.30.38.0/24

10. Answer:

    ■ Hides network details and protects against flaps

    ■ Reduces router CPU and memory consumption

    ■ Saves network capacity

Chapter 3

"Do I Know This Already?"

1. B

2. A and B

3.   A and D

4.   A and D

5.   B and C

6.   A

7.   D

8.   D

9.   B

10. C and D

11. A

12. C

13. A, B, C, D

Q&A

1.   If the router does not have a feasible successor in its topology table, it sends a query packet to its neighbors asking whether they have a feasible successor.

2.   The timers that the neighbor table keeps track of are the holdtime, the SRTT, and the RTO.

3.   An update is the routing information packet that a router will send out to inform its neighbors of a change in the network. In a query, the router has no feasible successor in its topology table for a network that is down. At this point, it queries its neighbors to ascertain whether they have a feasible successor. If they do, this route becomes the feasible successor for the original router.

4.   EIGRP recalculates the topology table whenever it receives a change input to the topology table. This could be a change of metric for a physically connected link; a change of status of a physically connected link; or an EIGRP routing packet—either an update, a query, or a reply packet.

5.   The rules for scaling an EIGRP network include the following:

   ■ Addresses should be summarized.

   ■ A hierarchical tiered network design should be used to allow summarization.

   ■ Sufficient network resources (both hardware and software) should be used on network devices.

   ■ Sufficient bandwidth should be used on WAN links.

   ■ Appropriate EIGRP configuration should be used on WAN links.

- Filters should be used.

- Network monitoring should be used.

6. The packets that EIGRP sends reliably are updates, queries, and replies. EIGRP uses RTP. This is necessary because EIGRP does not send out periodic updates, and the RTP mechanism ensures a loop-free synchronized network.

7. The holdtime is three times the Hello timer. The holdtime is 15 seconds on a LAN or 180 seconds on a low-speed WAN.

8. The topology table contains all links received with a metric other than infinity, in other words, every valid path. The topology table does not include all links because of split horizon. The topology table holds the metric for every path along with the metric from the next logical hop or neighbor. The table contains the outgoing interface on the router through which to reach the remote network and the IP address of the next-hop address. The status of the route (passive or active) is also recorded. The topology table also keeps track of the routing protocol packets that have been sent to the neighbors.

9. Advertised distance is the metric that is reported by the neighbor routers. Feasible distance is the metric that is reported by neighbor routers, plus the cost associated with the forwarding link from the local interface to the neighbor routers.

10. The Diffusing Update Algorithm (DUAL) is run on the topology table. It is used to determine the best path and to build the routing table.

11. EIGRP places a network into active mode when there is no feasible successor in its topology table.

12. By default, EIGRP summarizes at the classful network boundary.

13. Stuck in Active (SIA) is a state in which a router will place a route after it has failed to hear a reply to a query that was sent to a neighbor.

    EIGRP sends a query when a route is lost and another feasible route does not exist in the topology table. The SIA is caused by two sequential events: First, a route has gone away. Second, an EIGRP neighbor (or neighbors) has not replied to the query for that route. When the SIA occurs, the router removes the neighbor that has not replied to the query from the neighbor table.

14. A hierarchical tiered design and summarization are both critical to being able to scale an EIGRP network. If these are in place, it is possible to summarize the network, which reduces the network resources needed for large tables and limits the query range of the router.

    It is also important to ensure that the router has sufficient memory, the network has sufficient bandwidth on its WAN links, and, where appropriate, the bandwidth command has been configured.

15.   The reply packet is used to update the topology table. It is a response to a query sent out by a neighbor asking about suspect routes.

16.   To become a neighbor, the following conditions must be met:

■   The router must hear a Hello packet or an ACK from a neighbor.

■   The autonomous system number in the packet header must be the same as that of the receiving router.

■   The neighbor's K-values must be the same as that of the receiving router.

Chapter 4

"Do I Know This Already?"

1.   B

2.   A

3.   B

4.   D

5.   B

6.   C

7.   D

8.   B

9.   A

10.   A, B, C, D

11.   C

12.   B

Q&A

1.   The **passive-interface** *interface* command prevents EIGRP from speaking on an interface. If it cannot speak, it cannot form neighbors. In the example, **passive-interface serial0/0** would prevent the serial interface from being involved in EIGRP.

A second way to limit EIGRP interfaces is to use the **network** *network wildcard-mask* to specify the interface that should run. In the example, network 10.1.1.1. 0.0.0.0 would limit EIGRP to fastethernet 0/0.

2. The preferred configuration for a hybrid multipoint NBMA network, in which one circuit is lower than the other circuits, is to create a point-to-point subinterface for the lower circuit and then to configure the bandwidth to reflect the CIR of the link. Another subinterface should be created as a multipoint interface with a configured bandwidth that equals the aggregate CIR of all the circuits—in this instance, 5 * 256 kbps, or 1280 kbps. An alternative solution is to configure each PVC as a point-to-point link.

3. EIGRP will assume each PVC is 56 kbps because it divides bandwidth evenly between PVCs on a multipoint interface. By default, EIGRP will limit advertisements to half that (28 kbps).

4. The command **no auto-summary** is used to turn off automatic summarization, which EIGRP applies at classful network boundaries. With automatic summarization off, manual summarization can still be used to summarize appropriately.

5. The **ip bandwidth-percent eigrp 63 100** command overrides the default bandwidth of 50 percent that is allocated to EIGRP for network overhead. This command sets the bandwidth allocation to be 100 percent of the link for the EIGRP autonomous system of 63 on the interface upon which it is configured. This command would be used if the **bandwidth** command had set the logical bandwidth of the link to be artificially low.

6. The hold time is three times the hello timer. The hold time is 15 seconds or 180 seconds, depending on the medium.

7. The **variance** command is used to determine additional paths to be included in load-balancing traffic to remote networks. The command is used in conjunction with the multiplier number. This number multiplies the path with the best (lowest) metric by the number stated as the multiplier. Any paths that the router knows of that have a metric value equal to or less than this value are included in the paths for load balancing. The amount of traffic sent across each path will be proportional to the metric value of the path.

8. The command **show ip eigrp topology** shows the passive and active state of the routes that are contained in the table. The route is passive if the route is operational; it is set in an active state if the router must query its neighbors for alternative paths to a network. This command also shows the number of successors and the neighbors and distance information.

9. The interface command **ip summary-address eigrp** *autonomous-system-number address mask* is used to define the summary address to be used.

10. The command **debug eigrp packet** displays the types of EIGRP packets that are both sent and received by the router.

11. Summarization reduces the amount of resources needed by both the network and the routers within the network. Summarization limits advertisements, minimizes the size of advertisements, and optimizes routing table lookups and recalculations. It also reduces the scope of the queries sent out by a router.

12. The stub configuration is typically used on small-capacity routers in a hub-and-spoke WAN environment. The router has a limited set of neighbors and does not need to be involved in convergence. It is not necessary, therefore, for this remote router to have a complete routing table that might overwhelm its limited resources. The remote router needs only a default route to the distribution router that can serve all its needs.

    Another reason to configure the remote router as a stub is to optimize queries in the network. When a query is sent to a stub router, the router will immediately respond, thus accelerating the process.

13. Descriptions of the parameters are listed in the following table.

Parameter	Description
connected	(Optional) Advertises connected routes
summary	(Optional) Advertises summary routes

14. Any feasible successor in the topology table can be used in the **variance** command.

15. The command **ip eigrp hello-interval** *timer* is typically used to decrease the time between hellos to ensure that the network is more stable and converges more quickly. Although this increases the amount of bandwidth consumed, it is a minimal cost. It becomes very useful in WANs, particularly when NBMA clouds are used. NBMA technologies (such as Frame Relay) assume a low bandwidth medium (less than T1 speeds) and set the hello timer to 60 seconds by default.

16. EIGRP will assume that bandwidth is evenly distributed between PVCs on a multipoint interface. The bandwidth command serves two purposes in this situation—it is used as part of the EIGRP metric and it is used to determine how much traffic EIGRP will send over an interface. Generally, the best way to configure this interface is to take the slowest PVC and multiply it by the number of PVCs. In this case 5 * 56 = 280. A better solution would be to divide the PVCs into separate subinterfaces.

    Another solution is to configure many subinterfaces, each with a point-to-point link.

17. If the multipoint network has differing speeds allocated to the VCs, it is much easier to configure and manage an environment that has used subinterfaces, where a VC is logically treated as if it were a separate interface or point-to-point. The **bandwidth** command can be configured on each subinterface, which allows different speeds on each VC. In this second solution, subinterfaces are configured for the links with the differing CIRs. The links that have the same configured CIR are presented as a single subinterface with a bandwidth, which reflects the aggregate CIR of all the circuits. Cisco recommends this as the preferred solution.

Chapter 5

"Do I Know This Already?"

1. D

2. B

3. C

4. D

5. B

6. B

7. A

8. A

9. C

10. C

11. A and B

12. D

13. D

14. A

Q&A

1. The **ip ospf priority** *number* command is used to determine the DR manually. The higher the priority, the greater the likelihood of winning the DR election.

2. By default, the OSPF metric is calculated as 100,000,000 bps divided by the speed of the line. For instance, a 10 Mbps Ethernet interface has a cost of 10 and a 1.544 Mbps T1 interface has a cost of 64.

3. To have more than one OSPF process on a router, simply identify two separate processes. For example:

   router ospf 1

   router ospf 2

   You might do this to create two different domains with separate routing policies.

4. Answer:

```
network 192.100.56.10 0.0.0.0 area 0
network 192.100.56.8 0.0.0.7 area 0
network 192.100.56.0.0 0.0.0.255 area 0
network 192.100.56.0 0.0.7.255 area 0
```

5. The most straightforward way to change the metric on an interface is to set the cost:

   ```
   Router(config-if)# ip ospf cost cost
   ```

   Cost is a 16-bit value (0 to 65,535) and lower values are preferred. A second way to deal with high-bandwidth paths is to change the numerator in the automatic calculation.

   ```
   Router(config-if)# ip ospf auto-cost reference-bandwidth reference-
       bandwidth
   ```

6. **show ip ospf neighbor** or **show ip ospf interface**

7. The **show ip ospf database** command displays the contents of the router's topological database and the different LSAs that have populated the database

8. **show ip ospf neighbor**

9. **debug ip packet**

10. Process ID is shown by a number of commands, including

    show ip ospf

    show ip ospf database

    show ip ospf interface

11. LSAs are labeled with sequence numbers so that they can be distinguished from each other. LSAs are marked with sequence numbers so that older or newer versions of an advertisement can be recognized. LSA sequence numbers start at 0x8000 0001 and iterate to 0xFFFF FFFF before wrapping back around to 0x0000 00000.

12. The field specifies how long to wait to start SPF after receiving an LSA to prevent running SPF too often. The default time is 5000 msec.

13. The **show ip ospf interface** command allows you to verify that a given interface is active in OSPF, verify its area, and look at the DR and BDR.

Chapter 6

"Do I Know This Already?"

1. B

2. C

3. D

4. C

5. A and D

6. True

7. D

8. A

9. C

10. A and C

11. B

12. A

Q&A

1. Answer:

   ```
   Router(config-if)#ip ospf network point-to-multipoint broadcast
   ```

   The broadcast option is a default, not a keyword option.

2. The **ip ospf priority** *number* command is used to determine the DR manually. The higher the priority is, the greater the likelihood of success.

3. It is necessary to have one subnet per connection. Thus, if there are four point-to-point links, four subnets are required.

4. The **ip ospf network point-to-multipoint non-broadcast** command was introduced with Cisco IOS Release 11.3a. You can find more information online at Cisco.com by searching for "OSPF point-to-multipoint network with separate costs per neighbor." This feature was added to support customers using point-to-multipoint on nonbroadcast media, such as classic IP over ATM.

5. The syntax of the **neighbor** command is

   ```
   Router(config-if)#neighbor ip-address [priority number ] [poll-interval sec]
       [cost number]
   ```

6. Multiaccess topologies, such as those found in NBMA and broadcast OSPF network types, rely on DRs and so are best applied to full-mesh topologies. If the topology is not a full mesh, then the DR should be manually selected, using priorities, to be a router with permanent virtual circuits (PVCs) connecting to all other routers.

7. 4—30/120 (NBMA, point-to-multipoint) or 10/40 (broadcast and point-to-point)

8. The configuration options proprietary to Cisco for NBMA are

   - Point-to-multipoint nonbroadcast

   - Broadcast

   - Point-to-point

9. In a point-to-point network, the concept of multicast is not relevant because the communication is direct to another router. There is very little network overhead. An IP subnet is required for each point-to point link.

   With multipoint interfaces, OSPF network traffic is replicated and sent down each PVC.

10. The default OSPF network type for serial interfaces is nonbroadcast multiaccess.

Chapter 7

"Do I Know This Already?"

1. C

2. C

3. B

4. D

5. D

6. C

7. A and E

8. D

9. B

10. A

11. A

12. A

13. A and D

14. A and D

15. A

16. B

17. A

18. A

19. D

20. D

21. B

22. A and C

23. A, B, D

Q&A

1. There will be no summary or external routes propagated by the ABR into the area. Thus, there will be no Type 3, Type 4, or Type 5 LSAs sent into the other area.

2. No, a virtual link cannot contain a stub area. A stub area cannot accept external LSAs, and by definition, the virtual link is traversing a different area.

3. An ABR must be resident in Area 0, as well as in the area that is connecting to the backbone area. It has two topological databases, one for each area in which it is resident, so that it knows how to forward traffic.

4. The ABR forwards summary LSAs. It forwards both Type 3 LSAs and Type 4 LSAs. Type 3 LSAs are forwarded to the other ABRs, and Type 4 LSAs are forwarded to the ASBRs. ABR also forwards Type 3 LSAs from other areas into its own area. If the ABR has multiple links in the same area, it also forwards Type 1 and Type 2 LSAs in its capacity as an internal router.

5. The advantages in creating areas in OSPF include the following:

   ■ It is easier to manage and administrate smaller areas, where hopefully many of the design considerations, and even configuration, are standardized.

   ■ It uses a smaller topology table, which reduces the CPU, memory, and network bandwidth consumption.

   ■ Fewer SPF calculations are involved because the topology table is smaller and there is less likelihood of change in the network.

   ■ It uses a smaller routing table if summarization is in operation.

   ■ Convergence is faster with smaller areas.

6. An external route is a route that did not originate in the OSPF domain. It has been redistributed from another routing protocol or static routing. An external route is introduced into the OSPF domain by an ASBR.

7. Summarization is important in the design of OSPF because it supports a hierarchical design and allows for the summarization of IP subnets between areas, which reduces the size of the routing tables, which in turn reduces the CPU and memory requirements. It also speeds convergence.

8. 40–80

9. Some restrictions govern creating a stub or totally stubby area. The following restrictions are in place:

- No external routes are allowed.

- No virtual links are allowed.

- No redistribution is allowed.

- No ASBR routers are allowed.

- The area is not the backbone area.

- All the routers are configured to be stub routers.

10. The virtual link provides a disconnected area with a logical path to the backbone. The virtual link must be established between two ABRs that have a common area, with one ABR connected to the backbone. It can also be used to connect two Area 0s together. This might be necessary when two companies merge, each with its own Area 0, or if, due to the loss of a link, the Area 0 becomes bisected.

11. Having a Frame Relay NBMA cloud within one OSPF area causes summary LSAs to be flooded throughout the NBMA network. This results in a large number of routers recalculating whenever there is a change that requires the topology table to be updated, and the Frame Relay cloud can become saturated. If the Frame Relay cloud has a problem, the entire network could suffer.

12. One advantage of this design is that any flooding of external LSAs is prevented from entering the Frame Relay network, because it is a stub network. This reduces the network overhead.

13. The number of SPF calculations is reduced because the size of the topology table is reduced. This lessens the likelihood of a change in the network and, thus, SPF calculations.

14. A stub area differs from the backbone area in that it does not propagate external routes into its area. The backbone is obliged to forward these LSAs to ensure connectivity throughout the network.

15. A totally stubby area differs from a stub area in that it propagates neither external routes nor summary routes from other areas. This is a Cisco solution to minimize the amount of CPU and memory required of the routers within the area. Interarea connectivity is achieved through the use of default routes, which are advertised to the internal routers (intra-area connectivity is handled as usual).

16. The different LSA update types are as follows:

   - **Router link**—Sent by the router, stating the links directly connected. These are flooded through the area. This update is identified by the type code Type 1.

   - **Network link**—Sent by the DR, stating the links for the LAN for which it is the DR. These LSAs are flooded throughout the area. This update is identified by the type code Type 2.

   - **Network summary link**—Sent by the ABR into the backbone, stating the IP subnets within the area that are to be advertised into other areas. This is where summarization would be configured. This update is identified by the type code Type 3.

   - **AS external ASBR summary link**—Sent from an ABR to a router that connects to the outside world (ASBR). It contains the metric cost from the ABR to the ASBR. This update is identified by the type code Type 4.

   - **External link**—Sent to the ASBRs to which the organization is directly connected. This update is identified by the type code Type 5.

   - **NSSA External LSA**—These LSAs are created by the ASBR residing in an NSSA. This LSA is similar to an autonomous system external LSA, except that this LSA is contained within the NSSA area and is not propagated into other areas.

17. OSPF has special restrictions when multiple areas are involved. If more than one area is configured, one of these areas must be Area 0. This is called the backbone. When designing networks, it is good practice to start with Area 0 and then expand into other areas later.

   The backbone must be at the center of all other areas—that is, all areas must be physically connected to the backbone. The reasoning behind this is that OSPF expects all areas to inject routing information into the backbone; in turn, the backbone will disseminate that information into other areas.

18. The two types of summarization are as follows:

   - **Interarea route summarization**—These routes are sent between areas. The ABR will summarize routes if the network within the area was designed using contiguous addresses, conforming to both a physical and a logical hierarchy.

   - **External route summarization**—These are routes sent into OSPF from another routing protocol. This summarization also demands a hierarchical design using contiguous addresses. This is employed at the ASBR.

19. The ABR creates the LSA Types 3 and 4.

20. The command **show ip ospf** *[process-id area-id]* **database network** displays the network link-state information.

21. The command **area** *area-id* **stub no-summary** will create a totally stubby area. This is a subcommand to the **router ospf** *process-id* command. The command is necessary only on the ABR, but all the other routers in the area must be configured as stub routers.

22. A virtual link is a link that creates a tunnel through an area to the backbone (Area 0). This allows an area that cannot connect directly to the backbone to connect virtually. The command to create the link is **area** *area-id* **virtual-link** *router-id*. Note that the *area-id* that is supplied is that of the transit area, and the *router-id* is that of the router at the other end of the link. The command needs to be configured at both ends of the tunnel.

23. Summarization is done at area boundaries. The command to start summarization is the **area range** command, with the syntax **area** *area-id* **range** *address mask*. To summarize external routes, use the **summary-address** command on the ASBRs.

24. The command **summary-address** *address mask* is the command that you would use to summarize external routes before injecting them into the OSPF domain.

A virtual link is used when an area is not directly attached to the backbone area (Area 0). This may be due to poor design and a lack of understanding about the operation of OSPF, or it may be due to a link failure. The most common cause of an area separating from the backbone is link failure, which can also cause the backbone to be segmented. In these instances, the virtual link is used to join the two backbone areas together. Segmented backbone areas might also result from two companies merging.

25. The command to define the cost of a default route propagated into another area is **area** *area-id* **default-cost** *cost*.

26. It is appropriate to define a default cost for the default route when a stub area has more than one ABR. This command allows the ABR, or exit point for the area, to be determined by the network administrator. If this link or the ABR fails, the other ABR will become the exit point for the area.

27. The default cost for the default route is defined on the ABR. The ABR will then automatically generate and advertise the route cost along with the default route.

28. The command syntax to configure a stub area is **area** *area-id* **stub**. This command is configured on the ABR connecting to the area and on all the routers within the area. Once the configuration is completed, the hellos are generated with the E bit set to 0. All routers in the area will only form adjacencies with other routers that have the E bit set.

29. The **area range** command is configured on the ABR because it dictates the networks that will be advertised out of the area. It is used to consolidate and summarize the routes at an area boundary.

30. The commands are as follows:

network 144.111.248.0 0.0.7.255 area 1

network 0.0.0.0 255.255.255.255 area 0

31. The syntax is as follows:

summary-address 144.111.248.0 255.255.248.0

32. The **area range** command is used to summarize networks between areas and is configured on the ABR. The **summary-address** command is used to summarize external networks on an ASBR into the OSPF routing domain.

33. The command **area 1 stub no-summary** creates a totally stubby area. The number after the word *area* indicates the area that is being defined as a totally stubby area. This is necessary because the router might be an ABR with connections to many areas. Once this command is issued, it prevents summarized and external routes from being propagated by the ABR into the area. To reach the networks and hosts outside the area, routers must use the default route advertised by the ABR into the area.

34. The reason to configure the router process to log adjacency changes to syslog as opposed to running debug is an issue of resources. It takes fewer router and administrator resources to report on a change of state as it happens than to have the debugger running constantly. The debug process has the highest priority and thus everything waits for it.

35. Many OSPF problems stem from adjacency problems that propagate throughout the network. Many problems are often traced back to neighbor discrepancies. If a router configured for OSPF routing is not seeing an OSPF neighbor on an attached network, do the following:

- Make sure that both routers are configured with the same IP mask, MTU, InterfaceHello timer, OSPF Hello interval, and OSPF dead interval.

- Make sure that both neighbors are the same area type and are part of the same area.

- Use the **debug** and **show** commands to trace the problem.

36. The configuration is between the ABRs, where one of the ABRs resides in Area 0 and the other in the area that is disconnected from the backbone. Both of the ABRs are also members of the transit area. Having created the virtual link, both ABRs are now members of Area 0, the disconnected area, and the transit area.

37. The command **area 1 default-cost 15** will assign a cost of 15 to the default route that is to be propagated into the stub area. This command is configured on the ABR attached to the stub area.

38. The parameter *area-id* is the area ID of the transit area. Thus, if the ABR in Area 0 is creating a virtual link with the ABR in Area 3 through Area 2, the area ID stated in the command is Area 2. The router ID is the router ID of the router with whom the link is to be formed and a neighbor relationship and adjacency established.

Chapter 8

"Do I Know This Already?"

1. A and D

2. A and B

3. B

4. B

5. B and C

6. A

7. C

8. B, C, D

9. A and B

Q&A

1. Standard, stub, totally stubby, and NSSA.

2. All (standard, stub, totally stubby, and NSSA).

3. All except totally stubby.

4. Standard

5. Temporary LSA assigned to routes redistributed by an ASBR attached to an NSSA.

6. The only path out of the area is via a default route, which may be suboptimal should there be multiple exit points.

7. Minimizes the routing table and associated computations (SPF, event-driven changes).

8. Standard, non-backbone areas.

9. All internal routers in a stub area must have this same command so that all hellos agree on the stub area flag.

10. Null indicates no authentication, plaintext means that the password can be read with the aid of a protocol capture tool, and MD5 authentication uses a key number in combination with a password to create a hash value that is not decipherable if captured on the network.

11. A message digest is a hash value used to secure a password.

12. N1 or N2

Chapter 9

"Do I Know This Already?"

1. A, B, D

2. A, B, D

3. C

4. B

5. D

6. D

7. D

8. A

9. A and B

10. A, B, C, D

11. B

12. A

13. C

14. A and B

15. A

16. B and C

17. B

18. A, B, C

19. B

20. B and C

21. A

22. C

Q&A

1. The DIS generates the pseudonode, using its own system ID and setting the following octet to be a nonzero number.

2. The complete sequence number packet describes every link in the link-state database. It is sent on point-to-point links when the link comes up to synchronize the link-state databases. The DIS on a multicast network will send out CSNPs every 10 seconds.

3. Partial Sequence Number Packets are sent on point-to-point links to explicitly acknowledge each LSP they receive. A router on a broadcast subnetwork will send a PSNP requesting the LSPs it needs to synchronize its link-state database.

4. The routers exchange Hellos and immediately see that both routers have the same priority. If the new router had a higher priority, it would take over as the new DIS. However, if both routers have the same priority, the router with the highest MAC address will reign as the DIS.

5. There is no backup designated router in IS-IS. Therefore, if the DIS meets an untimely death, a new DIS would be elected, based on priority or highest MAC address. If another router comes online with a higher priority, it will dislodge the existing DIS and rule in its place. This behavior is different from that of OSPF. Once a new DIS is elected, the link-state databases are purged and new LSPs are flooded.

6. IS-IS is capable of carrying both IP and CLNS.

7. The DIS sends out hellos every 3.3 seconds, three times the speed of other routers on the multiaccess link.

8. The name of the link-state algorithm is the Dijkstra algorithm.

9. The default dead timer is three times that of the Hello timer; thus the path will wait for 30 seconds before declaring the path dead and flushing the LSPs from the link state database.

10. Integrated IS-IS areas are similar to OSPF stub areas.

11. There is only one hard and fast rule for the design of a Level 2 network: Level 2 routers must be contiguous; that is, the area cannot be fractured.

12. The address is a NET address because the last octet is set to 0x00. Thus, there is no network service defined. This is the address of a router, not an end system.

13. The pseudonode is the LAN identifier for a broadcast subnetwork. The pseudonode is the system ID of the DIS plus the Circuit ID. The pseudonode has links to each of the ISs, and each IS has a single link to the pseudonode. The use of the pseudonode reduces the number of links required. Instead of n-1 links between each of the ISs, there is one link per IS to the pseudonode. The DIS generates link-state PDUs on behalf of the pseudonode. These LSPs are sent to all the connected ISs.

14. For an adjacency to be formed and maintained, both interfaces must agree on the following:

    ■ The same MTU.

    ■ Both are Level 1. If both are Level 1, they must be in the same area.

    ■ Both are Level 2.

- At least one is Level 1-2.

- The authentication must be the same.

The Hello timers (including the holddown timer) must match. If one router has a Hello timer of 40 seconds, the defaults on the other router would time out the holddown timer and purge the LSP, resulting in a flapping link and endless SPF calculations.

15.   The system ID is the unique identifier for the area. The first part of the address is a very long area address, of which only the last six octets are available for addressing the router or host.

16.   TLV is the same as CLV, but some literature refers to the variable length fields as Type/Length/Value in accordance to the IP terminology. Although the IS-IS PDUs are fixed, the TLV fields are variable length and can expand as needed. This design allows great flexibility and movement to develop in step with technological advances. The development of TLV code 128 extended IS to carry integrated IS-IS.

17.   A Level 1-2 router has two SPF (link-state) databases, one for the Level 1 routes and the other for the Level 2 routes. A separate SPF algorithm is run for each database.

18.   IS-IS packets run directly on top of the data link layer.

19.   The NET address is associated with the end system, but not with a process on the end system.

The address is that of an entire system, as opposed to an interface on the system, as is the case with IP. Because the NET (unlike the NSAP) does not identify a process, the address is that of a transitional or intermediate system. Therefore, the NET address is associated with the router or IS and is the destination address of the next hop in the life of a routed or routing packet.

20.   Characteristics of a Level 1 IS include the following:

- An intra-area router.

- Similarity to an OSPF stub router.

- Knowledge of the network limited to the area.

- A link-state database with all the routing information for the area.

- The address of the closest Level 2 router to which to send traffic destined for another area.

- Neighbors must be in the same area.

- A DIS is elected on LANs.

21. It is necessary to configure routers that straddle more than one area as Level 1-2 routers so that they can receive updates from both Level 1 and Level 2 routers and thus forward datagrams from Level 1 routers out of their area. Some designs allow for every router to be configured as a Level 1-2 router; this is the default configuration on Cisco routers. This eliminates errors but is a drain on network resources.

22. The four stages of the routing process are update, decision, forwarding, and receiving.

23. An LSP contains the list of neighbors connected to the originating router.

24. LSPs are generated whenever there is a change in the network, often because of a configuration change. However, any of the following instances trigger a new LSP to be flooded throughout the network:

    ■ An adjacency comes either up or down (for example, a new router comes online).

    ■ An interface on the router changes state or is assigned a new metric.

    ■ An IP route changes (for example, because of redistribution).

25. The following list describes the flooding process on a point-to-point link:

    a. When an adjacency is established, both sides send a CSNP packet with a compressed version of their link-state databases.

    b. If there are any LSPs in the receiving router's database that were not in the CSNP it received, it sends a copy of the missing LSPs to the other router.

    c. Likewise, if the database is missing any LSPs received in the CSNP, the receiving router requests the detailed LSP to be sent.

    d. The individual LSPs are requested, sent, and acknowledged via PSNPs.

    e. When an LSP is sent, the router sets a timer. If no explicit acknowledgement has been received before the timer expires, the LSP is resent. This timer is the minimumLSP-TransmissionInterval and can be configured; the default on a Cisco router is 5 seconds.

26. The LSP contains three fields that help determine whether the LSP that has been received is more recent than that held in the database and whether it is intact or has been corrupted. These three fields are as follows:

    ■ **Remaining Lifetime**—This is used to age-out old LSPs. If an LSP has been in the database for 20 minutes, it is assumed that the originating router has died. The refresh timer is set to 15 minutes.

    If the lifetime expires, the LSP has the content removed, leaving only the header. The lifetime is set to show that it is a new LSP, and then it is flooded through the network. All receiving routers accept the mutilated LSP, recognize that this means the route is bad, and purge the existing LSP from their databases.

- **Sequence Number**—This is an unsigned 32-bit linear number. The first LSP is allocated the sequence number 1, and the following LSPs are incremented by 1.

- **Checksum**—If a router receives an LSP and the checksum does not compute correctly, the LSP is flushed and the lifetime is set to 0. The router floods the LSP, all routers purge the LSP, and the originating router retransmits a new LSP.

27. Each router builds a shortest path tree (SPT) with itself as the root. This is achieved by taking all the LSPs from the link-state database and using the Dijkstra algorithm to create the SPT. The SPT is used in turn to create the forwarding table, which is also known as the routing table.

28. If there is more than one path to a remote destination, the criteria by which the lowest cost paths are selected and placed in the forwarding database are as follows:

    - If there is more than one path with the lowest value metric, Cisco IOS places up to six equal-cost paths into the table. The default number of equal-cost paths is four.

    - Optional metrics are chosen before the default metric, but because Cisco supports only the default metric, this is a moot point.

    - Internal paths are chosen before external paths, because going outside the autonomous system is likely to be a suboptimal route and might be the result of a routing loop.

    - Level 1 paths within the area are more attractive. If the path is within the area, not only is it more efficient to route directly to it, but also going outside the area and returning can be the cause of a routing loop, demanding greater resources and time.

    - The address with the longest match or most specific address in IP is the address with the longest IP subnet mask. This ensures that the closest router is chosen, because prefix routing is configured by summarization that can occur only on area boundaries.

29. A narrow metric is the default metric, which has a 6-bit field. Cisco increased the size of the field to 24 bits; this 24-bit field is referred to as a wide metric.

30. The IS-IS metric is applied to the outgoing interface.

31. If an LSP fragment is incomplete, the routing process ignores it, safe in the knowledge that it will be retransmitted if the sending router does not receive an acknowledgment within a specified time frame.

32. Suboptimal routing decisions occur when Level 1 areas have knowledge of networks only within their own areas. To reach another area, packets are sent to the nearest Level 2 router.

    Without additional configuration, the Level 1 router determines the nearest Level 2 router to be the one with the lowest hop count. The metrics used are the default metric of 10 on each outbound interface; therefore, the best route translates to that with the lowest hop count. As you know, the router two hops away might include a 16-Mbps Token Ring and a 56-kbps link as opposed to the three hops of Fast Ethernet and ATM.

33. Route summarization can be configured on a Level 1-2 router at the area boundary.

34. A DIS is elected on a WAN when the NBMA cloud is configured as multipoint.

35. Frame Relay and ATM are examples of NBMA networks, which are not accommodated in Integrated IS-IS. OSPF has a point-to-multipoint configuration option, but Integrated IS-IS does not. The solution in Integrated IS-IS is to configure the link as multipoint, allowing the election of a DIS. The alternative is to configure the interfaces with subinterfaces that are point-to-point.

Chapter 10

"Do I Know This Already?"

1. B
2. C
3. D
4. C
5. B
6. A
7. D
8. C
9. B, C, D
10. B
11. B, C, D
12. C and D

Q&A

1. The **router isis** global configuration command starts the routing process for integrated IS-IS.

2. By default, the routing process for Integrated IS-IS runs as a Level 1-2 router.

3. The **ip router isis** interface command is used to start Integrated IS-IS routing on the interface.

4. Under the command that started the routing process for Integrated IS-IS, enter the **net** command followed by the full Network Entity Title.

5. The **show clns neighbor** and **show clns interface** commands both display the adjacencies. The **show clns neighbor** command shows information on the state of the link, the type of routing performed on the link, the data-link address (SNPA) of the link, and the holdtime, or how long since it received the last Hello.

6. The designated intermediate system (DIS) is identified in the output screen of the **show clns interface** command or any **show** command that shows the pseudonode, such as **show isis database** or **show clns neighbors**. If the medium is multiaccess broadcast, the Circuit ID field shows the ID of the pseudonode. The pseudonode is identified by the nonzero value in the octet following the system ID of the DIS (for example, R2.01).

7. The **show isis database** command displays the LSPs in the link-state database. This database should be identical on every router in the area.

8. The **show isis spf-log** command shows the trigger for the last 20 occurrences for which the SPF calculation was run.

9. The **frame-relay map** command with the broadcast parameter is used in a fully meshed environment and when the network is multiaccess. This allows the election of a DIS, streamlining of adjacencies, and efficient use of IP subnets.

10. The command that shows all the Integrated IS-IS packets both sent and received by the router is **debug isis update-packets**. These packets are the CSNPs, PSNPs, and LSPs that are detected by the router.

11. The command **show isis database detail** shows the LSPs in detail.

12. The commands that display the interface and the adjacency on the local router are **show clns neighbor** or **show clns interface**.

13. The steps required for a basic configuration in IS-IS are

    - Define the areas and addresses.

    - Enable IS-IS on the router.

    - Configure the NET address.

    - Enable IS-IS on the appropriate interfaces.

14. The commands required to summarize the networks 10.10.0.0 through to 10.10.255.0 into another area of IS-IS are

    - **router isis**

    - **summary-address 10.10.0.0 255.255.0.0**

15. The command **show clns interface** shows both the circuit type, or routing level, of the interface and the IS-IS metric for outgoing packets.

16. In an NBMA multipoint configuration, subinterfaces and a point-to-point IS-IS network should be configured. NBMA multipoint topologies should be avoided, because, although they can be made to work, they require complex configuration and do not work with the strengths of the IS-IS routing protocol.

17. It is necessary to map CLNS to the DLCI in a NBMA Frame Relay network that is using a point-to-multipoint topology.

    The **frame-relay map ip** command maps the IP destination address to the outgoing DLCI and defines the interface as a broadcast interface. Integrated IS-IS uses the links as if they were truly a broadcast link and elects a DIS.

    The **frame-relay map clns** command maps to the CLNS process on the destination router.

    Without the second command, no routes appear in the IP routing table because CLNS does not receive the frames to populate the LSDB. Remember that these are IP routes carried in the IS-IS routing protocol. It is IS-IS that updates the IP routing table.

18. The field that shows the DIS is the circuit ID. This field shows the pseudonode ID, which is the system ID of the DIS. It is easily identifiable, as it has a value greater than 0x00 in the octet after the system ID.

Chapter 11

"Do I Know This Already?"

1. C

2. A

3. A

4. A and C

5. B

6. C

7. A and B

8. A, B, C

9. C

10. C

11.   B

12.   B, C, D

13.   B

14.   C

15.   A, B, C

16.   E

Q&A

1.   Answer:

- Passive interfaces

- Static routes

- Default routes

- The null interface

- Distribute lists

- Route maps

2.   Answer:

- If there is a WAN link where the cost of the link is based on network traffic. This might also have the added disincentive of being a WAN link that is a dial-on-demand link, which is raised and maintained by the presence of traffic attempting to flow across the interface.

- When trying to prevent routing loops.

3.   EIGRP will automatically redistribute between IGRP and EIGRP if the AS number is the same.

4.   The **show ip route** command displays two numbers in brackets: the route metric, followed by the administrative distance.

5.   When there is more than one routing protocol for IP running within the organization and when every part of the network needs connectivity to all the networks.

6.   Overlapping routing protocols will increase network traffic, router CPU processing, and memory requirements because of the additional protocol updates. The additional traffic and CPU and memory requirements complicate the routing process. The decision is not simply between multiple paths, but also between the various routing protocols that are advertising the paths.

7. Lower metrics are preferred when choosing among multiple paths to a remote network.

8. Answer:

    ■ The organization is transitioning from one routing protocol to another because the network has grown and there is a need for a more sophisticated protocol that will scale.

    ■ There is a mix of vendors used within the network, and some equipment does not support the preferred solution.

    ■ The organization is transitioning from a set of smaller networks to form one large enterprise network.

    ■ After a merger or a takeover, redistribution allows the status quo to be maintained while planning for a combined network.

    ■ There are ideological differences among the different network administrators.

9. Answer:

    ■ Suboptimal paths chosen.

    ■ Routing loops.

    ■ Convergence time increases.

10. Answer:

    ```
    Router(config-router)#distribute-list {access-list-number | name} out
    [interface-name | routing-process | autonomous-system-number]
    ```

11. A passive interface is an interface that listens to updates but that will not propagate updates for a given routing protocol. OSPF and EIGRP will not learn routes over a passive interface because they cannot exchange hellos.

12. There is no way to algorithmically compare OSPF cost to EIGRP metric, nor—with the exception of IGRP and EIGRP—is there a way to compare any two routing protocols. Routes from different protocols are therefore chosen on the basis of a Cisco-defined ranking, called administrative distance.

13. If two routing protocols both have a path to the same destination, the path for the routing table will be selected based on administrative distance. Potentially, this path is not the best path.

14. Costs are lost during redistribution, and setting a default metric provides some idea of how a route should be preferred. Also, RIP and EIGRP set the default metric to infinity. If you do not specify a default metric, nothing will be passed.

15. Answer:

```
Router(config-router)#distance weight [address mask] [access-list | name]
[ip]
```

For EIGRP, the administrative distance command is

```
Router(config)#distance eigrp internal-distance external-distance
```

Chapter 12

"Do I Know This Already?"

1. C

2. A, B, C

3. B

4. D

5. B

6. B

7. C

8. C

9. A

10. B

Q&A

1. The command is used to match criteria in establishing the policy-based routing. Access lists are used to specify the addressing of the packets to be affected.

2. Matching routes are modified with the **set** command. If the criteria are met in the **match** command and the action was to permit, the **set** criteria is initiated to control the routing as specified.

3. The **match** command determines whether the packet will be routed using the route map; the **set** command determines how the packet will be routed.

4. Within a route map, each route map statement is numbered with sequence numbers and, therefore, can be edited individually. The sequence number is also used to specify the order in which conditions are checked. Thus, if there are two statements in a route map named BESTEST, one with sequence 5 and the other with sequence 15, sequence 5 is checked first. If there is no match for the conditions in sequence 5, then sequence 15 will be checked.

5. A route map statement might contain multiple match statements. All match statements in the route map statement must be considered true for the route map statement to be considered matched. This is a logical AND.

6. When editing a route map statement with the **no** version of the existing command line, if you forget to type in the sequence number you will delete the entire route map.

Chapter 13

"Do I Know This Already?"

1. D

2. A

3. A, C, D

4. D

5. A

6. B

7. A

8. D

9. D

10. A, B, C, D, E, F

11. C

Q&A

1. DHCP traffic flow:

   — A client broadcasts a DHCP DISCOVER message for IP settings

   — The server responds with an OFFER

   — The client picks an OFFER and responds with a REQUEST

   — The client issues a gratuitous ARP to verify that no one else is using the address

2. To configure DHCP for a device with an interface assigned an IP address of 192.168.1.1/24:

```
Router(config)#ip dhcp pool 1
Router(config-dhcp)#network 192.168.1.0 /24
Router(config-dhcp)#default-router 192.168.1.1
Router(config-dhcp)#lease 3
Router(config-dhcp)#dns-server 10.1.1.1
```

3. Answer:

```
Router(config)#interface type number
Router(config-if)#ip address dhcp
```

4. Answer:

```
Router(config-if)#ip helper-address address
```

5. NTP (UDP 37), TACACS (UDP 49), DNS (UDP 53), DHCP (UDP 67 and 68), TFTP (UDP 69), NetBIOS name service (UDP 137), and NetBIOS datagram service (UDP 138)

6. server, relay, and client

7. Answer:

```
Router(config)#ip forward-protocol udp 5000
```

8. Answer:

Step 1   Create a pool of addresses to assign to clients.

Step 2   Assign a network to the pool.

Step 3   Specify the lease with default of one day.

Step 4   Identify the DNS server.

Step 5   Identify the default gateway.

9. Answer:

```
Router(config-if)#ip address dhcp
```

10. **show ip dhcp binding**

Chapter 14

"Do I Know This Already?"

1. A and D

2. C

3. D

4. A

5. A, B, D

6. A, B, C

7. C, B, A

8. C

9. A, B, C

10. B, E, A, D, C

11. C

Q&A

1. It is ill-advised to use BGP in certain conditions:

   ■ When the company has only one connection into the Internet

   ■ When there are limited resources on the network

   ■ When the user is not familiar with BGP configurations or policy-based routing

2. BGP is classified as an External Gateway Protocol (EGP), as opposed to OSPF, EIGRP, RIP, and so on, which are known as Interior Gateway Protocols (IGP). BGP can send a summary of the networks known within an organization to maximize security and minimize bandwidth overhead. It is used to convey routing information between autonomous systems.

3. The easiest way to connect to the Internet is to take default routes from all providers. This provides your company with a backup path if one provider fails. Because you are only receiving one route, the processor and memory utilization is quite low.

4. Before iBGP can propagate a route, the route must be known from another source.

5. Idle, Connect, Open Sent, Open Confirm, Established.

6. Answer:

   ■ Neighbor

   ■ BGP Table

   ■ Routing Table

7. The established state should display if the neighbor relationship is working correctly.

8. Load sharing.

9. For the majority of autonomous systems, synchronization is disabled—most autonomous systems are not transit autonomous systems.

10. Several answers are possible: path vector, exterior gateway protocol, interdomain routing protocol.

Chapter 15

"Do I Know This Already?"

1. A
2. C
3. D
4. D
5. C
6. C
7. B
8. D
9. A
10. A, B, D
11. C and D

Q&A

1. The command resets BGP peer associations, clears the BGP routing table, and re-establishes BGP connections to the neighbors. It should be used cautiously because the loss of connections will drop packets.

2. The command tells the router the IP address of the BGP neighbor and the autonomous system to which the neighbor belongs. This information allows the router to create a TCP session with the neighboring router and exchange BGP routing information.

3. The four message types of BGP are

   - Update messages: Contain paths to destination networks and their attributes. Routes that are no longer available or withdrawn routes are included in updates.

   - Open messages: Used to establish connections with peers.

   - Keepalives: Sent periodically between peers to maintain connections and verify paths held by the router sending the keepalive.

   - Notification: Used to inform the receiving router of errors.

4. A peer group is a group of BGP neighbors that share characteristics. The use of peer groups simplifies the configuration of BGP because one configuration effectively configures every router in the peer group. They are also more efficient because updates are generated once per peer group instead of on a per-router (peer) basis, reducing the resources required to support BGP.

5. In external BGP, there is no difference between a neighbor and a peer. A peer is the BGP term for a neighbor. Both terms refer to a router that is directly connected, with which routing information is exchanged. In iBGP, these routers are not necessarily physically adjacent, but they are the next logical hop router running BGP.

6. The **network** command permits BGP to advertise a network if it is present in the routing table. It is not responsible for starting the BGP process on an interface; instead, it identifies which networks the router originates.

7. On a broadcast multi-access network such as Ethernet, the next-hop address is the IP address of the advertising router. This command forces BGP to advertise itself as the next-hop router instead of letting the protocol determine the address to be used. This avoids problems seen on NBMA networks or nonmeshed environments, such as X.25 and Frame Relay.

Chapter 16

"Do I Know This Already?"

1. A and B

2. C

3. A and E

4. B

5. D

6. B

7. A and C

8. B

9. B

10. C

11. C

12. B

13. A

14. B

Q&A

1. BGP attributes include weight, local preference, AS-path, Origin, MED, Community, and Cluster ID.

2. The Cisco-proprietary weight attribute selects the exit when there are multiple paths to the same destination. The higher the weight value, the better the path. Weight is local to the router and the attribute is not propagated to other routers. Weight values range from zero to 65,535. The default weight is zero, unless this router sources the route (in which case the weight defaults to 32,768).

3. Local preference is used inside an AS to select outbound paths. It has a range from 0 to 4,294,967,295 and higher values are preferred in selecting routes. The default value is 100.

4. The AS-Path attribute is a list of AS that the route has passed through (the shortest path is preferred).

5. Origin describes how the route was learned. It can be i (native to BGP), e (EGP), or ? (redistributed).

6. Multi-exit discriminator (MED) is advertised to external neighbors to try to influence path selection into an AS. MED is an optional, nontransitive attribute and lower MED is preferred. The default MED is zero.

7. Router(config-router)#**neighbor** *{ip-address peer-group-name}* **weight** *weight*

8. Router(config-router)#**bgp default local-preference** *value*

9. Answer:

```
router bgp AS
  neighbor ip-address route-map question9 out
access-list 9 permit 192.168.25.0 0.0.0.255
route-map question9  permit 10
  match ip address 9
  set metric 90
route-map question9 permit 20
```

10.

Order	Preference	Description
0. Synchronized	TRUE	Use only routes that meet the synchronization requirement
1. Weight	Highest	Administrative override
2. Local Preference	Highest	Used internally to pick path out of AS
3. Self Originated	TRUE	Used to prefer paths originated on this router
4. AS-Path	Shortest	Minimize AS-hops
5. Origin	i<?	Prefer stability
6. MED	Lowest	Used external to come in
7. External	EBGP<IBGP	Hot Potato routing
8. IGP Cost	Lowest	Look for more information
9. EBGP Peering	Oldest	Prefer stability
10. RID	Lowest	External path preferred over internal path

Chapter 17

"Do I Know This Already?"

1. C

2. A

3. D

4. C

5. B

6. D

7. D

8. B

9. B

10. B

Q&A

1. Answer:

   - Unicast—One-to-one routing.

   - Broadcast—Sent to destination 255.255.255.255; used to transmit from one to everyone.

   - Multicast—Sent to a destination in the 224/4 range, used to transmit from one to a group.

2. Broadcasts are not forwarded by a router by default.

3. A router does not forward these packets by default unless some form of multicast routing is enabled.

4. A Layer 2 switch cannot learn the location of the destination multicast address, so the packets are flooded to all ports on the destination VLAN by default.

5. The first four bits of a multicast IP address are 1110.

6. The host must receive and examine every frame that has the MAC address it is interested in, regardless of for which of the IP addresses the frame is destined. The host then looks at the destination IP address in the packet header to verify that the more specific IP multicast address is a desired multicast group. If not, the packet is discarded.

7. 224.0.0.0/24

8. 239.0.0.0/8

9. Scalability—bandwidth used by multicasted content does not increase with the number of receivers.

10. Multicasting is efficient in terms of end-system processing because it allows network cards to throw away traffic based on destination MAC.

Chapter 18

"Do I Know This Already?"

1. A

2. D

3. C

4. B and D

5. B

6. A and C

7. D

8. A

9. C

10. B

11. B

Q&A

1. Every 60 seconds, one router (the *querier*) on each network segment sends a query to the all-hosts address (224.0.0.1) to see if there is at least one host still interested in receiving the multicast group.

2. In version 2, when a host decides to leave a group it has joined it sends a *Leave Group* message to the all-routers address (224.0.0.2). All routers on the local segment take note, and the querier router responds with a group-specific query message (sent to the group address), asking if others are still interested in receiving that group. Interested hosts must reply with a membership report, or the querier assumes there is no need to continue forwarding the group on that segment.

3. IGMPv3 adds support for multicast source filtering.

4. A router running IGMP can coexist with routers running older versions. To do this, the router must degrade itself to the highest common IGMP version in each multicast group.

5. CGMP is a protocol that runs between switches and routers. When routers receive IGMP messages, they pass the MAC of the requestor and the multicast group requested on to the switch. The switch then cross-references the requestor with its MAC table and enables the multicast group for a port.

6. IGMP snooping enables the switch to recognize IGMP and act on it as the IGMP packets cross the switch. This allows the switch to understand the requested multicast group and the port of the requestor.

7. All routers start as queriers and transition to non-queriers if they hear another querier with a higher IP address.

8. Router# **show ip igmp group**

9. IGMPv3 (RFC 3376) adds support for multicast source filtering and is backward compatible with v2 and v1.

10. **show ip igmp interface**

Chapter 19

"Do I Know This Already?"

1. A
2. E
3. A
4. C
5. C
6. D
7. C
8. B
9. A
10. C
11. D
12. A
13. A and D
14. E

Q&A

1. *Reverse Path Forwarding (RPF)* checks to make sure traffic always flows away from the root of the tree—from the source toward the recipients.

2. Protocol Independent Multicast (PIM) is a routing protocol that can be used for forwarding multicast traffic between IP subnets or network segments. PIM makes use of the IP unicast routing table and does not keep a separate multicast routing table.

3. PIM routers can be configured for *dense mode*. The source of the multicast traffic becomes the root of the tree, and the multicast tree is formed from the source to each of the recipients. This is also termed *(S,G)* multicast traffic, where the path between the source and group members is unique and well-defined.

4. With PIM *sparse mode*, the multicast tree is not extended to a router unless a host there has already joined the group. The multicast tree is built by beginning with the group members at the end-leaf nodes and extending back toward a central root point. The tree is grown in reverse, from the leaves toward the root.

5. If a group has an RP defined, sparse mode is used; otherwise, dense mode is used.

6. Auto-RP is a Cisco proprietary means of automatically informing PIM-SM routers of the appropriate RP for a group. This is done by identifying a centrally located and well-connected router to function as the *mapping agent*. The mapping agent learns of all candidate RPs that are announced over the *Cisco-RP-Announce* multicast address 224.0.1.39.

7. PIMv2 uses a method similar to auto-RP. A *bootstrap router (BSR)* is identified; this router learns about RP candidates for a group and advertises them to PIM routers. You need to configure only the BSR and candidate RPs; all other PIM routers learn of the appropriate RP from the BSR.

8. Auto-RP is a PIMv1 function, whereas Bootstrap routers are used by PIMv2.

9. Enable Multicast Routing:

   ```
   Router(config)#ip multicast-routing
   ```

   Turn on PIM in appropriate mode on selected interfaces:

   ```
   Router(config-if)#ip pim {dense-mode | sparse-dense-mode | sparse-mode}
   ```

   Set up RPs:

   ```
   Router(config)#ip pim send-rp-announce {interface type} {scope ttl} {group-
       list acl}
   ```

10. Answer:

    ```
    Router(config)#ip multicast-routing
    Router(config)#interface s0/1
    Router(config-if)#ip pim sparse-dense-mode
    Router(config-if)#interface f0/0
    Router(config-if)#ip pim sparse-dense-mode
    Router(config-if)#interface s0/2
    Router(config-if)#ip pim sparse-dense-mode
    ```

11. Answer:

    ```
    Router(config)#ip pim send-rp-announce f0/0 scope 5
    ```

12. Routes that are not source-specific (routes to an RP) are (*,G). Routes to a source are listed as (S,G).

Chapter 20

"Do I Know This Already?"

1. C

2. D

3. C

4. A

5. D

6. B

7. B

8. D

9. A, B, C, D

10. B

11. B and D

12. A and D

Q&A

1. The benefits of IPv6 include

- Larger address space, because of its 128-bit addresses

- Simplified packet header, which can be processed more efficiently

- IPv6 mobility built in

- IPsec built in

- Many ways to transition from IPv4

2. The fields in the IPv6 header are described as follows:

- **Version**—A 4-bit field, set to the number six for IPv6.

- **Traffic Class**—Also called priority. Similar to ToS field in IPv4, this 8-bit field describes relative priority and is used for QoS.

- **Flow Label**— The 20-bit flow label allows traffic to be tagged so that it can be handled faster, on a per-flow basis; this field can also be used to associate flows with traffic classes.

- **Payload Length**—This 16-bit field is the length of the data in the packet.

- **Next Header**—Like the protocol field in the IPv4 header, this 8-bit field indicates how the fields after the IPv6 basic header should be interpreted. It could indicate that the following field is TCP or UDP transport layer information, or it could indicate that an extension header is present.

- **Hop Limit**—Similar to the TTL field of IPv4, this 8-bit field is decremented by intermediate routers and, to prevent looping, the packet is discarded and a message is sent back to the source if this field reaches zero.

- **Source Address** and **Destination Address**—These 128-bit fields are the IPv6 source and destination addresses of the communicating devices.

- **Extension Headers**—Zero or more extension headers follow the basic IPv6 header, for example before the transport layer data. The *next header* field within an extension header points to the next header in the chain.

3. Extension headers may follow the IPv6 basic header; possible extension headers include Hop-by-Hop options, Destination options, Routing, Fragment, Authentication, and ESP.

4. The following fields are significantly different in the IPv6 header and in the IPv4 header:

- **Version**: The value is set to six instead of four.

- **Flow Label**: This new field in the IPv6 header allows tagging and simplifies forwarding.

- **Source Address** and **Destination Address**: These fields contain 128-bit addresses instead of 32-bit addresses.

- **Extension Headers:** Extension headers are new in IPv6 and provide a flexible way to support other features.

Another difference is that the IPv6 header does not include a checksum, whereas the IPv4 header does. Fragmentation is also handled differently: in IPv6, intermediate routers do not fragment packets. Fragmentation is performed by the source node and fragmentation information has been moved to an extension header.

5. 2001:0:240E::AC0:3428:21C

6. Broadcast addresses do not exist in IPv6. Broadcasts can be thought of as a special case of multicasting, where every device is the intended recipient. In IPv4, sending a broadcast causes *all* devices to process the packet, even those that are not concerned with the contents. Using multicasts is much more efficient because the packets can be targeted to a subset of devices, such as to routers running OSPF.

7. The EUI-64 bit interface ID is derived from the MAC address by inserting the hexadecimal number FFFE between the OUI field (the upper three bytes) and the vendor code (the lower three bytes) of the MAC address. The seventh bit in the first byte of the resulting interface ID, corresponding to the U/L bit, is set to binary 1. Thus, the EUI-64 bit interface ID for this interface is 020C:0AFF:FE28:121C. This value could be used in stateless autoconfiguration; the EUI-64 format interface ID is appended to the prefix advertised by the local router.

8. An address may be manually assigned, or dynamically assigned through DHCP or stateless autoconfiguration.

9. An IPv6 anycast address is a global unicast address that is assigned to two or more devices. Other devices route to the *closest* active device with the anycast address; the routing protocol metric determines which is closest.

   Anycast addresses are created by assigning the same unicast address to more than one device; there is no reserved address space for anycast. Nodes on which the address is assigned must be explicitly configured to use and know that the address is an anycast address.

10. All IPv6 multicast addresses start with the prefix FF00::/8. The next four bits are flags; the four bits after the flags indicate the scope of the address and limit how far the multicast may travel. IPv4 uses TTL as a crude way to accomplish this, but there are times when the distance allowed by TTL is too far in one direction and not far enough in another. The IPv6 multicast scope is flexible enough to limit the multicast to a link, to a site, or to an enterprise.

11. The following IPv6 addresses exist on an interface:

    ■ Any global unicast or anycast assigned (in the range 2000::/3)

    ■ Link-local address (FE80::/10, using autoconfiguration for the EUI-64 format interface ID)

    ■ Loopback (::1/128)

    ■ All-nodes multicast addresses (FF01::1 and FF02::1)

    ■ Solicited-nodes multicast addresses (appending the last 24 bits of the corresponding unicast or anycast address of the device to FF02::1:FF00:/104)

    ■ Any other multicast group addresses assigned (in the range FF00::/8)

12. Routers must respond to the following additional IPv6 addresses on each of their interfaces:

    ■ Subnet-router anycast (the unicast address of the subnet with the interface ID—the host bits—set to ::0)

    ■ All-routers multicast addresses (FF01::2, FF02::2, and FF05::2)

13. Stateless autoconfiguration can be used to renumber a network, by changing the network information only on the routers. Each router advertises network information (either periodically or at the request of a host), including the 64-bit prefix, on each of its links. By listening for this advertisement, end-systems create a unique address by concatenating the new prefix and the EUI-64 format interface ID.

14.   An IPv6 mobile node has a *home address* on its home network and a *care-of address* on its current network. A node communicating with a mobile node is called a *correspondent node* of the mobile node. The association between a the home address and the care-of address of the mobile node is known as a *binding*. When a mobile node roams away from its home network, it sends a binding update to its *home agent,* a router on its home network.

A mobile node and a correspondent node can communicate either via the home agent or directly.

Chapter 21

"Do I Know This Already?"

  1.   B and C

  2.   C

  3.   D

  4.   B

  5.   C and D

  6.   B

  7.   D

  8.   B

  9.   A

 10.   C

Q&A

  1.   Cisco routers support RIPng, EIGRP for IPv6, IS-IS for IPv6, MP-BGP4, and OSPFv3. Static routes are also supported.

  2.   Like its predecessor OSPFv2, OSPFv3 is a link-state routing protocol that uses the Dijkstra SPF algorithm to select best paths through the network.

  3.   The link-local address, autoconfigured using the FE80::/10 prefix, is used as the source addresses in an OSPFv3 hello packet.

  4.   OSPFv3 is different from OSPFv2 in many ways, including the following:

  - Has 128-bit prefix support and runs within IPv6 packets; however, still uses 32-bit router ID, area ID and link-state ID

  - Uses multicast addresses FF02::5 and FF02::6

- Uses *links* rather than *subnets*; uses link-local address as source address

- Has a 16-byte packet header; authentication not built-in, uses IPv6 extension headers instead

- Support for multiple instances

5. Type 1 is a Router-LSA; type 9 is an Intra-Area-Prefix-LSA, new to OSPFv3.

   In OSPFv3, LSA types 1 and 2 no longer contain route prefixes, instead they contain 32-bit IDs. OSPFv3 type 3 and type 9 LSAs carry all IPv6 prefix information; in OSPFv2, IPv4 prefix information is carried in type 1 and type 2 LSAs (router and network LSAs).

6. OSPFv3 priority works the same way it does for OSPFv2—routers default to a priority of 1; a higher priority means a better chance of being elected DR or BDR, and 0 means that the router will not serve as a DR or BDR.

7. The commands used to implement IPv6 and OSPFv3 are as follows:

   ```
   RouterA(config)#ipv6 unicast-routing
   RouterA(config)#ipv6 cef
   RouterA(config)#ipv6 router ospf 1
   RouterA(config-rtr)#router-id 10.255.255.1
   RouterA(config-rtr)#interface fastethernet0/0
   RouterA(config-if)#ipv6 address 2001:0:1:1::2/64
   RouterA(config-if)#ipv6 ospf 1 area 1
   RouterA(config-if)#interface serial 1/0
   RouterA(config-if)#ipv6 address 2001:0:1:5::1/64
   RouterA(config-if)#ipv6 ospf 1 area 1
   ```

8. The following command is used to configure an OSPFv3 router ID:

   ```
   Router(config-rtr)#router-id 32-bit-router-id
   ```

   The router ID must be a 32-bit number in an IPv4-address dotted decimal format, and could be set to the value of an IPv4 address on the router.

9. Interfaces are assigned to areas in OSPFv3 in interface configuration mode, using the **ipv6 ospf** *process-id* **area** *area-id* [**instance** *instance-id*] command, instead of using the **network** command in router configuration mode, as is done for OSPFv2.

10. The **show ipv6 ospf neighbor** or **show ipv6 ospf neighbor detail** command can be used to verify that neighbor relationships have been established with the appropriate directly connected routers.

11. There are several transition mechanisms including

    - Dual Stack

    - Tunneling (manual, 6-to-4, ISATAP, and Teredo)

    - Translation

12.   The commands used to implement IPv4 and IPv6 are as follows:

```
RouterA(config)#ipv6 unicast-routing
RouterA(config)#ipv6 cef
RouterA(config)#interface fastethernet0/0
RouterA(config-if)#ip address 192.168.0.1 255.255.255.0
RouterA(config-if)#ipv6 address 2001:1:A:ABCD::1/64
RouterA(config-if)#interface fastethernet0/1
RouterA(config-if)#ip address 192.168.254.1 255.255.255.0
RouterA(config-if)#ipv6 address 2001:1:A:FEDC::1/64
```

13.   The 6-to-4 prefix is 2002:AC14.40C0, because AC14.40C0 is the hexadecimal representation of 172.20.64.192.

14.   NAT-PT maps IPv6 addresses to IPv4 addresses. If IPv6 is used on the inside of a network and IPv4 is used on the outside, a NAT-PT device receives IPv6 traffic on its inside interface and replaces the IPv6 header with an IPv4 header before sending it to an outside interface. Reply traffic follows the mapping backwards, enabling two-way communication.

Index

Numbers

N

CISCO

CCNP Prep Center
CCNP Preparation Support from Cisco

Visit the **Cisco® CCNP® Prep Center** for tools that will help with your CCNP certification studies. Site features include:

- CCNP TV broadcasts, with experts discussing CCNP topics and answering your questions
- Study tips
- Practice questions
- Quizzes
- Discussion forums
- Job market information
- Quick learning modules

The site is free to anyone with a Cisco.com login.

Visit the **CCNP Prep Center** at **http://www.cisco.com/go/prep-ccnp** and get started on your CCNP today!